THE STONES OF LONDON

Also by Leo Hollis

The Phoenix:
St Paul's Cathedral and the Men
Who Made Modern London

THE STONES OF
LONDON

A History in Twelve Buildings

LEO HOLLIS

Weidenfeld & Nicolson
LONDON

First published in Great Britain in 2011
by Weidenfeld & Nicolson

3 5 7 9 10 8 6 4 2

A CIP catalogue record for this book
is available from the British Library.

ISBN: 978 0 297 85082 3

Typeset by Input Data Services Ltd, Bridgwater, Somerset

Printed and bound by CPI Group (UK) Ltd, Coydon, CR0 4YY

The Orion Publishing Group's policy is to use papers that
are natural, renewable and recyclable and made from wood
grown in sustainable forests. The logging and manufacturing
processes are expected to conform to environmental
regulations of the country of origin.

Weidenfeld & Nicolson
Orion Publishing Group Ltd
Orion House
5 Upper Saint Martin's Lane
London, WC2H 9EA
An Hachette UK Company

www.orionbooks.co.uk

For Rose, home

CONTENTS

But London is more than a collection of streets and markets. It's Wren churches and ABC tea-shops. It's Burlington Arcade and the Temple. It's the Athenaeum and Adelphi Arches. It's Kennington Gasometer and the Zoo. It's the iron bridge at Charing Cross and the statue of Eros at Piccadilly Circus. It's the Serpentine and Moss Bros. It is Paddington Recreation Ground, and the Nelson Column. It's Big Ben and the Horse Guards. It's the National Gallery and Pimm's. It's the Victoria Palace and Ludgate Hill. It's second-hand bookshops and the undertakers and the cinema and the obscure back-street chapels. It's the waif-and-strays Societies and the fortune tellers and the pub on the corner and the trams. That's London.

And the people. They're London too . . .

Norman Collins, London Belongs to Me, 1945

INTRODUCTION

Stand on any street corner in the centre of London and you are on the edge of a historical journey. Look around you, and you will see a story that stretches across centuries. The glass and steel of the modern world reflect the stones of previous eras: you may catch a glimpse of the shimmering churches and royal houses of white Portland blackened with the soot of city life; the sandy yellow brick made from the city's very own clay; creamy stucco; the knobbly Kentish rag favoured by Romans and Saxons; imported marble from Italy and grey blocks from Norman Caen; burnt terracotta in imitation of Renaissance Venice; porches and decorations in the faux marble of Coade stone invented in the 1760s and sold off the Westminster Bridge Road; Dartmoor granite used to curb the cement pavements; fired tiles in every colour and sheen; rare coloured fragments of porphyry from distant ancient monuments. These are the stones of London.

The variety of the city's stones proves that the metropolis is not just one place, captured in a single moment, but plural, a series of layered narratives that need to be explored in the same way the palaeontologist excavates geological strata: Celtic, Roman, Saxon, Norman, Medieval, Modern, Georgian, Gothick, Modernist. What the stones remind us is that London is not a modern city, and it has never been. Despite its deepest desires to escape history, the city finds that its pockets are filled with the rocks of the past.

On the south side of Trafalgar Square, on an island constantly circled by the bustling traffic, stands a statue of Charles I upon his horse, the beast pointing towards Whitehall where his master met the executioner's axe in January 1649. This is the centre of the city from which are taken all measurements from the capital, London's ground zero. From the front of the statue, the main arteries of the city spiral in all directions and it is from here that Dr Johnson spoke his famous tribute to the metropolis: 'No, Sir, when a man is tired of London, he is tired of life; for there is in London all that life can afford.' From this place, the city reveals itself from its earliest origins to the present day.

When workmen began to dig the square in the 1830s they were surprised to find the skeletons of prehistoric animals – mammoths and hippopotami – that had once roamed the watery banks of the Thames. It was the Romans who first established the roadway that still runs along Fleet Street from the walls of the ancient city, through Ludgate, following the river towards the west. Once the Romans had left, this place remained an important Saxon enclave. Recent archaeological work at St Martin-in-the-Fields, on the north-east corner of the square, has uncovered an early Christian burial site. From the Norman era, the square became the meeting place between Royal Westminster and the walled city.

Looking around this square today one can still find evidence of the many layers of the city rubbing up against each other. Charles I's statue replaced the old Charing Cross, a commemorative cross built by Edward I for his wife Queen Eleanor, which is now preserved, in name only, at the nearby train station. Southwards one looks down Whitehall towards Westminster, the Gothick towers of the Houses of Parliament rising above Inigo Jones's 1619 Banqueting Hall, said to be the first modern building in London, and the last remnant of Whitehall Palace, the home of the Tudor and Stuart kings. Through the opening of Admiralty Arch to the west, one can now see Buckingham Palace, the present home of the royal family, at the end of the elegant Mall.

St Martin-in-the-Fields is a reminder of the changing city in the early eighteenth century, when the metropolis was growing so fast that a scheme for fifty-one new churches was announced. The completion of Trafalgar Square itself is a marker of the evolution of London a century later when first John Nash, and later Sir Charles Barry, were commanded to convert the dilapidated Royal Mews into a grand public space. This was once again converted in 2003 by the contemporary architect Norman Foster, who named the project 'World Squares for All', redefining the public spaces of the city for the twenty-first century.

The square was not just the centre of the city but also the fulcrum of empire, and the evidence of its imperial past is layered in stone. The column that rises high above the ground is the monument to Horatio Nelson who died in 1805 at the Battle of Trafalgar defending Britain against Napoleon. The column is set upon four resting lions, sculpted by Sir Edwin Landseer, symbols of the nation's might. Later statues have been added as reminders of distant valour: Major-General Sir Henry Havelock, who successfully quashed the Indian mutiny of 1857; General Sir Charles James Napier, who overpowered the Muslim regions of Sindh. In summer 2010, the vacant fourth plinth was filled by a massive ship in a bottle created by the Anglo-Nigerian artist Yinka Shonibare. The sculpture was a model of Nelson's HMS *Victory*, its sails decked out in vibrant African fabrics. On the edges of the square stand South Africa House, built in the 1930s, and Canada House (originally built as the Union Club by Sir Robert Smirke in the 1820s). Both imposing buildings remind us of the role of London as the world capital.

Yet the square itself also tells another story – of the public history of London, of the crowds that have gathered here in celebration and protest. Since its construction, the square has been a meeting point for political demonstrations: in the 1840s the Chartists held their meetings here; in November 1887 the mob, campaigning for Irish Home Rule and the conditions of workers in the East End, clashed with police, on what would be called 'Bloody Sunday'. This was repeated in 1990 with the Poll Tax riot, when mounted police charged into the crowd. An anti-apartheid vigil was held outside South Africa House for much of the 1980s, and it was a stopping point for the million-strong anti-Iraq War march of 2003. Yet the square is also a place for communal celebration: the euphoria of VE Day, 8 May 1945; the annual New Year's Eve revels; the announcement on 6 July 2005 of London's successful bid to host the 2012 Olympics.

Today, Trafalgar Square has been transformed into the front room of the city, a piazza linking William Wilkins's Greek Revival National

Gallery with the ornamental open space. Under the guidance of the Mayor of London, it has become the leading tourist site in London, with a full schedule of events including concerts, festivals and gatherings. It is the city in microcosm, ever-evolving, the confluence of layered narratives, of stones and memories.

In this book, I tell the story of London through twelve buildings. Arriving in any city for the first time, our sense of place is first informed by the physical setting: the density of the clustered buildings, the rush of the traffic, a feeling of verticality as our eyes rise to the top of the skyline. As we orientate ourselves we begin to understand the scale of the metropolis, the horizon point obscured by man-made vistas, streets and houses. We may start to acknowledge an emotional response to this evolving landscape – fear, loneliness, liberation; yet we are also almost unconsciously engaging with the spaces around us. It is the physical nature of the city – the stones themselves – that are the starting point for this adventure.

The nineteenth-century critic John Ruskin made it clear that the story of architecture is one of the most powerful viewfinders into history: 'great nations write their autobiographies in three scripts – the book of their deeds, the book of their words and the book of their arts ... of the three the only trustworthy one is the last'. Buildings do not lie. At the time of their creation, they are ideas made solid and permanent; they encapsulate, even by accident, the economic, technological and political realities of the age. Thus they tell a polyphonous narrative between the individuals on the building site – clients, architects, builders, observers – and the wider city in which the building is born. In time, buildings transform and change, and that too becomes part of the story handed down to us today.

It is for these reasons that we here look at the buildings themselves. Each of the twelve buildings, places and remnants in this book can still be found today in various states, either as ruins rebuilt or transformed. These places have been selected not because they are the finest buildings in London, nor even the most famous of each era, but because they reveal an essential narrative of the city.

The relationship between the individual building and the city as a whole is telling, and sometimes unexpected. The twelve or so buildings within this book are the launching point for some of the main themes not just of London but the history of urban life. These include the importance of trade, the performance of power, the balance between government and the freedoms of city life, displays of patronage or luxury. In each case the building begins as a dream, full of hope, but becomes entangled with everyday life. The stories reveal unexpected connections, a ghost map of the city that lives and works today.

But London cannot be revealed by the stones of the city alone; it is also a human narrative. The relationship between flesh and stone is uncanny, for the stories of buildings are the stories of people, the men and women who dreamt and lived their lives in London, leaving their imprint upon the fabric of the capital, and vice versa. Through the investigation of these buildings, we can come to understand something about ourselves: our need to project vast monuments; the way that we create a refuge, a personal space amidst the maelstrom; how we have coped with the problems of the mass within the confined spaces of our cities; the rise of consumption; the crisis of social housing; the organisation of crowds.

As a result this is not a work of architectural history, nor is it a complete story of London. Instead, each building is at the centre of a broad canvas, a panoramic view of the metropolis, and reveals some aspect of the ever-changing art of urban living. Thus it is a many-threaded narrative that tells of architects and patrons, kings and emperors, the relationship between work and pleasure, the impact of war and the effects of poverty. It is also a history of the present day, and an account of this city over 2,000 years from its first origins.

I hope that these stories will also help us to understand what we need in order to build the city of the future.

CHAPTER I

WORDS AND STONES

Fragments of an Ancient City

This is a journey to the end of the world.

Patrick Keiller, *London*

In London, history hides barely below the surface. On many occasions, the greatest treasures of the city – a cache of Renaissance jewels, an ancient Roman burial ground, a long-forgotten manuscript – have been uncovered by happenstance. In September 1954 it was, in the words of Professor William Francis Grimes, 'a fluke', but what he found was a striking reminder of the many layers of London's past.

Two years earlier, Professor Grimes, London's leading archaeologist, had begun work on the site of what was once Bucklersbury House, situated in the heart of the city, near to the Bank, before large-scale redevelopment began. Since the Victorian period it had been a thriving business quarter with various offices and shops including solicitors, insurance brokers and a Lyons Tea House, yet Grimes realised that the current buildings were set upon ancient foundations. For Bucklersbury House sat on one of the oldest thoroughfares, facing eastwards onto Walbrook, a street that had once been divided by an ancient river. The River Walbrook had been covered over in the eighteenth century but nonetheless over 2,000 years of history continued to exist beneath the modern street.

After the war the site had stood abandoned; rubble was strewn across the whole area from the Blitz ten years before, while stones and bricks choked the battered basements. The Nazi bombing in 1940–41 had laid waste to the fabric of London, from the docks to the east right into the very heart of the metropolis. In the years following VE Day, there had been hopes to revive the city out of the ashes of the Nazi onslaught; however, progress was painfully slow. It was not until 1952 that the landowners turned their focus to the Walbrook, which they planned to cover over with a new office block.

Before work began, the developers listened to the pleas of Professor Grimes, then Director of the London Museum, to explore the disrupted ground before it was lost for good. In 1947 Grimes had written in hope that out of the chaos of the Blitz some historical good might emerge: 'the cellars which are now open to the sky present archaeologists with an opportunity which they have never known before and are not likely to know again'.[1] Grimes and his team hoped to find evidence of the river that ran down the street towards the Thames to the south, and that summer they began cutting a number of exploratory sections. To begin with there was a scattering of interesting finds that were cleaned and taken to the Guildhall Museum for examination; but Grimes could not have predicted what he was to uncover on 18 September 1954.

Londoners have always been fascinated by their city's origin. The medieval chroniclers created myths from the few ruins they had found inside the walls, attaching their stories to the fragments and broken monuments that still remained. The antiquarian John Stow interwove these ancient stories into his account of the Tudor capital. When Christopher Wren began rebuilding it after the Great Fire of 1666, he excavated the classical origins of the metropolis. The eighteenth-century Enlightened thinkers hoped to rebuild Rome by the Thames, while the Victorians were aghast as they dug up the old city and found ancient buildings and the archaeological evidence for Londinium. In 1869, as they were tearing up the earth to lay a new sewerage system, engineers were fascinated by a mosaic found only a few yards from the Walbrook, evidence of a grand villa. Even today, we are still discovering new treasures: while the Jubilee line extension was being dug in Southwark in the 1990s, extensive Roman remains were recovered that have changed our understanding of the ancient city.

That September day in 1954 was intended to be the last of work on-site.

Through the slow and patient process of excavation, the archaeologists had peeled back the layers of time that had been hidden for centuries. The huge foundations of the modern building had compacted and distorted certain areas of the soil deposits, while the digging of basements in surrounding buildings had removed centuries of evidence. Yet, two and half metres below the street on the eastern side of the river, the remnants of a solitary building were uncovered. The soil was waterlogged, which made exploration difficult but had also preserved the stones, 'not as flimsy ghosts but as their solid original selves'.[2] As they delved there were more intriguing revelations. Grimes's discovery of a pagan temple in the heart of the capital in 1954 would reignite the city's passion for its classical past, just as it hoped for a brave post-war future.

By 18 September, the team had found the outline of a temple building and an altar stone, but on that day, 'as final recording work was being done', a sculpture was discovered – the head of a man wearing a cap. The following day *The Sunday Times* claimed to have identified the head as the god Mithras. The story caused a sensation as Londoners rushed to the site and hoped to make their own finds. By Monday *The Times* was calling for the preservation of the temple as a place of major historical importance.

As the archaeologists explored the evidence, they must have had a strange feeling of historical vertigo. The work had begun during a period of huge change as London attempted to find its feet again out of the debris of war, yet the devastations of the conflict had opened up the opportunity to uncover history that had lain hidden for over 1,700 years. They must have felt as if they were slowly revealing the foundation stones of the city.

London was born a Roman enclave and its stones have their beginnings with five ancient fragments that can still be seen today. A twisted stub of wood in the porch of St Magnus the Martyr church on Thames Street is the last remnant of the wooden London Bridge, which captures the earliest identity of the city – a crossing place on the River Thames. In the basement of a barber's shop in Leadenhall Market stands a portion of the second forum from the second century AD from where this outpost on the edge of the Roman Empire was administered, linking it to the wider Imperium through extensive trade routes. By the Tower, at the eastern fringes of the city, one can find the old Roman walls, built in AD 190 to protect the growing Roman capital, first called Londinium. The London Stone, a block of Oolite rock of unknown origin, today almost forgotten, links the city with classical myth and ancient origins. Finally, the temple of Mithras, originating in the third century, represents the sacred nature of the city.

The bridge, the forum, the walls, the temple, the stone are the genetic code of London, the building blocks of urban life: a place of crossing, movement, bustle; a centre of trade, a final destination for the goods of the world; a sacred space, the site of miracles as well as worship; a line of protection, a barrier as well as a definition of belonging. This is what made London, and what still characterises the city today.

Before the Romans London did not exist: there was nothing, except woods rolling down towards a river's edge, with few signs of cultivation or homesteads. The marshy littoral sprinkled with random shingle patches made it difficult to tell what was estuary and what was land; rivulets fed by springs wound between sandbanks, creating small islands within the tidal flow. Here the waters were shallow but wide and represented the boundaries between tribal lands, where the domains of the Celtic tribes – Catuvellauni and Trinovantes – merged. A space in between places, a waterway to be crossed.

In 55 BC, Julius Caesar, having vanquished Gaul, chased his enemies across the Channel and harried them as far as the River Thames yet saw no point in setting up camp. There was no need to stay; as he later wrote, 'there was nothing there for us to fear or rejoice at'.[3] He found a wide estuary that at high tide could stretch 1,000 metres across the low-lying southern shores. On the north bank, two hills rose above the marsh while, in between, small gravelly islands dotted the shallows of the river and were used as stepping stones across the water. Having 'achieved nothing', Caesar returned to Rome. Britain thus signified the end of the known earth, and was not even worth submission.

The Romans returned in 43 AD; the invasion was a political ploy intended to distract the native Italians from domestic travails, an act of

Caesarism performed by the Emperor Claudius to prove that he was imperial enough to quash nations. Britain was a soft target: many of the Belgic tribesmen who had fled Gaul after Julius Caesar's rout had settled in the south-east: the Catuvellauni and Trinovantes to the north of the river, the Atrebates and Cantii to the south. They had grown wealthy from the land and developed trade networks with their kin on the Continent. This was reason enough for Claudius to go to war once again; there was also the added bonus of completing the job that great Caesar himself had left undone.

As the troops gathered on the Gaulish coast, however, panic struck when the soldiers were gripped with fear 'since they strongly resented fighting beyond the limits of the known world'.[4] Yet as they sailed, a comet split the sky from east to west, a good portent. They arrived on the Kent coast and found no native army awaiting them; the tribesmen watched from afar and scattered into the woods and marshes as the invaders approached. When the Britons did stand and fight they were easily defeated, and at a fierce battle by the Medway, where the Thames 'discharges into the ocean', they were forced to retreat.

A forward party of soldiers gave chase and followed them to a river crossing: 'The British easily crossed the river, for they knew the firm fords. The Romans pursued, but failed to catch up with them. German units swam across, and others crossed a little higher upstream by a bridge. They attacked the British on all sides and cut off many of them; but rash pursuit led them into trackless marshes, where many were lost.'[5] The rest of the band waited on the southern bank for the remainder of the army, elephants and machines to arrive before crossing. The troops did not stay by the riverbanks, for as soon as they had fixed a pontoon of boats to span the water they continued their pursuit of the natives, whom they swiftly defeated.

Claudius returned to Rome, where he built a triumphal arch celebrating the vanquishing of twelve British kings. In addition a naval crown was placed above Claudius's palace to signify not just dominance of the Britons, but 'as a sign that he had crossed, and as it were conquered Ocean'.[6] Within a few years, Caratacus, lord of the Catuvellauni, was defeated and brought to Rome where he was paraded through the imperial city and, having been pardoned by the Senate, stood in wonder and said: 'How can you, then, who have got such possessions and so many of them, covet our poor tents?'[7]

From that shaky martial pontoon London was born and for the next 350 years or so it rose at the edges of the greatest empire in the world. The insignificance of that first settlement is made palpable in the paucity of written accounts, as if it did not deserve a chronicle; no law books, no set of regulations, no accounts or banking receipts, no love letters or memoirs have been discovered. The narrative can only be sought through the fragments of what has survived. What history we do have – Tacitus's account of the life of his father-in-law, Governor Agricola – was dictated second-hand and written for a Mediterranean audience. Similarly, Cassius Dio's *History* puts words more suited to the Appian Way into the mouths of British natives. Britannia appears in the tales of emperors when they visit or where the native legions are caught up in conspiracy. Elsewhere, in political and scientific treatises, the nation is little more than a reference point in a handed-down geography, a ragbag of myths and assumptions. History is told by the victors and Britannia spoke only through Rome.

On the rare occasions that words have survived in London, they are on coins, carved into funerary stones and an abundance of curse tablets. The first use of the word Londinium was not uncovered in some local record or official document but scratched onto the base of a bottle: *Londini ad Fanum Isidis*. Written letters and reports found at military bases on the northern boundaries offer names and flashes of London life but no more. Instead we are forced to reconstruct the city in broken fragments – the official stamp of the governor on baked tiles tells us who was in charge, the functioning of the building trade, the status of the commissioned building. Coins concealed beneath structures, sometimes discarded by accident or buried as a portent, give a rough dating system. It is the stones themselves that begin the story of the city.

The Roman Empire was founded on brutality, and the conquest of the Britons was a performance that had been practised and perfected throughout the Imperium. Rome did not cross the Channel to deliver civilisation to the Celtic tribes; rather, the imperial army advanced in pursuit of raw materials to feed the empire's appetites and to subdue the tribes that threatened their lands across the Channel. Such an invasion was expensive and the nation was first won with the sword: between AD 43 and 81 the Roman army was ruthless in suppressing the local tribes and it is estimated that nearly 250,000 natives were killed. In the first year, eleven British kings of the southern kingdoms surrendered after a battle at Camulodunum (Colchester), which was quickly converted into the first Roman administrative capital. In time the Durotriges, Dumnonii, Atrebates, Corieltauvi, Dobunni, Iceni, Cornovii, Deceangli, Brigantes, Silures, Ordovices and the northern Caledonii were also subdued with violence and their lands, settlements and goods conquered.

If the new lands were to deliver a return on Rome's investment it would be long-term, however: there was no gold or treasure to be found. The rowdy tribes would be expensive to control and at times demanded the services of one tenth of the army that was recruited from the various corners of the empire – regiments from Germany and northern Gaul, as well as a cavalry troop from Spain. The profitability of the project initially appeared poor: there were expensive start-up costs in administration and supplying these troops, with very few rewards in rare artefacts and valuables to satisfy the appetites of Rome.

Yet where the army marched, the traders were never far behind. Amongst the letters that were found at the northern fort of Vindolanda, in Northumberland, there are many receipts, lists of accounts and commercial demands that linked the front line with the profiteer's warehouse, such as that of Octavius to his brother Veldeius: 'I have several times written to you that I have bought about five thousand modii of ears of grain, on account of which I need cash. Unless you send me some cash, at least five hundred denarii, the result will be that I shall lose what I have laid out as a deposit, about three hundred denarii, and I shall be embarrassed. So, I ask you, send me some cash as soon as possible.'[8] London evolved from such urgent notices.

More importantly, London was born a crossing place, the most easterly point on the Thames estuary that could be safely traversed, from the ports to the south on the routes northward. The river was dangerous and unpredictable, a tidal basin that flooded daily, which was also fed by creeks, brooks and rivers that wound their way through the gravel hills and clay banks. Here, in time, the traders built a bridge and, as the historian R. E. M. Wheeler wryly noted, the settlement grew, a parasite, from the two bridge ends.

Nevertheless, the Thames-side site was not immediately earmarked for colonisation by the conquering invaders. The first evidence of a community was as a stopping-off point on the developing transport network, demonstrated by the discovery of dropped coins throughout the area that offer a ghost map of the first street plan. By AD 50, a road had been built that led from the southerly ports to the south bank of the Thames, present-day Southwark, on the water's edge. On the northern shore, thirty metres away from the waterline, signs of a road junction can be discerned, the first evidence of Watling Street leading to Verulamium (St Albans) and the west. In time the road also branched towards the east – Camulodunum and the garrisons of the north.

For the next few decades these two locations developed as the first Roman outposts, a nameless crossroads. Nevertheless, the crossing point evolved and to the north, on the summit of the gravelly hill, barns and houses began to be built. By AD 60, a small community had grown along the junction of the road; there were now three streets, the scattering of early wooden barns had been replaced with a more orderly housing scheme, houses made of wattle and daub. There were even signs of some luxury: coloured plaster, glass and marble decorations; even piped water; yet, as Tacitus wrote, the new community 'did not rank as a Roman settlement, but was an important centre for businessmen and merchandise'.[9]

The crossing place became a hub of exchange; small workshops grew up by the river's edge – a kiln, a forge for working in iron and bronze, even some gems (intaglios) were found that suggest that the site was already a disembarkation point for goods from the rest of the empire. It was a merchants' enclave, huddled at both ends of the wooden crossing, populated by frontiersmen who turned a profit manning the army supply routes.

1. The last remaining
   fragment of the Roman
   bridge in the porch of
   St Magnus the Martyr,
   Thames Street

The first evidence of a permanent crossing can be found from the AD 50s: a modest gravel embankment, a bridge pier, a few timber piles are all that remain of the first bridge, located at the bottom of Fish Hill. It is likely that this was constructed by driving timber piles into the river-bed and then building a latticed trestle across the span. It was said that this bridge was strong enough to withstand the attack by Boudicca, Queen of the Iceni, in AD 60, which destroyed the rest of the settlement. Nevertheless, repairs were necessary and an inscription was found on one of the quayfront timbers, naming the unfortunate soldiers, the 'Augustan Cohorts of the Thracians',[10] who were co-opted into the rebuilding project.

In the 80s this early bridge was quickly replaced by another, only a few yards to the east. It is very likely that this was also a temporary structure while a more permanent bridge was built on the original site. The new crossing was raised on brick piers with masonry arches that carried a road of timber decking. Proof of its existence is the large amount of coins and votive offerings found in the middle of the Thames just where it was assumed to be. The structure reinforced the status of the settlement as a permanent crossing place, but it also took on a second function: a barrier to all shipping arriving up the river. The bridge thus became a port as well as a crossing; in time this would be an essential part of the new enclave, administered by officials and marked by a tax. London would be a place not only of trade but also of government.

The bridge was to be repaired by successive generations but would remain at the heart of the Roman settlement. The bridge placed the city at the centre of the colony and allowed the settlement to profit and grow. By AD 100 the site beside the river had become more than a community of tradesmen and old soldiers; the population was now nearing 30,000, far larger than Camulodunum; more importantly, work had started on transforming the entrepôt into a thriving city. In the second century, London was mentioned in the *Geographia* of the Egyptian philosopher and stargazer Ptolemy and, just as he set the Aristotelian universe around the earth, so he charted the various places within Britain in their relationship to London, measuring their distance from the bridge.

In AD 60 the traders' nameless community was razed to the ground, and the new settlement of Londinium was born from the ashes. For archaeologists today, that brutal turning point is represented by a thin layer of ash, measuring half a metre, and fragments of broken pottery deep within the London soil. This second enclave saw the community expand into a substantial commercial hub, a market place in its own right with a wealthy elite and at the centre of a sophisticated business network. With trade came power, and the need for law to protect the rights of both buyer and seller; and the forum – the second foundation stone of London – was where enterprise and government combined.

Londinium was not a military outpost; a rudimentary ditch was dug around the site, perhaps marked with boundary stones. As a result, there was no hope for the settlement when Boudicca attacked. The origins of the unrest were predictable; the resentment that had brewed between conqueror and vanquished was uncorked with a dispute over land, resentment fuelled by a high-handed and vicious attack by the conquerors upon the conquered. Usually the Romans attempted to find accommodation with the tribal leaders by first brutally breaking their armies and then buying their acquiescence; but on this occasion something went wrong.

At that time the Roman army was pushing back the frontier of the empire; the governor, Suetonius Paulinus, was at the head of his troops attacking the island of Mona (Anglesey). At the same time, in the eastern counties, the death of the King of the Iceni, Prasutagus, gave the local magistrates the opportunity to plunder the royal lands; in addition 'his widow Boudicca was flogged and his daughters raped . . . The King's own relatives were treated like slaves.'[11] It was an act that shocked Romans as much as tribesmen and, in fear of further reprisals, the Iceni rose up alongside their neighbours, the Trinovantes, and marched towards Camulodunum, and then southwards towards Londinium.

With the bulk of the Roman army miles away, the Iceni were free to rampage. Eventually Paulinus was forced to march eastwards and hoped to meet the native army at the junction at the Thames. Once here he saw that the enclave could not defend itself against the hordes and so he decided to sacrifice Londinium and manage an evacuation. Any who remained were left to their fate. For Tacitus, the scene was more gruesome: 'the enemy neither took nor sold prisoners nor indulged in any of the traffic incidental to ordinary warfare, but massacred, hanged, burned and crucified with a headlong fury'.[12]

The site could return to Rome only if Boudicca was defeated and, on a field, Battle Bridge, long believed to be to the north of the city, the two armies met. Tacitus puts noble, rallying speeches into the mouths of both Paulinus and the British queen, yet the fighting itself was so brutal that even the baggage animals were added to the heaps of dead. Rather than accept defeat, Boudicca poisoned herself and her daughters.

The merchants' enclave itself was slow to re-emerge; new building began within two years of the fire but the settlement's rebirth was influenced as much by events in faraway Rome as by local issues. In AD 69, following the death of Nero, civil war rocked the imperial city and that year saw four emperors – Galba, Otho, Vitellius and Vespasian –

taking the throne. Vespasian held onto the prize and was able to establish the Flavian dynasty. He was determined to unite the empire and was willing to fight for it, yet at the beginning of his reign he faced revolt in Judea in the East and uprisings in Germany; he subdued both without mercy. Yet he also knew that his lands would never be secure without the suppression of the northern tribes of Britannia. He had participated in the first invasion of Britain and had seen the dangers with his own eyes.

In AD 71 legions began to arrive in Britain and were sent marching off towards the untamed corners of the empire: Wales, the north and Scotland. Under this new Imperium, a permanent Londinium was built for the first time as an administrative centre for the new territories, and with every marching step of the legionaries the enclave became stronger. Recent excavations along the north Thames shore have found significant evidence for a Roman port developed in the AD 70s: a timber waterfront terrace running along both sides of the bridge, likely commissioned by the civic officer and paid for by the city through tolls and levies. This new development may have coincided with Londinium finally gaining status as a *municipium*, and the permanent base for both the governor, the military leader, and the *Procurator*, the imperial lawgiver and tax man.

In AD 77 this was consolidated with the arrival of a new governor, Gnaeus Julius Agricola, who was commanded by Vespasian to seal the frontiers of his lands, which he did with breathtaking efficiency. He was also ordered to cement Roman rule within the conquered territories; and here he proclaimed a new phase in colonialism – the soft power of Romanisation, as his son-in-law, Tacitus, famously recounted: 'He therefore gave private encouragement and official assistance to the building of temples, public squares and good houses. He praised the energetic and scolded the slack; and the competition for honour proved as effective as compulsion.'[13] Thus, from the start, the stones of London were politics by other means, the embodiment of power within the bustle and rush of the city.

By now Londinium had gained sufficient size and wealth to become a destination for merchants; this trade encompassed not just rarities such as ivory bracelets from Africa, amber from the Baltic, gems from the Continent and the Middle East, but also more mundane but equally profitable stock – oil, grain, olives and wine sealed in large clay amphoras from the Mediterranean; building stone from further up the Thames coast, marble from across the Channel. Once the ships had docked official *negotiatores* worked the waterfront to set the prices for the commodities being offloaded that then were passed on to local customers or destined for the garrisons in the north. The haggle and trade did not move from this very site alongside the Thames for another 1,800 years, and then it only shifted less than a mile eastwards up the estuary; there the port remained until the 1960s.

There were other civic programmes in the AD 70s that further established Londinium as the leading colony in Britannia. A bathhouse was built at this time along the waterfront, and the work was so elaborate that archaeologists still dispute whether an adjoining annexe was part of the sports complex or was in fact the governor's palace. On the south bank of the river was erected a resplendent coaching inn or *mansio*, with a courtyard eighteen metres across. Meanwhile the population grew, pushing the boundaries of the enclave further outwards, across the River Walbrook and on to Ludgate Hill to the west. Here a fort was built and a temporary wooden amphitheatre. A new road scheme linked and divided the neighbourhoods. Many of these prized buildings were funded by private investment as Agricola encouraged architecture as an act of citizenship – one could become Roman by building Roman.

Nonetheless, the most important building in this emerging city was situated at the centre of the community, the forum. In fact, Londinium was growing so rapidly during the thirty years of the Flavian dynasty that two *fora* were built. The first forum was relatively small, 104.5 by 52.7 metres, and consisted of a wide, open market place ringed by a range of rooms, many of them shops that could also face outwards onto the street beyond. The main gate was on the south wall and at the northern end stood the impressive basilica, an aisled hall forty-four by twenty-two metres with a central space where the political business of the city was handled in public. The foundations were of stone – flint and brown mortar, probably shipped from the nearby county of Kent.

The rest of the walls above the ground were of local tile and then buttressed on the outside with bricks. The whole was then roofed in earthen tiles, made and baked outside the city boundaries.

The forum courtyard with its rooms and shops would be the first ancestor of the cries and hubbub of medieval Leadenhall Market, which rose on the same plot 1,200 years later and soon became the main meat market inside the walled city; it was also the antecedent of the loggias that encircled the Elizabethan Royal Exchange, the trading floor of the stock exchange, first established in a coffee house in Change Alley, yards away; and even the modern-day financial trading floors of international banks, within a minute's walk, encased in glistening modernity, steel and glass.

The basilica was intended as the most prominent building in the city, dominating the market place, raised upon a platform of rubble and gravel to ensure that it sat above the roofs of the surrounding dwellings. The long hall was now also the home for the *curia*, or council, that met and deliberated the regulations of the city, while at the east end of the room there was a magistrates' court, which saw that the law was followed. This too would be the forebear of many of the essential institutions of London: the Guildhall, built on the ruins of the once resplendent amphitheatre, home to the Lord Mayor and the Common Council that regulated the Corporation of London, once again making business and politics indivisible. The form of the basilica itself was a powerful influence on London: St Paul's Cathedral, the religious heart of the city, completed in 1708, was based upon a Flavian basilica, the Temple of Peace in Rome, identifying its role as a place of civic as well as divine power.

Here the two pillars of Roman power, politics and business, were based, and in the chamber the rulers debated questions of citizenship, the systems of trade regulation and the exploitation of the colony for the good of the empire. While no Londinium constitution, legal documents or decrees remain, as the community was transformed from a nameless enclave to an administrative centre, a *colonia*, and finally a *municipium*, it slowly became Roman. As a result the city government was forced to balance local demands by the new elite, rich from business on the island, with the pressures from the imperial centre.

The issue of citizenship – to Rome, not Londinium – was at the centre of an individual's legal standing within the community. Genetic studies of many of the remains within the cemeteries prove the diversity of the settlement's heritage: soldiers had marched here from Germany, Spain and Syria; there were also traders from throughout the empire who came and sought commercial advantage. Local elites, the defeated Celts, were also slowly acculturised into the imperial way of life – they were 'civilised' – and tempted with membership to the most powerful club in the world. Roman citizenship was the only bond that united these disparate people. Belonging encouraged uniformity of aspiration; more importantly, it set out the rules for property-owning, the freedom to conduct business and the exercise of political power.

As a market place and a political exchange, the forum regulated the internal politics of the community and as the city grew so the role of the institution gained prestige. The site was Rome in microcosm, just as the statues of the emperors that stood in the temples were the imperial presence itself. The place came to signify power. This was once again given added importance when, as the role of the army evolved from a conquering force to an administrative tour of duty across pacified lands, that of the governor changed from martial general to political figure-head. Thus, rather than deriving his power from the size of the garrison or his reputation in the field, he sought to find a more permanent base.

The Flavian dynasty came to an unpleasant end in AD 96 with the murder by court officials of Vespasian's grandson, Domitian. Despite the coup, the subsequent emperor, Nerva, inherited a stable empire that was set to prosper. Londinium, in particular, enjoyed a period of ambrosia for the next fifty years, when it reached the summit of its power and wealth. This was once again set in stone by the demolition and rebuilding of a new forum five times the size of the original (166 by 167 metres) – the largest building in Britannia. The structure took the same design: a wide courtyard surrounded by walls, with a basilica at the north end. It is quite possible that the original building may have stayed in place as they started to build around it, as it could easily have stood inside the courtyard. Yet the basilica itself was far more impressive, spanning 52.5 by 167 metres. Inside there were a number of arcade rooms, and here the power of the city sat. An elegant portico and herringbone tile floor were later added to offer a sense of grandeur. This established the forum as the most important space within the city, combining a trading floor, a law court and the main political chamber. And as a result, Londinium became the forum of Britannia.

Londinium by the AD 190s had risen and fallen over the century. It had grown rich on army contracts when the military was on the move pushing the frontier in the north. In AD 83/4 Agricola had led his army to victory at the glorious battle of Mons Graupius where, as Tacitus reported, 'Arms, bodies, severed limbs lay all around and the earth reeked of blood ... Only night and exhaustion ended the pursuit. Of the enemy some 10,000 fell.'[14] Yet the Caledonii tribes were not suppressed for long and the Romans failed to consolidate their victory. As a result, defending the northern frontier became a lengthy and expensive business – not that the Londinium merchants were complaining. Under the emperors Trajan (AD 98–117) and Hadrian (117–138) there were constant uprisings amongst the tribes. After Mons Graupius work was started on the northerly fort of Vindolanda, built by hand by the soldiers themselves, provisioned by traders brave enough to risk their stock in the badlands of Caledonia. Quickly a civilian community grew alongside the garrison providing for the soldiers' every need – merchants, craftsmen, slaves, wives and prostitutes.

In AD 122 Hadrian himself arrived in Britain to see the state of his northern frontier. He was concerned that this patch was costing him dear by absorbing so many of his troops when there were more pressing conquests to consider. On his arrival he initiated a project for a protective wall to run along the northern boundary. Hadrian's Wall was a barrier between the Romans and the northern barbarians; but that was not all it did. It had been planned to run through contested territory in which the enemy occupied both sides; it was not meant to exclude but to control the movement between the two zones. The new regime of surveillance brought with it an uneasy peace.

Stability in the north did not last long but there were greater threats closer to home, for the Imperium was on the verge of implosion. In A D 192 the Emperor Commodus was murdered, strangled by a wrestler called Narcissus. The next decade was marred by conspiracy and death as numerous factions fought for ultimate power. Britannia was not allowed to stand outside the fray, for, although far from the centre, events on the frontier had a habit of destabilising the empire. According to the historian Edward Gibbon, this was the beginning of the end of the Roman Empire. For fear that the military power of the governors could threaten Rome itself, the territory of Britain was divided into two colonies – Britannia Prima in the south and Britannia Seconda in the troublesome north. Britain now had two governors, neither powerful enough to topple Rome. Londinium was renamed Augusta, and designated capital of Britannia Prima. To be granted a wall, the enclave needed imperial permission: clearly, Londinium's role within the empire was changing.

Work soon began on the wall to surround the city, signifying not just the need for security but acting as a multi-faceted barrier, both figurative and real, and far larger than the needs of the urban community. On the western edge of the walls the city was protected by a natural defence: the waters of the River Fleet. Elsewhere a ditch was dug on the outer edge of the boundary, usually about five metres deep. The ditch was a standard defensive technique to make the outside of the wall as high as possible. In addition, the ditch took on the role of the city's liminal space – neither city nor country – symbolised by being swiftly transformed into a vast rubbish tip. From the Romans onwards the debris of 1,800 years has been excavated from this area; at Houndsditch, for example, there is extensive evidence that 'dead dogges were there laid or cast'.[15] The region remained on the edge of things for centuries to come.

The walls themselves exhibited all the fine engineering know-how of the Romans, two and a half metres thick and probably six metres high. The stone was Kentish rag, a very hard, fist-sized stone, not easily carved, transported thirty miles or so up the Thames from Maidstone, and used to face the outside of the walls. One of the three Roman shipwrecks in the estuary, at Blackfriars where the Fleet meets the Thames, was clearly used to bring the stones up to the capital. At certain stages there was a flat course of red bricks to stabilise the structure. On the inside of the wall a bank was created from all the moved earth, that then led up to a parapet from which the guardian troops could watch over the wall's edge. The parapet could also be reached by three towers with wooden staircases.

The four gates opened across the major routes out of the city – Bishopsgate, for the north-east and York; Cripplegate, where previously the garrison fort had stood, led to the north-west; Newgate, the west and Gloucester; Ludgate, Oxford and the south-west. Aldersgate was added in the A D 350s, towards the east. Evidence from Newgate proves that these were impressive structures: two towers stand either side of the two openings, a ten-metre-wide double carriageway. These gates remained the main crossing points of the city until they were finally destroyed in the eighteenth century, yet their names can still be found upon the street map, wards and parishes of the Square Mile.

The whole project was a vast undertaking that included mining, quarry work and transportation from the east up the Thames; shipping the huge amounts of stone to the city where they were prepared, alongside the local brick-making efforts. Large supplies of mortar and clay had to be found to bind the stones together. It is not known whether the army were used to construct the wall, as with Hadrian's Wall, but it must have taken at least two years' constant work.

The very act of building gave the wall – and the space it enclosed – its identity. Defence and prestige inspired the project, as a physical manifestation of the elevated status of Londinium within the empire, and the threat that such a status now held. But once work had started the economic identity of the barrier, the question of how the wall was going to pay for itself, must have come to the fore. Like Hadrian's Wall, Londinium's defences were as much a crossing point as a buffer and the walls now determined access to the richest markets in the colony. Just as all goods that arrived up the Thames would have been subject to a levy as they were docked on the quay, now all goods that arrived by land could be stopped, checked and charged. In addition, the market place was now protected and exchange could be conducted in safety. As with goods, so with people: unwanted visitors could be deterred or stopped from entering the city. The walls became a physical embodiment of the privileges of citizenship, defining who belonged and who did not.

A thousand years after the Romans left London, after the bridge had been rebuilt in stone and the forum lost, the temples smashed into the earth, the chimera of Roman Londinium remained. In that millennium the capital had withstood numerous attacks from Saxons, Vikings, Danes and Normans. It had also gained a cathedral and palaces, Gothic spires replacing the basilicas, guilds and new systems of regulation superseding the *curia*. Many of the original Roman roads had been built over, wooden houses mushroomed across the once regulated street plan, governed by a new idea of what London should be. Despite all these transformations, the upheaval of the stones of London themselves, the essence of the Roman city bound by the ancient walls remained.

It can still be seen and felt today. Bare remnants of the walls themselves stand awkwardly at random points in the city; in places they have been integrated into the foyer of a modern office block or encased in glass, while elsewhere they rise boldly amongst the traffic. At some times in later centuries the walls were rebuilt and extended, houses emerged from the defences. More significantly, where the walls have disappeared, a palimpsest of the original design can still be found in the street plan around the City that arches from the Tower in the east along Aldgate and Houndsditch towards Moorgate, along London Wall itself, where Professor Grimes discovered remnants of the old wall that now stand in the grounds of the Museum of London, and then returns to the Thames along Fleet Street and Blackfriars, once the course of the River Fleet. The Roman walls still define the Square Mile, the powerful financial centre within the city.

But a city does not solely find its identity in the relationship between businessmen, the exchange of goods, or even the stuff of politics and law. A city is a holy place, where the sacred and the profane must find accommodation. Places of worship sanctified sections of the city and blessed the inhabitants; they also regulated the order of the community, offering a transcendental hierarchy to consolidate the social. Roman

religion was a complex and very human affair that monitored the interaction between the divine and the mundane. The history of Roman
gods combined omens and rituals, sacrifices and promises in order to
balance the world and protect the supplicant; it was used to unite the
masses, binding them together in a common fate.

Armies conquer but nothing unites the conquerors and the vanquished in commonality like a shared fear of the supernatural. When
the Romans arrived in A D 43 they brought their own gods with them
and the victories on the battlefield were reflected in the defeat of local
deities by potent Latin-speaking powers. In the decades that followed
conquest native symbols, places of animistic power, secret rituals took
on Roman identities, with the latter absorbing the powers of the former
in a process that Tacitus termed *interpretatio*. This act of translation was
as powerful as the legionaries' cohorts and the merchants' wagons as
they trudged through the new colony.

Yet the Roman gods were not rational, obedient travel companions
and the Roman soldiers who arrived on British shores believed that,
as these wayward deities were necessary to protect and bring good
fortune in everything, prayers, offerings and altars needed to be made
wherever they marched. In addition, they brought with them a
complex celestial social system that incorporated local gods, professional protectors and imperial and official cults that they had picked
up throughout their travels within the empire. While worship of
personal protectors was a daily business, the year's calendar was
marked with festivals to celebrate the passing of the seasons, altars
were regularly serviced to guarantee victory, rituals performed to
sanctify the status quo, religious guilds and household shrines organised, talismen crafted to ward off spirits and wayside markers carved
to protect the traveller against evil.

Emperors themselves became objects of worship, giving the impression of distant rulers watching over their domains. Commodus was
partial to statues of himself as Hercules, while Domitian promoted the
worship of his favourite goddess, Minerva, the inventor of music and
protector of the parade ground. Hadrian even had the temerity to deify
his lover, Antinous, creating a series of statues that represented his

paramour as the Roman god Bacchus and Egyptian Osiris, both symbols of rebirth and youth.

The army were a superstitious lot and religious cults followed the military routes across the country. The first major temple to be built in Camulodunum was constructed almost as soon as the *colonia* was established, and dedicated to the divine person of the Emperor Claudius. There is similar evidence that the gods of Rome swiftly settled on the banks of the Thames in Londinium. Beside the first forum a small basilica was set up, while inscriptions indicate at least one temple to Jupiter, the father of the gods. On the south bank there was a temple to the Egyptian god Isis. The remains of a round building on Peter's Hill suggest another holy site. It is said that a temple to Diana was built on the place that has for the last 1,400 years been home to St Paul's Cathedral. A vast amount of altars, plaques, vows, dedications and curse tablets has been uncovered which proves that the Romans saw their gods walk the streets of the city, doing the bidding of dedicated petitioners.

By the mid-third century, the capital of Britannia Prima was also home to a new temple. Mithraism originated in Persia, possibly from the town of Tarsus on the eastern borders of the empire in modern-day Turkey. The first Roman mention of the cult was in a dedication by Sacidius Barbarus, of the XV Apollinaris legion, stationed in Austria. The legion had travelled extensively – to Austria, Armenia, Jerusalem and back. At some point, Barbarus had adopted a new icon of worship. Mithraism soon began to infiltrate the army, starting first in legions which saw service in the East but then finding rich soil in Germany and Gaul. It appears to have marched into Britannia near the beginning of the third century, by which time it had been officially sanctioned by the empire and became hugely popular amongst the cohorts on the northern frontier. A temple to the Persian god was consecrated on the eastern banks of the River Walbrook inside the walls of the city.

There is still much debate about what Mithraism was. Until recently it was considered to be a mutation of Zoroastrianism, or an initiatory cult involved in animal sacrifice. The London temple itself, uncovered by Professor Grimes in 1954, conformed to many similar temples – the mithraea – found on the frontier in Germany and near Rome. The building was made from stone, faced with Kentish rag and levelled with a series of courses of tiles; following the standard form of a basilica, it lay approximately east to west, in total nineteen metres long and eleven metres wide, with the portico on the east end and the altar to the west. Inside, there was a long nave that ran the full length of the interior, with two aisles, arcades of stone columns on both sides, where the cult members reclined. In the west end, a series of steps led down to a plinth, while to the south there was a well. It was here that Grimes uncovered his most unexpected find.

The tauroctony, the central icon of the cult, depicted the story of Mithras, combining the personality of the god, born of stone, who alongside a dog, a snake, a raven and a scorpion kills a bull. As a result many theorists have presumed that this was a cult dripping in blood and sacrifice. Recent research suggests, however, that Mithraism has a more rational explanation than most ancient cults. The symbolism of the bull-slaying can be read as an astrological prediction – the moment spring turns into summer. The figures each represent an astrological entity: the bull is Taurus, the dog the stars Canis Major, the snake Hydra. There is also evidence of the sun and moon, and the constellations of Scorpio, Leo and Gemini.

Tarsus was known as an intellectual powerhouse that held a library of over 200,000 books, including the work of Hipparchus, the Greek astronomer who bridged the scientific gap between the stargazers of Babylonian and classical tradition. The Babylonians had systematically observed and charted the night sky in order to predict eclipses and celestial portents; Hipparchus concluded that the whole universe worked to a single plan that could be discerned by careful observation. Mithras's tauroctony therefore mapped the hoped-for order within the universe with a system to appease the gods that controlled the fates and the seasons. Not just gods but also the motions of the heavens themselves predicted fortune and order.

As in the heavens, so on earth: Mithras's temple represented the unity within the empire, and the means by which it was made concrete. Starting as a military cult in which the necessity for order and fortune united soldiers who were themselves recruited from every nation,

Mithraism was soon adopted by the merchants. It linked the turning of the celestial spheres with local needs and fears and offered a celestial reason for belonging. Through a sophisticated system of initiation rites, it also embodied and sanctified the social order within seven levels of seniority: raven, bridegroom, soldier, lion, Persian, sun-courier, father; what secrets each rank revealed are unknown.

Christianity arrived in Britannia soon after the mithraeum was built and offered the prospect of one god rather than many. In the following decades the fortunes of the Church rose and fell on the whim of the emperor. A Christian basilica and a London bishop, a *vicarius* granted by Rome, are mentioned but no evidence has as yet been found. It is with a certain irony that Edward Gibbon, writing his masterwork *The Decline and Fall of the Roman Empire*, identified Christianity as one of the main reasons for the decimation of the great empire. While Mithraism united its adherents to the cosmic system and the empire, Christianity offered an alternative power, a religion that promoted private redemption above public service. Within a century, Rome was under threat and there was nothing the gods could do to save the empire.

When the Romans left Britannia in AD 410, Governor Honorius commanded the nation to 'look to its own defences' and departed. The temple still remains, however, one of the foundation stones of the city. In 2006 it was declared that the ancient stones were to be returned to their original setting beside the Walbrook, but this was not to be. Instead a new, prestigious modern block, the Walbrook Building, has been built here, designed by Foster + Partners, boasting office space as well as extensive shopping facilities. In a quirk of fate the temple has now been replaced by its most contemporary incarnation – the shopping mall.

Once the Romans had abandoned Augusta, Britannia was soon overrun by tribesmen who had little interest in cities; soon after, Rome itself was conquered. Without the centre the empire could not hold, and without Rome there was no need for London and the bridge, the forum, the walls and the temple were all allowed to break and decline. It was only centuries later, when the stones of the city were being rebuilt, that the story of London was told once again.

The myths surrounding the birth of a city often involve the descent of gods into the world of men, a period of nomadic wandering, the fulfilment of a prophecy, a sign of divine approval. The city needed its own genesis story, as John Stow commented: 'by interlacing divine matters with human, to make the first foundation of Cities more honourable, more sacred, and as it were of greater majesty'.[16] Both the Bible and the Qur'an recall that the very first city was built by Adam's son, Cain, the tiller of the ground, who murdered his brother, the nomadic keeper of the sheep, in jealousy and was banished by God. The mark of Cain can be found in the foundation myth of all cities.

The new history of London was written by the twelfth-century monk Geoffrey of Monmouth, a Welshman who lived most of his life in London. He claimed that he heard it first from Walter, Archdeacon of Oxford, and it may have come from 'a certain very ancient book written in the British language'.[17] Geoffrey may have also read the work of Nennius, the Abbot of Bangor and 'pupil of the holy Elvodug',[18] which told a similar story. London was not born with the spilling of fraternal blood, but had its origins in the fire that consumed Troy. Brutus was the great-grandson of Aeneas, the hero of Virgil's poem, who escaped the flames and wandered Europe before finding a refuge in ancient Italy. On the island of Leogetia Brutus was visited by the goddess Diana, who told him:

> Brutus, beyond the setting of the sun, past the realms of Gaul, there lies an island in the sea, once occupied by giants. Now it is empty and ready for your folk. Down the years this will prove an abode suited to you and your people; for your descendants it will be a second Troy. A race of Kings will be born there from your stock and the round circle of the whole earth will be subject to them.[19]

And so, after many travels – including Africa, the altars of the Philistines, the salt-pan lakes of the Middle East, Russicada and the Mountains of Zarec, sailing up the River Malve and landing at Mauretania, withstanding the temptations of the Sirens' call at the Pillars of

Hercules – Brutus and his men reached the coast of Albion, where they established their new kingdom at Totnes, in the south-west of the island. They soon discovered that they had disembarked onto an island of giants and, after many struggles, culminating in the defeat of Gogmagog, claimed the island for themselves. Meanwhile Brutus went in search of his own city and 'visited every part of the land in search of a suitable spot. He came at length to the River Thames, walked up and down its banks and so chose a site suited to his purpose. There he built his city and called it Troia Nova.'[20] A new Troy.

From Brutus, whose body was buried in the walls of the city he founded,[21] came generations of British kings. The last of the line was King Lud, who transformed the fortifications of London in the face of the threat from Julius Caesar, 're-buil[ding] the walls of the town of Trinovantum and gird[ing] it round with innumerable towers'.[22] On his death the city was renamed Kaerlud, Lud's city, which corrupted to Kaerlundein and finally, transformed by the tongues of foreign invaders, to Lundres. Lud's body was interred by the gate which soon bore his name, Porthlud or Ludgate, on the western fringe of the city; the name still lingers today, although the gate itself has had many lives. Ludgate may have also derived, less dramatically, from the Old English for a postern, 'ludgeat'.

Thus, a thousand years after the departure of the Romans the city was rebuilt from legend as well as stone. It was clearly Geoffrey of Monmouth's aim to find London's origins in an age before the Caesars, for Brutus's story proved that London was the equal to and not the servant of Rome. Thus London was no longer on the edge of an imperial history, but at the centre of its own narrative.

This genesis myth was consolidated in the story of the London Stone, the last of the foundation stones of the city. Just north of the Thames on present-day Cannon Street stands an ancient lump of Oolite stone, today encaged with a Victorian metal grille. For some, it was a stone statue that Brutus brought with him to mark his new city by the Thames; from this mythical origin comes a cascade of other stories that empower the stone: the mystic poet William Blake thought it might be a druid's altar; others, an altar to Diana. Mythic or mundane, the stone has acted

2. The London Stone, encased and forgotten on Cannon Street

as a centre-point of the city for centuries, a focus for civic power, and the place where myth becomes history. John Stow noted that the stone appeared in a 'fair written Gospel Booke' belonging to the tenth-century Saxon king, Ethelstone. The first Lord Mayor, Henry Fitz Ailwyn, had the additional surname De Londonestone, perhaps to enhance his authority, and it is recorded that all new proclamations were made with the striking of the civic sword against the stone. This act of political theatre was dramatised by Shakespeare in Henry VI, Part 2, when Jack Cade leads the peasant rebels into the city and announces, 'And here, sitting upon London Stone, I charge and command that, of the city's cost, the pissing conduit run nothing but claret wine this first year of our reign.'[23]

However, one must be cautious approaching the stone. All legends can be used and reinvented for all manner of purposes and the London

Stone, in particular, continues to attract speculation. It is often said that 'So long as the Stone of Brutus is safe, So long will London flourish'. This has since been uncovered as a Victorian hoax, concocted by a Welsh vicar, the Rev. Richard Williams Morgan, for his own entertainment. The myth-making continues to the present day, with the historian Adrian Gilbert claiming in 2002 that the stone was that from which King Arthur extracted Excalibur. Recent archaeological digs have uncovered a vast Roman villa nearby and suggest that the stone could merely have been a gatepost. It could also have been a *milliarium*, the centre-stone from which all Roman roads radiated and were measured. We will never know, and perhaps that is as it should be.

The myths of Brutus and the London Stone are as important as the rediscovery of the ancient stones of London themselves. Just as the bridge, the forum, the wall and the temple tell us of the foundations of the city, so the stories we tell each other of how the city was born teach us that London has risen and fallen, and been reborn; that it began by chance, as the result of a fluke; that its shape is determined by its function as a workshop, a fort, a wharf, a market place, a holy site. Carved in stone and later recreated in a genesis myth born out of the ruins, London has become permanent and in its origins can be found its many faces.

CHAPTER 2

WESTMINSTER ABBEY

Henry III's Heaven on Earth

Stone seems, by the cunning labour of the chisel, to have been robbed of its weight and density, suspended as if by magic.

Washington Irving, *The Sketchbook of Geoffrey Crayon, Gent.*

At 9.08 on the morning of 6 September 1997, the coffin was taken from its resting place at the royal apartments at Kensington Palace on the edge of Kensington Park, and returned to St James's Palace. In the days since the Princess of Wales's death, wreaths of flowers had been placed at the palace gates in front of Hawksmoor's classical villa, covering the gravel pathway and attached to the black metal railings. From St James's the coffin was carried upon a gun carriage, pulled by Hussars and draped in the Royal Standard, followed by members of the Princess's family and escorted by a phalanx of uniformed guards, as it wound its way through the tearful crowd, some having camped for nights along the roadside, towards Westminster Abbey.

Inside the ancient abbey, the sacred site of royal rituals for over 800 years, the nobles and grandees of the modern age assembled: the rump of the royal household and the Princess's family, political leaders from home and abroad, royalty from Europe as well as further afield. The modern saints were also there: pop singers, movie stars and fashion designers. At one point, the singer Elton John sang a song that he had written for Marilyn Monroe, transforming the lyrics to beatify 'England's Rose', which would later sell around the world, becoming a best-selling single in France, Norway and Japan. The whole ceremony was watched by 32 million people in the UK and by billions around the world.

Over 700 years earlier, on 13 October 1269, all the nobles of the realm were commanded to attend another ceremony, the translation of a royal coffin into the sacred space of Westminster. On that day the remains of St Edward the Confessor were raised from the reliquary where they had been resting since 1245 and carried around the unfinished abbey by Henry III, King Richard of Germany, the two princes, Edward and Edmund, the Earl of Surrey and Philip Bassett. The body was to be placed in the new tomb located behind the high altar, delicately ornamented with intricate stone carvings and surrounded by precious relics. As the hallowed saint was carried towards his seat of power, the assembled dignitaries, nobles and bishops, were encouraged to note that the new abbey that surrounded them, a vast edifice of towering stone and glass, was now England's holy of holies, rebuilt by Henry III for the glory of his royal line. The placing of the saint's body at the centre of the new abbey was proof not just of Henry's religiosity but also the sanctity of the English Crown.

The troop finally arrived at the shrine that now gleamed with gold and precious jewels. Ceremonial candles flickered at each corner, picking out the stones that had come all the way from the ancient monuments of Italy, Greece and Egypt. The stones themselves were part of a more intricate pattern that covered every surface; in front of the altar was a newly completed pavement, a sacred space where the royal rituals – baptism, coronation and funeral – would be conducted. This pavement, in its patterns of stones, symbols and forms, suggested the connection between the abbey and God's creation, a metaphysical puzzle that linked the earth and the heavens, and placed the throne of England as the intermediary between the two worlds.

The two events, although centuries apart, are similar and revealing. The power of the building itself was the means of transubstantiation, transforming the royal body into sainthood. Yet the story behind the creation of Westminster Abbey is not a transcendental one, but rather a story of how the stones of London were used to establish a new kind of power; and how a new style of architecture – the Gothic – was adopted

3. The shrine of St Edward the Confessor

for both political and religious purposes. The abbey was built at a turning point in the history of the English Crown, as well as the development of London itself, and these many personalities can still be found in the fabric of Henry III's monument.

In 1245 Henry III, 'inspired by the devotion he felt towards St Edward',[1] commanded that work begin on the rebuilding of the abbey close by his palace at Westminster. By this time he had sat on the English throne longer than most of his forebears, but his reign was never secure. There were threats at home from the powerful nobles who demanded that the limits of his kingship be recorded in law, as well as from abroad, where the French kings took advantage of England's weakness to covet Henry's lands. Unable to challenge his rivals on the battlefield, Henry sought other ways of consolidating his power, and found consolation and succour in his faith, especially in the veneration of St Edward, the former Saxon King of England, who first built the abbey at Westminster. The site had been a monastery and centre of learning since the tenth century, and its proximity to the royal palace had always lent it a particular potency; yet Henry was determined to shore up his rule by transforming the enclave into a heaven on earth – a new cosmology between God, kings, men and the city.

The abbey, like London itself, has a multitude of genesis myths. According to the fourteenth-century monk John Flete, it was first built in the sixth century upon the site of a temple to Apollo, thus restoring the sacred stones of the Romans. Other chroniclers claim the abbey was established by King Ethelbert of Kent in the following century and dedicated to St Peter, who mysteriously appeared and himself conducted the dedication of the church in AD 604, the same year that a chapel was first built on the site that would become St Paul's Cathedral. All these stories were concocted at various times to enhance the power of the site, enshrined in forged charters and inaccurate chronologies, to make the abbey older and more potent than its rivals.

The truth, however, was more humble: a Saxon church was established here after the seventh century, during the reign of Offa of Mercia. It was not until the dawn of the new millennium that the church became an abbey when, in AD 970, the Archbishop of Canterbury, Dunstan, was granted Thorney Island by King Edgar, who saw a network of religious communities around the country as the best way to consolidate his Saxon power base. Here Dunstan brought with him twelve monks who observed the rules set out by St Benedict, dedicated to the horarium, the daily cycle of prayer and work. Nonetheless, the abbey also came with a number of local estates, making it rich and influential. This 'Westminster Corridor' would later stretch across some of the most prosperous neighbourhoods of the burgeoning London suburbs – from Holborn to the Strand, and north to Hendon and Hampstead, tying the abbey's wealth to the success of the metropolis.

The abbey was therefore both of the city and yet separate, a prosperous landowner yet also an alternative to the mundane world outside the cloister. Within the walls of the monastery a holy community evolved offering an enclosed world, dedicated to the trade in souls. It was thus practising the doctrines of the first work of medieval theology, *The City of God* by St Augustine, written in the fifth century in response to the rise of paganism at the end of the Roman Empire. Augustine split the world into two cities: the City of Man and the City of God, which were created at the moment of Adam's expulsion from the Garden, confirmed by the birth of two sons: 'Cain was the first-born, and he belonged to the city of men; after him was born Abel, who belonged to the city of God.'[2] The abbey, therefore, was a refuge for those who wished to turn their backs on the mark of Cain, the temptations of earthly pleasures, and to work for the restoration of the New Jerusalem.

The abbey represented more than just a haven, for its establishment coincided with a revolution in monastic politics. As the millennium approached, a date many thought heralded the end of the world, the Benedictine Abbot St Berno at Cluny in east-central France hoped to build not just Jerusalem but a temporal paradise. The monastery at Cluny was separate from earthly politics and reported to the Pope rather than local lords, abiding by the law of God alone. By the twelfth century there were over 314 monasteries, as well as numerous houses and priories that adopted the Cluniac reforms. Westminster was certainly influenced by the reforms, and was a working monastery with a community of brothers dedicated to prayer and learning, yet its location would ensure that it was never far from the political debates of the nation.

From now on the monastery reflected the many faces of the city: it represented Augustine's City of God within the metaphysical realm, but also in relation to the walled city to the east. Since the seventh century, the Saxon settlement had grown outside the Roman enclave rather than seek safety within its crumbling walls. Here the tribesmen founded a new London, Lundewic (on the site of present-day Aldwych), where a beachhead of shingle made for a rudimentary port. This community thrived because, rather than docking at the old Roman quays, it was common for traders to drag their longboats onto the beach and sell their wares from the gunwales. This scrap of land was fought over and won by successive generations of East Saxons, West Saxons and Mercians; archaeologists have also unearthed here evidence of a healthy trade between the Saxon settlers and northern France, the Low Countries and the Rhineland.

It was not until the ninth century that King Alfred encouraged the tribesmen to return inside the Roman walls and London, named Lundenburgh, was revived. A new street plan was formulated around a settlement of about forty houses, and some of the principal routes of the medieval city laid over the old Roman thoroughfares. The wooden bridge remained the main crossing place of the city and central to the city's preservation; it was where the citizens made their last stand against the forces of Svein Forkbeard in 1013, while Olaf II attempted to pull it down with his Danish ships during a siege the following year, inspiring the folk song 'London Bridge is Falling Down'. The abbey, west of the walls, shared the dangers of invasion and nothing remains of that first monastery.

It was the victorious Danes themselves who transformed the fortunes of London when Cnut, son of Svein Forkbeard, conquered the city and began to build his royal palace inside the city walls. The Thames location and the good river navigation made the port an attractive proposition to a new ruler who still had lands across the North Sea. Like the Romans, Cnut chose London because of its proximity to the Continent, thus linking the city's fortune with Europe. Yet it came at a cost: in 1018 the new community that huddled around his palace was forced to pay one eighth of the whole tax demand placed on England.

Cnut's son Harold I was buried at Westminster in 1040, suggesting some royal link with the religious community. Nonetheless, his brother Harthacnut travelled from Denmark at the news and, not wishing his sibling the honour of a royal burial, had his body 'thrown into the fen'.[3] Harthacnut himself only held the crown for two years and was succeeded by his half-brother, the British-born Edward, the seventh son of King Aethelred and his Norman wife Emma (Harthacnut's mother), who had spent the past twenty-four years in exile. According to legend, Edward had promised St Peter that if he gained the throne he would venture on a pilgrimage to the saint's tomb in Rome. His nobles were against the idea; the last forty years had been treacherous and Edward was persuaded to ask the Pope to release him from the vow of a long and dangerous voyage on the condition that Edward dedicated himself to the rebuilding of the abbey at Westminster. Thus, the relationship between the monastery and the royal line was consolidated with a sacred oath.

By the 1050s work on the abbey was under way and, according to a later chronicler, William of Malmesbury, it was 'the first in England erected in the fashion which all now follow at great expense'.[4] The Romanesque was foreign and new, Norman even before the Norman Conquest. The heavy, impressive architecture was a resurrection of the Roman basilica, but with new influences and ideas picked up from the Byzantine Empire by soldiers marching to the Holy Lands and traders in search of eastern spices. The sense of mass, the effort of raising such stones, offered a monumental permanence in a world of uncertainty and change. Few records of Edward's abbey remain, however. Its first chronicle was written by the Benedictine monk Sulcard in the 1080s:

> ... the princely house of the altar, noble with its most lofty vaulting, is surrounded by dressed stone evenly jointed. Also the passage round that temple is enclosed on both sides by a double arching of stone with the joints of the structure strongly consolidated on this side and that. Furthermore, the crossing of the church, which is to hold in its midst the choir of God's choristers, and to uphold with like support from either side the high apex of the central tower, rises simply at first with a low and sturdy vault, swells with many a stair spiralling up in artistic profusion, but then a plain wall climbs to the wooden roof which is carefully covered with lead.[5]

The abbey was completed in 1065 and plans were made to consecrate the building that Christmas Day, but it was not to be. On the eve of the dedication Edward took ill in his new palace and, while he presented himself before his barons the next day, he was too weak to observe the festivities, and sent his wife Edith in his place. On 5 January 1066 he died. His body was carried to his new church and in solemn ceremony buried before the high altar. Almost immediately there were claims of the departed king performing miracles. His death transformed the abbey into a royal mausoleum; it also left an empty throne.

Within days Harold Godwinson, Edward's brother-in-law, was crowned at Westminster, but by the end of the year a new Norman dynasty was on the throne. In October Harold faced an army led by his old comrade, William, Duke of Normandy, who also claimed to be king and had the support of the Pope to prove it. The two armies faced each other outside the Kentish village of Hastings. By the next morning, the Norman victory was declared. England's king was dead, but the crown had not yet been won.

Like every conqueror, William knew that, to take the nation, he had to conquer London, which was protected 'on the left side by walls, on the right side by the river, [thus] neither fears enemies nor dreads being taken by storm'. William finally arrived on the southern banks of the Thames and the unprotected settlement of Southwark was put to the sword. Then, rather than facing the city walls head-on, William marched up the Thames and crossed, bringing his forces as far as Westminster, where he sent messages that he was building engines and battering rams to pull down the walls, threatening to 'bring the proud tower in rubble'.[6] Londoners – merchants, not warriors – capitulated.

On Christmas Day 1066, William, Duke of Normandy, was crowned William I of England in Edward's Westminster Abbey, thus consolidating the sacred relationship between the abbey and the throne. The ritual was delicately calibrated to show that William was the true heir of the Confessor and that a new dynasty was born out of the old. The Conqueror was also keen to show himself as the natural successor to Charlemagne, the father of the Holy Roman Empire, who had been crowned on Christmas Day 800 at St Peter's Basilica, Rome, by the Pope himself. The abbey was thus established as the powerhouse for a king who aspired to recreate the Roman Imperium, stretching from Scotland to Sicily. This, too, would be in Henry III's mind as he hoped to set his own reign in sacred stones 150 years later.

The City of God was swiftly becoming the enclave of kings as the village of Westminster itself grew around the burgeoning court and along the boundaries of the abbey. Although William, like many of his predecessors, rarely stayed in one place for long, Westminster became one of his principal centres for ritual and administration, and after his campaigns in the west and the north he returned and developed a palace under the shadow of the abbey. His son, William Rufus, who claimed the throne in 1087, added the magnificent Westminster Hall to the site as a symbol of his majesty and here he held his court sessions and the annual Whitsun banquet for 'the great men of the kingdom'.[7]

It was the most magnificent building and the largest hall in Britain, if not Europe, standing seventy-three by twenty metres, with walls twelve metres high. The room was a stunning work of medieval engineering. Particularly impressive was the way in which the roof spanned such a vast area, using an ingenious forest of timberwork columns, struts and arcades. The walls were whitewashed and covered in 'rich and minute paintings'[8] as well as hangings and, when glass was added in the twelfth century, stained windows. Here the fiery monarch turned political power into architecture, a space that would remain at the heart of government for the next 800 years.

The palace also became the fixed legal and administrative centre for the King's finances and councils, and Henry II moved his Exchequer here from Winchester, making it the fiscal centre of the nation, which soon attracted other spheres of power. As the court increasingly conversed in contracts and statutes the Temple, halfway between Westminster and the city and completed in 1185 by the Knights Templar, became home to the legal profession. Across the river at Lambeth the most powerful prelate in England, the Archbishop of Canterbury, built his palace, while the Archbishop of York set his palace nearby on the northern bank at Whitehall.

As the court's power increased, a community began to grow outside the royal walls that profited from the proximity to power and money. In the Domesday Book of 1086, Westminster was designated a 'Vill' and contained nineteen villeins and forty-two cottars; in addition there was housing for twenty-five knights and other men of the abbey. By 1200 this had become a vital, buzzing enclave. Many of the new population were lay staff – seneschals, stewards, clerks; some of these senior titles became hereditary and included housing near the abbey precinct.

Proximity to the royal court also brought with it a raft of officials and courtiers, many of whom settled on land rented from the abbey, swiftly turning the surrounding fields that had once been ploughed by the monks into teeming streets, many that we know today: King Street for royal servants, and rich merchants such as Odo the goldsmith and Ralph Vinter the wine-seller; Tothill and Longditch for favoured abbey workers; while craftsmen and courtiers hoped to profit from the market in the hamlets to the east – Charing Cross and St Martin-in-the-Fields. The neighbourhood was ripe for speculators like Nathaniel de Levelond, Keeper of the King's Palace, who lived near the gatehouse to Westminster Hall, and his neighbour John de Upton, the Marshal, who both found time to profit from the local housing market.

There was also a growing relationship between the court and the city to the east. Only a few weeks after his coronation William wrote to the bishop, portreeves and citizens of London 'in friendly fashion', and declared that the laws of the city 'be preserved as far as they were in King Edward's day.'[9] It was a wise move, for despite the amount of blood spilt and the continued brutality of the Norman lords across their newly conquered territories, London was little changed by its new masters. Over the next 150 years the city would fortify its identity as separate from royal Westminster, and increase its power as the trading capital of the island. In return for its freedom, and despite occasional dissent, London bolstered and funded the King's power and acted as a catalyst for change at the centre of the nation.

William gave the city its freedom but he consolidated his dominance over the 'fickleness of the vast and fierce populace'[10] in stone. At the eastern end of the walls he built the White Tower, thirty metres high with walls five metres thick, where he stationed his own marshal and armoury. At the western fringes he built Baynard's Castle and Montfichet Tower. These fortifications were principally to defend the city against Danish invasions, but it was also clear that they were there to watch the city. This was confirmed by the building of the Fleet prison, just to the west of the walls.

The city nonetheless benefited from the security of peacetime and the new opportunities to trade with Europe, exporting wools through the port of Calais and importing wine and precious metals from across the Norman Empire. London grew – it was possibly the greatest city in northern Europe: at the time of the Conquest the population was

10,000–20,000, doubling during the following century, and by 1300 was close to 100,000. It also grew rich, delivering the lion's share of the King's Exchequer. Thus the economic power of the Crown became increasingly reliant on the buzzing activity of the docks of the walled city.

The two cities – London and Westminster – thus grew together. Westminster offered a major market for many of the luxury goods that arrived up the Thames, and the city often protected the Crown in times of trouble. Yet London also sought its independence from the throne, and the Crown, in turn, could barely complain in moments of weakness when it was desperate for money or support. This, in time, became codified in a sophisticated political system of offices, charters and rights between the two cities that balanced and moderated the often volatile relationship.

William I inherited a city that was already divided into a series of wards, which looked after local affairs and were led by aldermen. Above this administrative layer he placed two sheriffs, royal officers with the task of gathering taxes. During the civil wars of the 1130s between Stephen and Matilda over their rights to the throne, the aldermen were able to bargain with the King to appoint their own sheriff in return for support. In desperation, Stephen was also willing to proclaim the city a 'commune', a self-governing city state similar to the independent cities in Italy or northern France. Once the war ended many of these privileges were rescinded by Henry II; however, a precedent had been set.

By the end of the twelfth century the Crown was in trouble again. Richard I, the Lion Heart, was lost in the crusades, and his proxy, the Bishop of Ely, William de Longchamp, was under threat from the King's brother John, who in 1191 marched on the city. Longchamp was forced to find safety in the Tower, which was surrounded by the citizenry. The city elders then negotiated to recognise John in exchange for the renewal of the 'commune' status. In addition, the city pressed for the creation of its own civic baron – the Lord Mayor. Henry Fitz Ailwyn – a cloth merchant who lived and worked near to the London Stone, was a leading alderman and had been closely involved in the negotiations with John – was elected as the first. In this role he represented the interests of the leading citizens to the King and the concerns of the King to the citizenry.

In time, the role was clarified and the system of annual elections organised, which continue to the present day.

As they gained power and wealth, the city leaders felt the urge to build their own halls and monuments. As the city administration grew it became increasingly important to find a site for the smooth running of government, but also the city elders wanted a court in which to exercise their new-found power. According to Gerald of Wales, cleric and chronicler, the first location for the meetings was a well-known tavern; however, the site of the ancient Roman amphitheatre, on the north-west corner of the walls, was soon adopted. It was said that the Saxon *folkmoot* had once made its home here in the ruined piers of the stone theatre, thus proving that the city government was older than the Normans or Plantagenets. It was, therefore, the ideal site for the Guildhall. The first mention of the hall is found in a 1127 charter, but the building that still remains today as the administrative centre of the Corporation of London was developed over the following centuries.

As the political identity of the city was becoming established, it was also being consolidated in the massive piers and the awesome width of the new London Bridge, which was started in the 1170s and completed in 1209. In times of uncomfortable peace, the bridge was one of the few points of union between the King and the city as the new crossing had been inspired by Henry II but controlled by the city elders. The priest/architect Peter de Colechurch designed the nineteen arches that spanned the river from the north bank to Southwark; it was an extraordinary work of engineering that symbolised the power of the city. In those days the ingenuity of building a bridge matched that of a cathedral, and the masters of each trade held tightly onto their mysteries and secrets; a bridge represented man's conquest of nature, the science of building bringing order and reason to the city of men. The man who could command such constructions had a very special power indeed. The bridge would thus also foreshadow the next great project within the city – Henry III's rebuilding of Westminster Abbey.

For the infant Henry III, an anxious mistrust of the city was bred in the bone. In May 1215, when he was only eight years old, he watched as

London turned its back on his father, King John, and supported the barons in a civil war that erupted on the question of the limits of kingship. John had been high-handed with his subjects, squeezing them for money to fund his foreign ventures; while his brother, Richard I, had bled the coffers of the nation but had returned with victories and honour, John had taken the money and lost the war. For his failures he gained two nicknames – 'Softsword' because of his martial failure and 'Lackland' for being the first English monarch since William I to lose all the royal lands in Normandy. That May the nobles could tolerate it no longer and, as they conspired, the mayor offered the walls of the city as protection.

John's failures highlighted the changing relationship between the Crown and the nation. The traditional feudal structure of kingship was no longer viable, and new ideas were beginning to enter the debate that reconfigured the shape of society; Robert Grosseteste, Bishop of Lincoln and the leading scholastic thinker in the land, proposed that the king was a part of the body politic, not a separate divine proxy above the law and answerable only to God. This was particularly felt by the barons, who had for a long time accepted that the king was the first among equals rather than a superior semi-divine class. These matters came to a head when John squeezed too hard for money and offered nothing in return. That summer, the barons strong-armed John out of his palace at Westminster to Runnymede, where he was forced to sign a charter that redefined the conditions of the Crown.

London was central in the rebellion that led to the Magna Carta and the clear definition of rights and liberties was the end of the feudal relationship based on obligations and duty. Clause 13 in particular dealt with the new relationship between Crown and city: 'The city of London shall enjoy all its ancient liberties and free customs, both by land and by water. We also will and grant that all other cities, boroughs, towns, and ports shall enjoy all their liberties and free customs.'[11]

King John signed the charter but had no intention of honouring it; and the rest of his short reign was spent in civil war. By the time of his death in October 1216 he had lost much of his land and, as legend goes, had seen his treasure sink into the Wash in a desperate attempt to escape his pursuers. Worse, some of the barons had invited the French Prince Louis to England to take the throne, and he had been rapturously welcomed into London. Within months, the Scottish army led by Alexander II marched over London Bridge. On 28 October 1216 the nine-year-old Henry III was crowned with his mother's chaplet rather than the sacred ornaments of kingship a long way from London at Gloucester Abbey. It was another four years before he was formally crowned at Westminster Abbey in the tradition of his ancestors.

On that occasion, the archbishop made Henry swear an oath to protect the Church and the people and uphold the law of the land; he was formally blessed with 'the insignia of royalty and crown of the most saintly King Edward'.[12] Thus Henry was united through the most sacred of ceremonies with England's royal saint, both as a 'kinsman' and in piety; it would soon become the central image of his kingship. When he started work on renovating his palace at Westminster in 1226, he commissioned the Painted Chamber, a private apartment that he turned into a colourful shrine to his forebear, and, by association, to his own divine kingship. Every surface of the room was decorated with scenes from the saint's life (two of the panels still exist in the British Museum). It was with some irony – and perhaps posthumous revenge against his father – that Henry's son, Edward I, allowed this room to be used as the first permanent home of Parliament.

The young Henry III had few other protectors to guide him; he had already lost his father and within months his mother fled to her family in France, forcing the boy king to rely on the power of others to hold onto his birthright. Subsequently, he spent his minority in a desperate search for father figures. Later chroniclers called Henry 'most pious' and 'simplex', an untranslatable word that for his enemies indicated stupidity or, in a more fair-minded diagnosis, naivety. He never found the wherewithal to take control of the events around him and, despite being England's longest-reigning monarch, failed to overcome his inheritance: the Crown was poor and dependent on the barons who forced him to confirm the charter. In the late 1220s he attempted to regain power from the nobles who had dominated his minority and he haltingly attempted to rule by himself through the 1230s.

The young man found consolation in prayer and in his piety Henry had a prodigious appetite: he increased the days that his choir chanted the *Laudes Regiae,* calling for Christ's aid; and it was said he fed over 500 paupers in Westminster daily. In particular he developed his special veneration for St Edward the Confessor as a means of enunciating his rule. In 1239, he even named his first-born son Edward. As his kingship was being redefined by charter, scratched into law by scriveners, and seemingly at the mercy of the barons, Henry III desired to promote the divine image of the English Crown.

Thus in 1245 he played his strongest hand and vowed to transform the sacred fabric of the abbey in the hope of consolidating his own rule: he would revive the shrine to St Edward and make the abbey the site for all royal rituals – baptism, coronation and a reliquary. The stones of Westminster themselves would become proof of kingship, dynasty and divine protection beyond lawyers' quibbles and nobles' threats. As Matthew Paris noted in his *Chronicle of Westminster:* 'In the same year the king, inspired by the devotion which he felt towards St Edward, ordered the church of St Peter at Westminster, to be enlarged. He therefore caused the old walls, with the tower on the eastern side, to be pulled down and new and handsome ones to be erected by clever architects at his own expense.'[13]

Henry also sought a new architecture, the Gothic, to announce his message to the world. The story of this architectural movement is one of the most debated in design history: for some, it was a historical period – the expression of the High and Late Middle Ages – a time of intellectual and political change; for others, it is best explained through its physical characteristics – the development of the pointed arch, the ribbed vault and the flying buttress – without reference to its historical context. It was, first and foremost, an urban invention, found in the new towns of France, rather than the secluded communities of the abbots with their old feudal powers. In this the Gothic reflected the rise of the city above the rural powerhouses as the new economic centre of the nation, and was therefore the ideal style for a new building that stood at the crossroads of both.

The new architecture was also a reflection of the scholastic revolution in learning, of man's place within God's creation; the Gothic cathedral was designed to convince and inspire, engage the mind as well as create a sense of physical change. The whole machinery of the building was focused on the creation of a magnificent interior, the manipulation of space within the walls, with every inch of the interior laden with meaning. The action of entering the abbey was intended to be a translation from one world into something else. Abbé Suger, Abbot of Saint-Denis and often named as the first proponent of the new style, wrote of this experience as if it were Augustine's City of God made stone:

> ... the loveliness of the many coloured gems has called me away from external cares, and worthy meditation has induced me to reflect, transferring that which is material to that which is immaterial ... then it seems to me that I see myself dwelling, as it were, in some strange region of the universe which neither exists entirely in the slime of the earth nor entirely in the purity of heaven.[14]

In all corners of the abbey, the ancient mysteries were illuminated in statues and symbols, wonder and reason bringing understanding to faith. In this it was both a temple to, and an exact physical expression of, the latest ideas that were emerging from the new University of Paris, which was already the alma mater of Peter Abelard, St Thomas of Canterbury and the Abbot of St Albans. At that time the professor of theology was the leading thinker Albertus Magnus, who was a pioneer in applying the ideas of Aristotle to Christian theology, later called scholasticism. The Gothic was this new reason turned into stone.

Luminosity became the defining feature of this marvel of engineering, the columns, vaults and decoration created with the intention of letting the stones melt into light. In the new scholastic age, as Robert Grosseteste noted, light was 'the mediator between the bodiless and the embodied substance, at the same time spiritual body and embodied spirit.'[15] For him, just as the study of the science of optics was the means to understand the natural world, reason was the spiritual light that God gave man to reveal His truths.

The Gothic interior was, therefore, both a symbol as well as an actual place of illumination; the architecture itself was as much a source of light as the stained blue, clear and red glass that intended to have the quality of gems 'glowing from within'.[16] Candles also highlighted the key areas of the space, so that the precious stones on tombs of kings shimmered and glinted. It was no accident that the shrine of St Edward, the centrepiece of Henry III's new abbey, was described as 'on high like a candle upon a candlestick, so that all who enter into the House of the Lord may behold its light'.[17]

As Henry III began work on his vision of heaven on earth at Westminster he sent his master mason, Henry of Reyns, to France to encounter the greatest examples of the Gothic for himself. In the 1130s the influential Abbé Suger started work on repairs to the church at Saint-Denis, the sacred mortuary of the French kings north of Paris. The designs stole and adapted where needed – the vaulting from Normandy, pointed arches from Burgundy – enlarging the basilica window and refusing to discard the lessons learnt from the Romans, nonetheless creating something new. After Saint-Denis, this revolutionary style was adopted throughout the Île de France where the Capetian kings held power: at Sens (1140s), Noyon (1150s), Laon and Notre Dame de Paris (1160s), Soissons (1170s) and Chartres (1190s).

As Henry planned his new abbey work was also still ongoing at Notre Dame de Paris, on the Île de la Cité in the centre of Paris. Begun eighty years earlier by Bishop Maurice de Sully, by the 1240s work was under way on the transepts and the extraordinary West End with its magnificent towers and rose window. In previous decades the Gothic had evolved its own language of ornamentation which added to the sense of lightness within the body of the church with an intense flowering of decoration, carving and manipulation of space. This was later called the Rayonnant style and had its apotheois in the nearby Sainte-Chapelle, built by Henry's rival and cousin, Louis IX.

The Sainte-Chapelle was a shrine to house Louis's newly acquired relics from the Holy Land, including Christ's crown of thorns which had been exorbitantly purchased from the Byzantine emperor. The Chapelle was a study in the limits of architecture, the stones attempting to melt into air as the arches between the columns and the rounded tops of the windows rose into a point, as if being lifted effortlessly to heaven.

Even the roof itself escalated into the sky, the ribs of the columns breaking off into fronds that crossed and anchored the vaulting in 'an incessant war against weight'.[18] The brand-new sciences of geometry and proportion, statics and load-bearing were tested with the creation of a latticework skeleton of stones that seemed to contain the space of the interior without mass, giving the impression, as Vasari commented, 'of being made out of paper'.[19]

This effect was made possible by the new learning, the abbey becoming the intersection between the light of reason and the science of architecture. In the 1160s, as Suger was working at Saint-Denis, the English monk Athelard of Bath translated Euclid's *Elements* for the first time from Arabic into Latin. These six volumes of mathematical proofs were the bedrock of all geometric science for the next 800 years. In the study of the rediscovered ancient texts God was an architect and the ordered universe an expression of his creation; it could be understood only through the laws of statics and geometry.

The universe was also harmony and proportion, and the same rules that governed the infinite also commanded the most mundane of objects. In the 1220s this was illustrated in the drawings of the Picardy architect Villard de Honnecourt, which dissected a number of objects – from a human face to animal bodies and architectural forms – into patterns and uniform shapes in relation to each other. Thus every object was reduced to geometric solids: the face into a series of symmetrical triangles, squares and rectangles. Villard was putting on paper the codes and knowledge of the master masons whose secrets could be found in the creation of the pointed arch, the wonder of a bridge spanning a river, the apex of a spire. Henry III's abbey was to be a microcosm of the sacred universe, built beside the Thames. The King had these architectural dreams in mind as he began work in 1245.

Matthew Paris, the Westminster chronicler, records that the project began in 1245 with the demolition of the eastern end of the old church and the central tower. A temporary choir was created in the nave for the monks while the shrine of St Edward was moved to safety. The foundations were laid the next year and work begun on the north-east corner while preparations were made to the Chapter House and vestibule within the abbey precinct. That April the sheriff of Kent was warned that the King expected 200 ships to arrive up the Thames bringing the first load of Caen stone, while marble was ordered from the Purbeck quarry in Dorset; the traffic clogged up the river with barges throughout the building season as they docked at the King's quay in Westminster. Freestone, Kentish ragstone and chalk were also used, arduously transported overland by cart along rough roads. At the same time Alexander, the master carpenter, visited the royal woods in the Weald and Essex to oversee the supply of timber for scaffolding and later for the roof.

The complete operation was to be funded by Henry III alone, just when the royal chest was nearly bare. Nonetheless, the abbey accounts show that there was no respite on construction throughout the 1240s and 50s. In 1248 the works cost £2,063, in 1249 £2,600, in 1250 £2,415; this was at a time when the whole royal income was no bigger than £35,000 a year. There are extraordinarily full accounts for the year 1253 which show the extent of the undertaking: between February and April 74 white (stone) cutters, 45 marblers, 24 layers, 4 carpenters, 13 polishers, 20 smiths, 15 glaziers and 131 labourers worked on-site. In the same period £203 12s 5½d was spent on individuals, such as 'to Matilda of Bexley for 51 dozen of gold' as well as 21s for 'William the swineherd for carting 1058 cart-loads of sand'.[20]

As the stones of the new abbey were being prepared Henry was investing in treasures to compete with Louis IX's Sainte-Chapelle. He bought silver vessels for the chrism, banners to be hung inside the building, candlesticks for the shrine, a silver crown for the candles, twelve 'obel de musc', a large cross for the nave, cherubims and jewels. These were mere baubles to illuminate the newest acquisitions: a portion of holy blood from Jerusalem; a footprint said to have been made at Christ's ascension; bones of one of the innocents slaughtered by Herod; a tooth belonging to one of the Magi; and the Virgin's girdle.

In 1247, there was much ceremony when the vial of Christ's blood was brought into the abbey. The sacred relic had been obtained from Jerusalem by the Knights Templar. The King had ordered that the nobles of the kingdom assemble at Westminster on St Edward's Day; all the priests, prelates, bishops and abbots were also summoned and similarly entered 'in their surplices and hoods, attended by their clerks, becomingly clad, and with their symbols, crosses and tapers lighted'. Amongst the finery and treasures of the land, Henry III himself was dressed in a poor cloak without a hood as he walked from the Bishop of Durham's palace to the abbey, his arms stretched upwards as he bore the crystal vial filled with the Lord's blood, supported by two assistants, 'lest his strength should fail in such an effort'. When he arrived at the gate, the collected throng burst into 'singing and exulting in a holy spirit, and with tears'; he then carried the vial around the abbey, the palace and his own chambers. Only then did it come to rest in the central shrine, now transformed into the most sacred site in Europe, in the words of Matthew Paris: 'a priceless gift, and one which made England illustrious, to God, the Church of St Peters at Westminster, to his beloved Edward and the holy brethren who at that place minister to God and his saints'.[21]

After this time, St Edward's Day was always celebrated as an especially holy day when the nation came together at Westminster to praise God. The incomplete abbey was now the most powerful pilgrimage centre in the nation, trumping Canterbury, the site of St Thomas à Becket, the archbishop murdered by Henry's grandfather. There was also the added incentive of a year's penance being offered to all the supplicants who made their way there. In addition, a fair was organised on St Edward's Day that ran over fifteen days to fill the King's pot for the rebuilding project.

By 1259, the east end of the abbey was transformed: the transepts, crossing, the choir including the presbytery, high altar and shrine, and Chapter House. Undoubtedly, it was more impressive than anything seen in Britain, but nor was it so foreign as to be considered an unnatural import; the Gothic was finding its English voice. At the centre of this first stage of the rebuilding sat the shrine, and the magnificent stones were laid carefully in veneration. The process was itself a prayer and a meticulous act of grace.

The abbey would be cruciform to remind the congregation that Christ saved the world by his sacrifice on the cross; the east end would contain the central high altar and shrine; the body of the church was then widened by the transepts that led off the central crossing. This east end, the apse, was wrapped by an ambulatory that was studded by small chapels that bubbled out from the main body – called a chevet, from the French for 'headpiece'. Henry III regarded this as an essential feature for the abbey, as he intended it to copy and out-champion the cathedrals at Rheims, Amiens and Beauvais.

This first burst of industry concerned not just the abbey itself but also the buildings within its precinct. By 1253 work had almost been completed on the Chapter House that stood along the cloisters on the west side. The octagonal room was the first clear indication of Henry III's majestic intentions: all eight sides of the high room seem to be built from coloured glass held together by a thin tracery of stone and iron, the eight corners offering only a kind of skeleton. The coloured, radiant walls reach a peak as the roof begins to incline towards the central point of the room, with an intricate web of vaulting. At the centre a single column stretches from the floor to the vaults; it is impossible to tell whether the stones extend from the ground up to support the covering or whether it is a stalactite cascading from the cave roof. Here was the administrative heart of the monastery where the abbey leaders planned the day-to-day running of the community; it was also here that the first King's Council met. This room would be the model for future governments that had their origins within these walls.

As the apse began to rise work was also afoot on the crossing, the ceremonial and architectural centre of the structure where the transepts met the east end. A building of the vast size of the abbey was a complicated system of engineering and proportions. If one were to cut a cross-section of the body it would reveal the complex relations between geometric forms – the quadratum (the square) and the triangulum (equilateral triangle) – that summed up the relationship between the inner space and the outer body of the abbey, a square within a triangle. This allowed for the sense of lofty proportion and symmetry; the abbey was shorter than many of its French competitors – 103 feet from the floor to floating vaults, compared with 140 feet at Amiens, 159 feet at Beauvais – nonetheless the relationship between its height and the rest of its dimensions still inspired awe.

Just as the major parts were in proportion, so too the elevation was broken into a rigid system of four sections: the aisle, triforium and clerestory reaching their apex with the radiating vaults. In 1254 Henry had visited and eyed with jealousy Louis IX's Sainte-Chapelle, on which every surface was radiant with colour and ornament, rising to impossible heights. At Westminster a repeated motif, a diaper, of roses ran across the surface of the blank spaces above the nave piers, dividing the main body of the church from the aisles, perhaps signifying the Rose of Provins, symbol of Henry's queen, the domineering Eleanor, as well as the blood of Christ. These, in their day, would have been highly painted, turning stone into resplendent bloom. Henry also commissioned a series of heraldic shields to run along the body of the abbey; those nearest the crossing included symbols of the nation, the throne, the dominion: Edward the Confessor, England, the empire, France, Provence, Scotland. Spreading westwards, the stones were emblazoned with the heralds of his leading barons, the pillars of the nation, many of whom would in a matter of years threaten his kingship – and jeopardise the work on the abbey itself.

Above the columns and spandrels of the nave walls rose the triforium, a further level of windows, and then the clerestory. On the exterior, this section was encased by a series of flying buttresses, a unique feature of Gothic architecture that made a work of art out of necessity. In the pursuit of weightlessness, the Gothic abbey became a web of stresses, forces and tensions that demanded a technological revolution. The stones of the abbey were in a constant battle to push outwards and downwards. The pointed arch in particular was a study in how to balance and control the pathway of weight through the body of the building. The buttresses made the lightness of the interior space possible, as if the skeleton of an insect, in the words of Sir Christopher Wren, had been turned inside out. This grew from unsightly to beautiful with an emphasis on structure, with pinnacles to highlight the verticality of the exterior, the stones rising into peaked spires in the air, carved with crockets and finials, giving a sense of natural forms, leaves and flowers. It was as if, when the building was rising out of the earth, it soared

4. Inside the transept showing the aisle, triforum, clerestory, and the radiating vaults

towards heaven, transformed from the mundane into the transcendental.

There is much debate as to the order in which a Gothic cathedral was built so that all the parts stood up during construction. According to the engineering historian John Fitchen, first the nave piers and the aisle walls were erected, which were then connected by the aisle vaults. The second stage included work on free-standing pinnacles rising up from the aisle walls at regular stages along the length, while at the same time the triforium and the clerestory walls were built up to the level of the roof. The buttresses that connected the pinnacles to the clerestory like ribs came next. It was only now safe to construct the vaults of the main body of the church. Then the wooden frame of the roof, lined with lead, was added. To top it all the spire or tower above the crossing, set around the large piers of the central space, was slowly built up in the lightest material possible so as not to overpower the fine balance of the building, the thrust down through the piers as well as the outward stress of the exterior walls.

Thus the main vaults, the arching geometrical ceilings, were the final task within the construction. The vaults at Westminster were very different to the ones found in many of its French counterparts. Most examples have radiating ribs, 'springing' from the summit of the columns that ran from the nave floor, either spreading out diagonally along the barrelled, geometric vaults to meet at a central carved boss, or crossing the body of the vaults to create a pointed arch with a corresponding rib from the opposite side. At Westminster, an innovative English vaulting was developed that gave the impression of a ribcage and seemed to be driven by a pragmatism that encouraged a nineteenth-century French engineer to note that they were 'no caprice or question of taste, but the rigorous application of a method followed to its deduction'.[22] This could be a definition of British architecture as a whole.

Nonetheless, despite all the disturbances, the abbey remained a place of worship at the centre of the city, a home for the abbot and his monks, a seat of learning. As the city beyond continued to grow, the abbey itself grew richer and more powerful, making the abbot one of the leading barons; yet the enclave remained outside, the City of God untainted by the mark of Cain. Despite the upheavals of the rebuilding the incumbent at that time, Richard de Ware, elected by the monks themselves, was determined that the abbey continued its rituals and commissioned a customary 'very necessary for the common utility of all, both for divine office and for the diverse customs of the monastery',[23] which set out the routines of the community within the cloisters. The directives of the 274-page notebook included everything from the privileges of the abbot to the gardener's job description. At the time there were about sixty monks within the precinct, with about thirty-five of them assigned official roles such as the cellarer, who looked after the provisions, sacristans, who protected the relics, as well as a number of mendicants who tended the sick and dying.

The church itself remained in use throughout the redevelopment, as a place of pilgrimage as well as for the rites of monastic life. The standard day began at matins at midnight, lauds at daybreak and prime at about 6 a.m.; terce, sext and none prayers were said at the end of the day. Most of the day was spent in and around the cloisters that stood on the west of the main body of the church. After breakfast the whole community gathered inside the Chapter House to hear a chapter from the rules of St Benedict and the day's business decided; afterwards each monk went on to his given task: tending the herb garden, treating the sick, educating the young initiates within the cloister itself or retreating to the scriptorium where the great works of literature were carefully copied out in elaborate illuminated scrolls.

Yet despite this secluded life, the abbey was at the centre of an intricate and dangerous political drama. In 1259, Henry III urged work to continue on the abbey with the command to demolish the next stage of the fabric 'as far as the vestry by the King's seat'.[24] However, this optimism hid a more desperate situation, for the King had reached a crisis both in his relationship with the barons at home as well as with his French rival, Louis IX: the English throne was on the verge of collapse once again. Henry's continued demands for money brought the many simmering disgruntlements of his lords to the surface. Henry had also finally admitted defeat in France and had spent part of the last year abroad negotiating the Treaty of Paris with Louis IX. Henry was now forced to deny any claim to French lands outside his Angevin inheritance, albeit under the reduced status of Louis's vassal.

It was a humiliation that drove the King finally to admit that he was no emperor, but only the Lord of England. He was forcefully reminded of this in April when, in the words of the Tewkesbury Chronicles, 'earls, barons and knights went to the court at Westminster, armed in excellent fashion and girdled with swords'. They did not come threatening violence and left their arms at the entrance of the King's hall 'and appearing before the king saluted him as their lord king in devoted manner with fitting honour'.[25] In fear Henry asked if he was a prisoner but was answered by Roger Bigod, Earl of Norfolk, that their complaint was not against him but his advisers, who were all members of his wife's family. The barons demanded that they had a say in the ruling of the nation and after some days of negotiation it was agreed that a new council of twenty-four men was to be drawn up to help the King govern: twelve elected by Henry, twelve by the barons. It was further agreed that they should meet up again in Oxford for more talks.

The Oxford council, sometimes called the Mad Parliament, was more belligerent. Henry had chosen his twelve men but at least three came from the hated Lusignan faction of his in-laws. They were marked men and in their attempt to escape were arrested and expelled from the country. Henry was now isolated and the barons pressed for reforms, led by Simon de Montfort, the King's brother-in-law. The Provisions of Oxford are often described as England's first written constitution. The King was to be aided by a council of fifteen elected members who would advise on all positions of power. There was another council, Parliament, that would meet at least three times a year to discuss matters further. The word 'Parliament' was not, in fact, new; it had derived from France and had been in official use since 1236 to describe a council designed to review 'the state of the realm and to deal with the common business of the realm and the king together'.[26]

Needless to say, Henry first sought peace with his barons and then, like his father, turned his back on his own treaty. For a man who had invested so much in enhancing the sacred nature of kingship, to be tied down by legal definitions was too much. In 1259 he revoked his oath and by 1261 had gained a bull from the Pope that absolved him from having to comply with any limitations set down in the provisions. Both sides began to sense that the time for conciliation was over. Two armies mustered, and civil war loomed.

The threats and overtures of war began in 1261 and the reformers soon gained ascendancy, yet no side won an outright victory. By early 1262, however, many of the barons were willing to fall in with Henry, but not all. De Montfort remained resolute in his determination to oppose the rights of the King, who was now once again claiming absolutism. The Second Barons' War eventually ignited in June 1264, and London was at the centre of the conflict. The city joined with de Montfort in his condemnation of the King's favouritism and arbitrary taxes. They saw an opportunity to extend their own powers in the demands for reform, and the battle was fought on the city streets. As Henry sought refuge once again in the Tower, his queen, Eleanor, was abused and pelted as she tried to escape.

De Montfort assembled his troops in Oxford and marched south; he secured the Cinque Ports along the Kent coast to ensure that no reinforcements could come from France and marched on London, where he was greeted with joy. When, in December 1263, de Montfort's troops were caught unawares at Southwark, the citizens opened the city gates so they could withdraw in safety. However, things did not all go his way and he was forced to retreat, successfully facing the King's army at Lewes on 14 May 1264, imposing a new set of provisions on Henry, the Mise of Lewes. It was only a temporary victory and at Evesham, on 4 August 1265, the two armies met again and de Montfort was outnumbered and overpowered. His body was hacked to pieces on the battlefield and the parts were later sent as prizes to the leading barons; the rest of his remains were denied a religious ceremony and discarded under a tree near Evesham Abbey.

This had terrible after-effects for London, for the King's faction were swift to impose control once again. A fine of 20,000 marks was exacted from the citizenry for their waywardness and their chartered liberties were revoked for two years. The city had to wait for a new king before its voice was heard again.

Throughout this ruckus, however, work progressed at Westminster. Despite the wars Henry still found £2,000 to spend on the abbey in 1265, and a further £1,096 on refurbishment of the palace; nevertheless he was forced at one moment to pawn some of the treasures of the shrine to pay for it. The abbey grew painfully slowly: the tower that was meant to rise high above the crossing remained little more than a stump of stone as work on the nave that ran northwards trundled at a lesser pace. It would remain incomplete for the rest of Henry's reign and it was only in 2009 that it was announced that a corona would be added to the abbey in celebration of Queen Elizabeth II's coronation, to be finished in 2013. Meanwhile glaziers and painters busied themselves on the surfaces and windows. On the walls of the eastern transept it is still possible to see traces of painting upon the fabric: a portrait of St Thomas touching the wounds of Christ.

At that time, Italian paviors had already begun to lay out the intricate stonework in front of the high altar. In 1260 the Abbot, Richard de Ware, travelled to Italy to seek blessing in his new role from the Pope, whom he found at the citadel of Anagni outside Rome. Here he encountered extraordinary stonework by the Laurentius family from Rome, Cosmas and his two sons, Luca and Jacobo, and in the father's honour the style was called Cosmati work.

There was also work to be done on the two magnificent rose windows on the north and south transepts. The round window celebrated the intricacy of its own design, and owed its origins to the classical and Romanesque. Rose windows, the first of which was found at Saint-Denis, became an integral part of Gothic architecture. Recent innovations within the Rayonnant style had made the designs and construction of the windows increasingly intricate, with thin metal tracery dividing the surface into swirls, circles and shapes.

At Westminster the window filled the clerestory level of the transept, high above the highly carved porch and doors. Unfortunately there is little information about the original windows. In the early maps, there is insufficient detail to note anything more than the four impressive buttresses that clasp the side of the transept. In 1654, the inestimable Wenceslaus Hollar made a sketch that showed the dilapidated state of the building, which was called 'a skeleton ... shrivelled by the north wind and the fretting of the smoke of sea coal' by one writer in 1683.[27] It was finally repaired by Sir Christopher Wren in the 1710s, and then adapted by George Gilbert Scott in the 1870s.

Work was also continuing on the shrine, ready for the return of the body of St Edward, which currently lay in a side aisle. By 1259 the monks' stalls, west of the crossing, were complete. The high altar itself, in front of the shrine, was also nearly finished; only an eleven-foot panel remains. It was highly painted and studded with jewels, glass and enamels, described by Viollet-le-Duc as 'unique in Europe ... one of the most ancient of the great moveable retables known'.[28] The front piece of the altar was also spectacular and took four women three years to complete, costing a staggering £280.

The Cosmati pavement, laid in front of the high altar, expressed many of the mysteries within the abbey – the microcosm within the macrocosm, the vision of heaven on earth. Steps rose from the crossing floor to the elaborate stones that were now nearly finished. Around the edge of the stones brass lettering was added to the assemblage. The inscription further enhanced the mystery of the stones. Henry was creating not just the City of God but out of that he was showing how his sanctified reign was part of an ordered universe. To challenge his kingship was to question the great chain of being. The abbey was of this world but also a conduit to something beyond. Like Plato's shadows on the cave wall, the stones of Westminster left flickering outlines of the perfection of God's creation as well as of knowledge beyond the con-templation of scholars.

The pavement was twenty-four feet and ten inches long and included over 30,000 pieces of stone and glass. John Flete reported that the 'merchants and workmen' who accompanied de Ware back from Italy brought 'with them those stones of porphyry, jasper and Thasos marble which he had brought here at his own expense'.[29] The stones themselves were laden with significance – remnants of ancient civilisations, of mystical properties.

5. A plan of the Cosmati pavement

The purple porphyry had been mined in the remote deserts of Egypt during the age of the pharaohs and used in ancient temples. The green stone was also ancient, found only in the mines of long-lost Sparta, but raided from ruins by the masons for their intricate designs. There was yellow marble from Tunisia, pink *beccia giallo*, black Egyptian gabbro, rare alabaster, native Purbeck limestone. There was opaque glass, handmade in cobalt, red, turquoise and white, as well as transparent glass in the same colours. At the centre of the designs was a huge disc, two feet three inches wide, of veined alabaster.

The laying of the stones was a labyrinth of shapes and significance.

They came from the ruins of the Roman Empire but were brought to order within London's royal abbey. The patterns incorporated motifs gathered from Christian, Byzantine and even Islamic designs, and all completely distinct – of the sixty roundel bands that are wrapped around the shapes within the design, forty-nine are unique. On the large scale, the pavement was a square border that encased an inner square at 45°, forming a cross, then enveloped a quincunx, swathed with roundels, that then held the central alabaster orb. Within the border there were eight panels, and within the four corners intricate patterns of five hexagons.

Each pattern is itself a maze of meaning: rational geometry, conforming to the defined laws of Nature, intertwined with theology and pagan philosophy in order to find a new representation of God, Man, Time and the Universe. Each shape has its own meaning – the perfection of the orb signifying eternity, as well as the earth; the square reminds the viewer of the fourfold symmetry of the elements – the seasons, points of the compass, the humours of the body. The quincunx forms a cross within a square, centred round a circle, and offers a simulacrum of the cosmos. The powerful iconography of three reminds the viewer of the Trinity, the beginning, middle and end, the passage of the soul through time, as, three times three, the nine spheres of the firmament rotate to make heavenly music.

The stones represented a reordering of Nature that can only gesture through their imperfection to the wondrous beauty of God's perfect plan. But in this very human effort, the stones offer a portal into another world, reconciling the chaos of everyday life with the rational and geometric order of God's creation.

And around the outer border of the pavement, the dedication was set:

> Four years before this year of our Lord 1272,
> King Henry III, the court of Rome, Odoricus and the Abbot
> Set in place these Porphyry stones.

The stones then offer a riddle – nothing less than the nature of the Prime Mover, and the date of the end of the world:

If the Reader wittingly reflects upon all that is laid down
He will discover here the measure of the prime mobile:
the hedge stands for three years,
add in turn dogs, and horses and men,
stags and ravens, eagles, huge sea monsters, the world:
each that follows triples the years of the one before

Finally, encircling the central stone of the work, as if looking out of the sun-filled mouth of Plato's cave, God's vision is transcribed:

Here is the perfected rounded sphere which reveals
the eternal pattern of the Universe.[30]

Finally the abbey was ready for the translation of the saint's body to rest at the heart of the shrine, as Henry III and the princes carried his remains around the church. In celebration the Pope had granted a special indulgence of forty days in purgatory for any pilgrim who wished to worship at the new tomb. A banquet was organised at which Henry provided the venison of 125 deer for the assembled dignitaries, knights and commoners. Yet even this only highlighted the divisions within Henry's realm: thirteen bishops refused to process behind the Archbishop of York, who appeared to be usurping the privileges of the more important Archbishop of Canterbury. Representatives of Winchester and London bristled in contempt of each other over who had primary rights to serve the King. Henry III made the diplomatic decision to attend the ceremony without his crown so as not to stoke the antagonism. Elsewhere, however, there were reports of miracles that day in Winchester and Ireland following special prayers for the intercession of St Edward.

Thus in the very fabric of the abbey, the whole interconnected complexity of medieval life – from the Creator to the most humble supplicant – was set in stone. In his attempts to shore up his political weaknesses Henry III created a City of God in opposition to the City of Cain that lay outside the abbey walls. However, Henry was never to see the completion of his building, and the fate of the structure is perhaps even more revealing about the changing nature of kingship and the rise of London beyond.

Henry died in 1272 and was buried close by the shrine of his beloved St Edward. At this stage work had only progressed to halfway along the western nave of the church. While there was for a few years following his death a cult for Henry III, his claims for sainthood never materialised. By contrast, Louis IX, master of Sainte-Chapelle, who died in Tunis on his second crusade, was named St Louis in 1297. Instead, Henry has gained the accolade of being the longest ruling king in British history and perhaps the least distinguished. This reputation was further battered as the Victorians raised Simon de Montfort to hero status as the man who created the first parliamentary system in his defence of the Provisions of Oxford.

Henry's successor, his son Edward I, possessed many of the gifts that his father desperately lacked. He had fought alongside de Montfort and after the defeat of the reformist faction had made himself scarce, joining a crusade to the Holy Land. He heard of his father's death abroad and was only crowned at Westminster on 19 August 1274. He spent the first years of his rule reforming the convoluted machinations of the royal court, protecting the rights of property and setting down in statutes the limits of feudal power. During the rest of his reign he tried to win back the lands in France lost by his father and grandfather. Yet he would be the first to continue the rituals of his father and establish Westminster Abbey as the royal shrine, the place of coronation and burial.

This had a particular impact on the relationship between the Crown and the city. Edward had none of his father's weaknesses and held onto London from his palace in Westminster. If he had inherited a passion for architecture, it was for the fortification of the Tower of London and the defensive walls. Henry III's monument to sanctified kingship was left to stand and there was scant work done on the abbey in the decades following the funeral. Edward I had little of Henry's deep devotion to the veneration of royal saints, and better things to spend his money on. The existing fabric was made safe and the monks made do.

Edward nonetheless followed his father into a tomb near the shrine at Westminster, as would every English monarch thereafter. What is more, Edward would also build a coronation chair, and under it place the Stone of Destiny, stolen from the Scottish monastery in Scone; upon this chair every British monarch was crowned. Edward proved that it was not just the fabric of the building that gives it significance but also the rituals and practices that occur within.

In 2010 Elizabeth II visited the site to review the restoration work of the Cosmati pavement. At her own coronation in 1953, the ancient stones had been almost forgotten and hidden beneath a carpet. Today it shines once again after painstaking work on each of the thousands of pieces of mosaic by English Heritage. And here, in time, the throne will sit once again.

CHAPTER 3

THE ROYAL EXCHANGE

Sir Thomas Gresham and the
Birth of the Atlantic World

'I pray you, let us satisfy our eyes
With the memorials, and the things of fame,
That do renown this city.'

William Shakespeare, *Twelfth Night*

In 1598 the antiquarian John Stow published his *Survey of London*, a compendious, sometimes obsessive, hymn to the 'inward pith and substance'[1] of his home city. He had been born and lived his whole life within the neighbourhood that became the Exchange, but he was also in mourning for London's passing. In his lifetime he had seen it transformed from the medieval capital to a more modern metropolis, and he was determined to chart the receding splendours before they disappeared completely.

In his book, Stow recalls the images of his childhood, a time of charity and ritual, of 'the lordly munificence and pomp of prelates and nobles'. At St Paul's he recalled the dean standing at the high altar, his head crowned with roses, as a buck was led through the nave to commemorate the patron saint. He transcribed the memories of citizens who could recount what life was like in the reign of Richard III. There were regrets for lost buildings and how fields that he remembered as a boy had turned into streets. Yet he still believed in London: 'the propagation of Religion, the execution of good policy, the exercise of Charity, and the defence of the country, is best performed by towns and Cities: and this civil life approaches nearest to the shape of that mystical body whereof Christ is the head'.[2]

In his lifetime he had witnessed the Reformation, the desecration of churches, chapels, priories, hospitals and abbeys that ringed London at Blackfriars, Bridewell, Clerkenwell and Holywell, St Bartholomew the Great, Smithfield, St Mary's Bethlehem, in Moorgate, Spitalfields beyond Bishopsgate, Crutched Friar. The ancient sites were made into aristocratic houses or reduced to 'tenements for brokers, tiplers and such like'.[3] Westminster Abbey itself was turned over, the monks reduced to citizens and the relics broken, but the body of St Peter's church preserved as a royal mausoleum. Stow was witness to the persecution and the horrors of the burnings at nearby Smithfield as heretics, Catholic and Protestant, all tasted the fire. He had also seen the devastations of war and economic uncertainty, failed harvests and rising prices, the city streets clogged with itinerant poor, while rumours circulated of the incalculable riches of the New World, and mountains made of silver.

Stow bemoaned the loss of the old London and the voracious appetites of the new metropolis; his mourning would be repeated through the centuries as every successive generation regretted the loss of the old city and the rampant ruthlessness of the new. It is a distant echo of the cries that can be heard today as the old buildings are being replaced by skyscrapers. Stow was born into a city that was centred round the cathedral; he died in a city that circled the trading floor of the Royal Exchange. He was also observer to something that might not have been noticed yet – the birth of London, world city.

Today, despite the upheavals of the global banking recession, London is still considered the world financial capital. Ideally situated between America, Asia and Europe, 550 international banks have offices within the City, and enjoy a lion's share of the world markets including (in 2008) trading $1,679 billion foreign currency every day, seventy per cent of the Eurobond market, $268 billion turnover in insurance business, with a total sum of funds managed a staggering $4.1 trillion a year. The Square Mile generates the same revenues as the combined economies of Denmark and Portugal. Despite the recession, the Mayor, Boris Johnson, still claims the City's supremacy, and in the 2009 Global Financial

Centres Index it remained top of the table, equal with New York despite losing fifteen points in the overall ratings. This status has its origin in the machinations of the sixteenth century and the dreams of Sir Thomas Gresham, one of the leading Elizabethan merchants, to build a bourse for his home city.

Standing today in front of the third Royal Exchange, built in 1842 by Sir William Tite, yet still on the same ground as Gresham's original, one can feel at the crossroads of the centre of the world, where six principal streets converge. Until 2000, LIFFE, the London International Financial Futures and Options Exchange, stood at the corner of Lombard Street and still trades over 1,000,000 contracts a year. To the north-east stands the darkened glass facade of the London Stock Exchange. The skyline is dominated by the most modern examples of contemporary design dedicated to the arts of capital. Tower 42 was built for the National Westminster Bank in 1980; looming over Leadenhall Market is Richard Rogers's Lloyd's building; and nearby stands the Swiss Re Tower at 30, St Mary Axe – iconic edifices to the world of risk which had their origins in a coffee house on Lombard Street. On a more human scale, Sir John Soane's Bank of England, set up in the 1690s to manage the national debt, runs along Threadneedle Street, while along Cornhill are the small enclaves of Change Alley, the first stock exchange, home to the first trades in joint stock companies that proliferated from the seventeenth century onwards, the corporations of their day. Here also one finds Mansion House, the elegant home of the Lord Mayor, the powerhouse of the City of London Corporation.

The contemporary Royal Exchange stands out like a temple to capital. It is no longer a trading floor, having closed down in 1991 to be replaced by electronic screens and large open-plan office space, but continues as an exclusive shopping mall offering super-brands such as Tiffany and Co. and Louis Vuitton, as well as perfumeries and racy lingerie. At the centre of the covered courtyard, Gresham's original cobbled floor of Turkish stone still intact, is a European-style café and restaurant, packed with the 'masters of the universe' from nearby offices. Although the building has been transformed, the stones themselves still hold the story of its past. The heraldic emblem of the City Corporation, the maiden's head of the Mercers' Company, has been carved into the fabric, while around the ambulatory Sir Frederic Leighton painted frescoes from the history of trade; high above, a statue of Sir Thomas Gresham still stands, as well as his family emblem, the golden grasshopper.

On the evening of 4 June 1561 a flash of lightning struck the ancient steeple of St Paul's and set the cathedral on fire. As the flames spread across the vast field of wood and metal that spanned the largest building within the city walls, the cross and eagle that had once sat high above the city collapsed, crashing through the south transept. Within an hour the flames were devouring the body of the church, and the bells in the tower began to melt. Troops and locals with ladders and tools scaled the building and began to break up the covering in advance of the flames; by dawn the church had been saved but at a huge cost.

In the following days Elizabeth I commanded an Italian inspector to make a survey of the damage; he claimed that it would cost over 100,000 ducats to repair. This was too much either for the monarch, who had inherited empty coffers and hated to spend money unnecessarily, or for the deep pockets of the city elders; in the end the great symbol of London was patched up and allowed to decay, the tower made safe while the hopes of a new spire above the capital's roofline were allowed to fade.

Rather than a temple at the heart of the Elizabethan capital, the cathedral became a shopping mall, renamed St Paul's Walk, described by one observer as 'the land's epitome, the lesser isle of Great Britain . . . a great exchange of all discourse'.[4] London, it seemed, had adopted a new religion. This was confirmed within six years of the fire at St Paul's when new stones dedicated to the glory of London were laid on Cornhill, near to where the original Roman forum once stood. Unlike St Paul's, this new building did not act as a link between the world and heaven but as a meeting place between men, and the pursuit of a more material profit.

The Exchange was created to celebrate the arts of capital and to elevate the role of merchant. The building of the Exchange offered a new epicentre within a city at the moment of anxious transition. The edifice, an immaculate study in the northern European Renaissance style, rose above the medieval huddle and was as modern in its day as anything a contemporary architect could imagine.

London had been born out of trade and built on gold. Before the first evidence of the stones of the capital, archaeologists have charted the rise of the settlement – the street plan, the location of the first river crossing – by the trail of uncovered coins dropped or planted by the first Roman visitors. Coins were often placed in the foundations of buildings for good fortune, and have been used to date the early stages of the city. In the centuries prior to Henry III, London was established as the principal market place of the nation. The cleric William Fitzstephen, who died in 1190, observed that already London was the city 'whose renown is more widespread, whose money and merchandize go further afield, and which stands head and shoulders above the others'. The port in particular was filled with ships from around the globe:

> Gold from Arabia, from Sabaea spice
> And incense; from the Scythians arms of steel
> Well-tempered; oil from the rich groves of palm
> That spring from the fat lands of Babylon;
> Fine gems from Nile, from China crimson silks;
> French wines; and sable, vair and miniver
> From the far lands where Russ and Norseman dwell.[5]

Yet, while London was powerful within England, it began the sixteenth century as an isolated city on the edge of Europe, a satellite to the major ports of the Continent. The origins of this were old: when Henry III's son, Edward I, banished the Jews from the city at the end of the thirteenth century, Italian merchants were eager to take their place as the capital's moneylenders. The Lombards had originally arrived in London in order to farm taxes on behalf of the Papacy, yet the cash-strapped king soon also granted these aliens tax exemptions, right of residence and even their own court, the Piepowder Court, named after *pied-poudre*, the dusty feet of the travelling salesman. In time, they used their privileges to take the majority of the lucrative wool trade away from local dealers and by the 1470s it was said that the Florentine bankers, the Medici, 'rule these lands, having in their hands the lease of trade in wool and alum and other state revenues'.[6]

It was on Lombard Street that this small community settled their business, congregating there twice a day, as Thomas Gresham later complained:

> The merchants and tradesmen, English as well as strangers, for their general making of bargains, contracts and commerce did usually meet twice every day (at noon and in the evening) ... but their meetings were unpleasant and troublesome, by reason of walking and talking in an open narrow street ... being there constrained either to endure all extremities of weather ... or to shelter themselves in shops.[7]

By 1527 this had become so rowdy that a chain had to be drawn across the top of the street during trading hours to keep order.

Another community of alien traders congregated around the Steelyard, or Stillyard, on Thames Street, west of London Bridge. The Hanseatic League were a dominant trading force in the city made up of merchants from the northern ports of the Baltic and Germanic states, where they traded in grain from Poland, timber, tar, herring and honey. The Baltic ports of Lübeck, Danzig, Tallinn and Riga all grew from Hansa wealth, and in the fourteenth century the League were so strong that they were willing to wage war against Denmark in order to protect their interests.

The Steelyard, as well as a string of warehouses among the leading wool towns along the east coast, was the centre of operations in Britain. The yard, which was dominated by big grain stores and a hall 'large, built of stones, with three arched gates towards the street',[8] was granted a special charter in 1303 by Edward I in exchange for the promise of looking after the repair of Bishopsgate. The German merchants negotiated their own privileges and were given preferential rates on goods coming into and out of the yard. While all English traders were obliged to give fivepence in the pound to the Crown, the Hansa had only to sacrifice threepence.

No wonder, therefore, that the sixteenth-century English businessman found it so hard to make his way in the world. He was being undercut on his home territory by foreign competitors, as well as being governed by the restrictive practices of the civic guilds. The real money was to be found in selling British goods on the European market, but this entailed large investments and risks. The men who could succeed in the global market would undoubtedly become vastly wealthy. They were called the merchant adventurers and the source of their power was first established not amongst the docks and quays of the Thames, but across the Channel in the Flemish port of Antwerp.

In time, however, this new-found preponderance would accord with a change of political ambition within the English court. Elizabeth I came to the throne at a time of trepidation, yet she was determined to strengthen the nation in defiance of the very great threats from Europe. England should not remain so dependent on the Continental markets, and should also seek trade routes of her own to find the treasures of the New World.

This would have an impact on the way in which business was run at home: London needed to embrace the modern economy. Where once the many deals and promises had been negotiated in all corners of the city, based on a complicated system of privileges, royal charters and civic dispensations, the Exchange heralded the radical overhaul of the capital's trading centre, a new enterprise zone that enshrined the modern rules of capital. London, which had once been dominated by the medieval guilds, was now run by a new class of nobility: traders, bankers and retailers. These so-called 'masterless men' neither held allegiances or obligations to ancient institutions nor defined themselves by their bloodlines, whose power came from wealth, education and civic position. They were the merchant princes and the Royal Exchange was their palace.

The building connected London to the global markets as merchants of all nations gathered twice a day, at midday and late afternoon, inside the main quadrangle. Here, the square itself became alive with the huddle and buzz of business as the merchants congregated to practise their art. Investment was sought and new ventures planned that could send ships across the globe. Bills of exchange were arranged to ease the international traffic of goods; thus a merchant in London could see his money or goods travel to any port on the Continent. Commodities, which were now piled up on the quays or safely deposited in warehouses along Thames Street, were haggled over as credit was sown and harvested.

In December 1558, Thomas Gresham wrote to newly crowned Elizabeth I, following the death of her sister Mary. He did so in haste, as the new nation was on the verge of collapse. However, his letter did not set out the best religious policy for a nation divided after the tumults of Bloody Mary's persecutions, nor did he offer succour for the threats from Catholic Europe; instead, he focused on the economic foundations of the new reign:

> ... the exchange is the thing that eats all princes, to the whole destruction of their commonwealth, if it is not substantially looked unto; so likewise the exchange is the chiefest and richest thing only above all other, to restore your Majesty and your realm to fine gold and silver, and is the means that makes all foreign commodities and your own commodities with all kind of vitals good cheap, and likewise keeps your fine gold and silver within your realm.[9]

Thomas Gresham was the heir to a family business that had been at the heart of the London market for two generations. His father, Sir Richard, had made his first fortune in the lucrative transportation of wool to Calais, but in time he speculated on the purchase of his own fleet and hired them out, making trips to Prussia and the Baltic as well as 'beyond the straits of Morocco'. He was also able to navigate his way through domestic politics and grew close to Henry VIII and his leading courtiers, most of whom soon became his debtors. He inevitably rose within the city, first becoming Sheriff and then Lord Mayor in 1537. Soon he was given the role of King's Agent in Antwerp, charged with negotiating foreign loans to pay for the King's extravagant and costly wars against France.

Thomas followed in his father's footsteps. Born inside the city walls, he gained an education at Caius College, Cambridge, and endured an eight-year apprenticeship within his uncle's office. For the son of a master merchant this lengthy initiation into the Mercers' Company was unnecessary, but Thomas later confided that the experience did him good and he gained 'knowledge of all kinds of merchandise'.[10] He was then placed within the family business, where he soon turned his attention to the wool trade with Antwerp.

In 1544, just as he was starting his career, Gresham stood for a portrait, considered to be the first of a commoner in British history. Unlike an aristocratic painting, there are no estates or fine houses in the background; Gresham stands against a bare, blank wall; he is dressed in sober black, rich yet unshowy; he is a serious young man. In his right hand he holds his glove; the little finger bears a family ring. By his right foot is a human skull, reminding the viewer that death comes to all. In this pose, Gresham is not just finding his own emerging self but also projecting the image of the idealised businessman, offering nothing except his name and his good reputation for posterity. He would soon meet every example of the type when, in 1551, he followed his father as the King's Agent at the great nursery of global capital across the Channel, Antwerp.

Antwerp, on the bank of the River Scheldt in the Spanish-controlled Duchy of Brabant, was the most important trading city in Europe, its rise to prominence one of the opening chapters in the history of globalisation. Before the sixteenth century Venice dominated the oceans, carrying goods from the Ottoman East to the West; however, the world was changing: the capture of Constantinople in 1453 by Sultan Mehmed II tolled the end of the Byzantine Empire, cutting off the eastern trade routes. In 1492 Christopher Columbus sailed west and discovered the New World, which soon offered riches beyond imagination. In 1497 the Portuguese explorer Vasco da Gama navigated around the Cape and found a maritime trading route to the spice islands of the East. To the north, by the beginning of the sixteenth century, the Hanseatic League were also losing their monopoly as individual nation states hoped to regain control of their own trade.

Antwerp was blessed by geography and found itself at the centre of things at just the right time. The port was sited between the Baltic and the Mediterranean, allowing Dutch merchants to steal a march by sailing south in spring and returning before the Hanseatic ports had even thawed. From the east, the port was also adopted by German traders from Cologne, Aachen and the Rhineland who dealt in the overland transportation of metals – copper, gold, lead. This further attracted the Portuguese King, who in 1499 selected Antwerp as the location for his northern European factor, which swiftly made the port the centre for the northern spice market, 'by which means it drewe all Nations thither'.[11] It was also the ideal site for overland business from Rome, and gained the monopoly on the papal alum trade, which was essential for dyeing all types of cloth. Alongside the exchange, it swiftly became an industrial centre for the finishing of cloth.

The city's governance was also important in raising the port's profile. It was first famed for its trade fairs that ran twice a year, where it gained a reputation for good business practice and regulation. This started to attract leading bankers who wanted to get involved in the rapidly expanding market, and soon Antwerp was judged not just by the number of ships in the harbour but also by the amount of currency and bills of exchange passing through its halls. In time the finance houses of the Fuggers, 'the Medicis of Germany',[12] Welsers and Hochstetters set up offices. It also gained a reputation as a tolerant city and a refuge for the persecuted Jews from Spain and Portugal, who brought with them skills as well as wealth.

In 1567 the Florentine merchant Ludovico Guicciardini visited Antwerp and was astounded by what he saw, summing up its diversity and energy: 'as to what and how many are the trades used, actually in this city, this can be expressed in one word – all'.[13] It was calculated that in one year 2,500 ships transported over 250,000 tons through the harbour; Guicciardini suggested that in a similar period 12 million crowns changed hands, and the majority of all international banking.

It was a cosmopolitan city that had doubled its population in less than seventy years. The majority of new arrivals were foreign merchants – estimated in the 1550s as 300 Spaniards, 150 Portuguese, 200 Italians, 150 Hanseatics, 150 Germans and 100 English. As Guicciardini noted:

> ... it is a wonderful thing to see such a great coming together of so many people and nations. It is even stranger to hear the many different

languages: as a result, without the need to travel, one can discover, or even follow the nature, habits, and customs of many nations. It is because of this accumulation of strangers that there are always new tidings from all over the world.[14]

This also placed Antwerp at the cutting edge of the exchange in ideas and culture from across the Continent. Printing and publishing proliferated within the atmosphere of freedom.

This confidence was also expressed with grand architectural projects to reflect and enhance the new-found prominence of the city. Most impressive of all amongst the civic programmes – fortifications, the completion of the Cathedral of our Lady, the town hall – was the new bourse which was completed in 1531 and adapted the newest ideas of the Italian Renaissance to the local civic style.

Many of the foreign merchants built within the city to house their trading associations and on Wolstraat, near the bourse, the fellowship of English Merchant Adventurers found its home. In 1558 they then moved to the House of Liere, renamed the English House, admired by the artist Dürer, who confessed, 'In sum, I didn't see such a marvellous house in all of Germany.'[15] There was room enough here for the governor and his deputy as well as meeting space for the Court of Assistants and General Court of the fellowship. In addition, there was a chapel and a chaplain who conducted services according to the Book of Common Prayer.

The English House was the focus for permanent English residents as well as the seasonal traders who came to seek their fortunes. England produced the finest wool, which was much in demand throughout the Continent; but until the fifteenth century, most of this had been exported in bulk as raw material by foreign merchants via the Staple in Calais. Yet it soon became clear that there was more profit to be had in selling woven cloth and in time an unregulated export market of finished cloth began to dominate the port, controlled by the fellowship. Rather than working the trade through Calais, which was managed by the guilds and marshalled by foreign ships, the English merchant adventurers made Antwerp the main clearing house for their goods. By the

1550s the new route was changing the economic landscape of the nation: wool constituted eighty per cent of all England's exports, and seventy per cent of that was controlled by London merchants; most of it was now sold in the Antwerp mart.

Guicciardini estimated the English cloth market was worth nearly 5.25 million crowns and in exchange for the fabric, the local merchants returned to London laden with foreign luxuries for the London rich: 'jewels, pearls, and precious stones, silver unwrought, quick silver, clothes of gold and silk, silks, gold and silver thread, chamlets, Grogains, Turkey work, spices, drugs, sugar, cotton, Gauls, linen cloth, sayes, russels, tapestries, madder, hops, glass, powdered fish'.[16] The merchants were making themselves rich like never before, and were starting to be able to afford the goods that had once been reserved for kings. In 1559, almost all the richest men in London were connected to the fellowship.

The Merchant Adventurers were unlike any other trading organisation in London. Many of the merchants were members of the principal liveries – the Mercers and Grocers – yet the fellowship had no company hall within the city walls, there was no system of apprenticeship, or permanent seat on the administration. Nevertheless, the wealth accumulated abroad soon made its way back to London and, with it, heralded a change in the balance of power within the city. By the 1560s the Merchant Adventurers had a sizeable majority within the Corporation as well as influence in court, while their concerns – the freedom to trade without restrictions, the end of privileges for foreign traders, the promotion of international business at the centre of the Crown's foreign policy – were presented as the desires of the city as a whole.

In 1558 Thomas Gresham was renamed the Royal Agent in Antwerp by the newly anointed Elizabeth, regaining the position he held under Edward VI and Mary after a short hiatus. He was the best candidate for the job and by this time was very familiar with the ways of the mart, having worked the system since 1551. The primary purpose of an agent was to raise money for the Crown while also managing the ever-burgeoning national debt. This was no mean feat, as the Tudors had bankrolled their reigns and martial ambitions on the market for a number of decades. For this he was offered the paltry sum of twenty shillings a day, which was more than enough encouragement for him to continue his own private business at the same time; and he did not do badly. In the 1550s he saw an annual fifteen per cent net profit on the wool he sold through Antwerp, effectively doubling his investment in five years.

This was enough to keep anyone busy and, either in his London office on Lombard Street or the house he rented at Lange Nieuwstraat, on the main street of the Antwerp new town. In addition, he was in continuous correspondence with his own team of agents around the Continent: John Eliot in London, Richard Clough in Antwerp, Edward Hogan in Seville, John Gerbridge in Toledo, as well as his post riders, William Bendelowes and Thomas Dowen. His human network was proof that, even in the sixteenth century, information and speed were at the heart of a successful international enterprise.

Gresham was unimpressed by the labyrinthine mess of the nation's finances. Henry VIII had been fooled into a bad deal in order to fund his failed sorties into France; and to make matters worse the King had then debased the English currency, reducing its value on the international money markets. The Crown now owed 260,000 Flemish pounds, with an annual interest payment of 40,000. The deal also had a kicker, for if any payment was late the interest rate escalated and Gresham was required to purchase unnecessary jewels to keep the lender sweet. He faced a huge dilemma: the exchange rate was sixteen Flemish shillings to a native pound and moving large amounts of English sterling would only cause it to lose its value further.

Gresham was a keen observer at the centre of a hugely complex system, and was alive to the possible advantages and opportunities in the ever-changing market. In his letter to Elizabeth at her accession he outlined the intricacies of the currency market: 'The double ducat of Spain all without the Andrew Cross ... is worth here 18s ... the half of the same ducat after the rate 9s 3p; the single Hungarian ducat is worth 6s 10p ... the Kaiser's reals of fine gold – 11s ... the Crusados of the long cross – 6s 11p ... the French crown 6s 8p,' ending with a warning, 'the exchange rises and falls daily, which is the thing most expedient in our commonwealth to be looked upon.'[17] In his letter he then set out a five-point plan for fiscal prudence: borrow less and borrow not from the international market but from home-grown London merchants; end the advantageous privileges of the alien traders in London; develop the London market so that it can compete with foreign ports; stabilise the English currency after decades of debasing and clipping; finally do not go to war.

Elizabeth was not able to heed her agent's words immediately and Gresham was sent to Antwerp once more in search of cash. He was also named Ambassador to the court in Brussels, where the Duchess of Parma governed the Spanish Netherlands on behalf of Philip II of Spain. Here, Gresham had to tread gently on two accounts: Elizabeth I had acceded to the throne after her sister Mary and by the Act of Settlement was determined to return the nation to Protestantism. This inflamed Mary's husband, the Catholic Philip, who had shown little interest in England while he had been king but now was determined to oppose Elizabeth's heresy. Secondly, Philip had also turned his attention on tolerant Antwerp itself and had begun to tighten the screws on the city to conform to his zealotry. As a result, both in his diplomatic role as well as on the market floor, Gresham found himself forced to practise the dark arts of cunning subterfuge.

Yet there was also reward: Thomas became Sir Thomas and, as befitted a new noble, he turned his merchant's fortune into land with the purchase of two estates outside London – Mayfield in Sussex and Osterley in Middlesex. He also became increasingly lavish in his entertainment and luxuries, as behoved a courtier; he became known for his extravagant gifts, such as the first pair of silk stockings for his queen, who was so charmed by them that 'she never wore any cloth garment again'[18] and banned her ladies-in-waiting from wearing them in case they looked more beautiful. He converted his Lombard Street house into the control centre of his trading operation and set about building an urban palace, Gresham House, by the eastern gates at Bishopsgate.

As a final confirmation of his new status, Gresham commissioned a portrait by the Dutch painter Antonio Mors in which he presents a vision of the seasoned, prosperous merchant. Again, he is modestly dressed in black, apart from his crisp white ruff and cuffs. There is no

6. Sir Thomas Gresham –
self-made man turned
nobleman (*Getty*)

decoration around him and instead he presents himself as a self-made, modern man, confidently holding the viewer's gaze. In another study of the period his change of status is marked by a nobleman's sword swaying nonchalantly on his side.

Yet, despite adopting the garb of a fashionable courtier, Gresham kept his eye on the main game. He continued his endless journeys between London and Antwerp, claiming to have travelled forty times across the Channel between 1560 and 1562. This was despite a horrific riding accident in 1560 when he broke his leg in a fall. The bone was badly reset and would never heal, causing him terrible pain for the rest of his life.

As Royal Agent in Antwerp Gresham's first task was to reduce the royal debt abroad. While Queen Mary had been married to Philip II, there seemed to be no problems finding lenders in Antwerp and Mary had borrowed more than was wise. Initially Elizabeth commanded her agent to get his hands on any cash available; he was so successful that he feared for his safety from other merchants; soon, however, everyone was after him for repayment. Nonetheless, business was good, and he was able to ride the undulating waves of the mart and pay the interest rates. In time the rate of borrowing was lowered from fourteen per cent to twelve per cent and then finally to just above nine per cent. Within five years Gresham was able to reduce the debts from £280,000 in 1560 to £20,000.

Yet while this liberated the Crown from foreign bankers, it did not deal with the question of how to improve the English domestic economy itself. Part of the problem was the state of the English currency, which had been debased and was considered unreliable on the international market; thus Gresham and others set about persuading Elizabeth to call for a programme of recoinage. On 27 September 1560, Elizabeth announced that the old coins were to be replaced; she also announced that the value of old shillings and groats was to be reduced; and to speed up the process she offered threepence for every pound delivered to the Mint. A firm of German refiners, Wohlstaht, was brought to the Mint, housed inside the Tower of London, to purify and restamp the new currency. The whole process was dirty and dangerous and many of the workers sickened with metal poisoning. It was said that the only cure was to drink milk from a skull and so the city fathers donated the heads of criminals previously displayed on spikes at the gatehouse of London Bridge.

This did not stop the Queen needing more money. Instead, Gresham made a bold plea for Elizabeth to look to local bankers and merchants rather than let foreigners get wealthy on English interest. There were now London traders who could afford to lend to the Crown and were willing to trust the Queen's bond. For the merchants, these rational business decisions were intertwined with a hint of patriotic pride, as lending to the Crown was an investment in the Protestant cause.

In parallel, there was a concerted effort to clean up and rationalise the port in London and ensure that a steady stream of customs revenue entered the royal coffers. The customs had to be made fair and Gresham used his position to whisper advice to his new sovereign, joining widespread calls for the suppression of the Hanseatic merchants who had special privileges to dock their ships at the Steelyard rather than at the Legal Quay. They also campaigned for the special excise rates to be abolished and insisted that the German merchants pay the same as everyone else. Eventually, Elizabeth was persuaded to close down the Steelyard completely in 1598.

Secondly, Elizabeth was advised to develop the Legal Quays that ran east of London Bridge between the Tower and Queenhithe to handle goods from foreign and domestic markets. The whole scheme was devised by Sir William Paulet, the Lord High Treasurer, through consultation with leading Londoners like Gresham in order that 'her majesty must first bring herself from debt to treasure'.[19] In 1558 Paulet had planned a revised book of rates, setting out the new levies on all goods passing into the city. The rate book increased the number of commodities to be taxed, from 700 to over 1,000, reflecting the variety of goods now for sale in London. Paulet also raised the basic rate to five per cent and in one instant enhanced the annual revenue by £80,000 a year.

However, it was one thing to increase the rate, another to enforce it, and a new bureaucracy was created to police the wharves. A team of searchers and weighters examined every cargo that was hauled upon the quay. The riverbank soon became so congested that the quays were separated by markets: the Customs House Quay for general stuffs; neighbouring Bear Quay for Portuguese merchandise; Billingsgate for fish and food; the Vintry for wine, wainscotting and oil. Despite the new regime there was still plenty of room for smuggling and bribery of officials.

There were also calls for the Thames itself to be improved for the benefit of river traffic. In 1514 Henry VIII had incorporated the Fraternity of Mariners of Trinity House, based in Deptford, who were dedicated to control the piloting of ships in and out of the port. This service was further expanded in 1565 by an Act of Parliament that allowed the mariners to monitor all ships within the Pool and gave permission for sea-marks to be laid along the length of the river to aid navigation from the Channel.

Thus every effort was made to develop London as a working port and a trading floor in its own right. However, it was not just the economists' attempts to rationalise the domestic market place that heralded

London's rise as a trading capital; rather, that most unreasonable pursuit, religious war, would have the greatest impact. In the 1559 Act of Supremacy Elizabeth I announced her commitment to Anglicanism as the national established religion. This bold assertion placed England in continual danger, from the internal threat of insurrection and betrayal and international aggression from her nearest neighbours. Elizabeth was determined to avoid any form of conflict at the beginning of her reign: the Crown was not strong or rich enough to make enemies.

From now on, diplomacy in hand with subterfuge would dictate England's dealings with her brother-in-law, Philip II, as well as France, which was suffering its own religious civil war. The Catholic empire had a low opinion of its neighbour and, with the arrival of Gresham in Brussels, took the opportunity to belittle the diplomat, warning that it was in its power to make England 'another Milan to set the princes by the ears,'[20] a colonial duchy rather than a princely state.

Precautions were necessary, and while Ambassador Gresham was sent to negotiate with the court of the Duchess of Parma, he was also arranging the transportation of barrels of munitions to England, code-named 'velvet' in his letters to the Queen's first minister, William Cecil. The merchants almost got into hot water when Gresham's under-the-counter relationship with a couple of customs officers in Antwerp was nearly exposed. This cold war became a crisis in 1563 when – under the pretext of protecting the port from the plague – the government in Brussels decided that the English wool trade should be banned from Antwerp.

The ban did not last for long but it was a prelude to further disturbances, and for Gresham in Antwerp things were tense. His high level of borrowing on behalf of the Crown at times gave the impression of draining the exchange dry of all currency. On occasion, he feared leaving his house during trading hours due to the suspicions of his fellow dealers. Nonetheless he continued to supply armour and, crucially, intelligence that he gained from across the Continent. In 1560 an invasion of Scotland by France caused shock waves as it was feared that Spain might take sides with their Catholic co-religionists, yet Gresham reported with glee that, despite their power, neither France nor Spain could raise any cash in Antwerp, as 'for credit they have none'.[21]

In 1564, all this enmity spilt out into a choatic trade war. That winter a group of British sailors were arrested after fighting with French merchants in Cadiz, causing a diplomatic row. Philip II complained about pirates while Elizabeth accused the Spaniards of heinous brutality. There were also accounts of piracy in the English Channel and claims that the British had halted over thirty Dutch ships and inspected them under the pretext that they were carrying French goods. This volatile situation made it all the more necessary for the merchants of London to take control of their own fate.

On 3 May 1560 Sir Thomas's only son, Richard, died of pleurisy, which plunged his father into deep mourning. The shock sent Thomas's mind in new directions for, now without an heir, he sought new ways in which to establish his legacy. Within nine days he was thinking about the future of the Gresham name within London and seemed determined to commemorate it, as in the words of one contemporary biographer: 'from this time he seems to have devoted himself, in a large measure, to the service of his fellow citizens'.[22] On 11 May, it is noted in the records of the Court of Aldermen that Sir Lionel Duckett was commanded 'to move Sir Thomas Gresham for and concerning his benevolence towards the making of a burse and understanding his pleasure therein'.[23]

The Gresham family, influenced by their experiences in Antwerp, had long been promoting the idea of an exchange for London. The trading city needed its own place for the promotion and practice of their particular arts, and it should be a building that rivalled any livery hall or cathedral. Thomas's father, Sir Richard Gresham, had been the first to raise the issue of a bourse for London in 1521 but had been voted down by the Common Council. Sir Thomas himself had attempted this in 1534 but had also been rejected by a vote of hands. Now that the oligarchy of merchant adventurers held the reins of power, there would be no such opposition. In 1561 Gresham had discussed the plan with his agent in Antwerp, Richard Clough, in a letter: 'considering what a city London is, and that in so many years they have not found the means to make a Bourse! . . . I will not doubt but to make so fair a Bourse in London as the great Bourse in Antwerp, without molesting any man more than he shall be well disposed to give.'[24]

On 4 January 1565 he kept his promise and made a formal offer to the city for 'erecting and building at his only costs and charges of a comely burse for merchants to assemble upon'.[25] This time the Corporation accepted the proposal. Yet while Gresham was willing to pay for the fabric of the building, it was up to the Corporation, and private donors, to find the right location for the new Exchange and to make all the arrangements for building to begin. In the crowded jumble of London this was not an easy task, as space had to be found in the already densely packed streets. The first plan was to appropriate a house owned by the Merchant Taylors' Company near Lombard Street, but the land had been bequeathed to the guild with certain restrictions and the sale was deemed illegal.

Five days later an 'apt place',[26] thirteen houses, a storehouse and garden belonging to the Dean of Canterbury, was found on nearby Cornhill and appeared available; the Corporation would also need to purchase the surrounding houses. Already the costs were escalating: £2,208 for the freeholds, £1,222 for compensation, £101 for legal fees; yet the donation fund remained bare: few individuals wanted to give to the cause, however much they might benefit from it later. Nonetheless, by May 1566 the site was demolished and ready for the masons to begin their task. On 7 June Gresham laid the first stone with a group of city elders, each man carefully tossing a gold coin into the foundations for good fortune.

Gresham was clear in his aspirations for the Exchange: it was a personal gift to the city that would both glorify him and would set London on a standing with its rivals, perhaps even surpassing them. Yet this was not necessarily reflected in the design of the bourse itself. Gresham was a merchant and an importer of Continental luxuries rather than an architect; thus when he cast around for a design for his Exchange he not only chose an Antwerp master mason, Hendrik Van Paesschen, but also chose a design that almost replicated the Nieuwe Beurs that he knew so well. As would happen so often within its history, London adopted ideas, plans and designs from abroad and naturalised them, making them its own, so that the foreign becomes British and London becomes a trading floor of more than just commodities and materials but the central mart of urban life itself.

While many might have been surprised by the foreignness, the brazen modernity of the Exchange, they were certainly angered by the importation of foreign labour in order to see Gresham's vision come alive. The London bricklayers were up in arms, while the masons looked on in disbelief as carved stone was brought from across the Channel. By the autumn of 1566, the carcass of the building was already standing. The timbers were from Gresham's family estate at Ronghalls, wainscotting was gathered by Clough from Antwerp and the slate for the roofs came from Dort. It was now clear that this was a building intended to stand out, a new palace for commerce, a temple of exchange. The Exchange dominated the skyline, where once only the tower of St Paul's Cathedral rose above the daily hubbub of the city.

By the end of 1568, the Exchange was complete and the doors were open for business. The visitor entered by two gates, from the north or south. From the outside the southern end appeared the most grand, and unexpected – it was the first Renaissance building within the city walls, and for many citizens the first they had encountered. The main body of the building, rising over four storeys, had been made with brick, stuccoed and inlaid with intricately carved stone. The ground floor was given over to rough stalls ready for business, and above were two rows of windows, capped with the broad grey slate roof, studded by dormer windows. On each dormer, a chimney and on all four corners, the golden grasshopper reminded the visitor whose building this was.

The southern entrance was situated beneath an imposing tower with a clock – which marked the trading hours at twelve and six – and a belfry; on top of the tower reigned another golden grasshopper. Entering the building here, the visitor walked under the royal crest into the open courtyard, eighty paces wide by sixty, and on the opposite northern end, the first thing the entrant would see, stood a Corinthian column holding up yet another golden grasshopper. Around the walls of the quadrangle were thirty niches in which Gresham planned to place bronze statues of all the kings and queens of England since William the Conqueror. One

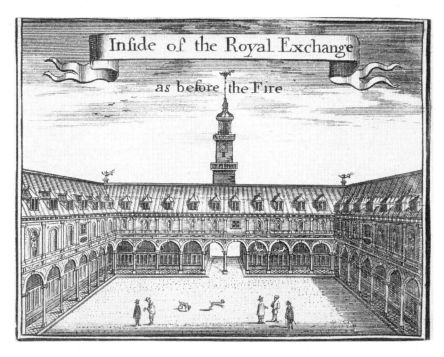

7. The interior trading floor of the Royal Exchange, surmounted by the North Tower and the golden grasshopper of the Gresham family (*Guildhall*)

special niche on the northern wall was reserved for the figure of Gresham himself.

The quadrangle floor was cobbled with an ornamental design of Turkish stone, large enough to hold over 4,000 merchants deep in negotiations. For inclement weather there was a loggia that ran around the ground floor, six paces wide and paved in black and white stone, punctuated by thirty-six twelve-foot stone Doric columns surmounted by a curved arch. This was also the location for the first row of shops and stalls.

The purpose of the Exchange was more than just money deals and goods. Foreign traders could visit in order to pick up their post, tips or just gossip, as the courtyard was soon the sounding post for the whole fleet; it was also the grandest shopping mall within the city. To begin with, Gresham found it slow leasing out the 150 stalls on the three levels that encircled the quadrangle; however, by the 1570s he was able to raise the rent from forty shillings a year to £4 10s. Everything was for sale, from the rarest of commodities from the farthest shores to the most basic of domestic appliances: 'mousetraps, birdcages, shoeing-horns, lanthorns, and Jews' trumps. There were also sellers of armour, apothecaries, booksellers, goldsmiths, and glass-sellers.'[27] In time it became the most fashionable place to shop, where the gallants went 'from shop to shop like bees from flower to flower if they had that fountain of money that could not have been drawn dry'.[28]

Gresham was also determined to control the conduct of all those who did business inside his building. Only orange and lemon vendors were allowed to put their barrows by the main south entrance. In 1590, women selling apples were arrested for 'amusing themselves in cursing and swearing, to the great annoyance and grief of the inhabitants and passers-by'.[29] The Exchange also attracted its own collection of chancers who sought to take advantage of the less wily customers – 'young rogues' gathered in gangs to make mischief and soon became so loud that the sermon in nearby St Bartholomew's was drowned by their mirth.

Nonetheless, the Exchange altered the face of London. This was given the royal imprimatur on 23 January 1570 when Elizabeth I entered the city to dine with Gresham at his house in Bishopsgate. The merchant had prepared well and the richly detailed damask tablecloth and napkins, which still exist, are testament to the lavish occasion. In the words of John Stow,

> After dinner, her Maiestie returning through Cornehill, entered the Bursse on the southside, and after that she had viewed euery part thereof above the ground, especially the Pawne, which was richly furnished with all sorts of the finest wares in the City: she caused the same Bourse by an Herald and a Trumpet, to be proclaimed the Royal Exchange, and so to be called from thenceforth, and not otherwise.[30]

The transformation of London into a major trading capital was a royal act, part of a wider foreign policy as Elizabeth negotiated England's relationship with the world. Gresham's Exchange was just part of a broader plan to place England as an imperial nation with possessions and influence globally. Yet in truth, Elizabeth was putting her name to something beyond her grasp, as the city had now become a public sphere beyond the manipulations of Crown and courtiers. For Gresham the royal approval was good business, for, in the words of historian Charles Macfarlane, the Exchange was built not by 'the munificence of a donor, but the calculation of a projector and capitalist'.[31] The edifice was the cornerstone of a national project that involved the Crown, private enterprise as well as the ordinary people.

The Exchange acted as a magnet for the many disparate arenas of the business city and gave it its exclusive zone, a place where new rules were observed and where an emerging class of 'masterless men', the first bourgeoisie, could assemble in common pursuit of profit. In this public space, goods from around the world found their price, men who had something to sell found a customer, credit was negotiated on the basis of a man's good name and trust. The public man was a trader whose reputation was made not by noble blood, advantageous marriage or title but his reputation as a man of sound business, a man of 'long head and deep pockets'[32] who owed allegiance to nobody but his business partners. Thus was born the modern Londoner from the corridors of Gresham's Exchange.

It took another century for London to surpass Antwerp as the entrepôt of the world and much happened in those decades; however, the seeds were first sown in the foundations of the Exchange. In 1566 the Protestants of Brabant began to rise against their Catholic overlord, Philip II, and broke the relics housed in the cathedral. Gresham himself was on hand to offer assistance, and the discreet approval of Elizabeth I. Yet he also travelled having repeated his advice to the Queen that it was perhaps time to look for more local sources of loans, 'to take up money she needed of her own merchants, which would be both for her honour, and their benefit, while she allowed them the same consideration she had done strangers before,'[33] as the foreign exchange market was no longer dependable or safe.

Elizabeth showed her hand in opposition to Philip II and legitimised a policy of state-sponsored piracy against all ships, which soon made any serious trading with Antwerp impossible. 'Married men' members of the Merchant Adventurers were called home and there was a positive effort to find new ports to exchange their goods: Emden in east Friesland offered itself to the Adventurers, promising to advance 20,000 thalers. They also made plans to ensure that the streets and alleys could cope with the merchants' traffic, and that there were adequate wagons and wheelbarrows to transport the goods. Amsterdam in Holland also proposed itself, and quickly became the new banking capital on the Continent.

The fatal blow was finally dealt to Antwerp in 1576, when Philip II's forces sieged the city without mercy and in one night, called the Spanish Fury, slaughtered over 7,000 citizens. The English merchant George Gascoigne watched in horror and later reported: 'I set not down the ugly and filthy polluting of every street with the gore and carcasses of men and horses ... But I may not pass over with silence the wilful burning and destroying of the stately town houses and all the monuments and records of the city; neither can I refrain to tell their shameful rapes and outrageous forces presented unto sundry honest dames and virgins.'[34] The bourse was broken and the town hall destroyed. Antwerp was rebuilt but never regained its position on the European stage. Gascoigne's account of the massacre haunted London, and was transformed into plays and broadsheets that burnt in the hearts of many men in 1588 when Spanish forces were mustered in Netherlands ports, ready to sail with the Armada. Only by the vagaries of the weather did London survive that onslaught unscathed.

Gresham died in November 1579. In his complex will he left Gresham House and the rents from the Royal Exchange to his wife. However, he also decided that after her death both should be given to the city: the Exchange would be shared by the Mercers' Company and the City Corporation. Following the terms of the will, the house was transformed into Gresham College for the education of the city's traders in the latest arts and innovation in business and natural philosophy. The college would, by chance as much as by design, become a focus for the business revolution within London.

The college was the first university for the city merchants, with an emphasis not on the scholastic arts but the pragmatic laws of business, mathematics, astronomy and navigation to instruct the future masters of the bourse. Rather than enrol students or offer qualifications, Gresham made money available for the appointment of a group of professors in divinity, music, physic, law, rhetoric, geometry and astronomy who were commanded to lecture six times a year, first in Latin and then again in English, to a public audience. The hope was that the college would become the Harvard Business School of the Renaissance world, offering lessons in the latest technology and know-how, giving London the commercial advantage to dominate the seas.

With the fall of Antwerp, there was increased pressure on London itself to become a trading capital in control of its own destiny. Rather than relying on foreign traders to find routes to the spice islands of the East Indies, the precious gold from the West African coast and the fortunes that were being shipped from the New Colonies to the West, why shouldn't native adventurers be establishing British settlements and creating their own trade routes across the globe?

The building of Gresham's Exchange happily coincided with a generation of adventurers enthused by the spirit of discovery. The lives of Sir Walter Raleigh, Sir Francis Drake and Sir John Hawkins have been handed down to generations of schoolchildren as idols; the truth is less edifying and the image of rugged individualism should be replaced by that of state-sponsored thuggery in the pursuit of establishing London as a leading trading capital of Europe. London would thrive, not just from the import and exchange of goods with the European powers, but also by expanding its own domain within the unknown world, carving out its own empire.

This expansionist drive flourished in the ambitious atmosphere of Elizabeth's court, where self-made men like Gresham and Paulet hoped to place the economy at the centre of the Crown's policies. At the time, London provided seventy-five per cent of all England's tax revenues and so its voice was heard; but there were also calls for adventure and a number of courtiers, glamorous but penniless second sons, were more than willing to take a risk on the waves of fortune.

Such adventures cost money, and there were plenty of merchants who stayed at home but went in pursuit of profit with the creation of new joint stock companies, pooling their investments to pay for long-distance trips that needed large capital reserves. The first of these adventure companies were in the reign of Elizabeth's brother, Edward VI, when Sebastian Cabot, the son of the Venetian adventurer John Cabot, was named 'governor of the mystery and company of the Merchants Adventurers for the discovery of regions, dominions, Islands and places unknown'.[35] He hoped to find a route to the Indies from the north, thus bypassing the heavy traffic of the Portuguese route around Cape Horn. Two hundred subscribers – shareholders – donated a total of approximately £6,000 to fit out three ships that sailed from London in 1553.

The trip was a disaster; all three ships became stuck in the cold waters of Lapland. One of them got lost and made its way to the White Sea where the captain, Chancellor, trekked overland to Moscow; there he was taken to the Golden Court of Ivan the Terrible. Chancellor was fortunate to be able to deal with Ivan and an agreement was negotiated, launching the Moscovy Company, which was later granted a monopoly by Queen Mary to control the exclusive trade in all regions 'Northwards, Northwestwards, and Northeastwards'. In time the merchants found an overland route from Moscow to Persia and hoped to do business in the southern hemisphere without sailing via Africa.

There was much to be gained from such private enterprise, but this desire for mercantile profit went hand in hand with the issue of national security. There were many London merchants who looked enviously at trade with the Atlantic world, and desired to dominate these new markets. However, England had been slow in finding and establishing new dominions and if Elizabeth was to succeed upon the oceans she needed muscle to back up her ambition. In 1577, nine years after the completion of the Exchange, Elizabeth I's leading court intellectual, Dr John Dee, wrote *The Petty Naval Royal*, setting out the nation's ambitions to be at the heart of global trade, and for the first time in history foresaw the formation of the 'English Empire'.

The defence of the kingdom could only be guaranteed by a vigorous merchant market protected by a navy. Sir John Hawkins, the first admiral of Elizabeth's Navy, was the epitome of this new breed. Born in Plymouth, where he began his trade, he was established in London by 1559, shipping to the Canary Islands, where he heard about the Portuguese trade in Africans. Forming a syndicate, he took three boats to Sierra Leone and captured at least 300 natives. One ship then headed to the Caribbean, where it was confiscated by Spanish officials; a second ship was boarded at Lisbon and seized. Only the third ship made it to London and, although Hawkins claimed he lost £20,000 in the two missing vessels, he still made a profit from the one ship that came in.

Hawkins made two further trips. Both voyages drew complaints from the Spanish ambassadors in London, who claimed that Hawkins was nothing less than a pirate, breaking established trading monopolies. On the occasion of the voyage of 1567, the accusations were true: on 23 September, Hawkins was on the Mexican coast and got into a fight with the transatlantic Spanish fleet carrying a year's cargo of silver. Although Hawkins's ships were devastated, he limped home in two captured boats, having transferred his treasures at the last minute. It was Britain's final slaving voyage for this century, but the events at San Juan d'Ulúa inspired a generation of nautical adventurers to even greater feats.

Perhaps the most romantic of these reckless buccaneers was Sir Francis Drake, state pirate, slaver and the first British global circumnavigator. In 1577, Drake sailed off on the command of the Queen to fight the Spanish on the Pacific coast of the Americas. Returning three years later with only fifty-nine men alive, he proved that an Englishman could command the seas, face his enemies in any waters and claim victory. Drake was also the admiral who led the fleet against the Armada in 1588. His success meant that England could harvest the wealth of enemies rather than establish colonies. The foundation of the Empire would be postponed for a generation.

Many of these great escapades found their way into the work of the cleric Richard Hakluyt, who was born in London in the 1550s, spent time in the embassy in Paris and became one of the most popular travel writers of the age. In 1589 he published the first two volumes of *The principal navigation, voiages, traffiques and discoveries of the English nation, made by sea or over-land, to the remote and farthest distant quarters of the earth;* a third volume came out in 1598. The books were the strongest possible argument for England's right to explore and found colonies in the New World. Thus the desire to profit from the wealth of others, the 'harvesting of the seas', was soon transformed into the ambition to capture the nation's own territories.

This was first seen in the creation of new joint stock companies hoping to establish permanent trading routes. In 1579 the Eastlands Company was founded to challenge the monopoly of the Hanseatic League in Scandinavia and the Baltic states. The following year, the charter for the Levant Company was presented to Elizabeth I with the aim of finding new routes to the Middle East. Rather than setting up colonies, the company intended to establish factories in Aleppo, Constantinople, Smyrna and Alexandria. In the first decade of the seventeenth century the rise of such companies was prodigious: the London and Bristol Company (1608), for example, hoped to exploit the fisheries off Newfoundland.

The most famous was the East India Company, established in 1600. The idea for the venture had emerged in 1588, after the English had defeated the Spanish Armada, when a group of merchants hoped to take advantage of the relatively open seas; of the three ships that sailed in 1591, only one returned. Nevertheless a new consortium campaigned and raised funds throughout the 1590s, aiming to compete with the Dutch hegemony in the Indian seas. On the first voyage they were able to establish a factory on Bantam, which was ideal for exploiting the pepper trade from Java. They also founded an entrepôt in Surat, on the Bay of Bengal. In time the East India Company would come to dominate the trade with Mughal India.

While many companies were looking for well-known ports in which to develop trade ties, there was also a desire to found new colonies in uncharted territory. These adventures were authorised and funded in the same way, but the establishment of communities in the New World was a hugely different operation. The first attempt to found a new England in America was a disaster: in 1585 Sir Walter Raleigh gained a charter to explore and set up a colony in the Virginia territories in order to find treasure for England as well as create a port for privateers raiding Spanish lands to the south. In 1584 he sent an expedition to scout out the region, and the first cargo of settlers were sent out the following spring, disembarking at Roanoke Island in Chesapeake Bay. The following June Sir Francis Drake sailed by and found the community in desperate straits; he took them back to London.

A second trip was set for 1587, with 117 settlers establishing a colony on Roanoke Island. Swiftly the natives began to show their dislike of the invaders and it was decided that the expedition leader, John White, should return to London to get reinforcements. By the time he came back in August 1590, there was no one left in the settlement – what happened to the ninety colonists who disappeared is still a mystery today. Nonetheless, the Virginia Company was set up in 1606 and in May the following year the London Company founded Jamestown along the James River leading into Chesapeake Bay. The community would find good fortune despite difficult conditions, and America was born.

At the dawn of the seventeenth century – as John Stow was publishing his *Survey of London,* charting the transformations of the city within the short period of a generation, and as Hakluyt set out the early history of the English Empire – London was becoming a world city. It would take a century for this to be made firm.

In 1666, the original Royal Exchange was destroyed in the flames of the Great Fire and it was said that, as 'the fire ran around the galleries, filling them with flames, then descending the stairs … giving forth flaming vollies, and filling the courts with sheets of fire',[36] the smell of burnt spices lingered over the broken and charred stones, while only the tower and the golden grasshopper survived. It was rebuilt by 1669, almost forty years before Sir Christopher Wren would complete St Paul's Cathedral; the speed of rebirth was a testament to the importance of the trading floor for the revival of the capital, which was now at the heart of a new empire that stretched from Sumatra in the East to the recently captured New York. This was the protean empire that would soon outstrip Spain and France, and make London the capital of the Atlantic world.

CHAPTER 4

GREENWICH

Theatre, Power and the
Origins of Modern Architecture

> Architecture has its political use; public buildings being the ornament of a country; it establishes a nation, draws people and commerce, makes the people love their native country; which passion is the original of all actions in a commonwealth.
>
> Sir Christopher Wren, *Tract on Architecture I*

Anne of Denmark was a woman of appetites and could more than hold her liquor alongside her husband, James I, who was himself a legendary imbiber. She adored the joys of court life and worshipped the theatre. On her arrival in London in 1603, she swiftly became instrumental in introducing the masque to the cosmopolitan court. The first such performance of *The Masque of Blackness*, organised for Twelfth Night 1605, was an intricate and lavish display, part drama, part tableau, combining classical allusion, gods and angels, acted out by players and courtiers in which the heavily pregnant Queen herself and her ladies-in-waiting wore dark make-up and took to the stage.

The royal performance was a very different drama to that found on the other shore of the Thames at William Shakespeare's Globe, and the gulf between the two would widen through the following century. Whereas the masque was carefully calibrated to enhance the image of the Crown, that same year Shakespeare was penning his two great studies in the tragedy of power, *Macbeth* and *King Lear*. While Shakespeare's players imagined the human drama that drove an ambitious man to murder or destroyed a great man through vanity, the court masque was an act of political conjuring. Through the ropes and pulleys of the theatrical arts, the well-ordered lyrics and the chaos of the revels, true power was articulated, with only one conclusion: the adoration of the sovereign. On one such occasion, the first performance of *The Golden Age Restored* at the Banqueting Hall in Westminster, the stage was placed at one end, facing the King's throne, garlanded by a large canopy. On either side, stools were arranged for foreign ambassadors. In front of the stage, an orchestra of violins and wind instruments whirred in anticipation. At last the King arrived, flanked by his most favoured ambassadors, and the drama was allowed to begin.

The curtains were pulled back to reveal an arcadian vision. The stage was a devastated landscape but the audience's eye was drawn to a figure hanging in the air. Pallas, the goddess of wisdom, stood upon her chariot and by some ingenious device was descending from the sky. Over the soft fuzz of music she delivered a message from her father, Jove, that the Sun, Astraea, had been commanded to return and bring to England an 'Age of better metal'.[1] Pallas then hid behind a cloud and watched as the Iron Age and a cohort of Evils conspired to make war and ruin the nation. They danced in dreadful delight until they were turned into statues by Pallas. The goddess then heralded the return of Astraea and the Golden Age, who appeared singing a song of rebirth. Yet they demanded a court and Pallas thus called forth 'Chaucer, Gower, Lidgate, Spenser ... to wait upon the Age that shall your names new nourish, Since Virtue press'd shall grow, and buried Arts shall Flourish'.[2]

The New Age was once more celebrated with a dance that soon spilled from the stage into the hall itself. First the players danced with the ladies of the court and then, with 'Galliards and Corantos', the whole assembly joined the throng. The drama became life, and the restoration of the Golden Age was no longer an illusion. At her parting, Pallas reminded her audience who was responsible for the transformation, not even needing to point to the King amongst them: 'To Jove, to Jove, be all the honour given, that thankful hearts can raise from earth to heaven.'[3]

Since the first masque, the royal court had come to depend on the wonder of fantastical worlds formed in the imagination of the set designer, Inigo Jones, and the words of Shakespeare's heir and rival, Ben Jonson. From his first adventures in the creation of theatrical wonders, crafting other worlds with pulleys and canvas, Inigo Jones proceeded to acquire the accolade of England's first architect. Born the son of a cloth worker, he was raised in the parish of St Benet Paul's within the London city walls. As with so many pioneers, his origins were mythic and self-serving, as he later recorded: 'Being naturally inclined in my younger years to study the Arts of Designe, I passed into foreign parts to converse with the great masters thereof in Italy.'[4]

Almost the first concrete fact of his life records that in 1601 he travelled to Italy, where he almost certainly visited Venice. Here he purchased a copy of Andrea Palladio's *I Quattro Libri dell'Architecttura*, a work that would change his life, and quite possibly he also met Palladio's pupil, the leading designer Vincenzo Scamozzi, who guided the untutored Englishman in his first glorious encounters with the Italian Renaissance. This immersion in the ancient and the foreign would have a profound

8. Inigo Jones in the pose of an Italian maestro

(*Bridgeman*)

impact on the young Londoner for, as Sir John Summerson later wrote, 'he knew, probably, more about Italian design than any Englishman living. He had the whole thing at his fingertips.'[5] In a later portrait by Anthony Van Dyck, when Jones was at the height of his fame, he is every inch the modern Renaissance man, a design for his latest invention held lightly in his left hand. This is the first painting of an English architect – the position did not even exist before Jones returned from Italy.

Jones came back transformed, his mind full of schemes as to how he would transform Britain; yet he had to bide his time and for the moment restrict his visions to working as the designer for Queen Anne's lavish masques. As he continued with his curious devices, he was determined to develop his new-found belief that the painted world could be as potent as the written word. In Italy, he had been encouraged to consider that architecture could create, inflame and reorder as forcefully as the lines of a poet or the demagogue's oratory. Design, he argued, could be used to express the many faces of modern power, just as the Medici had used the stones of Florence to consolidate their rule. His ambitions did not have to wait long and, in a note written in December 1606, the poet Edmund Bolton raised the hope that, through Jones, 'sculpture, modelling, architecture, painting, theatre work and all that is praiseworthy in the elegant arts of the ancients, may some day insinuate themselves across the Alps into our England'.[6]

This fascination with the visual world was enhanced by a second voyage to Italy. Following the wedding of Princess Elizabeth to Frederick V, the Elector Palatine, in 1613, Jones accompanied the royal train back to their new home in Heidelberg. He then continued over the Alps to Italy, alongside Thomas Howard, the Earl of Arundel, a Catholic nobleman already recognised as one of the most learned men of the age. Together, they would conduct what one historian called the most significant Grand Tour ever taken. On his return Jones would be offered the first chance to put his new-found philosophy into practice.

In July 1613, while hunting at Theobalds House in Hertfordshire, Queen Anne shot the King's favourite hound, Jewel, and James I's rage was of such proportions that within days he was forced to placate his wife with a £2,000 diamond and give her the royal Tudor palace at

Greenwich and the surrounding parkland, on the southern outskirts of London. It was a considerable gift with a distinguished history, yet from this moment a new saga would be written here: of royal power and pleasure, of the sea and of space, of the nature of kingship and the changing identity of Englishness, revolution and the birth of modern British architecture. This ground, caught between the city and the countryside, hugging the south bank of the Thames, would become the unlikely parchment upon which was written the script of the seventeenth century.

There had been a palace at Greenwich since the fifteenth century. The first manor was the home of Humphrey, Duke of Gloucester, the youngest brother of Henry V, who tried to usurp the Crown in the 1420s. His house was the epitome of chivalric good taste, named Plesaunce or Bella Court, with a vast library that would later be the foundation of the Bodleian Library in Oxford. After the Wars of the Roses the manor became a royal residence for the new Tudor dynasty, and a favourite hunting ground of Henry VII, who demolished much of Humphrey's designs and replaced them with Placentia, a sprawling range of brick houses set within walls. Great feasts and celebrations were planned but, as Henry's moods become increasingly ill-disposed, the palace was passed over to his boisterous son, Henry.

It was here that Henry VIII held jousting tournaments as a young man, as well as feasting and hunting. It was also a place for the rituals of courtly love: at Christmas 1511, a mock castle was erected within the grounds and the vainglorious Henry and his gang stormed the battlements to win the six ladies who were hidden inside. Yet as Henry grew older he too lost interest in many of the pastimes of his youth, including Greenwich, which was passed over to his children. Elizabeth, in particular, grew fond of the old palace. It was from here that she sailed to Westminster Abbey on her coronation day, and she would spend most summers at Greenwich 'for the delightfulness of its situation'.[7]

It was also during the Elizabethan reign that Greenwich was closely tied to the aspirations of the Atlantic empire. It was from the palace that

9. Greenwich in the time of Elizabeth 1 before work on the Queen's villa

Elizabeth could observe the shipbuilding in nearby Deptford, while many of her seafaring courtiers often spent time in the grounds, which lay close by the port. It is often suggested that it was within the palace that the Queen first encountered Walter Raleigh, who famously laid his cloak across a puddle to save the royal foot from getting muddied. More certain is the fact that Elizabeth travelled from Greenwich to Tilbury in 1588 to deliver her speech in defiance of the Spanish Armada that was threatening the Channel.

In 1617, when Queen Anne first inquired of Inigo Jones for his plans, the palace was broken and old. Anne began by enhancing the grounds of the old site with a new garden, designed in the latest European styles, with an aviary, a grotto, a water maze and fountains with statues. The new scenery expressed an arcadian ideal in contrast to London, a place where the government of Nature and man were in balance, an allusion to a time of Eden before cities, politics and war. It was in this perfect setting that Anne wished to place her new palace and, as John Chamberlain wrote in a letter in July 1617: 'The Queen is building somewhat at Greenwich, which must be finished this summer, it is said to be some curious device of Inigo Jones, and will cost above £4000.'[8]

Anne wanted a private pavilion away from the hubbub of the main palace, a world away from the nearby city, and, as Jones was considering designs for the Queen's villa, he was determined to bring all of the lessons he had learnt on the Continent to bear. What Jones would produce would be unlike anything seen in England before: the Queen's House would be the first example of modern architecture north of the Channel; the villa would represent the shock of the new enclosed within an earthly paradise. Inigo Jones was called upon to deploy his great learning to the task to ensure that the retreat was the perfect expression of the philosophy of order, proportion and balance. He loosely based his designs on a villa built in the 1480s for Lorenzo de' Medici at Poggio a Caiano, near Florence, an exercise in the Renaissance doctrine of dignified symmetry.

Unlike any English builder before him, Jones set out his ideas on paper before approaching the building site. On his designs there are often references to actual measurements in feet and inches and he drew all his devices to scale so that they could be replicated exactly. But, more importantly, he also measured his work through a basic system of ratios, each part connected with and reflected by the other. His original plans are scored with the pockmarks of a pair of dividers. In his mind, the perfect form was the square and the cube, with the ratio of 1:1 and 1:1:1 respectively; while the rectangle had a variety of ratios: a square and a third, 3:4; a square and a half, 2:3; and a square and two-thirds, 3:5, as well as the double cube, 1:2. For Jones the unity of a building, and the skill of an architect, were to be found in the relationship between its various parts.

Jones also balanced this divine geometry with an appreciation of the classical laws of architecture, priding himself on being the best-read and most knowledgeable man in England. He had been the first to visit the ruins and sites of Italy, but he also developed an extensive library of books. He distilled the conventions of classical architecture that had been forged in ancient Rome and revived in the Renaissance and hoped

to translate them to seventeenth-century northern Europe. From Vitruvius, Alberti, Palladio and the other masters he learnt the identity of the
five orders – columns – that represented the basis of all architecture. He
also understood that the essential unit of measure for all ratios was the
module, the diameter of the column. He absorbed the delicate rubric
that characterised each order within a hierarchy of ornamentation, each
style expressing the virtues of a particular type of building – villa,
temple, baths, theatre.

At the very beginning, however, Jones also had to cope with an
unusual circumstance: the Queen's House at Greenwich was to be built
over the London–Dover road. Reasons for this are obscure: the villa was
to replace a gatehouse that opened out onto the road. Perhaps Jones felt
that it would be better for the road to be hidden by the house rather
than ruin the view and therefore devised an H-shaped villa raised upon
two wings to the north and south of the road, connected by a floating
bridge room. Both these wings on the first floor would be of rough
stone – rusticated – and within, there would be cellars where rowdy
drinking sessions were planned. The main rooms of the house would
be accessed on the north side via an oval staircase leading up to a
terrace. On the south side there would be a colonnaded balcony, a
loggia, from which the Queen would able to watch the hunt in the park
beyond.

Little did Jones know in 1617, however, that he was beginning a project
that would span a century or more, and become the weathervane for
the pitching fortunes and personalities of the Stuart dynasty. From the
outset things did not go to plan, for Queen Anne grew sick over the
winter of 1619 and died on 2 March. At Greenwich, work stopped almost
immediately; the builders had only completed the two wings on the
south and north to the height of the first floor. There was as yet no
masonry connecting the two halves of the building. James I was dis-
traught at his loss and, after a final performance of a rustic masque, *The
Shepherd's Holiday*, the royal arcadia was abandoned. A roof of thatch
was laid across both ends of building site and the court returned to
Whitehall. Greenwich Palace was forgotten even before the villa had
been completed.

Jones's villa was the very first modern building in Britain, but now stood empty to the south end of Placentia, the crumbling Tudor hulk, along the river. Yet this plot would have many lives, and through the development of Greenwich one can chart the story of the tumultuous seventeenth century. Most clearly, it is the story of architecture, the introduction of the classical template into the English tradition. This radical modernity would begin with the completion of the villa in the following decade and later be joined by a series of grander plans that would replace the old palace with a new Baroque monument, growing out from the villa. The parkland that surrounded the Queen's House would also be transformed from rough hunting grounds into a royal park, including an astronomical observatory, the most advanced scientific institution of the age. The scheme was never completed but the site was then passed over to create a people's palace, a royal hospital for the care of old sailors. The final construction, Greenwich Hospital, was far grander than any other royal project.

Yet how the arcadian retreat became first a prince's pleasure palace and finally a hospital, a royal gift to the people, is bound up with the complex and perilous journey of the Stuart dynasty and the changing role of kingship. The Stuarts, as in the masques, saw themselves as divinely ordained monarchs; however, the reality was closer to the human dramas to be found at the Globe. Continual unrest rumbled into civil war over the question of the limitations of dynastic kingship and it was not until the Glorious Revolution of 1688 that the written contract between Crown and subject was finally inked. This dangerous transition – from God's lieutenant to the people's sovereign – would also have an impact upon the buildings at Greenwich.

The transformations at Greenwich are also interlinked with the changing fortunes of London. The capital was at the heart of the tumults throughout the century, the crucible where the conflict between the Crown and the nation was most keenly felt. London was, in the words of the Earl of Clarendon, 'the nursery of our present troubles'.[9] It was also, in the aftermath of the Civil Wars and the horrors of the Great Fire, the first modern city. This intellectual revolution was expressed in the city's buildings. It also found its way to Greenwich, which was not immune to these changes, especially as the main figures who rebuilt London out of the ashes of 1666 were also those who created some of the most enduring works of architecture here: Sir Christopher Wren, Nicholas Hawksmoor and Sir John Vanbrugh.

James I died in 1625 and was succeeded by his second son, Charles, a very different man to his father. James had won rather than inherited the crown, while Charles saw it as his God-given right to rule; where the father made treaties, found accommodation, judiciously exercised favours and threats, and manipulated the Church to bind the nation together, his son, by contrast, saw negotiation as compromise. Charles I's reign heralded the second act in the drama of the Stuart dynasty: a period when dark clouds appeared to gather over the arcadian scene. For a second time also, Greenwich was converted into a stage set for the sophisticated theatre of power.

'French queens never brought any happiness to the English,' observed Lucy Hutchinson, a Puritan lady of the court;[10] yet in 1625 Charles married the French princess Henrietta Maria, daughter of the notable Henri IV. It was foremost a political match but did little to bind the fissures that were beginning to appear inside Britain – which were made worse when it was clear that, despite marrying God's Protestant lieutenant on earth, Henrietta Maria was to hold onto her Catholic faith. A papist chapel was built at Whitehall and a vast French retinue swarmed around the Queen at her official palace on the Strand. The marriage did not start well, yet, as in *A Midsummer Night's Dream* where the quarrel of Oberon and Titania was quelled by sympathy, the King and his queen finally fell in love; and, as the Earl of Carlisle observed, 'at such a degree of kindness as he would imagine him a wooer again and her gladder to receive his caresses than he to make them.'[11]

The revival of works at Greenwich was an expression of the royal bond. The palace grounds were considered a vale of health and nurture, away from the pollution of the court, and here Charles and his queen hoped to reform their marriage and build a temple to their affection. Here, Protestant princes would be born to cement the royal union and to offer a beacon to the nation, a focus for the future happiness of the

British polity. In 1629 Henrietta Maria was staying at the Tudor palace when she gave birth to her first child, Charles-James; unfortunately he was born ten weeks early and was too weak to survive more than a day. Despite the sad news, work began anew on the Queen's House.

In a painting of 1632, *A View of Greenwich Park* by the Dutch masters Adriaen Van Stalbemt and Jan Van Belcamp, the royal party are seen surveying the ground from the hill above the palace. Charles, Henrietta Maria and the young prince, Charles, are placed at the centre of the scene; the King's right arm is raised as if to indicate with a gesture his power over the scenery, if not Nature itself. Behind him, the Queen's villa is still covered over with a temporary thatched roof, yet Inigo Jones is also here, to the side, dressed in a blue cape, an Italianate cap on his head, caught in conversation with the learned courtier, Endymion Porter. The portrait seems to be showing us the old palace on the cusp of renewal through the intercession of Charles, whose wishes are fulfilled by the genius design of Jones.

While Anne of Denmark's villa had been designed as a place of retreat, the work on the new house transformed it into a sanctuary of royal love, a symbol of the perfect marriage, a commonwealth of mutual benefit. If Henrietta Maria's villa were a play, the Queen intended her new house to revive the ancient story of Daphne and Apollo portrayed in a portrait Charles I had commissioned from the Dutch painter Gerrit van Honthorst the previous year. In the picture, the Greek god of music is struck by Eros and falls for the mortal Daphne, who initially spurns his advances. In the heat of pursuit, Daphne turns into a laurel tree and Apollo vows to venerate her for the rest of his life. In Ovid's account of the tale in *Metamorphoses*, the story of escape becomes a narrative on the evergreen constancy of love. Thus Inigo Jones was once again called to work on the plot that had lain covered in thatch for ten years, and his new designs would transform the painting of Apollo and Daphne into stone.

Since 1619, Inigo Jones had continued to refine his philosophy of building. That year he had started work on the Banqueting Hall at Whitehall, the grandest theatre of Stuart power and the architect's most adventurous exploration so far of classical conventions. From the outside, the building was raised on a basement of rusticated stone with two sets of windows, the lower level with simple Doric pediments holding up a range of more ornate Corinthian columns. Inside the main room was 110 feet long, 55 feet wide and 55 feet high – a double cube. It was opened on St George's Day, 23 April 1621, and was so revolutionary in its foreign 'newness' that few knew how to interpret it; for some it was 'too faire and nothing suitable to the rest of the house',[12] but Jones was placing a Roman basilica, inspired by his veneration of Andrea Palladio, in the centre of a medieval huddle. He would bring the lessons he learnt here to bear on the new work for the Queen's House.

The thatch was stripped from the roof of the old villa and work began immediately on raising the house to the first floor. Meanwhile Jones also developed a terrace on the north side of the building on the first floor and a curved pair of stairways leading up to it. This had an immediate effect on the interior spaces of the house, for as one approached the villa from the river and ascended the stairs the entrance led into the great hall. The hall itself would express everything that Jones had learnt since 1619: the central room was a forty-foot cube, a perfect unity of space and light. The villa presented itself as a private space but with a very public purpose: the personal affection between Charles I and his queen was also a projection of the love between the nation and its Crown.

By raising the house onto the second floor, still floating above the London–Dover road, Jones was also able to link together the two sections with an ingenious bridge room. This allowed, with a deft Palladian touch, access from the great hall into an open loggia, an enclosed, pillared balcony that looked out southwards towards Greenwich Park. Jones even remarked, in his own copy of the Italian master, that such a feature was one of the greatest ornaments that a country house could have. Thus the Queen's House was renamed the House of Delights.

Inside, the villa was resplendent. Chimneypieces were designed and built in France and shipped down the Thames, while the Tuscan artist Orazio Gentileschi devised the ceiling panels, which held a series of paintings expressing the blossoming of the arts within the royal union.

There was also a commission for a portrait of the couple enacting the myth of Cupid and Pysche by Jacob Jordaens that was set, according to Apuleius, in 'a worthy mansion for the powers of heaven'.[13] This theme of eternal affection was acted out in a masque, *The Temple of Love* by Sir William Davenant, in 1635, with scenery by Jones. It was the last masque to be performed for Charles's court.

In addition, the King filled the house with his latest collection, making the villa a retreat for a Renaissance leader. Charles considered himself something of a connoisseur, loved anything that was not British and was determined to accumulate a portfolio of artwork that signified his position as a modern European prince. He bought wisely and widely; Europe was in the grip of the Thirty Years' War and many small principalities were looking for ways to fund their armies. In 1627 he purchased a cache of paintings from the Duke of Mantua that contained over 175 works by Peter Paul Rubens, who also made a handsome profit as a go between on the deal, buttering up his customer by noting that Charles was 'the greatest amateur of paintings among the princes of the world'.[14] At the centre of the collection, placed within a niche in the great hall, was a bust of Charles by the Roman maestro Bernini.

The great arts of Europe found a home within the English court, bringing prestige to the Crown. In the process Inigo Jones was establishing what modern British architecture could be. Within these rules, Jones was also developing his own grammar of ornamentation. As one observer commented, he 'hath so finished and furnished, that it surpasseth all other of that kind in England'.[15] This was a worthy endorsement of the architect's skill, but it was a dangerous compliment to pay a monarch in a time of adversity.

By the end of the 1630s, Charles's royal performance was starting to look ragged and isolated. As Lucy Hutchinson so perceptively observed as she watched the royal masques, 'viewed from outside the Banqueting Hall, the masque could be seen to provide the monarchy with an impenetrable insulation against the attitudes of the governed. This vision was a perfectly accurate project of the way Charles saw his realm.'[16] At some point the royal drama lost its ability to command the adulation of the nation and the performance of sovereign power proved to be an illusion.

In January 1642 Charles and Henrietta Maria, along with their children, fled from Whitehall; London was no longer safe for the King or his family. They left in such haste that they arrived at the Palace of Hampton Court before their messenger and found that their beds had not been prepared. Within weeks they travelled to Greenwich, on the way to Dover, where Henrietta Maria took a boat to France carrying the royal jewels, hoping to sell them on the Continent in preparation for war. Husband and wife, the King and Queen, did not see London again together. After leaving his wife, Charles travelled to the north where, seven months later, he raised his Royal Standard and declared war on his subjects. Abandoned once more, Greenwich Palace was immediately seized as civil war swept the nation. In November 1642 Parliament commanded that the tools, arms and armour inside the palace – over £200 of weapons – be removed to the Tower. The royal site was neutralised and forgotten.

In contrast, Inigo Jones was swept up in the maelstrom of war and, before leaving London, he hid his fortune in a Lambeth marsh. In July he was asked by the King for a loan of £500 and the architect sent his nephew by marriage, John Webb, to deliver the money sewn into his jacket; it was a dangerous mission and one that would return to haunt the young courier. Jones was also called to assist the King on the battlefield and use his architectural knowledge in the preparation of fortifications. In October 1645 he was caught by the Parliamentary army at Basing House, Hampshire, and was forced to make accommodation with the ascendant power in the land. He was then allowed to retreat into obscurity while his royal master continued the increasingly hopeless fight.

After six years of relative peace, the Civil Wars eventually returned to Greenwich in the spring of 1648. The previous autumn Charles I was captured and then allowed to escape. In a last throw of the dice he called for a desperate uprising against Oliver Cromwell and his New Model Army. The Second Civil War was brief but bloody. In May, a local militia of 800 men marched to Greenwich and camped in the grounds of the royal park. Finding no weapons in the nearby houses, these royalist rebels raided the outlying ships, as well as seizing 'carts, harrows and such like materials',[17] and prepared to face the enemy which they expected to advance from London. At dawn on the 28th, mist rising from the Thames, two regiments appeared from the west and 'like the devil himself' scattered the ill-disciplined horde. It was a weak, impotent attempt to swing the tide of events that was running away from Charles and his supporters.

The Civil Wars came to an end on 30 January 1649, when Charles I was led to the Banqueting Hall, Inigo Jones's perfect, symmetrical space that had been built thirty years earlier to symbolise the harmony of the Stuart dynasty. The geometric room was further emphasised by the ceiling paintings above the gathered huddle that now surrounded Charles. The paintings had been commissioned by Charles himself from Peter Paul Rubens and in the central panel stood a celestial James I, from whom the light and order of the nation emanated. Charles I was driven forward across the hall towards one of the windows which had been dismantled, and led out to a platform that ran along the front of the building. He said his prayers, forgave the executioner, and addressed the throng that waited in anticipation. Laying his head upon the block, he spread his arms and was beheaded. The second act of the Stuart dynasty ended with the swing of an axe. For some it was a royal martyrdom; for the new regime it was just punishment for the King's betrayal of his own people.

What is a palace without a king? The Crown was replaced by a Commonwealth, an uncomfortable balance between Oliver Cromwell's army and an increasingly desperate series of parliamentary constitutional experiments. This was not a time for grand architectural gestures and the Puritan wind quickly reached Greenwich, where the Queen's House was neglected, but not altogether lost. With Cromwell's triumph the villa was unceremoniously stripped of the royal collection of art: 'The noblest collection that any prince out of Italy could boast of,' noted one commentator, 'but those barbarous rebels, whose quarrel was as much to politeness and the liberal arts, as to monarchy and prelacy, dissipated and destroyed the best part of it.'[18] The villa was briefly passed over to the parliamentary lawyer Bulstrode Whitlock, while the old Tudor palace nearby was turned into a stables and then a prison for enemy sailors captured in the First Anglo-Dutch War of 1652–4.

Yet even in these years of neglect, the stage set of Greenwich was not completely abandoned. For the Stuarts the park and the palace had always been a place of royal pleasure; perhaps now it could be transformed for the benefit of the new regime and given a new power, one connected to the Lord Protector's ambitions to make England overlord of the seas. Greenwich was the place where London met the world. It was often here that foreign dignitaries arrived on their trips to the metropolis (a word that was first used in the 1650s), docking at the palace steps and then, after a rest, travelling overland or by barge into London. Perhaps the palace could be converted from a place of private pleasure into a centre of national pride.

In the 1650s Cromwell devised his first Navigation Act, which set out the rubric for the British Empire; by peculiar precedent Greenwich was already at the centre of these schemes. By some unlikely quirk of feudal tradition, all the grants for settlement in the New World were said to be 'of the manor of East Greenwich'.[19] Thus the charters for the lands of Virginia (1606), the Fellowship for the Discovery of the Northwest Passage (1607), Newfoundland (1610), Guiana (1613), Bermuda (1615), New England (1620) and Maine (1639) were all drawn up as within the manor lands of Greenwich park. In effect, the British Empire was nothing more than an extension of the palace grounds.

Cromwell began a systematic overhaul of the Navy to protect British ships as they uncovered new trade routes and settlements with a massive programme of shipbuilding at the Deptford docks. Things swiftly led to war against the Dutch, who also coveted the treasures of far-off colonies. And war creates heroes. Because of the combination of its maritime connections and social distinction the Queen's House was soon co-opted for the veneration of the new national leaders, a mausoleum for the fallen warriors who died in the service of the Commonwealth. In 1653 the body of General-at-Sea Richard Deane, who had died at the victorious Battle of the Gabbard, thus ending the First Anglo-Dutch War, was laid in state at the villa. From Greenwich, his coffin was ceremoniously carried up the river to Westminster Abbey, where he was buried in the Henry VII Chapel.

In 1657 the villa was used once again solemnly to record the death of Robert Blake, Deane's fellow General-at-Sea, so brave and skilled that even Horatio Nelson would later be in awe of his victories as an admiral. Wounded in battle outside Cadiz, having captured over £200,000 in American bullion, Blake died within sight of Plymouth. He was given a full state funeral despite the fact that, while his body lay in state at Greenwich, all his internal organs remained in Plymouth.

The Commonwealth years proved that modern architecture was a fluid thing, that a royal building designed to project the glory of the Crown could be converted for a different kind of performance; that the stones that had once sung of the divine right of kings could be used to praise the valour of the whole nation. Yet, as Cromwell grew ill in 1658, the future of the republic seemed dark, and no one knew what was to come. Cromwell's son, Richard, was named as his heir but he could not bend the interests of the Army and Parliament to his will. The Army, led by General Monck, then attempted a coup and marched from Scotland to London, inciting a parliamentary conspiracy. It was only after every other option was found lacking that a ship sailed to Holland, where Prince Charles was waiting in exile. He returned to London and claimed the crown but, despite his own desire, his kingship would be very different to that of his father, and this would be reflected once again in building at the Palace of Greenwich.

On the morning of 29 May 1660, the old Tudor palace still stood in a desperate state. Beyond, one could see the Queen's House on the lea of the hill and the fields of Greenwich park beyond. The parkland, the popular hunting ground of James I and Charles I, rose dramatically up to Blackheath Common which ranged across the top of the mound. Here, Charles II was greeted by the Lord Mayor of London, who offered the returning King the ceremonial sword of the city. Also on the field were a troop of dancing girls, dressed in blue and white, who scattered flowers and herbs in front of the King's horse. Charles then made his way into London, which he had not seen for over eighteen years, and towards his palace at Whitehall.

Charles II returned a king, but not a conquering hero. As he travelled through the city he was torn between the temptations of absolutism that he had witnessed in the rule of his cousin, Louis XIV, who had proclaimed 'L'état c'est moi', and the prospect of being as powerless as a Venetian doge. With the definition of his role left unclear in the Restoration settlement Charles II desired to project himself as a Baroque prince; and if this could not be achieved by law, or swift victory on the battlefield, he hoped to do so through architecture. During his exile he had watched with envy as Paris was transformed into a modern capital, Louis XIV impressing his authority upon the nation through stone. As the playwright Corneille observed, 'An entire city, built with Pomp, seems to have arisen miraculously from an old ditch.'[20] Why should Charles II not do the same for London?

While in theory architecture could be used to project boundless power, it took money to turn paper projects into stone and Charles soon discovered that he could do little more than plaster over the cracks of a troubled inheritance. When he moved into Whitehall the King was perturbed by the years of neglect at the hands of the Lord Protector but was only able to afford a few new decorations and additions, allowing a visiting French courtier, Samuel Sorbière, to note that, beyond the elegance of Jones's Banqueting Hall, which had survived intact, the rest of the palace was 'nothing but a heap of houses erected at divers times'.[21]

Beyond the palace gates, Charles also had little control over the revival of the city. He could not afford grand monuments, and he was in no position to command change. He passionately desired to improve his new capital but could only do so by encouragement rather than patronage. Fortunately he returned from the Continent with a number of courtiers who were more able to afford new houses; where once the Strand was the aristocratic quarter, new grand *hôtels* built on French and Dutch designs began to rise on the green fields of Piccadilly. At nearby St James's, Henry Jermyn devised London's first square, based on the Place des Vosges in Paris, a noble enclave of large houses around a garden plot in St James's Square. Men such as John Evelyn, who had spent the Civil War years touring the sites of France and Italy, also began to debate the new identity of modern English architecture, taking Inigo Jones as the first master and combining his work with the latest marvels of the Baroque that they had encountered abroad.

The same could not be said about the Queen's House at Greenwich. With the Restoration, the villa was returned to Henrietta Maria, but rather than being a retreat for a glorious queen, the House of Delights became a dowager cottage, the permanent home for an elder noble-woman. Some improvements were made to the fabric of the building and John Webb, Inigo Jones's kinsman and his architectural heir, worked on expanding the living space, devising two new salons either side of the bridge room. There was also a concerted effort to retrieve the art collection that had been stolen during the Commonwealth. The Queen arrived back in England in 1662 and stayed only briefly at Greenwich. In June 1665, in the midst of the truest indication of the failures of London, the Great Plague, which brought the city to its knees, Henrietta Maria left England for good, moaning about the cold, and returned to Paris. Among her retinue was a young scientist, Christopher Wren.

The villa was then given by Charles to his new wife, Catherine of Braganza, but rarely used except by visiting ambassadors. In 1674 the Dutch minister visited and recorded how the house was a reminder of England's recent history: 'looking out on the floor and beautiful pictures of art and sciences; spacious rooms with marble chimneys, but the marble leaf-work mutilated; the noses of all the faces cut off from love of mischief, committed in the times of Cromwell'.[22]

How, therefore, would Charles II prove his new kingship in stone? The answer lay with John Webb who, soon after the Restoration, pre-sented Charles II with a brand-new plan for Whitehall. The new palace would rival El Escorial, Phillip II's monumental residence outside Madrid, but for the moment Webb did not gain the prized commission – he was not in favour with the new court, who had spent many years abroad absorbing the latest styles while he had sat out the Com-monwealth at home in England. Nevertheless, in 1663 he was offered another opportunity that far surpassed his hopes of Whitehall: the chance to build a palace for the Baroque prince in Greenwich.

Work had already begun on dismantling the old palace and Webb was allowed to dream of building an English Versailles to match Louis XIV's lavish hunting lodge outside Paris. In his initial plans he devised a building that filled three sides of a square facing the river front: a range topped with a cupola connected two wings. John Evelyn visited the site and was concerned that it would lie too close to the river's edge, but apart from that it was very uncontroversial. Except that, by using a conventional format for a Baroque *hôtel,* it did not take into account the building that already existed and the southern range had the unfortunate result of blocking the view from the Queen's villa towards the Thames. It was quickly made known that this was unacceptable. Thus, in the final drawings, the southern range was soon done away with and the palace would become a study in perspective, the two large wings running away from the river with the Queen's House as the eye's focal point. At the far end of the gaze, as the hill rose to a summit, Webb also devised a grotto.

The palace complex therefore dominated the whole of the park, a vast stage for the display of royal power and the interaction between architecture and Nature. For the approaching dignitary, arriving by barge to the broad stone steps at the river's edge, the sight was impressive: the ornate, formal solidity of the King's Palace dominated the eye; through the careful mathematical balance of space and perspective, the two wings receded and gave way to the refined elegance of the rustic Queen's House in the mid-distance; beyond, the garden rose finally to the fantastical ruin on the horizon.

The Baroque palace was intended as a thing of magnificence and power, an expressive mass of stone composed like frozen music, informed by the latest innovations in natural philosophy. The rigid codes of construction and classical correctness, as preached by Inigo Jones, were replaced by an overpowering determination to impress. As befitted such a grand scheme, the plan for the garden was as important as the buildings themselves. The Baroque garden was an exploration in form and reason on a monumental scale. Often a house would stand at the centre of Nature and from this fulcrum ran, first, a series of intricate parterres, displaying the owner's dominance over his land; beyond, vast avenues divided the landscape, occasionally punctuated by statues, canals, fountains and rooms. The overall impression was of power and grace. By 1662, Charles had already broken up the old hunting ground, dug a series of giant steps into the hillside and planted regiments of trees; the following year he hired André Le Nôtre, the famed French designer who had laid out the parks at Versailles, to draft a scheme for Greenwich. Unfortunately, Le Nôtre never visited the site and when he produced his plans it was clear that his ideas had not included the dramatic gradient of the hill to the south. In the end work was never progressed on the cascade and Le Nôtre's vision remained on paper.

On 4 March 1664 Samuel Pepys, diarist and member of the Navy Board, who often travelled through Greenwich on business, recorded that he 'did observe the foundacion laying of a very great house for the King, which will cost a great deal of money'.[23] Work began, but in recognition of the expense of building on such a scale, Webb was commanded to complete one wing before starting the second. Nonetheless, costs soon began to escalate and by 1665 the palace had racked up £75,000 as Webb continued doggedly on the west wing, later called the Charles II wing. Yet by the end of the 1660s, Charles was forced to admit that his dreams of being the British Sun King were in tatters. Nearby, London had fallen victim to a disaster that would change its history for ever.

On the morning of 2 September 1666, a fire began in the house of Thomas Farriner, the King's baker, on Pudding Lane, to the north of the gatehouse of London Bridge. Over that night the flames began to spread along the street and into the surrounding neighbourhood; within three days the fire had devastated much of the city, burning an area of over 400 acres, making more than 130,000 Londoners homeless and reducing to ash many of the major institutions of the city including the ports, the Royal Exchange, the Guildhall, numerous parish churches and consecrated chapels as well as St Paul's Cathedral. As John Evelyn noted in his diary that week: 'London was, but is no more.'[24]

The fire finally showed up Charles's attempt to act the Baroque prince for what it was. In 1672 Webb's work at Greenwich was brought to a sorry end, with only the western range completed. Webb retreated to

Somerset and would never build in London again. But while work on the palace was ended, it did not mean that Charles had abandoned Greenwich for good; it would revive, in a new form, and in the hands of the next generation of planners, who sought to find a modern language in architecture.

At the time of the Great Fire, Christopher Wren was the Savilian Professor of Astronomy at Oxford University, the leading stargazer in England and one of the most renowned scientists in Europe. On the Restoration, Wren had been one of the New Philosophers, pioneers of the empirical scientific method, who had persuaded Charles to institute a club as a permanent chamber for their activities in London, the Royal Society, and meet weekly for the pursuit of experiments, demonstrations and debate.

The New Philosophy was also at the centre of architecture and the idea of what a city could be. Following the 1666 fire Wren devised a fresh plan for the city that radically altered its street layout and rationalised the medieval huddle destroyed by the flames. Wren saw that architecture – the science of building – was an essential expression of the social dimensions of the New Philosophy, while the determination to rebuild the city would herald its rebirth as a modern, rational capital. Wren's plans were never put into practice, but the same spirit of reason informed the rebuilding of the city when, in 1667, Robert Hooke began to measure out the revised street plan for the capital.

That same year, Louis XIV had commissioned an astronomical observatory outside Paris, which was completed in 1671. The accurate charting of the stars by telescope was the space race of its day, at the heart of the early modern military-industrial complex, and Charles II was determined not to be left behind. The exploration of the heavens promised to bring glory to its royal patron and valuable knowledge to the market, improving navigation of the nation's fleet and ensuring that it got into port safely and ahead of the competition. Louis's *observatoire* was built by Claude Perrault, a noted architect and mathematician, one of the first members of the French Academy of Sciences, founded in 1666 in response to the Royal Society. Charles would similarly ask his own architect and geometer, Wren, to build one for England, to devise a building for 'Rectifying the Tables of the Motions of the Heavens and the Places of the Fixed Stars, in order to find out the so much desired Longitude at Sea, for the perfecting the Art of Navigation'.[25]

Thus at Greenwich, at the King's command, Wren's passions for science, architecture and stargazing combined in the creation of the Royal Observatory, the most ambitious project at the heart of Charles's imperial ambitions. The Observatory would be the first purpose-built scientific research centre in England but, needless to say, as befitted the times it was to be constructed on a shoestring budget. As most astronomical readings in those days were conducted in the open air, the building was intended as a basic structure to stand on the edge of the hill above the Queen's House, far enough away from the fug of the capital for a clear night sky. Wren devised a protected courtyard with plenty of waterproof storage for the instruments as well as a small house for the 'observator'. He was also allowed to add 'a little for pompe'.[26] for this was a royal building that was to be visited by interested dignitaries and courtiers.

Costs were kept low and, rather than setting new foundations, Wren reused those of an old house which had once stood there. There were consequences, however; as the building did not face due north, every calculation would be thirteen degrees off, which had to be factored into each observation. Wren also made savings by recycling 'bricks from Tilbury Fort ... [and] some wood, iron and lead from a gatehouse demolished in the tower'.[27] Progress, thankfully, was swift as John Flamsteed, the first Astronomer Royal, noted: 'the work carried on so well that the roof was laid, and the building occupied by Christmas'.[28]

The Observatory was a very subtle shift in the performance of power, and the role of Greenwich as a royal domain. The person of the King was no longer the sole object to be glorified through architecture; instead of a palace of pleasure, the site became a meeting place between royal patronage and national interest. The King was using his authority to promote the innovations of the New Philosophy in the service of merchants and tradesmen, as well as the Navy, who were at that time establishing Britain as the maritime superpower. Thus the power of the throne was expressed, not by magnificent stones or architectural awe, but in a new relationship between the king and his subjects: patronage, not absolutism, was the new order of kingship.

Charles never lost his hopes of building a palace for a Baroque prince, but it would not be in London. In the 1680s, as he was growing fearful of the political machinations of Parliament, which was once again crying out for limitations upon his sovereignty, he decided to build a new royal house at Winchester, far from the capital. Wren was commissioned to develop new plans and work began with uncommon haste. The palace was never completed; in 1685, as Wren was rushing between Winchester and the metropolis, the King suffered an apoplectic fit and died four days later.

In the early hours of 21 May 1692, seven years after Charles II's death, a messenger arrived at Whitehall Palace from Portsmouth with news of a great naval victory. The French fleet had been destroyed off La Hogue and the victorious Admiral Russell had returned to port with the injured. In her joy Queen Mary, wife of William III, gathered together fifty surgeons from the various London hospitals and sent them to help the wounded. The following week the Queen also granted 'of Greenwich as a hospital for Seamen'.[29] The building would be a fitting symbol of a new era of kingship, an expression of the Crown's thanks to those who had sacrificed so much for the nation. It was to be a place of rest after war, a magnificent shelter to show how the Crown bestowed charity upon the most needy. Greenwich Hospital would make solid the new understanding between the King and his people. But it was not to be just any hospital for, as the Spanish tourist Don Manuel Alvarez Espriella sagely observed in the following century, 'the English say that their palaces are like hospitals and their hospitals are like palaces'.[30]

Four years earlier, on 5 November 1688, William of Orange, the Dutch stadholder, had disembarked at Brixham, Devon, with a vast army and slowly made his way towards London. The last invasion of Britain was by no means bloodless, but it was swift. On 19 December William was welcomed into London by a crowd that called out 'Welcome, welcome, God bless you, you come to redeeme our Religion, lawes, liberties and lives, God reward you'.[31] Four days later Charles II's brother, James II, who had only been on the throne for three years, fled to France and lost his crown for ever.

The Glorious Revolution redesigned the political theatre of England. Who was to be the succeeding monarch? What was the nature of this new kingship? In the ensuing debates it was agreed that not one but two crowns were needed and that William would reign with his wife, Mary. Secondly, on their coronation day, the 'double bottom'd' king was presented with a Bill of Rights that outlined the ancient rights of the Crown so that sovereignty was defined within a written constitution. The new contract finally answered the problems that had haunted English power throughout the Stuart dynasty, and enshrined them in law: on what authority did the monarch reign? What were the limits of the throne? What were the bonds between the Crown and Parliament?

This public statement of royal power, however, needed a new symbol. Neither William nor Mary were interested in the grandiose Baroque gestures of their Stuart forebears; when they declared that they wished to move their court outside London as the metropolis's smoky pollution affected the King's asthma, they decided to rebuild Hampton Court to the west and to convert Kensington Palace as a quiet retreat away from the centre. William would almost instantly find glory on the battlefields of Europe to confirm Britain's predominance abroad, and Queen Mary's plans for a new hospital at Greenwich offered a very physical representation of the new reign. In October 1692, the Treasury drew up plans to finance the new project and within a year a Royal Warrant was issued. In addition, a commission of over 200 nobles and grandees was set up to oversee the building. Sir Christopher Wren was named architect and the treasurer was Wren's old friend, John Evelyn.

In January 1694 Wren visited the site with a number of masons and his assistant, Nicholas Hawksmoor, to make a survey. He found that Webb's wing, left in 1672, was now being used as a gunpowder store and £500 was made available to clear the rubbish and move the ordnance. Hawksmoor also noted the masons' advice that the Charles II wing 'was nothing but a heap of stones',[32] knowing that they got paid whether working on construction or demolition. Nonetheless, Mary demanded that the old building remain and, in addition, that any plans should not obstruct the view from the Queen's House to the Thames. This posed a sticky design problem for Wren that tested his skills as both architect and geometer.

Yet all proposals were thrown into the air in December 1694 when Mary died of smallpox. Plans for the hospital could easily have been stalled but William, having initially expressed concern about such expensive undertakings, pledged as a token of his heartfelt love for his wife the determination to see her project through. He promised £2,000 a year to ensure the memorial to his beloved was completed.

At that time, Wren was in his sixties and for the last twenty years had dedicated himself to the rebuilding of London after the Great Fire of 1666. Many of the fifty-one city parish churches were now in hand; he had also finished the Monument, the Customs House and other royal institutions within the walls, yet he was still building his cathedral, St Paul's, which was more than a decade away from completion. He was also working on reviving the Tudor palace at Hampton Court for William and Mary. As he began his first designs for Greenwich, Wren focused all his experience, learning and dreams in creating a magnificent new symbol for the monarchy.

Almost immediately he was forced to break the rules: traditionally, building around a central square, the two wings would connect with a central range that often contained a portico or cupola for dramatic effect. However, as Mary had stipulated that nothing disrupt the view from the Queen's House to the Thames, there was to be no central range at all. Like Webb before him, this challenged Wren's inventiveness as he hoped to create a central domed chapel to compete with Les Invalides, Louis XIV's hospital for old soldiers in Paris. Instead, viewed from the north, Wren was offered the puzzle of how to devise two parallel ranges running southwards from the river that were somehow balanced and gave the impression of being parts of a single building, combining with the Queen's villa in the distance. Despite such restrictions, Wren produced perhaps the most eye-catching design of his career.

Wren's solution was to abandon attempts to compose a single building but instead design a complex collection of different forms and shapes in a landscape: at the river front two blocks run either side of a large quadrangle, each with a double portico facing out towards the Thames. Beyond, rather than a central range, he invented two further blocks in parallel, each with a cupola at the southern end high above a colonnaded pavilion, a loggia, that ran away from the river towards the south. This clever device gave an elevation to the centre of the design while also creating a vista that channelled the gaze towards the Queen's House beyond. The effect was startling and seemed to bring the villa into relation with the new buildings, balancing the various parts of the site into a single whole.

Yet, as with all projects in the Stuart era, money was a problem. The hospital was fortunate in the integrity of the treasurer, John Evelyn, who never once took a salary (nor did Wren) or, as was common practice, siphoned off funds for his own profit. Like all great projects, the commission of nobles who were initially desperate to be attached to the scheme hardly ever met and when they did it was a costly affair: in 1697 a meeting of the fabric committee made its way through 'four ribs of beef, a leg of mutton, six chickens, two loaves of bread, and ten half flasks of wine'.[33] As a result Evelyn was forced to fundraise almost single-handedly. And fast: a year after the first stones were laid Evelyn calculated that he had raised £800 but had already spent over £5,000. Other possibilities were suggested, including a contribution of sixpence from every sailor; lotteries were held; all prizes gained from naval engagements were also press-ganged into service. Perhaps the unlikeliest donation came from the notorious pirate William Kidd, whose property was confiscated – £6,500 in all – and given to the fund. By 1702 Evelyn had spent £128,384 and racked up £19,000 in debts.

Building began with haste on all parts of the complex. A special model was constructed in wood to show how everything fitted together, and was clearly so useful that it was said in 1707 that it needed to be repaired by 'gluing the parts that were unglued'.[34] The Charles II wing originally built by John Webb in the 1660s was remodelled while work started on the Queen Anne wing opposite. To the south, the foundations were dug for the corresponding King William wing, to the west, and Queen Mary wing, to the east. The central space between the buildings was also transformed to give unity to the cluster of forms: a grand square was set at the Thames's edge. The Charles II and Queen Anne blocks were then divided from the south ranges by a wide road. Beyond this the William and Mary buildings were raised and between them a broad set of stone stairs led up to a paved court, bringing the two wings together yet also allowing the visitor a clear view of the Queen's House beyond. To complete the sense of visual unity, Wren added a colonnade on either side of the villa.

While Wren was the master planner of the project he placed his assistant, Nicholas Hawksmoor, in day-to-day charge on the ground; his choice of deputy was wise. Hawksmoor had started his career as a copyist within Wren's office at St Paul's, and had worked alongside him on many of his major undertakings. By 1700, Hawksmoor was also expressing his own architectural voice. Initially working as Wren's 'gentleman', he devised country houses at Broadfield Hall and Easton Neston, where he refined his distinctive English Baroque style. In 1700 he joined up with John Vanbrugh, the playwright who had recently turned his hand to architecture. Together they designed Castle Howard and Blenheim Palace, two of the greatest stately homes in England. Hawksmoor, like Wren, believed that good architecture had its founda-

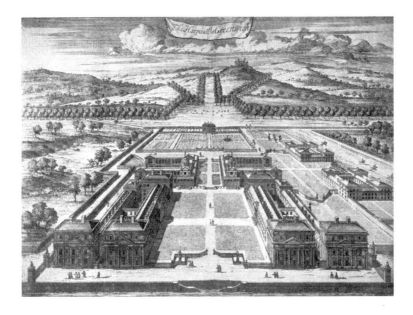

10. A panorama of the Queen's House and the hospital from the south

tion in geometry and reason: 'strong reason and good fancy, joyn'd with experience and tryalls, so that we are assured of the good effect of it'.[35] Like Jones, Webb and Wren before him, Hawksmoor took the essence of classical architecture and looked at it in a different way: they spoke the same language but with very different accents, all to be found at Greenwich.

After 1703 Hawksmoor was aided at Greenwich by Vanbrugh, who was named a commissioner at the hospital that year. Born in London in 1664, Vanbrugh had tried many careers before settling on architecture: he had travelled to Surat in Gujarat as an employee of the East India Company, joined the Army, been arrested in Paris for espionage, spending four years in the Bastille, written successful plays for the capital's stage and run the Haymarket Theatre, as well as being a deft political manipulator and ardent Whig. As an architect, despite his lack of training, he brought society connections and an unerring flamboyance to Hawksmoor's deep understanding of the necessities of design.

The work would continue through the reign of William III, who died in 1702, having stumbled on a molehill while riding. He was succeeded by Queen Anne, the second daughter of James II and the last of the Stuart monarchs. Despite the change of personalities, the role of kingship itself did not alter – political stability was ensured by the agreements established in 1689, following William III's revolution. Queen Anne supported the many architectural projects that she inherited; she was passionate about Wren's work on St Paul's and personally attended the celebrations held for victories abroad conducted in the cathedral. Greenwich was also a project close to the Queen's heart and it was during her reign that the hospital finally began to accept old sailors into its elegant halls.

In 1705, forty-two pensioners were allowed to take their lodges in the renovated Charles II wing. The following year this had increased to 300 and by 1738 there was a full complement of 1,000. The life of the new arrivals was to be heavily regulated: everyone wore a uniform with a grey coat and blue lining; there was daily chapel and strict rules against drinking and swearing. If caught drunk, the culprit was docked a day's food; if found telling lies, he had to stand in the hall for three meals holding a broom; the punishment for whoring was bread and water for a week. Despite the threats the pensioners were well fed. Every man had a pound of beef or mutton every five days, and a double ration of cheese twice a week.

In time, the four wings were divided up into dormitories for the old sailors, as a visitor noted, each sailor being given his own small cabin, with 'a little more room than he is like to enjoy in the Church-yard',[36] but it was better than living in poverty on the streets, which was the common fate for many ex-Servicemen. Later, in 1786, the German tourist and writer Sophie von La Roche would be more complimentary: 'their dormitories are very pleasant: large light and lofty, with cubicles containing glass windows on the side, where each has his own bed, small table, tea and smoking outfit which he can lock up'.[37] A teacher was hired in 1715 to instruct the pensioners, although a library was not made available until the 1820s.

The whole project came to a climax in the great Painted Hall. From the outset Wren and Hawksmoor were thinking about how to decorate the King William wing. At its southern end, they had projected a dome that would add symmetry and rhythm to the complex. Without the possibility of constructing a central range to link the two wings of the building, the cupolas on either side of the central space drew the whole together. In Hawksmoor's exquisite hand, the two architects started to plan their dome for Greenwich. At the same time, Wren was devising his grander dome for St Paul's Cathedral. The dome of the hospital was the first to be completed and, although far smaller, is perhaps even more elaborate than that of St Paul's.

Under the dome, the magnificence continued, especially in the rich painting of the interior of the Great Hall. On 17 July 1707 the business minutes note that, 'as soon as the scaffolding in the hall is ready Mr James Thornhill do proceed upon the painting thereof . . . and that he make such alterations in his designe, in inserting what more he can relating to maritime affairs'.[38] Thornhill was a young historical painter who drew in the Italian Baroque style; he was commissioned to tell the maritime history of Britain and its conquest of the seas upon every surface of the hall. He worked on the project for the next seventeen years and in 1724 delivered a bill for '540 yards of history with figures etc. on the ceiling of the Hall at £3 a yard … 1341 yards of painting on the sides with trophies, fluting etc. at 26s a yard'. In total he would be paid more than £6,600.

In 1726 Thornhill also produced a guide to the paintings for interested visitors, *An Explanation of the Paintings in the Royal Hospital at Greenwich*, which gave a clear description of the mixture of allusion, history, allegory and myth that combined in his art. Just as, over a century before, Inigo Jones had claimed that 'Picture is the invention of heaven: the most ancient and most akinne to Nature', and that the artist can use his tools to manipulate the world as powerfully as the orator or poet, now Thornhill was writing his new vision of the nation in paint. Where Jones had first set his masques with canvas and pulleys, Thornhill set out his theatre of power for posterity. At the centre of the Lower Hall ceiling sit William and Mary, who 'present Peace and Liberty to Europe, and trample on Tyranny and Arbitrary power'.[39] At the far end of the hall is the main image of a British man-of-war, filled with trophies taken from its enemies. The ship is sailing towards London up the Thames, while the other great rivers of England – the Severn, Humber, Isis and Tyne – are portrayed. The New Philosophy is also represented by the great astronomers, including the Astronomer Royal, John Flamsteed. In the Upper Hall the nationalistic celebration continues; here, the world itself, and even the four elements, pay obeisance to the British Crown.

Yet, even as Thornhill was working on his masterpiece, the state of the Crown was once again in question. In 1714, Queen Anne died childless and as a result the hopes of the Stuart dynasty passed with her. By the terms of the Act of Settlement, her half-brother, Prince James, the Old Pretender, was denied the crown as punishment for his Catholicism. Instead, genealogists had to work their way through the Stuart family tree all the way back to James I's daughter, Princess Elizabeth, who married the Elector Palatine in 1613. It was following this wedding that Inigo Jones had travelled to Italy for the second time with the royal party. Elizabeth's daughter Sophia of Hanover was the closest Protestant relative, but on her death, just months before Anne's, the inheritance of the throne of England was passed to her son George, who was named George I.

It was at Greenwich that the new King first stepped on English soil on 17 September 1744. One of his first acts was to knight the captain who brought him there and John Vanbrugh, who had campaigned for his coronation. In time, Thornhill was to weave a portrait of George into his fresco, as master of the seas and the munificent King of Britain.

Thus the stones at Greenwich tell the story of one dynasty as well as the first years of the next. Work on the hospital would continue for many decades. By 1713, Wren was rarely to be found at Greenwich; at over eighty years old he was still active, but the plan for the hospital had been established and the second phase of building, which began that year, could go ahead without the Surveyor General. He officially retired in 1716 and was replaced by Vanbrugh. It is often assumed that this change heralded an alteration in the plans for the project, Vanbrugh adding a hint of Baroque flamboyance to Wren's rational design. This is not true at all; Hawksmoor later complained that Vanbrugh did not need the title of Surveyor as he had so little to add to the design. A new chapel was not completed until 1742 and then rebuilt in the 1780s by James 'Athenian' Stuart.

Unlike Westminster Abbey (a building whose function has been consistent but its architects several), Greenwich Hospital has always been Wren's creation but has continued to change its purpose, offering itself as a stage set to successive generations. It remained a hospital until 1869, when it was converted to a naval college for the education of young officers, a use which continued until 1998. Since then it has served as the Main Campus of the University of Greenwich and, from 2001, as home to Trinity College of music. It has often been used, with a nod to its former role as a stage set for the Stuart dynasty, as the *mise en scène* for numerous films, including a recreation of London in the eighteenth century for *The Duchess*, the nineteenth century in *Sense and Sensibility* and the late Victorian era in the thriller *The Secret Agent*, as a replacement for Buckingham Palace in *Patriot Games* as well as a Venetian palazzo in *Lara Croft: Tomb Raider*. It is proof of the flexibility of architecture to change over time yet remain constant.

CHAPTER 5

19 PRINCELET STREET

Spitalfields and the Rise and Fall of English Silk

> We are all Adam's children, but silk makes the difference.
>
> Old Proverb

The history of Spitalfields is a cautionary tale, a story that starts in a field and ends in the slums; a narrative of immigration, naturalisation and how a neighbourhood is found and subsequently lost. Located to the east of the city walls, the enclave evolved in the decades following the Great Fire of 1666, and became renowned as a centre for the textile industry. At the same time it was also recognised as one of the centres of Huguenot culture within London – the French Protestants finding refuge in Britain away from religious persecution at home. The Huguenots brought with them their own customs and industry, in particular highly skilled weaving techniques, importing raw material from the far corners of the emerging British Empire and threading it into delicate, finely woven fabric. The production of and burgeoning demand for luxuries in the eighteenth century, goods that had been the preserve of the court in previous centuries, gave birth to the modern consumer market.

In time, however, changes in the supply and demand of the silk trade transformed Spitalfields and London became a fluid city, exposed to the tides of taste and money. The Huguenot community began to divide; some integrated with the rest of the city and naturalised, adopting Anglo-Saxon names, moving away from Spitalfields to other neighbourhoods; the less well-off were left behind. In addition, the opening-up of new markets created competition that had a dangerous impact on the weaver's livelihood. Cheap foreign goods as well as the development of industrial methods – mechanisation and the rise of the factory – forced the traditional craftsmen to take to the streets in protest. It did little good except to incite riots, murder and, eventually, execution.

Spitalfields had been built out of the fields by speculators hoping to provide desirable housing for the new bourgeoisie. Yet within a century a thriving Georgian community and industrial centre calamitously declined into a Victorian slum. This story can be told through one house, 19 Princelet Street, how it was built and the family that first lived there. The house itself is a reflection, and a victim, of the decline of the neighbourhood and the many faces of Spitalfields from its first moments in 1717 to the present day. In time the house has been a home, a factory, a place of worship, and now a museum.

In 1720, the ecclesiastical historian John Strype published an updated edition of John Stow's 1598 *Survey of London*. Strype's purpose was not just to edit out the errors that had crept into the work, but also to take note 'of the great Enlargements of the Compass of the two Cities; of the Fire of London, and of the new Buildings thereof, with the new Streets, Courts, Monuments, Churches, and Alterations'.[1] London had been transformed in the previous 122 years in ways that the long-dead Stow could not have imagined. Strype himself had been born in Spitalfields, a new neighbourhood that was developing from the old ground of St Mary Spital, a medieval priory founded in 1197. He was the oldest son of Dutch refugees who had been forced 'to fly for shelter to England'[2] following the persecution of Protestants during the Thirty Years' War.

His father was a successful silk throwster and thrived in London, developing his own workshop and rising to the role of master of the Silk Throwsters' Company, which had been set up in 1627 in response to the rise of the immigrant silk industry in London. John did not follow his father but, like many immigrant sons, sought naturalisation and pursued the most English of professions, becoming an Anglican cleric based in the rural parish of Low Leyton in Essex, where he soon gained a reputation as a fine Church historian. However British he became he could not leave his past behind; he travelled into London weekly and had the opportunity to observe the transformation of his childhood neighbourhood as he entered the city along Bishopsgate Road.

Since the dissolution of the monasteries in the 1530s the land surrounding the priory had been divided and sold, creating a number of different estates. Some plots were in the hands of private individuals, other were controlled by ancient rights attached to manors and liberties. Many of the open fields were used as 'tenter grounds' where the cloth workers and dyers hung their fabrics to dry. It also attracted Nonconformists, as it stood just outside the jurisdiction of the City Corporation; Baptists and Quakers found refuge here during the first years of the Civil Wars of the 1640s. The radical Nicholas Culpeper, author of the famous *Complete Herbal*, was raised at the house on Red Lion Corner (now Commercial Road). William Lilly, Cromwell's astrologer, who was jailed after predicting the fire of 1666, also lived here. By the time of the Restoration, however, the land was too valuable to be left to outsiders and Puritans and was ripe for speculation.

Matters became more businesslike after the Great Fire when demand for land outside the city was at a premium. The tax returns of 1674–5 calculated 1,336 dwellings within the Spitalfields parish; many of these may have been old cottages that had stood for some time, but it was noted that 140 were currently unoccupied, waiting for their first owner. Where once building was only commissioned for a specific need, now whole regions of the metropolis were being built in the hope of profit, in the expectation that once the shells of the houses were completed they would be snapped up by eager customers.

In 1681 it was declared that a market was needed at Spitalfields to supply the burgeoning community; bids for tender were requested from all the leading builders of the city with the warning that no offer should be less than £4,000 for the ground, or £5,200 for the ground and the right to control the market. Dr Nicholas Barbon won the contract for the land while the market franchise ended up in the hands of a George Bohun.

To the east there was also work along Brick Lane, for London was being rebuilt in brick and stone and the local clay was particularly prized. Here, too, there were housing developments emerging on plots owned by the Wheler estate. Sir William Wheler had the unusual honour of being knighted by both Oliver Cromwell and Charles II and was described as 'a Comely Old Gentleman with a round plump Face, a rudy cheerfull countenance, addorned with curled grey hair'.[3] He had inherited eight acres that had once been called the Bishop of London's Field and on his death in 1666 it was noted he left a 'Capitall Messuage now divided into three Tenements'[4] in Spital Yard, one of which had been rented to a silk throwster.

In his will the remaining land was divided up between his widow and seven daughters, who took one portion of the estate, and his kinsman Charles Wheler and his son George. George was 'a very worthy, learned, ingenious person, a little formal and particular, but exceedingly devout'.[5] They did not gain control of the land until 1670 when Sir William's widow died, and it was not until 1675 that Sir Christopher Wren gave his permission, as Surveyor General and the 'police architectonic' (a one-man planning tsar), for building to commence. The land left to the daughters was held in trust with two Middle Temple lawyers; later it was revealed that they had tried to deprive the heirs of their rights. In the meantime a merchant, Thomas Joyce, had added a few houses, the petitions cataloguing 'a messuage, garden, shed and two little houses (in all, three acres); a brick messuage, workshop, garden and two tene-ments; and two brick messuages and an orchard on which at least another six messuages had been erected'.[6]

It was not until the next century, however, that the daughters won back the leases and a new trust was set up to manage the land, run by two lawyers, Charles Wood and Simon Michell, to oversee the legal and financial intricacies of turning the pastureland into streets. From that moment the transformation of the Wheler ground into profit became a serious going concern; and from such speculations a whole new neigh-bourhood was born.

London is an immigrant city that attracts people, goods and money from the far ends of the earth. And in turn, the city itself is transformed by the people and goods that arrive on the Thames shoreline. Its great strength throughout history has been its ability to absorb influences and ideas from outside and make them its own – the first modern melting pot. This was made clear at the beginning of the eighteenth century, when it was calculated that only one in three people who died in London had been born there. In a poem of 1701 Daniel Defoe told the truth – too often forgotten – about the origins of Englishness:

> A True Born Englishman's a contradiction
> In Speech an Irony, in fact a fiction.[7]

What was true of England was even truer of London. By 1700 the metropolis had become for some the fount, for others the drain, of the nation's youth, who made their way there in search of work, lured by the prospect of higher wages; that year there were between 27,000 and 30,000 apprentices learning their trade in city workshops. This influx was augmented by tides of immigrants from the Continent who were arriving on the wharves looking for a new life. London was thus built by outsiders who settled and naturalised it. This process of renewal filled the streets with people but also brought fresh ideas, techniques and inventions to the city from beyond its boundaries.

While many found their way to London cross-country, others arrived by water, entering the busy port, now establishing itself as the entrepôt of the world. Some came with things to sell, others arrived with nothing, haunted by the recent horrors that had forced them to abandon their homes. In Paris in 1572, five days after the sumptuous marriage of the Catholic princess Marguerite and the Protestant prince Henri of Navarre, there had been a terrible riot, the St Bartholomew's Day Massacre, in which so many Protestants died that the only accurate figure for the murdered was the 1,100 that were dragged out downstream from the Seine. Like tremors after a quake, religious persecution rippled through the rest of the nation, wrecking major provincial capitals including Lyon, home to the French silk industry.

Elizabeth I made it known that England was a haven for the persecuted Protestants and many Huguenots made their way across the Channel, finding safety and a new life on the outskirts of the major cities – Canterbury, London, Norwich – where there was a ready market for their sought-after skills. They were soon followed by Dutch Protestants who fled Antwerp after the sacking of the port by the Spanish in 1585. It was said that one third of the Antwerp craftsmen left for London and Spitalfields soon gained a reputation as a major centre for refugees.

The silk industry of Spitalfields – the nature of silk, the creation of wondrous designs, crêpes, ribbons, lustrings, velvets, damasks, Alamodes tabby and taffeta – was at the heart of the new revolution. Before the eighteenth century the English silk industry had been largely unsuccessful, and restricted to the court (for example, the pair of silk stockings Sir Thomas Gresham gave Elizabeth). Silk remained exclusive for other reasons: there were few home-grown skills, so most fabrics had to be imported. In addition, there was the problem of raw materials: England had thus far failed to cultivate silkworms. James I was determined that England should have its own silk industry and set up his mulberry orchard at Charlton House, under the watchful eye of the master horticulturalist M. Vetron from Picardy; trees were also planted in the gardens of St James's Palace. Despite these efforts England would remain dependent on foreign imports of raw silk from Italy and eventually India and China.

This state of affairs changed with the arrival of desperate Huguenot families from France and Holland. One such family who made the dangerous voyage was that of Pierre Ogier from Chasais L'Eglise in Bas-Poitou, where he had run a prosperous business with his wife and thirteen children. Pierre died in 1698 and his clearly formidable wife, Jeanne, emigrated to London in 1700 along with a number of her children, settling in Spitalfields. It is probable that there were already members of her own family, the Bernardin, in the neighbourhood. The voyage, in most cases, was undertaken in great danger and in the face of extreme persecution. According to the testimony of a M. Claude, who escaped in 1685, first their neighbours turned against them, then, when garrisons arrived with their sabres drawn, they were forced to pray to Rome at knifepoint. Those who refused had their homes pillaged: 'taking from them whatever they could see, money, rings, jewels, and in general, whatever was of value ... Afterwards they fell on their persons, and there was no wickedness or horror which they did not put into practise, to force them to change their religion'.[8] Making their way to a port was perilous and the harbours were eagerly watched for any *réfugié* (the origin of the word 'refugee'). London represented a bastion of liberty.

The Ogier family soon integrated into the Spitalfields community, and the local industry. One son, Jean, began his apprenticeship as a silk weaver, but later became a wealthy coal merchant. Another brother, Andree, learnt his trade with his brother-in-law Pierre Ravenel, and in time became his own master specialising in the much desired half-silk trade, weaving silk and linen. Two of the sisters, Louise and Elizabeth, married weavers. The fourth son, Pierre Abraham, also entered the silk industry, serving his apprenticeship under a foreign master, Samuel Brule, and gaining his freedom in 1716. Four years earlier he had married Ester Dubois and they moved into 19 Princess Street (later renamed Princelet Street), at the heart of the Huguenot community. He became a member of the Guild of Weavers in 1741.

The story of his elder brother, Pierre Ogier, was even more dramatic. Pierre had remained in Bas-Poitou; however, by the 1720s life was becoming difficult and the family was constantly being watched by spies. In one report to the Abbé Goued it was noted, 'there is one very rich merchant ... who contemplates leaving the country'.[9] Pierre sent his children ahead and arrived in London in 1730, taking a house on Spital Square. With much of his family already established in London, he quickly used his contacts and considerable capital to enter the silk market. He had seven children, of whom three sons followed him into the same profession: Peter III, Thomas Abraham and Louis. Within two generations the Ogier family made London their home, and through judicious marriage arrangements, business partnerships and appren-ticeships placed themselves at the centre of the new community. As the historian Natalie Rothstein notes, 'it would be possible to write a history of the industry from this one family'.[10]

Yet this rapid transformation of the city's population brought its own anxiety. The immigrants were welcomed as refugees, and brought skills in weaving, clock-making and banking that England desperately needed; but their arrival also inspired the perennial fear that these foreigners stole jobs and undercut prices. As one 1709 poem, 'The Canary Birds Naturalised in Utopia', stressed:

> Here they grew fat, and liv'd at ease
> And bigger look'd than refugees . . .
> Them we so well did entertain
> They would not choose to go Home again.[11]

There were also occasional threats of violence. In 1683, English weavers began to congregate in the pubs of Spitalfields and stir up agitation against the new arrivals. When Charles II heard of the disquiet he ordered his Horse Guards to be stationed in nearby Devonshire Square. In the end the ruckus passed but, a week later, in Norwich full-blown riots occurred and the local weavers 'thronged all the streets, dragging the French about, sacking their houses and actually killing a woman'.[12]

Nevertheless, the French weavers offered London something that it could not hope to possess on its own. In 1684, the Weavers' Company invited the newly arrived refugee Jean Larguier from Nîmes to present his samples of shot silks – with the warp thread of one colour and the weft thread of another – and asked him to demonstrate how to perform this previously unseen technique, 'conceiving the like hath never been made in England, and that it will be of great benefit to this nation'.[13] The city therefore had to find a balance between the allure of the new and the threat of the strange. At the dawn of the eighteenth century, London was still in search of its identity following the upheavals of the previous era: civil war, plague, fire, invasion and revolution. The city was now suffering the birth pangs of modernity, changing from a medieval community into a bustling world city.

The metropolis had grown so large in the forty years since the Great Fire that some feared it was becoming a fragmented place, as Thomas Brown noted in 1702: 'London is a world by itself. We daily discover in it more new countries, and surprising singularities, than in all the universe besides. There are among the Londoners so many nations differing in manners, customs, and religions, that the inhabitants themselves don't know a quarter of them.'[14] How, amid the confusion, could the city find its voice against this polyphony of different races and beliefs?

The new century announced itself with a series of terrible storms that racked London. At lunchtime on Wednesday, 20 September 1703, a brisk gale began to blow that by Saturday had stirred into the most formidable tempest in the city's history, recorded by Daniel Defoe. When the winds first hit, the lead roof of Westminster Abbey rolled up like a parchment scroll. The chimneys of the houses were blown clean off, killing over twenty people, one missing Defoe only by a whisker. The wind caused the Thames to rise and Westminster was flooded, while in the docks at Poplar 500 wherries, 300 boats and 120 barges were destroyed. It was estimated that the damage cost more than £1 million. Four years later an infestation of fleas plagued the city, so that 'many of the streets were so covered with them, that the people's feet made as full an impression on them as upon thick snow'.[15]

Even in that nascent age of reason many read these disturbances as God's judgement upon the city for its religious tolerance. This was not helped by the uproar five year later when Parliament had passed the Foreign and Protestant Naturalization Act, which offered citizenship to refugees willing to profess their faith in a Protestant – but not necessarily Anglican – congregation. This was further enforced in November 1709, when Henry Sacheverell, a priest from Southwark, preached a vitriolic sermon against tolerance from the pulpit of St Paul's Cathedral. The subsequent trial whipped up even more support and erupted into riots; Puritan meeting houses and Presbyterian conventicles were broken into and set alight. The many congregations of the Reformed Church appeared to be tearing themselves apart. How could society remain united if it worshipped in so many different ways?

The storms returned in 1710 and in Greenwich village, on the edge of the royal park and hospital, the devastating winds broke the roof of the ancient St Alfege parish church. The parishioners petitioned Parliament for money to repair the damage; but the appeal touched a far more sensitive nerve. Greenwich was fortunate to have a church; what about the new communities beyond the city walls that had no such place to worship? A parliamentary report of 1710 estimated that over 342,000 souls, over half the city's population, lacked a local place of worship. The next year the vicar of Deptford aired his concern that if something was not done soon over 12,000 souls in his parish would be lost to the Presbyters and Nonconformist sects.

In fear of this spiritual drain, the grandees of the Anglican Church and Parliament did not just repair the roof of St Alfege but also set out a bold project to create fifty-one new parish churches in the burgeoning suburbs. The Anglican Church hoped to reach out to the new communities and make sure that they were in their control, yet there were two crucial questions: where to build? And what? The new project was as ambitious as Wren's rebuilding of the fifty-one city churches out of the ashes of the Great Fire and gathered together the new generation of architects – Nicholas Hawksmoor, Thomas Archer, James Gibbs and John James – to complete the task. Needless to say, on top of questions of architectural style, there was a tireless debate on what a church was, how it expressed the new notions of Anglicanism, the size of an ideal congregation and, crucially, how to pay for the new structures.

To begin with, the bureaucrats decided 'one General Modell be made and Agreed upon for all' to express the uniformity of the Anglican vision in the city; the new churches would stand out from the neighbouring houses, according to Sir John Vanbrugh, with a handsome portico at the western end. They would conform in the face of the rising tide of Nonconformity. This might work in theory, but whose design would be selected? Colin Campbell was one of the first to offer a plan, while Thomas Archer hoped the City Church commissioners would soon show 'their good opinion of him'. Yet it was not in the architects' interest to follow just one scheme, neither did it fit the purpose; thus, when the planners gathered together to look at the outline, they scratched out 'model' and replaced it with 'design or forme'.[16] As a result, the sites would be divided up amongst the leading Baroque practitioners of the day – Hawksmoor, Gibbs, Archer – who were allowed to devise the many different faces of the established Church in the modern city.

Spitalfields was soon earmarked by the commission as one of the first priorities and the site was quickly settled. It would be an

impressive plot of land carved out of the Wheler estate covering
'Smoke Alley' and an as yet undeveloped tenter ground. Nevertheless,
negotiations took longer than expected; Wood and Michell were
unwilling to reduce their price for the commission, knowing full well
that they could sell the land to a more speculative client at any
moment. Nicholas Hawksmoor was then given the task of finding a
design that fitted the surroundings as well as the spirit of the age.
The foundation stone was laid in 1715.

Christ Church, Spitalfields, completed in 1724, is Hawksmoor's
London masterpiece and perhaps the clearest expression of his own
philosophy of design, for here he was able to tell his own narrative of
the history and future of English architecture. For some critics, like Sir
John Summerson, Hawksmoor showed 'that slightly childish fascination
in everything Latin',[17] but this is without merit. The poet John Betjeman
was also far off the mark with his observation that it appears 'a huge
heavy galleon of white Portland Stone'.[18] Certainly, encountering the
church for the first time today, reflected off the steel and glass of the
new Spitalfields Market, one is struck by a sense of 'extreme stran-
geness',[19] but it is anything but infantile.

Hawksmoor has an unusual role within the story of English architecture. He was the ultimate autodidact, a classicist to his marrow, yet
he never visited the sites of ancient Rome or Greece. Born in Not-
tinghamshire, his early promise led him to work in the draughtsmen's
shop of Sir Christopher Wren's office. He took many years to develop
behind the shadow of his formidable master and can be identified as
perhaps the only student of 'the school of Wren', a peculiar cul-de-sac
of English Baroque that emerged and disappeared within a generation.
He was fascinated by the rules of architecture, but swam against the tide
of Neo-Palladian orthodoxy that was about to swamp London. Like his
master, he was well versed in the canon of Renaissance design. But he
was equally bold enough to look beyond the received wisdom of the
Italian maestros. In coffee houses and in notebooks Hawksmoor and
Wren debated and drew the shape of ancient monuments, speculating
on the form of the mausoleum of Halicarnassus, the tomb of Lars
Porsenna, the temple of Bacchus at Baalbek and that model of archi-

11. Christ Church, Spitalfields, built by Nicholas Hawksmoor: a history of church architecture in stone (*Guildhall*)

tectural perfection, Solomon's temple in Jerusalem, decimated in AD 70. In addition they were fascinated to hear travellers' reports of Hagia Sophia in Constantinople and other treasures of the Levant. Hawksmoor was determined to explore this further in his own designs, once he had become an architect in his own right.

As he was drawing up his plans for Christ Church, Spitalfields, Hawksmoor was also thinking of the role of the new church. Since the Glorious Revolution of 1688, a new spirit of comprehension and tolerance had arisen; the Church was a place of persuasion and reason rather than authority and persecution. This went hand in hand with a growing fascination with the history of the early Christian Church, the age of the Desert Fathers, and the moment when there was only one, universal congregation. Hawksmoor was determined to find a design that not only expressed the singular origin of Christianity but also overcame its contemporary divisions, bringing unity to the melting pot of the city.

By the end of the building season in 1715 progress was steady: the walls of white Portland stone had risen to fourteen feet, and at the close of the following year it was hoped that the workmen might start on the final phase, the roof. Yet by 1719 they were still a long way from completion; some shoddy brickwork made progress on the upper levels impossible. As work ground to a halt Hawksmoor was forced to set out his concerns in a report. The problem was more than just poor carpentry: money lay at the heart of the crisis. Hawksmoor had projected costs of £9,129 16s, but he would eventually underestimate by four hundred per cent. In 1720 there was only one craftsman working on the roof, who was owed 'a great Debt at this Church and in other Parishes due to him of above £2,000'.[20] It would take another three years before the church finally gained its covering.

The main body of the church was a tall, single-height room running from the west end to the altar in the east end. Along both sides were galleried aisles with bays covered by broad balconies with tiered seating. The plan conformed with Wren's own recommendations for the ideal shape of a church and were similar to city churches such as St Bride's, Fleet Street, and St James's, Piccadilly. This emphasised the importance of light – the illumination of reason – that burst through clear barrelled glass windows as well as audibility, being able to hear the preacher's words. The new church would be a place of inclusive persuasion, not doctrine and ritual.

It was, however, with the western facade and the dramatic design of the portico that Hawksmoor truly expressed his vision for the universal Church. The portico stands out to the west of the body of the church, raised up on a broad flight of white steps; it was designed to be seen above the bustle of the nearby market and was visible along the clear vista of Norton Folgate (now Brushfield Street) from Bishopsgate. The church was both part of the industry and trade of the neighbourhood and also stood above it.

The facade was split into three layers: the portico held up a tower and finally a steeple. It was a peculiar concoction which encouraged one later eighteenth-century critic to denounce it as 'one of the most absurd piles in Europe',[21] but it was in itself a history of architecture and a potent claim for the future of London. The tetrastyle portico, using four columns to create a shaded entrance, alluded to the earliest temples, the classical origins of all sacred places. The early Church, therefore, was a place of public worship, not a tabernacle or conventicle. The tower that emerged from the portico looked like a Romanesque triumphal arch and from this grew organically a Gothic spire. In this design, Hawksmoor seemed to be suggesting a new history of religious architecture. For his contemporaries who squabbled over questions of good taste and correct form, Hawksmoor's church combined all styles – the classical, the Romanesque and the Gothic – and showed that they developed out of each other rather than evolved from painful rupture. These different architectural voices were not discordant, but sang in harmony. They were all historical attempts at articulating a universal truth, the common pursuit of eternity expressed in forever changing ways.

In a time of such great upheaval and within a neighbourhood of such diversity, Hawksmoor perhaps hoped that architecture brought unity to society, turning the Church's new-found hopes for the city into solid form. In addition, a sense of historical continuity, dressing up the modern in ancient attire, would defuse the threat of the new.

As the walls of Christ Church were slowly rising, building work surrounding the churchyard was gathering pace. The land to the north, owned by the six surviving daughters of William Wheler, and handled by Wood and Michell, was still undeveloped. Despite making a small profit from the sale of the land to the new Church Commission, it was not until 1718 that the lawyers began to speculate on the value of the surrounding land and grant leases. The first leases were offered to Samuel Worral, a local carpenter with connections to the Guild of Masons, and Marmaduke Smyth, carpenter and blacksmith. These two tradesmen took the majority of plots and were at the centre of the project to develop the enclave. Worral and Smyth were typical of the new breed of speculative builders who had transformed the city since the Great Fire. This was not just a response to the demand for housing for a burgeoning population but was also a revolution in the way buildings were constructed and profit could be squeezed from the many stages of the process.

Dr Nicholas Barbon, the speculator who won the contract for the land surrounding Spitalfields Market, was synonymous with the new system of leasehold speculation. Barbon was the son of the Baptist preacher PraiseGod Barbon and had been baptised 'If Jesus Had Not Died For Thee Thou Wouldst Be Damned'. In the years following the Restoration he had trained to be a physician but after the Great Fire discovered another calling and in the subsequent decades he developed suburban housing throughout the west of the city in the Strand, St James's, Leicester Fields, Bloomsbury and Holborn as well as in the east at nearby Devonshire Square and the Old Artillery Ground. For the first twenty years at least he seemed to have a preternatural talent for coming out on top in every deal.

Barbon's life offers us the image of the original developer and speculator. His first project, a row of houses off Mincing Lane in the city, collapsed within years, but he ran a very tight office packed with a 'gang of clerks, attorneys, scriveners, and lawyers',[22] who kept him one step ahead of the law, and the opposition. He was deft at scheming, a master of divide and rule whenever he met obstacles to his plans. Where possible he held onto his capital for as long as he could; if a lender came to his house looking for payment, he allowed them to wait in his lavishly decorated drawing room, giving them time to notice his personal wealth, before entering swathed in a rich dressing gown, hoping to delay any payment request through charm.

He had powerful backers among the merchants and bankers who were riding the waves of prosperity of the new empire. After starting from only a few plots bought in the immediate aftermath of the Great Fire, his plans expanded, as he told the lawyer Sir Roger North: 'it was not worth his while to deal little ... that a bricklayer could do'.[23] He worked on a grand scale, rebuilding whole neighbourhoods rather than just single houses, and made sure that it was done in time, and under budget; he rarely paid a supplier until he had been paid himself. In this way he developed what became for the next 300 years the archetypal terraced house.

Compared to Barbon, Worral and Smyth were small-time speculators on the lower rungs of the business, but the Wheler estate had the potential to change that. The demand was clear as the nearby streets of the neighbouring estates on all sides were filling up, while the big merchants' houses on Spital Square had already become the leading addresses in the area. It swiftly became apparent that the new estate should offer a range of housing for all levels, from merchant masters to the lowly throwsters, within the silk community: Church Street (later renamed Fournier Street) was to be home to the grand *hôtels* for the merchant princes. Off this ran Princess Street, Hanbury Street, Wilkes Street, Puma Court, supplied with houses for the middling sort, weavers and freemen on the up. On the fringes there was still a profit to be made from small two-storey workmen's houses that would fit a family and a loom.

In most cases Wood and Michell leased out designated plots to the speculators on a new street scheme for terms of sixty, sixty-one and ninety-nine years. It had been calculated that the landowner earned the most by setting as many dwellings on the street front as possible, so therefore the plots were narrow at the front but two rooms deep, with a courtyard at the back. Once the lease had been arranged, the speculator would hope to build the new house as quickly (and cheaply) as possible, then profit from the sale of the lease; meanwhile the landowner topped up his balance by collecting ground rent. There is good evidence that Samuel Worral was given the role of principal surveyor to the estate and as a result had the pick of the plots on which he wanted to develop. Work began first on a range of houses on the north side of Princess Street in summer 1718. No. 17 and No. 19 were completed by Worral by that autumn, and quickly sold on to the purchaser.

No. 19 was part of a pair of houses, made with common London brick. It was single-fronted, with three storeys and a basement cellar below. It looked exactly like many of the other houses that were growing up along the street front, the archetypal London terraced house. This uniformity stemmed from a number of reasons: following the Great Fire, the 1667 Rebuilding Act defined the proportions of the new London house. It had to be made from stone or brick and, as a fire precaution, avoid bulks, jetties, windows, posts, or seats that pushed out into the street. Each house was to conform to one of four types:

> ... the first or least sort of houses fronting by lanes; the second sort of houses fronting streets and lanes of note; the third sort of houses fronting high and principal streets; the fourth and largest sort, of mansion houses, for citizens, or other persons of extraordinary quality, not fronting either of the three former ways; the roofs of each of the said first sorts of houses respectively, shall be uniform.[24]

No. 19 Princess Street was certainly of the second order, and therefore of good stock but not the highest quality.

With these proportions enshrined in law and the commercial incentives for setting out narrow plots on the street front, it soon became possible to create a template for new housing and the speculator quickly saw the advantage of standardising the design down to the smallest detail. Following on from Barbon's lead, the preparation of bricks and timber cut to length in the yard allowed for increased uniformity, but standardisation also helped reduce the cost of skilled labour that was now paid by the measure. In addition, there seemed no sense in building to last longer than the lease.

There were also Building Acts in 1707 and 1709 that imposed further restrictions upon what the speculative builder could do. These included a number of seemingly disparate ideas that distorted the design of the standard-plan terraced house in order to safeguard it against fires. Wooden cornices were banned, the party walls between houses were thickened and had to rise above the level of the roof as a fire barrier; these partitions would more often than not also hold the chimney. Windows had to be recessed so as not to attract flames, encouraging the use of sash windows. Thus evolved the unornamented face of the standard Georgian house, apart from a porch that was sometimes added and offered a silk weaver protection against the elements as he enjoyed a pipe at the end of the working day.

In his 1689 celebration of the speculator, *An Apology for the Builder*, Barbon made it clear that his aim was not the pursuit of architectural beauty: 'To write of architecture and its several parts, of situation, platforms of buildings, and the quality of materials, with their dimensions and ornaments ... [would] but misspend the reader and writers time'.[25] Speculators like Worral were not designers and were just as likely to copy the latest fashions from the refined neighbourhoods of Westminster and Holborn as designs from a pattern book. William and John Halfpenny's *The Modern Builder's Assistant* was a *Vitruvius Britannicus* for the jobbing artisan, giving detailed sketches of whole houses and plans that could be recreated off the page. There were also pattern books for carpenters offering an array of porches and interior wainscotting.

By these methods the luxuries once enjoyed only by the wealthiest were mass-produced and made available to the new fashion-conscious middling sort, who were enticed by the trappings of modern interior design. In the sales material for one Barbon project newly built near Soho, each house boasted the latest amenities: 'wainscotted and painted ... All the fireplaces had painted chimneypieces, firestone and marble hearths, and were set with "galley" tiles. At the rear of the house was the kitchen and a "Lardery", the former fitted with a buttery and supplied by a pump with New River water.'[26]

Pierre Abraham Ogier and his wife, Ester, moved into 19 Princess Street soon after the building was completed; his name first appeared on the 1743 register, two years after he had joined the guild. Unlike many on the street, he bought the freehold of the house. Other Huguenots and silk merchants had also settled there: Daniel Lee of Stepney, weaver, moved into No. 17 in 1718; in 1722, No. 6 was leased to a framework knitter, who also used it as a warehouse; Jean Sabatier lived at No. 16, where he lined the basement with Dutch tiles; Daniel Gobbee lived at No. 21, while John Baker, 'gold and silver brocade and silk flower weaver', settled at No. 23.

It was a very respectable neighbourhood, although perhaps not quite the grandest address. That was reserved for Church Street to the south, facing the soon-to-be-completed Christ Church, the last street to be built on the estate, once again by speculators such as Worral and Smyth. The rectory at No. 2 set the tone of the street and was designed by Hawksmoor, but most of the houses conformed to the larger scale of town house, the third type in the 1667 Rebuilding Act, and competed with anything found in Westminster. The names of those who first occupied the new dwellings were an indication of the attraction of the enclave: Smyth himself moved into No. 4–6 and had his initials emblazoned on the iron rainwater head. It was then taken on by a merchant in 'Striped and plain lustring mantua and tabby', Peter Campart.[27] No. 12 was first bought by George Garrett, who then sold it to the Huguenot minister Benjamin du Boulay. No. 14, later called Howard House, was a double-fronted terraced house and by far the grandest on the range. It was built by the mason William Tayler, who quickly passed it on to Judith Sequeret and Co. It then was home to a number of other silk families. In 1837, the fabric for Queen Victoria's wedding gown was woven here.

Even the grandest houses in this neighbourhood were places of work. Entering No. 19 Princess Street, one found a long panelled corridor, with a room leading off to the left and a back room. The stairs ran alongside the party wall on the right, and wainscotting was used throughout the house to cover the walls. At the beginning of his career Pierre Abraham Ogier would have worked at his loom on his own fabrics or on behalf of a master merchant, perhaps his uncle, who lived in nearby Spital Square. The loom was where the skilled weaver turned the twisted threads into elegant silks, damasks, lustrings and velvets and Pierre Abraham later became a weaver of flowered and intricately designed fabric for the luxury end of the market. However, throughout the neighbourhood, looms were found in the front rooms of many houses and made everything from simple handkerchiefs to the delicate laced mantua that became so popular amongst the most fashionable and demure London ladies.

The design of this front room had a specific impact on how the terraced houses of Spitalfields gained their idiosyncratic appearance. In 1696 a tax was levied on windows; glass was expensive and some indication of the wealth of the owners. The weavers needed good natural light for their intricate work, and on the ground floor at 19 Princess Street two large windows with shutters reached almost the full height of the wall. In addition, the room itself was larger than normal to accommodate the loom. While most terraced houses in London were fourteen to fifteen feet wide, so that the speculator could pack as many along the street front as possible, the average Spitalfields house of the Wood–Michell estate was seventeen to eighteen feet wide. Later looms made their way to the top of the house, where the garret was turned into a factory floor for any number of machines. This changed the face of the building as the dormer windows were replaced by wide windows, 'long lights', devised especially for the weavers' industry, that allowed sunlight into the rooms throughout the day.

The back room may have been a kitchen or storage space – for bales of thread, fabric to be finished, accounting books gathering dust. Beyond was a small yard where the Ogier children may have played. The Huguenot community were renowned for their love of horticulture and 'advanced the use and reputation of flowers',[28] in particular the cultivation of cut flowers. This rage for blooms exploded in flower feasts and competitions; nearby Columbia Road Market, which still runs every Sunday, was said to have Huguenot origins. The air was filled with the chirping of caged canaries, which were bred by Huguenot weavers and competitively displayed at society meetings and taverns. Until recently, a bird market was still held on Bacon Street, off Brick Lane, a modern echo of this forgotten tradition, adopted by the East Enders long after the French community had departed.

The community soon gained a reputation as an industrious and devout group who were prepared to help themselves. In William Hogarth's entertaining drawing 'Noon', a family of well-dressed French worshippers are seen coming out of a church only to be confronted by English squalor – a rebuke on native laziness. The Huguenots swiftly set up nine chapels within the neighbourhood, as well as a number of societies and charities. 'La Soupe' was one of the first benevolent societies established in the 1690s to help new refugees, run by members of the leading Huguenot families. There were also debating societies and the Spitalfields Mathematical Society, started in 1717 by Joseph Middleton. Some of the more famous members include John Dollond, who later become the founder of the famous spectacle company, Dollond & Aitchison, as well as the mathematician Thomas Simpson, who was born a weaver's son in Leicestershire but came to London to teach at the Royal Military Academy at Woolwich. The society was absorbed into the Royal Astronomical Society in 1820.

The newly arrived refugees in London but hoped to weave themselves into the fabric of London; however, like many immigrants, their initial isolation forced them to rely on their fellows. Often family and business were one and the same; it was certainly true for the Ogiers who, within a matter of years after their arrival, were connected to every major family in the neighbourhood in all aspects of the silk trade. Amongst the three sons of Pierre II, Pierre Abraham's elder brother in Spital Square, Thomas Abraham, made mantuas, the formal day headdress, and water tabby with its distinctive stripe and shimmer. Louis, who anglicised his name to Lewis, described himself as a weaver of flowered velvets. Peter III set up a company with two others, Vansommer and Triquet, and supplied the very heights of the luxury market with delicate flowered silks that were said even to have furnished the house of Lord Egremont at Petworth.

Those children who did not go into the silk trade still kept within the community. Pierre Abraham and Ester had eight children; the eldest, Peter, became a notary and his name appears on a number of family legal documents, as well as numerous wills of local weavers. Daughters were married into leading families to consolidate business partnerships and thus the Ogiers were tied with the Bigot, Byas, Godin, Grellier, Maze and Merzeau clans. In 1749, Louisa Perina Ogier married the goldsmith Samuel Courtauld. When he died in 1765, she continued the business and gained fame, being acknowledged by the Guild of Goldsmiths who allowed her to create her own gold mark. Yet in the end the family would return to the silk trade, establishing the Courtaulds factory in Essex the following century, industrialising on a huge scale what had once been completed in the Spitalfields garrets. At the beginning of the twentieth century, the chemical age, they would become famous once more for creating synthetic silk: rayon.

Yet while expressing their many differences in work, worship and community, the Huguenots also aspired to become Londoners and it was not a clerical error when some of the major names in the silk industry began to Anglicise their names. Pierre Ogier later became Peter; Bachelier became Batchelor; De La Croix translated to Cross. In addition, by the 1708 Act of Naturalisation, full citizenship was given to any foreign Protestant who swore allegiance to the government and received the Sacrament in any Protestant church. The clearest sign of this desire to belong was displayed in 1745, when a number of leading merchants offered their own employees to quell the Jacobite Rebellion in the north. Six Ogier companies made over 160 men available to leave their looms in Spitalfields and march to the battlefield of Culloden to fight the Catholic pretender, Bonnie Prince Charles.

In time, however, the ultimate indication of success and belonging was when the richer merchants departed Spitalfields and the security of the French community for good. Thus Ogier, Vansommer and Triquet opened offices in Bath and planned a shop in Exeter. Peter Ogier III was successful enough to build and retire to a country house to the south of the city at Lewisham. It is probably this same Peter Ogier (although by this time four Peter Ogiers were living in Spital Square) who in 1767 sent his son, Peter, with $50,000 to establish a silk market in Quebec, Canada. However, it is telling that Louisa Perina Courtauld, née Ogier, decided to be buried in the crypt at Christ Church, Spitalfields, despite having moved to Hackney.

Thus many of the most fortunate Huguenots went from being producers of fine fabrics to consumers. This was the perpetual story of immigrants who made their way to London and first settled to the east of the walls, only to move within one or two generations as they were integrated into the city. Over the next three centuries successive peoples arrived and laid foundations in the enclaves of Spitalfields, Whitechapel and Stepney, to begin the journey towards naturalisation.

This is exemplified by a building on Fournier Street that was erected as a Huguenot temple in 1743, just as the last stones were being laid at Christ Church. Since then it has been a Wesleyan chapel; then in 1809, as the community became a refuge for Eastern European Jewry, a meeting house for the London Society for the Promotion of Christianity amongst the Jews; a Methodist chapel; and 'Machzike Adass', the Spitalfields Great Synagogue. Finally, in the 1970s, it was transformed into the London Jamme Masjid, a mosque catering to the large Bangladeshi community that have settled here. On the south side of the building the original sundial remains, with the motto 'Umbra Summus' (we are shadows); Spitalfields has been lost in the city's shade for over three hundred years.

The emerging consumer culture of the eighteenth-century city made equals of every man with money. As early as the 1680s Barbon believed that consumption, the demand and supply for new goods, was driven by emulation, the desire to improve one's own situation: 'all men by perpetual industry are struggling to mend their former condition: and thus the people grow rich, which is the great advantage of a nation'.[29] One way to emulate one's social betters was by education, another was by shopping. The combination of new wealth from the port, as well as the banking enterprises within the city walls, the drop in prices as a result of increased supply, and the rise in demand for exclusive items, was an explosive mix. The early eighteenth century was the moment of the birth of the age of consumption. This new acquisitiveness brought with it two discerning handmaidens: taste and fashion.

The royal monopoly fell away in the seventeenth century and the popular fashion for silk was exponential. There are few courtly portraits by Van Dyck or Peter Lely whose sitter was not clothed in shimmering silk and taffeta, so that by the 1660s the taste for French fancy had reached so far down the social scale there were fears that 'every maid-servant became a standing revenue to the French King of one half of her wages'.[30] By 1721, it was estimated that the silk trade was worth £1.2 million per year.

The process of manufacturing a piece of cloth gave important insights into why silk was such a luxury. As the large merchants, such as the Ogiers, began to govern the market, the many stages of production were divided into a series of tasks. The throwster, who twisted the silk from the cocoon into a thread, was only a semi-skilled artisan, yet there was always tension between those who had served their apprenticeships and wished for more recognition and those who had not. The thread was then dyed, either by the master merchant himself or a dyer, who dried their threads on the tenter fields and then sold on the piecework to a middleman or the weaver. The role of the weaver, however, was more regulated and was protected by the Company of Weavers with a pro-scribed regimen of a seven-year apprenticeship and journeyman status. By 1733 there were nearly 6,000 members of the livery.

Nevertheless there was a vast number of semi-skilled and unliveried weavers in the neighbourhood competing on price for any job. In the main, these weavers were employed by a master, sometimes via a journeyman-foreman, sitting at their own loom in their attic rooms. Some masters would have over 150 weavers working for them at one time, each paid on delivery rather than a wage. When times were good, the community thrived; when the demand for silks ebbed, the streets quickly filled with disgruntled craftsmen, hungry children and the threat of violence.

Amongst the weavers there were grades of respect based on skill and the type of fabric worked. At the top of the tree, some were given the status of artists in their own right, were suitably rewarded, and made their way to the elite corps of the grand families. The flowered branch silk market was the very pinnacle of the industry. Where once the weaver would have devised his own designs and worked out his own methods, now the merchant hired a designer to predict and draft the fashions of the age. The paper designs were either for individual pieces for the best customers and special occasions, or less flamboyant fabrics to be sold by the yard. Yet this high-end market was precarious: a whole season could be unexpectedly ruined by the death of a royal or leading dignitary, which ironically sent the price of black crêpe and taffeta sky-high.

Like the silk itself, French fashions dominated London taste. Despite the Glorious Revolution and, after 1714, a Hanoverian prince on the British throne, *à la mode* London was still in thrall to Paris. However, the local industry soon sought its own advantage by absorbing and manipulating the varying styles, ideas and fashions from Continental Europe and making them at home, as seen in the delicate designs of Anna Maria Garthwaite, the daughter of a Lincolnshire cleric, who 'by the force of mere natural taste and ingenuity has made the English loom vie with the Italian pencil; very different from the gaudy patterns of the French'.[31] Garthwaite had arrived in London in 1726 and settled on Church Street. She was probably well-educated and her father had left her a legacy of £500 and his complete library. From this point she established herself as one of the leading silk designers in Europe. In particular, she was dedicated to recreating natural forms and botanical images upon the material: fruit, flowers, ribbons. In one design from 1742 Garthwaite combined carnations, blossoms, roses; in another there were pomegranates and the spiky leaves of aloe. Through her friendship with the horticulturalist Peter Collinson, she was also able to view the latest botanical specimens shipped from America and incorporate them as images of New World wonders into her fabrics.

Garthwaite's designs changed with the seasons, but after her arrival in London she worked on about eighty patterns a year, never taking a holiday, and dominated silk designing for the next twenty years. Her work was appreciated in the same tones as that of a court painter, with much discussion of 'the understanding of light and dark and the art of colouring a fabric to an astonishing point'.[32] Garthwaite produced a number of drawings for Pierre Abraham Ogier at 19 Princess Street, as well as for the company Ogier, Vansommer and Triquet who had their address at Spital Square.

Such designs in dress and upholstery went hand in hand with an explosion of luxury commodities: fine porcelain from China to drink tea or coffee imported from the new British settlements in the East, brought home by the powerful East India Company. The cup was sweetened with Jamaican sugar, cultivated in cruelty by slaves who were themselves part of the cycle of triangular trade between the West African coastline, the new colonies in America and the ports of Britain. The demand for new goods brought the world to London, and made the city a burgeoning bazaar.

Anna Maria Garthwaite, however, knew the fickle dangers of passing fashions and the dominance of Parisian styles over more native designs. In an anonymous article, 'Of designing and drawing of ornaments ... for the use of flowered silk manufactory, embroidery and printing (of the various kinds of flower'd silks)', which she contributed to the 1759 handbook *The Laboratory or School of Arts*, edited by G. E. Smith, she noted: 'a new pattern drawer will come into vogue and the old experienced one will be discarded. These ungenerous proceedings I have experienced myself.'[33] The silk industry of Spitalfields itself was not above the pitch and tempests of fluctuating taste and economics and the luxury market had its dark and desperate side.

In 1849, a century or so after the Ogier family had established themselves in Spitalfields, the journalist Henry Mayhew visited the area in search of a story. Thus far, he had made his name in exploring the shadows of London that the respectable city had forgotten; he sniffed out the deprived and downtrodden, the brutalised and strange and found plenty of copy. As he noted in his essay 'And Ye Shall Walk in Silk Attire': 'Such were the Spitalfield weavers at the beginning of the present century, possessing tastes and following pursuits, the refinements and intelligence of which would be an honour and grace to the artisan of the present day, but which shone out with a double lustre at the time when the amusements of society were almost of a gross and brutalising kind.'[34] The Huguenot community, in his opinion, had once been a beacon of taste for the city; now, no more.

In his survey Mayhew visited a velvet weaver who made drab for coat collars. Where once the street had been filled with children, it was now empty and quiet; there was no time for play or education, all hands were set to work. He was ushered into the house and scaled a flight of stairs until he pushed through a trapdoor into the 'shop' attic where three looms stood at the centre. The space was lit by a 'long light' attic window that stretched the length of the room; the whole family lived and worked in this area, filled with 'looms and some spinning wheels, at one of which sat a boy winding "quills". Working at the loom was a plump girl busy making "plain goods". Along the windows on each side were ranged small pots of fushias [sic].'[35]

The weaver complained that his prices had been squeezed – since 1824, they had dropped from 6s a yard to 3s 6d – until he could barely scrape a living. He worked fifteen hours a day, and only got meat once a week. In turn, his masters had now moved away and he was driven by underhand middlemen who exploited the surplus labour to reduce prices further: 'Weavers are all getting a-poorer, and masters all a-getting country houses. His master had been a-losing terrible, he said, yet he'd just taken a mansion out of town.'[36] The merchant princes who had first brought such glory and culture to Spitalfields were now deserting the forsaken neighbourhood; those remaining were to be left to their own survival.

The decline of Spitalfields had been slow and painful, but the seeds had been sown almost as soon as the silk industry had begun. It was a story that placed the small neighbourhood at the centre of a financial web that stretched from the cantons of India to the settlements of America. Spitalfields was the victim of the first stirrings of the Industrial Revolution and birth pangs of globalisation. The Ogier family, who made their wealth in the first decades of the silk boom, had now moved on. In time, 19 Princess Street was sold and then split into workshops so that, rather than housing one family and a loom, it would now be the home and workplace of a number of families crammed into the rooms. It is recorded that the house was at some point home to Mrs Mary Ellen Hawkins, who ran an industrial school, as well as Isaiah Woodcock, a carver. Where the attic was once a storage space, it was converted – as Mayhew noted – into a 'shop'.

Breaking up and dividing the old housing stock had instant advantages for rack-renter landlords who could charge rent on each room, but it drove the neighbourhood downwards. The rise of lodging houses, catering for itinerant workers, no questions asked, sent the area clattering towards desolation. The silk workers who could not leave only became more dependent on the decreasing prices for their wares. Thus a slum slowly began to emerge.

Ironically, it was the slum that preserved the silk weavers' houses, no matter the deleterious state of the fabric. It was not worth the landlords' time to demolish and rebuild new houses when the carcasses of the old would suffice for a penny a night. Where there was new building at the fringes of the community, towards Bethnal Green in the east and Whitechapel to the south, a new type of housing was devised. The demand for single-family houses had disappeared, yet the speculators saw there was a growing demand for workshop homes for a fluid population of short-term journeyman tenants with a family in tow. Smaller two- or three-storey cottages replaced the elegant town houses. On each floor there were wide latticed windows to spread as much light as possible into the interior where the loom worked every hour of the day. The house had turned into a factory, the buildings were one room wide, so that light could penetrate from both sides without obstructing walls. The fronts of the houses were stripped of all decoration, even a delicate lintel above the windows.

The new housing developed in response to the industrialisation of the weaving process and the growth of international competition. The industry had risen on a wave of demand, but it had been protected by Parliament, which had imposed high tariffs on all – in particular French – imports; yet this did not last for ever. In 1697 weavers had rejoiced outside the Palace of Westminster after the MPs inside had voted to ban the East India Company from importing Indian silks into the home market. Rather than accepting the restriction, however, the EIC flooded the market with cheap, printed calico. This coincided with the 1713 Peace of Utrecht, a cessation of the long wars against the French, which allowed trading to begin again. Suddenly the silk weavers were in peril on all sides.

The weavers did what they could to make their voices heard. They demanded a ban on French goods and a tax on all imports from the empire. When they thought they were not being listened to, they took to the streets. Where they found women wearing Indian calico they

LAMBETH { A GENERAL FAST in } SPITAL FIELDS.
{ Consequence of the WAR!! }

12. A Cruikshank cartoon highlighting the disparity between the rich merchant
princes and the impoverished weavers (*Guildhall*)

would tear the new skirts and fabrics, 'sousing them with ink, aqua
fortis, and other fluids'.[37] If they discovered French or Italian silk being
worked on a loom, they cut the fabric from the frame and shamed the
weaver. Yet by 1741 it was estimated that nearly £500,000 of French fabric
was making its way to English markets. Parliament listened and did its
best to impose restrictions on foreign imports, but the die was cast: the
weavers would have to lower their prices to remain competitive.

In response the workers attempted to protect their own and formed
'combinations', unions, in order to negotiate in strength with the
masters. They soon gained the nickname 'cutters' for their methods of
breaking looms and tearing out fabric belonging to unscrupulous
bosses. They gave themselves pirate names, such as 'the Defiance Sloop',
and were outlawed by Parliament in 1749. This did not stop them
meeting secretly in Spitalfields pubs, under low candlelight so no one
could be identified.

The unrest continued. In 1765, the King had been assaulted by a protest at Westminster against the decision to allow French silks in at a thirty per cent levy. The weavers formed a procession of red flags and black banners and bayed outside Parliament until the House of Lords were forced to adjourn. They then attacked Bedford House, the mob claiming that the Duke had taken the French king's bribe. The following year there was a law against 'cutting', yet the journeymen still threatened foreign weavers and masters, like Mr Chauvet who refused to pay the shilling per loom to support the union. Agitation continued until it exploded again onto the streets in the summer of 1769.

During that spring some of the masters had attempted to reduce their prices once again; in addition, Chauvet demanded that his workers refuse to associate with the unions. Scuffles broke out between union men and Chauvet's workers. Tension began to brew and gangs congregated outside the pubs. On 17 August, a mob went on the rampage and attacked fifty looms belonging to Chauvet's men, ripping the fabric from the frames. Over the next four nights the mob grew, as did their courage, and they prowled the streets, shooting pistols in the air. In response, Chauvet placed an advertisement with a reward of £500 for any information about the ringleaders. No one responded until 26 September when Thomas Poors, a small weaver, claimed the reward and passed on what he knew to the magistrate.

On 30 September Sir John Fielding, the blind brother of the novelist Henry Fielding, led a raid on the Dolphin pub, where he knew the Conquering and Bold Defiance combination of the handkerchief weavers were gathering. Hammering on the door behind which the meeting was being held, the constables were greeted by a volley of bullets that killed Adam McCoy 'without saying a word'. Mayhem then ensued and two customers inside the pub were also killed. The raid resulted in the trial and eventual execution of two of the conspirators, John Doyle and John Valline, outside the Salmon and Ball pub in Bethnal Green (which still stands today).

The outcome of the riots was the Spitalfields Act of 1773, which allowed the aldermen of the city to regulate the wages of the journeymen. Further Acts were passed in 1792 and 1811 with the aim of protecting the silk industry. In fact they did the very opposite and made the intractable gulf between master and workers even wider. Rather than offer stability, the Acts guaranteed poverty for most of the weavers now stuck in Spitalfields without a living trade. Also, factories were beginning to be built beyond London by families like the Courtaulds that could produce silk at speeds and prices that were unbeatable. The neighbourhood crashed.

From the pit of despair 19 Princess Street, the home of Pierre Abraham Ogier, would, however, revive. After the Huguenot masters left, Spital-fields remained a shadow city, a refuge for the desperate immigrants who came to London in fear of persecution or in pursuit of a new life. In 1862 the 'Loyal United Friends Friendly Society' (Chevras Nidvath Chen), set up by a group of Polish immigrants living in Spitalfields, was registered at 19 Princess Street. The charity had been established to organise a place of worship for the burgeoning Jewish community. Initially, a space was rented on nearby Fashion Street. By the 1890s the temple needed considerable repairs so it was decided to relocate, and in 1893 a new temple was opened at 19 Princess Street; four months later the street was renamed Princelet Street.

The temple was sited at the back of the Ogiers' original house covering what used to be the garden, ranged over two floors, and continued as a place of worship until the 1960s, when the Jewish community started to move away from the East End and leave it to the next tide of immigrants. The parlour, where once the Ogier family had spent much of the day, was given over to Torah study, and after the closure of the temple was used for the teaching of English to Bangladeshi women. The last resident at No. 19 was a reclusive Polish scholar, David Rodinsky. One night in 1969 he went out, locked the door of his room behind him and vanished for ever; the mystery of his disappearance entered East End lore and is symbolic of the passing of the Jewish East End.

Since then the houses within the estate have been threatened with demolition as they sank into dereliction. Only a concerted campaign by architectural historians such as Dan Cruickshank saved the neigh-bourhood; and because of its proximity to the financial City, it has once again become a desirable enclave for rich merchants, the masters of the universe of the contemporary money markets. In many cases, the houses have been assiduously restored to their original state, as if they were returned to the 1740s. This has brought wealth into the area which still sits awkwardly next to impoverished immigrant communities.

Today, 19 Princelet Street itself is in a delicate state yet the temple is intact, its features sagging and rusty, and it contains Europe's first museum of immigration and diversity. Within the rooms of the building a permanent exhibition, 'Suitcases and Sanctuary', explores the many different races and peoples that have come to Spitalfields since the first *réfugiés* made this part of London the first stage of their new lives in the city. As you walk out of the house and into the street, illuminated at night by the flashing neon of the nearby curry houses of Brick Lane, history and the present seem to blend, proving that this story has not yet found its ending.

CHAPTER 6

HOME HOUSE

The Queen of Hell and the Art of Politeness

I took a walk up and down that lovely Oxford Street, so as to take a good look at all the houses and the numerous shops. Our imagination, dear children, is not nearly big enough to picture the quantities of inventions and improvements.

Sophie von La Roche, 1786

The exterior of Home House, facing out on the north-west edge of Portman Square, is deceptively restrained; there is no indication on the outside of the character of the interior. Even compared to some of the other houses on the square it is remarkably quiet. An elegant stuccoed portico links the house to the street and stands out because of its lack of ostentation. On the second storey there is a series of four plaques, framing simple classical swags, offering a lightness to the building's simple brick face. Elsewhere, there is a positive avoidance of ornament, the four sets of four windows have no pilasters or decorations. It was only later that a thin balcony with iron balustrades that run along the first storey was added as well as a solid, stone balustrade that runs along the roof.

Yet this plain facade disguises one of the finest interiors in London, a series of rooms decorated in colour and the best materials, each space a model of taste and decorum; the story of this house, the woman who commissioned it and the architect who designed it, uncovers an intriguing narrative about London in the age of the Enlightenment.

Architectural history often tells the story of a building through the life of its creator – patron or architect – using biographical detail to explore the decisions, travails and whims that make up the many different aspects of a place. The combination of structural necessities, architectural conventions, idiosyncratic philosophies and caprice are often perceived as an expression of an individual soul. But what if that human heart at the centre of the construction is hidden, and we can only find fragments of a life within the historical record? Rather than looking at a building through its creator, can we do the opposite and reanimate a haunting absence by uncovering their surroundings? Can we resurrect a life that has almost been lost to history by exploring the rooms and spaces they commanded into being, and then discover the patron?

Elizabeth, Countess of Home, died in 1784, leaving a detailed will. Apart from that, despite being at the upper end of society, a redoubtable hostess and patron, there is surprisingly little account of her life: records that mark the regular human rites of passage, the bills and contracts that contain her name; today, she is almost a ghost. There are only the rarest glimpses of her in the literature of the day: she was well known enough to feature in the scurrilous *Modern Characters from Shakespeare* that satirised Georgian figures under the Bard's cloak. The Countess of H–E appears in *The Merry Wives of Windsor*: 'she's a witch, a quean, an old cozening quean! ... Come down, you witch, you hag, you; come down I say! No doubt the devil will soon have her!'[1]

She also appeared in a dubious portrait from the mischievous hand of William Beckford, the richest young man in England, author of the Gothick thriller *Vathek* and as unreliable a social commentator as it is possible to find. At the time Beckford had just moved into a new house on Portman Square, near to where Elizabeth had also built her own elegant residence, Home House: 'I accepted yesterday [an invitation from] no less a person in short than the Countess of Home, known among all the Irish Chairmen and riff-raff of the metropolis by the name style and title of the Queen of Hell.' That was not all, and Beckford continued his lampoon of an excruciating evening: 'Aware of my musical propensities she determined to celebrate my accession to Portman Square by a sumptuous dinner and a concert of equal magnificence. Last evening it took place and you never beheld so splendidly heterogeneous a repast as the dinner or ever heard such a confounded jumble of good and bad music.'[2]

Beckford should be trusted neither as a judge of character nor as a stickler for the truth when a better story was on offer. His portrait of Elizabeth Home, however, is a prelude to a more complex narrative that stretches from the new settlements of the English Empire to the finest salons of London, and tells of Enlightenment and reform, of classical architecture and money, and decodes the chicanes and delicate rituals of the new art of urban living: politeness. At the centre of this puzzle is the house itself, why and how it was built, its role within the city, and how the carefully calibrated collection of rooms and decoration combine to tell of an intriguing moment in London's history. In addition, an exploration of the house might bring its patroness back to life and unlock the truth of who 'the Queen of Hell' really was.

William Beckford and Elizabeth Home had more than Portman Square in common. In 1661 Samuel Pepys recorded in his diary a visit from Beckford's great-grandfather, Peter, who planned to sail to Jamaica that summer. His uncle Richard was already trading in the Indies and Peter arrived with a handful of slaves and hired himself out as a horse catcher. On his death in 1710 he was the largest landowner on the island and its Governor, and could claim to be 'in possession of the largest property real and personal of any subject in Europe'.[3] His grandson William Thomas, son of William, was born in London, but at the age of ten inherited all the family's Jamaica estates, worth over £1 million.

Elizabeth Gibbons was also born at the beginning of the new century, in Jamaica, the only child of William Gibbons and his wife, Deborah. It is not known when the family had arrived on the island but Jamaica had been captured from the Spanish by Oliver Cromwell in 1655 and a number of opportunists made the voyage to seek their fortune in the early 1660s. The Gibbonses had a plantation in the parish of Vere that lay on Clarendon plain, a large, well-irrigated valley ideal for agriculture. The Gibbons's plot was certainly big enough, and profitable enough, for William to gain some standing on the island. It was a tough life yet Jamaica offered something that was not possible at home: 'a man born of mean and obscure parents, without learning, or any thing else but his courage to support him'[4] could rise to the front rank of society and possess riches that were beyond comparison in London. The new colonies also provided religious tolerance and political freedoms that would have seemed dangerous at home.

When the writer Charles Leslie visited the island in the 1740s he found that it was a community dedicated to trade, 'regard[ing] nothing but money, and value not how they get it'. The main towns were trading depots: Port Royal never had less than 300 ships in the harbour, either delivering slaves and goods, or preparing to ship rum, ginger, sugar and spices back to Britain. Here there were churches for every faith, but also markets where the human cargo from Africa landed after their brutal 'sea tyranny ... [of] hunger, handcuffs and a cat O' nine Tails'.[5]

The environment itself was dangerous. The heat dominated daily life and, despite the delicate trade winds that rolled in from the sea, high fevers, bellyaches and distempers were common and the island soon gained a reputation as 'the white man's grave'. In the first six years of the colony (1660–6), 12,000 settlers arrived but by the end of this period only 3,470 had survived. It was too hot in the day to dress in full outfit and men only wore their wigs on Sundays. Nature had other ways of asserting its dominance, and in 1692 an earthquake devastated Port Royal, killing over 1,500, while houses sank into the 'hot loose sand' never to be seen again.[6] This was followed by a fire in 1703 and a devastating hurricane in 1722.

There were also very real threats from within. Before the defeated Spanish fled the island in the 1650s they freed their slaves, the Maroons, who took refuge amongst the native tribes in the impenetrable central mountain range. In the 1690s there was a slave uprising in Clarendon when hundreds of rebels escaped their bondage and joined the liberated brigades, forcing the planters to set up militias and demand help from the homeland. Punishment of any recaptured slave was unspeakable; however, this did not deter the Maroon leader, Cudjoe, who initiated a policy of guerilla raids on plantations and small villages. It was not until 1731, after hundreds of soldiers had died from fever or ambush, that an uneasy peace was negotiated. Yet the threat of the Maroons and the fear of slave uprisings on a plantation (where there were usually twenty slaves to each European) were never far below the surface.

In addition, Jamaica was part of a wider tumult that involved the major nations of Europe in competition for the dominance of the global trade networks that stretched from the frozen forests of the Hudson Bay to the gold mines of West Africa and the cantons of Mughal India. The War of the Spanish Succession at the beginning of the century saw the French fleet in nearby Hispaniola drawing a flotilla led by Vice-Admiral Benbow into battle, where the English commander lost his life. In addition, British settlements also had to contend with pirates funded by enemy states. In 1706 Pierre Le Moyne laid waste to the islands of St Kitts and Nevis and was commanded also to harass Jamaica. Conflict flared up again in 1717 against the Spanish, as the two European powers squabbled over possession of Belize.

Yet, in defiance of this insecurity and danger, a semblance of tasteful life was encouraged. There was no desire for expensive houses – after the earthquake, few buildings were built over two storeys; however it was usual for a rich man to express his taste and fortune in commodities imported from Britain and Europe, 'it being no uncommon thing to find, at the country inhabitations of the planters, a splendid sideboard loaded with plate, and the choicest of wines, a table covered in damask, and a dinner of perhaps sixteen or twenty covers; and all this in a hovel not superior to an English Barn'.[7] While architecture was beyond the wont of most planters, the sugar lords understood the laws of consumption: it was desirable to live in comfort while on the plantation but, more importantly, it was imperative to prepare for a return home in style.

There was no school on the island and 'neither [did] they seem very fond of the thing'.[8] Those who hoped for an education sent their sons home; William Thomas Beckford, the grandson of Peter, was sent to Westminster School in London as a boy and did not return to the island until he was a young man. For Elizabeth Gibbons education, bar preparation for marriage, was not a priority and when she was sixteen she wed the twenty-three-year-old James Lawes, the elder son of Sir

Nicholas Lawes, Governor of the island. In 1732 the couple travelled to London for the first time.

James was nothing like his father. Sir Nicholas was a remarkable man who arrived in 1663 and, as he amassed his fortune, had time to introduce coffee-planting to the community, built the first printing press, and married fives times. James and a brother were produced from the fourth union; a daughter, Judith Maria, was the result of the fifth. Sir Nicholas was also famed for his incorruptible pursuit of pirates who sailed in Jamaican waters and preyed on the seaborne trade between the island and the motherland. 'Calico Jack' Rackham, Anne Bonny, Mary Read, Robert Deal and Charles Vane were all condemned in his court. He was, however, less successful in controlling his tearaway son, who left 'nothing untr'ed to create trouble'.[9]

In London James must either have changed his ways or used his father's considerable influence, because by the end of the year the couple were already planning to return to Jamaica, James having gained the post of Lieutenant-Governor. However, on 4 January 1733 he died, leaving Elizabeth a widow at only eighteen years old. Nonetheless, she resolved to remain in London, and there she stayed for the rest of her life. As a wealthy heiress she had financial security, but this did not necessarily protect her from all the dangers of the unfamiliar city.

It was to be another forty years before she started work on Home House in Portman Square, yet in the meantime London was in an era of dramatic change. The metropolis in the age of Enlightenment was a paradox. In 1726 the French philosopher Voltaire had fled to England and found a fount of liberty and reason. He fell in love with the satire of Jonathan Swift, and spent time with the poet Alexander Pope and the playwright John Gay, whose The Beggar's Opera was playing at Drury Lane. He marvelled at the newest theories of Isaac Newton and was a committed advocate of the new fashion of inoculation against smallpox. The different sects within the city fascinated him and in his series of Letters on England he wrote how tolerance was at the heart of English liberty: 'If there were only one religion in England, there would be danger of despotism, if there were only two they would cut each other's throat; but there are thirty and they live in peace.'[10]

Yet the capital was also a dangerous, violent cacophony, a political tumult in constant fear of the mob, the *Vulgaris Mobile*, that was first identified in the 1680s as the faceless mass, without family ties or obligations. London could no longer be counted by communities, trades, or parishes but rather was a vast nameless majority of apprentices, the poor, the ill and old who were demonised as the drunks of Beer Street, the deranged of Gin Lane, the baying hordes that threatened violence on a short fuse. As the city expanded beyond comprehension the streets became theatres to the public dramas of everyday life, depicted in the clear-sighted work of William Hogarth where the violent politics, culture and social extremes were played out in hideous tableaux. Riots were common, and contagious – born out of the liberty of free speech, the free press and a corrupt political system.

This was in stark contrast to the vision of Enlightenment and improvement to be found in the latest works of philosophy and poetry. The historian Mark Goldie has described the Enlightenment as less of a revolution than a 'tone of voice, a sensibility';[11] it was a dream rather than a reality, it had to be built rather than discovered. The Enlightenment metropolis hoped to express and enhance the best of man and suppress his natural self. Since the Great Fire there had been attempts to rationalise the urban landscape and this was not better symbolised than by the development of the archetypal London square that came to dominate the city.

On 31 January 1765 *The Public Advertiser* announced: 'it is said that Portman Square now building between Portman Chapel and Marylebone will be much larger than Grosvenor Square; and that handsome walks, planted with Elm Trees, will be made to it, with a grand reservoir, in the middle'.[12] At that time the ground north of Oxford Street was untouched, the rural estate belonging to Henry William Portman of Orchard Portman, Somerset. To the east work was well under way on the Harley estate; to the north and west there was nothing except pastureland with an untrammelled view all the way to Highgate Hill. Portman Square, at the centre of the new community, was to be the

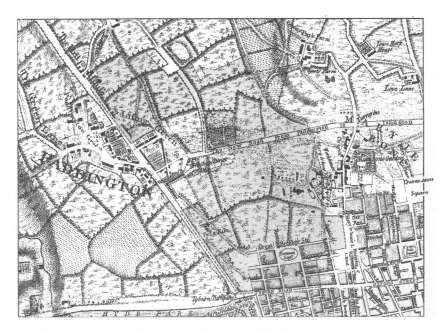

13. The Portman estate in 1745, on the verge of development

most splendid example of the urban square, and on 24 June 1772 Elizabeth Home, who was already living on the southern end of the square, at the very edge of the city, took a ninety-year lease on a parcel of land, 60 feet by 184 feet, to erect a brick house and office.

Like so many quintessential features of London life, the archetypal square had its origins elsewhere. In the 1630s, as Inigo Jones began to formulate his plans for Covent Garden on behalf of the Earl of Bedford, he had the piazza at Livorno in mind which he had first encountered on his ground-breaking Italian tour of 1614. Yet a passion for squares really began to change the shape of the metropolis in the decades following the Restoration of 1660. Aristocrats returning from exile on the Continent brought with them memories of Paris, especially the Place des Vosges, originally built by Henri IV to encourage a home-grown silk trade. The *place* proposed a new art of living by replacing the old-style *hôtels* with a number of elegant town houses around a central communal space. The aristocratic palace was superseded by an uniquely urban dwelling set around an artificially rural centrepiece.

The first person to propose this grand scheme in London was Henry Jermyn, the 1st Earl of St Albans, who in 1661 was granted a plot of land to the north of St James's Palace. He was determined to turn his royal gift to profit. In 1662 he built a *hôtel* for himself to signify his new status and then planned to lease out the surrounding land 'fit for the dwelling of noble men and other persons of quality'.[13] Jermyn then worked with speculators, such as Nicholas Barbon, who purchased the rights at No. 4 on the square, to develop high-quality housing for the wealthy. Other grandees followed and over the ensuring decades new, bold communities began to mushroom at the edges of the old city – St James's, Bloomsbury, Leicester Fields and Soho.

The houses themselves were very different from the Continental models and fitted both the rules of the speculative market as well as the British way of life. The main home for a leading family remained their estate in the country, but the matter of the right address was of crucial consequence and certain neighbourhoods fought for and defended their reputations at any cost. The houses were usually set over four or five storeys and were comfortable enough to accommodate a family, with a full complement of servants.

In addition to the changing ways in which people lived, this new fashion altered the dimensions of the city as the development of the squares tested the urban boundaries. In 1713 work began at Hanover Square, north of Piccadilly; four years later the Burlington estate to the west was developed by the exquisitely tasteful Earl using all the finest architects of the generation. In 1721, the Grosvenor family began to sell the leases that would plot the form of Mayfair, commanding that this most exclusive of locations was to be uniformly developed according to the vision of one designer, James Gibbs. Aristocratic settlements would rise out of the ground overnight, turning the rural fringes into dusty building sites. In 1725, Daniel Defoe stood in awe at the transformation of Mayfair: 'I passed an amazing scene of new foundations, not of houses only, but as I might say of new cities. New towns, new squares, and fine buildings, the like of which no city, no town, nay no place in the world can shew.'[14]

At the same time new projects were being built to the north of Tyburn

Road, quickly renamed Oxford Street, in the farmland of Marylebone. In 1717 the Cavendish Harley family devised the plotting of Cavendish Square. Until now, building this far north was almost inconceivable, yet the ravenous demand for the new tore up the fields on which, in the words of Defoe, builders need only 'like gardeners, to dig a hole, put in a few bricks, and presently there goes up a house'.[15] The whole northern side of the square was grabbed by the Duke of Chandos, the most powerful man in London, and work began on a suitably grand town house.

Unfortunately, such rampant speculation was always a victim of economic boom and bust. By the 1720s London had been overbuilt and the speculators' books began to fill with unsold projects. Further damage was done by another financial calamity in 1720, ironically instigated by the Earl of Oxford, Robert Harley, who was at that time ploughing his own profits into the estate. The South Sea Company had been set up as a monopoly on trade in the South Americas but soon secured the national debt incurred during the War of the Spanish Succession. Speculation on the company share price, which reached £1,000 in August 1720, sent London mad. When Isaac Newton was asked his opinion on the market he shook his head and mourned, 'I can calculate the movement of the stars, but not the madness of men.'[16] He had time to rue his wisdom as he lost over £20,000 when the bubble inevitably burst.

It was not until the 1760s, with a temporary outbreak of peace and stability, that building speculation in London recommenced. This new spurt of expansion picked up where the last boom had ended, transforming pastureland into fashionable squares and town houses. Work began again at Cavendish Square and the hinterland to the north of Oxford Street. Development also started to creep westward until it arrived at the edge of the Portman estate by 1765. The new rich once again went in pursuit of the kind of accommodation that suited their new position.

It was not, however, welcomed with universal acceptance. In 1772 the lawyer James Boswell, travelling back to London via the building site of Portman Square, complained, 'the increase of London is prodigious. It is really become too large.'[17] Four years later the architect John Gywnn produced an influential broadside, *London and Westminster Improved*, in which he gloomily contrasted the contemporary city with Sir Christopher Wren's graceful plans for the revived capital following the Great Fire. Gwynn's argument was that there was no city-wide planning, and that individual estates created their own roads, services and markets without reference to the needs of the capital as a whole. He proposed a new scheme for the metropolis, 'a general well regulated limited plan, the execution of which should have been enforced by commissioners, appointed by authority, men of sound judgement, taste and activity'.[18] It would limit the extent of the city boundaries, that were threatened by a 'fury which seems to possess the fraternity of builders and to prevent them from extending the town in enormous manner'.[19]

In short, London should not be left to the builders but should be managed into rationality by a new breed of town planners. This was the first attempt to see London as an integrated whole rather than a conglomeration of parts, parishes and vested interests, and would echo down the centuries. This question would be raised again nearly a century later, in the face of the most calamitous circumstances, when the city was gripped by cholera; and would soon come to define the way that it evolved over the following decades to the present day.

Gwynn's book came as the result of his work on drafting the 1774 Building Act, a most sweeping piece of legislation setting out minimum requirements at all stages of the building process. Each new building was to be graded according to four 'rates' and a corresponding level of regulation. Just as important as a statement of grievances, Gywnn identified the London of the Enlightenment as a dynamic place of constant movement. The modern city was a communications network through which bodies, money and goods should circulate unimpeded. This tolled the end of many of London's ancient foundations. In 1733, the Lord Mayor attempted to regulate the traffic on London Bridge by commanding that all traffic pass by the left-hand side in either direction, the origin of our present road laws. This was not enough and in 1759 it was decided to clear the ancient bridge of the buildings that had stood on both sides since its construction in 1209. Nevertheless, the bridge lost its monopoly as the only crossing place when in 1750 a bridge at

Westminster was proposed to aid the London traffic to the west of the old city. In 1759 plans for Blackfriars Bridge were also drawn up.

In 1760, the old gates – Ludgate, Newgate, Aldgate, Moorgate, Bishopsgate and Aldersgate – which had stood since the time of the Romans were dismantled in acknowledgement of the changing urban shape, as well as in an attempt to aid the traffic that ground to a halt at these ancient barriers. Work on cleaning up the putrid Fleet Ditch that ran along London's fringes was conducted between the 1730s and 1760s; parts were covered over, offering a new roadway into the city – from Ludgate to Blackfriars – from the west linking with the new Blackfriars Bridge. Perhaps the most unexpected ruling was the removal of all the old shop signs that identified each house and had for centuries acted as a means of locating addresses; from this point, house numbers began to be introduced.

This revolution in housing and city planning reflected a wider social revolution. Following the death of James Lawes in 1733, the story of his wife Elizabeth, the eighteen-year-old West Indian heiress, evaporates. It is not until nine years later, on Christmas Day 1742, that her name reappears, on a marriage certificate. On that day Elizabeth married William, the 8th Earl of Home, and took the title Countess of Home. The marriage did not last long and on 24 February the following year the Earl abandoned his twenty-eight-year-old wife, never to return. At least one historian has suggested that the Countess was pregnant, but later lost the child. After that, once again, she disappeared from the record until 1772, when she began work on her new house at Portman Square.

While the city was developing upon aristocratic land, the squares, theatres, pleasure gardens, fine houses and institutions that replaced the ancient pastureland were being funded by Britain's emerging empire. The marriage between the Earl and the Countess was for mutual benefit, not love, and reflected the changing nature of London. The rise of polite society reconfigured how one was defined, how one behaved, what one said and where one went; politeness created a filigree code of conduct that reinterpreted every gesture, scrutinised every purchase and imposed a political and moral significance on even the smallest matter of dress or appearance. The art of London life judged a book by its cover; it sought to comprehend from the outside in, to read the character of a person by the quality of her conversation, the delectability of her table, the exquisite choice of ornaments in her public rooms. Most of all, it reflected the changing balance between money and power.

The new squares were not just enclaves for the long-established aristocracy; where once power was in the hands of those who owned land in Britain, now merchants and traders who had made their names in the far-flung colonies of the nascent empire – the nabobs of the East India Company and the plantation owners of the Indies – were arriving with fortunes that were beyond belief. As the playwright Richard Cumberland noted in his light comedy *The West Indian* – about a young heir arriving back 'home' for the first time and the hilarious consequences as the avaricious natives attempt to snare his fortune – the master was so wealthy that 'he has rum and sugar enough belonging to him, to make all the water in the Thames into punch'.[20]

The cultivation of sugar had a huge impact on life in London. In 1663 150,000 hundredweight arrived in British ports; by 1700 this had increased to 370,000, the equivalent of 4lb of sugar for every Englishman; by 1800 the national annual average consumption had leapt to a massive 18lb. By the terms of the Navigation Acts only British shipping was allowed to transport these goods and they had to be delivered to British ports; as a result London, Liverpool and Bristol grew rich on Atlantic traffic. In the capital, the merchants soon found themselves wealthy enough to mix freely with the landed elites and the court, and in time these financial speculators, the MPs of Westminster and the nobles of the King's circle began to intermingle as equals.

The fusion of all these different factions in one place changed not just the city but also politics. Jamaican money had muscle and it soon assembled into vested interests and potent lobby groups. Initially the traders met casually at the Jamaica House, close to the Royal Exchange, inside the city. This was formalised in the Planters' Club in the 1740s, the Society of West Indian Merchants in the 1760s and the West Indies

Committee in the 1780s. They were powerful enough to persuade Parliament to vote for war in 1739 and to influence the peace in 1763.

The new money also changed the social landscape of the city, for the mixture of different classes demanded a new etiquette to ease relations between them. The vast wealth of the sugar lords overturned the old assumptions of power: their profits trumped more aristocratic sources of income, and purchased entry into any situation. If they were uncultured they could educate their sons to behave like lords; they could buy land and influence at will; Oxford Street soon developed into a luxury bazaar to cater for the sale of any accoutrement or new fashion to prove one's taste. Everything now had a price and a new social politics had to be formed, for it was no longer possible to judge a man by where he came from, who his father was or what he was selling. This was also reflected in the marriage market.

For Elizabeth Lawes her marriage in 1742 to the Earl of Home, however brief, offered the wealthy widow a title and social position in the established hierarchy; for the Earl, the family name was financially secure and he was free to pursue his own interests. Likewise, William Thomas Beckford, father of the writer, also hoped to turn his West Indian fortune into power in London. After his education at Westminster he returned to Jamaica in 1735 following the death of his father. A decade later he came back to London. To begin with he bought land – the Fonthill estate in Wiltshire – and was named MP for nearby Shaftesbury. Once there he threw himself into London politics, where he became an alderman for Billingsgate and was subsequently chosen to represent the city in Parliament. Eventually, he was twice elected Lord Mayor.

Both in Parliament and at the Guildhall, Beckford led the West Indian interest group; yet his passion was not restricted to protecting his own concerns – he also believed in political change. His family story showed that power should not rest in the hands of the nobility and landowning gentry alone but needed to be shared among the many different ranks both in the city and in the country. He was fortunate to find a close ally in William Pitt, the Prime Minister, and together they set out to spread reform, opening up the political process to all areas of middling sorts, as Pitt told the Commons in 1761: 'the manufacturer, the yeoman, the merchant, the country gentlemen [are] ... very sensible people who know better perhaps than any other nation under the sun, whether they are well governed or not'.[21] They hoped to recognise in legislation what had already happened in society, acknowledging the shift of power away from the landed classes towards the merchant, the financier and the bureaucrat.

What this new bourgeoisie wanted was to be represented within the political system, and to be left alone. Politeness was not just a response to the changing relationship between power and money at the top end of society; it was also a protection against the past. The age of liberty was born out of the terrors of the Civil Wars, revolution and struggles of the previous century. Despite the establishment of a constitutional monarchy and the Bill of Rights, the freedom-loving Georgian had to remain vigilant against the tyranny from above; but it also meant he had to deal with his fellow men with care. The Civil Wars had proven that men could do terrible things to their enemies, even if they were brothers or neighbours. In response the philosopher John Locke had promoted the concept of tolerance of the differences of others. Instead of instantly resorting to pistols, the Enlightened man must meet the enemy and find a language that engaged both – a reformation of manners and the suppression of emotions that could avoid violence. Every man became his own first minister and politeness was a form of disguise, as shown in advice Lord Chesterfield gave to his son in the 1740s: 'Of all things, banish the egotism out of your conversation, and never think of entertaining people with your own personal concerns or private affairs ... one cannot keep one's own private affairs too secret.'[22]

This was raised into the fine art of conversation, and the creation of its elegant forum: the salon. While men like Beckford played their politics in the public eye, women like Elizabeth Home were compelled to use their influence in subtler, albeit no less influential, ways. This was perhaps best exemplified by the Countess's neighbour on Portman Square and – if Beckford is to be believed – rival, Elizabeth Montagu, the patroness of the most celebrated salon in London, the Bluestockings. The salon was the intersection between the history of women and the culture of politeness. The eighteenth-century man was meant to be, in the words of Dr Johnson, 'clubbable'; however, the Georgian lady was not invited to the gambling dens or dinner clubs. The salon developed in the late seventeenth century as an intellectual gathering, usually circling around a dominant female figure. The grouping congregated for different purposes and each salon had its own personality, determined by the generosity of the patroness and the people she wished to associate with. They were centres of soft power, where influence and persuasion were played out rather than the coarse political debates of public men.

Conversation dictated the rules of engagement. This uniquely eighteenth-century phenomenon was summed up by Dr Johnson in exasperation: 'No Sir, we had talk enough, but no conversation; there was nothing discussed.'[23] Conversation indicated both the intellectual nature of a topic as well as the spirit in which it was discussed. It was serious entertainment, pedagogic without being dull, avoiding conflict at all costs. For Johnson, the correct way of engaging in talk regulated the passions, improved the mind and cultivated the bonds of community.

Elizabeth Montagu did not come from Jamaica but, like her counterpart, the Countess, came from a wealthy family and was born outside London, in York. She was well-connected and often stayed with her grandmother in Cambridge, who was married to the noted classical scholar Conyers Middleton; it is said that he was the inspiration for her later intellectual flowering. At Cambridge she also became friends with Lady Margaret Harley and through her was introduced to London life.

Elizabeth thought little of love, but wanted to come to London and be at the centre of society; in a letter, she wished for a husband with 'much wit to divert me, beauty to please me, good humour to indulge me in the right, and reprove me when I am in the wrong; money enough to afford me more than I can want, and as much as I can wish'.[24] She found some of these qualities in the fifty-five-year-old bachelor Edward Montagu, an eminent mathematician who owned a number of coal mines in the north. They married in 1742 but, following the tragic death of their first son, the partnership seemed to decline until the two barely lived under the same roof. Despite this setback, Elizabeth Montagu soon gained a name for herself as the den mother of an intellectual gathering.

'Brilliant in diamonds, solid in judgement, critical in talk,' noted Hester Thrale of her friend.[25] For Elizabeth Montagu the Bluestockings were dedicated to the education and promotion of the mind, an idealised community of writers, artists and thinkers. Montagu herself was the 'Queen of the Blues' and was sufficiently lauded to publish her own work, *Essay on the Writings and Genius of Shakespeare*, in which she attacked Voltaire's criticism of the nation's Bard. Amongst others, she was joined by Elizabeth Vesey, Frances Boscawen and the poet Hannah More. Male guests included the leading cultural figures of the age: Horace Walpole, Dr Johnson, the actor David Garrick as well as distinguished aristocrats.

Both Elizabeth Home and Elizabeth Montagu built their houses on Portman Square as places to hold their salons. For Montagu, there was an emphasis on conversation; as Hannah More wrote in her poem *Bas Bleu: or, Conversation*, the salon was an exchange of the most virtuous commodity:

> But tis thy commerce, Conversation,
> Must give it use by circulation;
> That noblest commerce of mankind,
> What precious merchandize is MIND.[26]

For Countess Home, as Beckford noted in his scurrilous pen portrait,[27] music was at the centre of her salon, and her rooms were designed accordingly. Yet this was very serious entertainment indeed and both women had their own political interests to promote.

Work began on Home House soon after the Countess had secured the lease in June 1772. To bring her vision of the perfect house to life she had chosen a twenty-six-year-old architect, James Wyatt, who, although at the very beginning of his career, had already made a name for himself within society. The previous year all London had been astounded by his new Pantheon on Oxford Street. The opening night, Monday, 27 January 1772, was unparalleled for glamour, with over 700 'of the first people of this Kingdom' as well as foreign dignitaries, one of whom commented that it appeared to him like 'the enchanted Palaces described in the

French Romances, which are said to have been raised by the potent wand of some Fairy; and, that, indeed, so much were his senses captivated, he could scarcely persuade himself but that he trod on fairy ground'.[28] Even the arch-arbiter of taste, Horace Walpole, admitted that it was the greatest building in the whole empire.

Wyatt had come from a family of Staffordshire builders, and while one of his brothers, Samuel, trained as a carpenter and another, Joseph, learnt a mason's trade, James showed early artistic talent. He was sent to Italy, where he spent six years painting as well as studying the ruins of the classical world, which fascinated him more than the glories of the Renaissance and Baroque that had reformed the modern city. The Pantheon was his first commission on returning to London and was as dramatic an entrance to the city as was imaginable. The building had been developed as a 'winter Ranleigh', an all-year-round pleasure garden where entertainments, spectacles and delights attracted the better end of society, offering a modern, 'public' alternative to the court. For his design, Wyatt resurrected the Emperor Hadrian's Pantheon in Rome and transformed it into a theatre set. Sophie von La Roche described her visit in 1783:

> The astonishingly high hall, cut down by colonnades and surrounded by a gallery . . . is excellent for masquerades; from these broad galleries where the statues of the graces and all the gods and goddesses are arrayed I should very much like to see English Nymphs and sylph-like figures wandering in and out; for when the many thousands of wax candles are alight, the building is said to be entrancing.[29]

Wyatt became so fashionable after the opening that when Catherine the Great of Russia came sniffing for a new court architect, it was said that a consortium of grandees set up a fund to ensure that Wyatt stayed in Britain. Needless to say, he was swamped by commissions and amongst the first were Elizabeth Home and her neighbour on Portman Square, William Lock. Wyatt was quick to draw up designs for both buildings, and some of his plans for the ceilings of Home House still exist, but he was in huge demand and was unable to focus his full attention on the projects. Instead, he began to travel around the country visiting the country houses that he was improving; as a young man in a rush he was forced to convert his coach into a mobile office with a draughtsman's desk and, at the height of his career, would claim to drive 4,000 miles a year.

This did not impress the Countess, who fired Wyatt in January 1775 when the building was probably at some advanced stage. In 1774 the house was rated, which suggests that it was close to completion; and the following year there was a paid invoice for the stuccoist Joseph Rose, indicating that work had begun on some of the ceilings. In Wyatt's stead the Countess placed the responsibility of completing her dreams in stone on Robert Adam. Thus Adam inherited a design from Wyatt, his great rival, but was determined to develop a whole new plan for the house. Home House became the most dazzling expression of Adam's accomplishments in London, and the perfect articulation of the Countess's aspirations.

Wyatt's sudden rise to fame had been a blow to Adam's hold upon fashionable London. Born in Kirkcaldy in 1728, he was a product of the Scottish Enlightenment: his architect father moved in the circles of leading intellectuals such as David Hume and William Robertson. While a boy, Robert was in the same class as Adam Smith, who would later lay the foundations for modern economics with his *The Wealth of Nations*. It was accepted that these new ideas found their expression in the revival of ancient architecture where only the most academic representations of the past were permitted – the belief in common sense, logic and order reflected in the strict appreciation of the rules of classical architecture. Adam, however, found something more exciting in his study of the past.

Adam began his education in his father's library, which was stuffed with ancient texts as well as a wealth of architectural tracts from France and Italy and their English translations. Here he also found a number of prints, mainly drawn in Holland, which he diligently copied as he hoped to discipline his eye. He was learning the art of landscape, cultivating his artist's hand. After university, like so many of his generation, Adam sought to complete his education in France and Italy. He was already determined on an artist's life, so the study of the ancient sites and the development of learned taste were essential. He departed in 1754 and soon arrived in Rome, where he fell in with a group of artists surrounding Charles-Louis Clérisseau, a pensioner at the French Academy at the Palazzo Medici. Here he also made friends with the architectural artist Giovanni Battista Piranesi. Both men would have an unexpected impact on Adam's architectural vision.

From Clérisseau he learnt academic exactitude, the ability to observe and measure and the powers of patience: thus he was encouraged to 'forebear invention or composing either plans or elevations till I have a greater fund' of knowledge.[30] As a result he spent his time observing, measuring and drawing. It was also a prerequisite to study and publish a monograph on monuments discovered on the student's Grand Tour in order to gain a reputation back home, and every respectable home was filled with youthful studies of the antiquities of ancient Greece, the ruins at Palmyra, the classical orders. Adam himself travelled to Split on the Dalmatian coast to chart the ruins of the palace of the Emperor Diocletian with the hope, as he wrote to his brother, of completing 'a very tolerable work to rival Stuart and Revett [authors of *The Antiquities of Athens*] in three months and return home laden with laurels'.[31]

On the other hand, Adam also became enraptured by Piranesi's more daring view of the classical past. Like many architects, Piranesi set about the accurate measurement of the ruins of Rome, yet in his resulting *Vedute* (Views) he infused his designs with emotion and imagination. He manipulated the scale of his buildings to make them appear imposing, imagining what the original architect's intentions were and then over-laying them, in the words of the art critic Robert Hughes, with 'heroic misinformation'.[32] The results were a dramatic, visceral response to the stones of the eternal city rather than an academic study of scale and proportion. As he formulated his own vocabulary of architecture Adam would struggle to balance the cerebral demands of academic study with the desire to use architecture as a means to manipulate emotions, distilling this dilemma into a fascination with the architecture of 'movement':

... the rising and falling, advancing and receding, with the convexity and concavity and other forms of the great parts have the same effect in architecture, that the hill and dale, foreground and distance, swelling and sinking have in landscape; that is they serve to produce an agreeable and diversified contour, that groups and contrasts like a picture.[33]

With the publication of his work on the royal palace, Spalatro, Adam set up his office in Lower Grosvenor Street in London and filled the newly completed house with bas-relief, statues and drawings in order to 'Dazzle the eyes' of potential clients. He slowly gained commissions, firstly small jobs such as improving the new drawing room and glass house at Gordon House, a ceiling and chimneypiece at Hatchlands. In time, however, he acquired a reputation and was adopted by eminent patrons and offered major projects. By 1760 he was the leading architect at the country house at Kedleston and of a refurbishment at Syon House; and he was given a number of commissions by his fellow Scot, the current Prime Minister the Earl of Bute, including a London town house on Berkeley Square and a country villa at Luton Hoo. In 1761 Adam was offered the official role of Architect of the King's Works. Over the next thirty years he would have nearly 300 different clients.

In London, Adam soon dominated the architectural field. In 1764, the 1st Earl of Mansfield commissioned him to remodel Kenwood House in Highgate, as an ideal stately home within reach of the city. Four years later he had his eye on a bigger prize: the Adelphi, a block of twenty-four grand terraced houses between the Strand and the Thames. The project was one of the most ambitious of the century and also nearly ruined the Adam family. In the year before starting on Home House Adam was nearby working on Portland Place, commissioned by the Duke of Portland to create the most exclusive street in the metropolis.

Adam arrived at Home House in 1774, and the work was to be the finest expression of his philosophy of movement, in which he sought to 'seize, with some degree of success, the beautiful spirit of antiquity, and to transfuse it, with novelty and variety'.[34] Within the constraints already imposed by Wyatt, Adam hoped to create a dynamic sequence of rooms, an adventure in interiors, driven to invention as he struggled to overcome the obstacles he had inherited. This pursuit started at the front door and made its route through the rooms of the ground and first floors. The organisation of the different spaces and the carefully selected assembly of decorations and ornaments was no accident; Adam designed everything, down to the candlesticks in the library, to perform a parade that 'gradually swells the mind ... towards a climax'.[35]

The front door opened into a square hallway. It was a remarkably simple design with few features, but acted as an interim space between the street and the interior of the house. Even here, however, Adam had shown his subtle dislike of the straight line and, despite the lack of decoration, he carved a niche on the east side of the room to contain an ornate brazier in the shape of a twelve-foot obelisk holding a lamp. The walls were marbled and offered no hint of the drama to come. There were four doors along the walls; three concealed cupboards while the fourth led into a dark passage.

Remaining on the ground floor, the visitor turned left through a small antechamber into the parlour, which ran along the length of the front of the house. The morning room and the withdrawing room were important spaces in the house for a *salonnière*. Here the Countess would receive her morning guests, and it was where the ladies retired after dining in the evening. Elizabeth Montagu set out her morning room with great care: it was 'lined with painted paper of Pekin, and furnished with the choicest moveables of China',[36] and she sat at the centre, her guests in a semicircle around her. At the home of another Bluestocking, Mrs Vesey, the chairs were scattered around the room in clusters and the patroness would move from one group to another, leaning in with her ear-trumpet to hear the discussion.

Robert Adam had devised the Chinese Room for Lady Montagu at her house in Hill Street; his designs for Countess Home were very different, constrained by Wyatt's design of a functional rectangular space. He attempted to break up the monotony of the room by placing a porphyry column in each of the four corners. The pillars offered no purpose except to add depth and break down the edges of the room. The walls and ceiling were decorated in stucco, with the oval panels painted a light blue. At the centre was a series of sphinxes in relief. He also added decoration above the mantelpiece with a relief of honey-suckle, husks and vases. Adam's use of such ornaments went against the severe classical rules of his contemporaries, as he preached in his first volume of *Architectural Works*, published just as he was working at Home House:

> We have adopted a beautiful variety of light mouldings, gracefully formed, delicately enriched and arranged with propriety and skill. We have introduced a great diversity of ceilings, friezes, and decorated pilasters, and have added grace and beauty to the whole, by a mixture of grotesque stucco, and painted ornaments, together with the flowering rinceau, with its fanciful figures and winding foliage.[37]

Adam valued variety and movement as highly as classical accuracy in his designs and noted that the ancients had so many forms of ornament that a modern artist was allowed to be innovative. In addition, it was essential that every room was different, the function and personality of each space reflected by its decoration to give a graphic expression of the various different modes within the 'art of living'. From the parlour, a door led into the dining room, in many houses the most masculine of rooms. Again, Adam had to find a way of 'exploding' Wyatt's static rectangular space. At one end the walls were thickened and then two niches scooped out to add variety and novelty to the surface of the wall. There were no tapestries or fabrics draped around the room so 'they may not retain the smell of victuals'.[38]

Throughout the house Adam had complete control of the whole design process and often used the same craftsmen on all of his projects, including master craftsmen such as the furniture maker Thomas Chippendale. In 1779, when Elizabeth Montagu first discussed plans for her house on Portman Square with Adam, she was surprised that 'he came at the head of a regiment of artificers ... the bricklayers talked an hour ... the stonemason was as eloquent ... the carpenter thought the internal fitting up of the house not less important; then came the painter, who is painting my ceilings in various colours according to the present fashion'.[39] The same level of attention was lavished upon Home House.

He devised the complete painting scheme and commissioned the

Venetian painter Antonio Zucchi, who had been discovered by Adam's brother James on his own Grand Tour. Together they travelled to London and the Italian worked on a number of projects for the brothers; he was also married to the portrait painter Angelica Kauffmann. The images were not just for the Countess's private contemplation and a pamphlet was produced, *Subjects of the Pictures Painted by Antonio Zucchi for the Different Apartments at the Countess Dowager of Home's Home, In Portman Square*, which clearly outlined the nature and subject matter of his designs. Homeric legend and the story of Dido, Queen of Carthage, and the refugee Aeneas, play a significant part throughout the house, perhaps illustrating the Countess's long journey from Jamaica to London, and acting as a commentary on her abandonment.

The paintings in the library, or asylum, which stood off the dining room were even more compelling. This was a private sanctuary overlooking the garden, and here the decoration celebrated the triumph of wisdom over youth in the form of twelve small medallions emphasising British genius including Sir Isaac Newton, John Locke, Sir Francis Drake, John Milton and (no less) Robert Adam Esq. Drake seems a strange choice, except that the library also had a nautical theme; above the mantel there was a frieze of Britannia amongst marine instruments and allusions to the Navy and sea power, perhaps a hint at the Home family's fortune across the ocean. The family motto, 'True to the end', sat uncomfortably on a plaque above the chimneypiece.

The parade around the Countess's house often ignored the ground floor completely and, entering through the hallway, the fashionable visitor was conducted through the dark doorway into the light-filled stairwell that led up to the first floor. Adam's staircase is rightfully acknowledged as one of his greatest achievements. Wyatt had bequeathed the architect a square space with a stairway running along the walls, yet the Countess had confidence in her new designer when he demanded to rip out the existing set-up and start again. He then created a rounded vestibule and an imperial staircase that rose to a single flight and divided, curving around the walls towards the first-floor landing. Above, the well space rose the full three storeys of the building and was crowned by a dome. On each level, Adam had devised a series of columns, niches and painted fancies to catch the eye as the visitor climbed to the next floor. His attention to effect even went as far as designing the ornate banisters that accentuated the curve of the steps. Most importantly of all, the design used light within the confined circular space to give a riveting sense of movement and elevation. From the darkness of the hall, the visitor rose into brightness as they ascended towards the main rooms.

Yet, before entering the main salon, there was another antechamber to heighten the emotions and delay the critical moment of entrance. This was an elaborate version of the hallway on the ground floor, but on this occasion the transition was not from the street to the house but an anticipation of what was coming next. The 'Sattin Room', or music room, was the most resplendent of all. Here, once again, Adam explored his philosophy of movement: circles were carved on the ceiling to give a sense of motion, while on the panels between the windows and walls, long mirrors reflected the action of the room back in on itself.

14. The famous staircase at Home House, one of Robert Adam's masterpieces (*Bridgeman*)

The music room was the first design Adam completed for the Countess and they clearly spent much time searching for the perfect solution. As with the morning room below, Adam broke down the static regularity of the space and, bearing in mind the Countess's request for an organ to be on hand for her famed music evenings, Adam decided to make a feature of the instrument, placing it on the west wall, opposite the entrance, the first thing the visitor saw. Unfortunately, Wyatt had installed a fireplace here, which was removed and put on the north side, facing the windows. Typically, Adam eschewed the easy solution and was determined to make novelty out of necessity. Moving the fireplace also meant moving the chimney, and so he built out the north wall by three feet; this allowed him to add drama by creating three large arches corresponding to the three large windows that faced out onto the square: in the central space he placed his grate and on the two flanking arches he created doorways into the second drawing room or ballroom. Thus the regular-shaped room had been adapted into an exciting space that encouraged dynamism, reflected in the swirling ceiling. It was as if the elegant music played within the room had, in a moment, been made visible.

It was in this room that the Countess conducted her evening in honour of William Beckford; unfortunately, the night was not a towering success. The Countess had hired the services of Felice Giardini, a celebrated Italian violinist, who may even have had a permanent position in the household. However, as he was devising the entertainment that morning, the Countess had 'happened to meet with a brace of tall, athletic negroes in flaming lace jackets, tooting away on the French horn as loud has their lungs permitted'. By whim they were instantly hired for the night, much to the consternation of the maestro. When asked his opinion on their talents, Beckford feigned politeness: 'I was just able to assume a civilized expression of countenance and praised these charming examples of original talent as warmly as their patroness could possibly desire. "There," said the Countess, turning round triumphantly to the rueful Maestro, "did I not tell you so? Mr Beckford is a real judge." '[40]

After the music room, via one of the doors on the north wall the visitor finally entered the ballroom, where the Countess most emphatically expressed her ideas and ambitions. This was also where Adam attempted to out-do Wyatt's Pantheon once and for all. By this time the guest, despite Beckford's snipes, would have no question as to the Countess's position and character, but here they would have found final confirmation for above the mantelpiece Adam had designed spaces for two paintings. Each space had a canopied throne with an individual pelmet adorned with ducal coronets and royal insignia; they were specifically designed to hold the portraits by Thomas Gainsborough of the Duke and Duchess of Cumberland that had been given to the Countess by the couple after their exhibition at the Royal Academy in 1777. The paintings were to be the most important ornaments in the house.

The Duke, Henry, was the sixth child of Frederick, Prince of Wales, and a younger brother of George III. The two boys had little in common and the division would be even more apparent as adults: as a young man George had been smitten by Lady Sarah Lennox, daughter of the Duke of Richmond, but had been persuaded that royal blood should not marry out. He wrote with a heavy heart that duty was more important than passion. When he inherited the throne from his grandfather in 1760, he dedicated himself to a moral and blameless life. Henry, on the other hand, behaved like every royal spare son in history. In 1767 it was claimed he married the commoner Olive Wilmot, who supposedly produced a daughter, Olivia. He had also been caught squiring Lady Grosvenor in a number of hostelries between London and the lady's estate in Cheshire. In 1771, he married again – Anne Horton, the widow of Christopher Horton of Catton Hall and daughter of the 1st Earl of Carhampton, Simon Luttrell, an Irish MP and rake who was often called the 'King of Hell', and his wife Judith Maria Lawes.

The marriage caused uproar. Days after the clandestine union, rumours began to circulate in the *Public Advertiser* that 'It is now happily for this country within the limits of possibility that a Luttrell may be king of Great Britain.'[41] The King himself was more concerned by the dilution of royal blood and demanded that Parliament pass a law, the Royal Marriages Act, that regulated with whom princes could tie the knot. As many noted, it was a law that encouraged mistresses rather than ensured dynastic purity.

The Countess was an ardent supporter of the newly married couple, as family ties running all the way back to Jamaica still governed her concerns; Judith Lawes was the half-sister of the Countess's first husband, James Lawes. Thus, as she commanded Adam to make the two portraits the centre of her home, the Countess undoubtedly had political intentions beyond family pride. It is perhaps possible that the whole of Home House may have been created in order to establish a resplendent port for the Luttrell faction. It was a dangerous party to ally oneself to, as the Luttrells had a reputation within political circles as troublemakers. Simon Luttrell had come to England from a distinguished Irish family and with the marriage to Judith Lawes gained great wealth that was quickly turned into an estate in Warwickshire, Four Oaks, and a seat in Parliament. In a satire of the time, when the Devil searched around for a successor, Luttrell pushed himself forward with glee. This passion for the rough and tumble of politics was inherited by his sons and in 1774 Luttrell, recently created Baron Irnham, returned to Parliament with three of his brood, the most noted being the eldest, Henry Lawes Luttrell.

Four years earlier, Henry had made a name for himself in the midst of one of the key debates of the age. In 1769, the radical journalist and outlaw John Wilkes had returned from exile in France and stood as prospective MP for the seat of Middlesex on a ticket of parliamentary reform. He had previously failed to secure the seat for the City of London but, in a finely organised campaign that harnessed a wave of popular enthusiasm, won the Middlesex seat. The government refused to accept the result, however, and threw Wilkes out of Parliament.

At the second election, Wilkes won again; but was once more barred from Parliament. In February 1769 he was the only candidate standing and yet he still did not win the seat. In March, the government placed Henry Lawes Luttrell against the agitator, commenting that they needed 'a man of the firmest virtue, or a ruffian of dauntless prostitution' for the task.[42] Luttrell had first set his heart on a military career but the rumours of his private life suggest that he fitted the second description better than the first. In his maiden parliamentary speech he attacked Wilkes and, after guarantees that he would win no matter the result, he offered to stand. Nonetheless it was a dangerous business and before the election it was said that gamblers took bets on whether Luttrell would survive. He was hissed at the theatre and 'did not dare appear in the streets or scarce quit his lodgings'.[43] The vote was taken on 13 April and Wilkes outstripped Luttrell by 1,143 to 296; yet the Commons voted that Luttrell should take up the seat. The episode split the city between those who wanted to maintain the status quo and those who felt that Parliament needed change.

Wilkes was an unlikely champion of liberty; he was a poor orator but wrote with a wicked pen that often got him into trouble. He had a squint and claimed that it took twenty minutes of talk before the impediment disappeared in the interlocutor's eyes. Often his fights had their origins in self-protection, getting himself out of the hot water into which he had inadvertently plunged himself, but he had an uncanny ability to make them sound like issues of universal liberty. He fought for the freedom of the press when his own journalism was seized; he argued against arbitrary arrest and for the right to privacy when he was threatened with gaol. The hiatus of the Middlesex election was soon transformed into a campaign against government control over who should or should not be elected.

National politics was slow to reflect the new economic reality of life in London: the rise of the urban bourgeoisie questioned the dominance of the landed interest, the wealth of the mercantile classes forced governments to consider Britain's relationship with the rest of the world. The Middlesex election was one of the defining moments within Georgian London, and raised the issue of parliamentary reform: the city was brought to the brink of uprising, the likes of which had not been seen for over a century. No one involved needed to be reminded that London had been the 'nursery' of the Civil Wars that had torn the nation apart. Nobody wanted to return to those dark days, but neither was it conscionable to stand in the way of liberty. How was the revolution to be conducted? Was it to be by violent leaps and fits, or could it be managed and controlled?

It is amid this turmoil that the person of Elizabeth, Countess of Home, and her creation, Home House, begin to reveal more than architectural conventions and decorative schemes. The house was not just a home, it was a political meeting hall, a salon and an exhibition space for the interests and ambitions of Elizabeth Home and her family. The design was devised as a marker of the patroness's taste as well as offering a very particular narrative that led Elizabeth Home all the way back to her birthplace, Jamaica, and her first husband's stepsister, Judith. Without heirs of her own, Elizabeth allied her interest with those of the Luttrell family.

This is made clear in Beckford's poisoned pen portrait of 1782. Despite the niceties, Beckford was a Wilkeite; his father, William Thomas Beckford, had supported Wilkes's pursuit of liberty in the 1770s as the rabble-rouser was released from gaol, and by 1774 Beckford was named Lord Mayor of London. Thus two neighbours, finding themselves living on the same square, also found that they stood on opposing sides on the key issue of the day, which had already spilt blood across the city's streets. Within Beckford's account, however, the two warring factions were able to put their animosity aside, to control their passions, regulated by the conventions of politeness, and live in liberty. Adam's carefully designed rooms had created a space that reflected the many changes within eighteenth-century London, and in which the hopes of the Enlightenment might thrive.

The Countess died in 1784. In her will the house went to her 'relation' William Gale, son of Henry Gale of St Elizabeth's, Jamaica. As he was still at school the house was rented out and in 1788, a year before the attack on the Bastille, was in use by the French Embassy. Meanwhile, the portraits of the Duke and Duchess of Cumberland were bequeathed to the city of London; however, the Duke himself vetoed this clause and took possession of the paintings. Despite the fact that the couple were never fully accepted back at court, the portraits are now in the Royal Collection.

Portman Square remained at the height of fashion up to the end of the century, associated in particular with the West Indies. In Jane Austen's *Mansfield Park* the Crawfords stay in Wimpole Street in a house once rented by Lady Lascelles, of a well-known Jamaican sugar family. Mansfield Park itself was built on sugar money as Sir Thomas

Bertram spends much of the narrative on his plantations in Antigua, a telling reflection of how the merchants of the eighteenth century became the landowners of the subsequent era. In a recent survey by the historian Nick Draper of compensation claims by former slave owners following the abolition of the Africa slave trade in 1833, Marylebone remained one of the most attractive neighbourhoods for plantation families from the West Indies.

Today, Home House is a private members' club, offering fine dining, a Zaha Hadid-designed bar, a gym and spa, conference rooms and beds for members. Private clubs are the salons of the modern age; membership is regulated and restricted, heightening the allure of belonging. Many of the original features have been carefully restored to bring Adam's genius back to life.

REGENT STREET

John Nash and the Creation of the World Capital

Augustus at Rome was for building renown'd
And of marble he left what was of brick he had found:
But is not our Nash, too, a very great master?
He finds us all brick and leaves us all plaster.

Quarterly Review

In 1776, four years after work started on Home House, Sir John Rushout, the future Lord Northwick, purchased the leases to land to the north of Bloomsbury Square, the first plots of what would become Great Russell Street, leading towards Russell Square. At that time the square, which was first developed in the 1630s, was on the northern edge of the city; beyond the grand houses on the north side, elegant gardens rolled into the surrounding countryside, giving an unimpeded view across fields to wooded Highgate and the windmill upon Hampstead Hill. In the following spring the Baronet signed contracts with a young, twenty-five-year-old south London builder, John Nash, to build two large houses on the north-east side of the square and six smaller residences along Great Russell Street. For a one-year-only peppercorn rent, Nash was tasked to develop the sites and then attempt to sell them off. Nash also signed a contract and entered into a bond that promised to complete the project by September 1778.

Nash was as much a businessman as he was an architect, the progeny of both Dr Nicholas Barbon, the speculator, and Sir Christopher Wren. Throughout his life he was driven by the desire for profit and seemed to stumble across taste by accident. He once described himself as looking like a monkey, and it is said he kept his Cockney accent until the grave; he had a weakness for luxury and money, and a passion for the grand gesture. In many ways, therefore, he was perfect for his time.

Nash was born in 1752 in Lambeth, south of the Thames. His father had originally come from Wales and was a successful 'engineer and millwright' in one of the many factories that huddled along the southern riverbank. On his mother's side, he was connected to the Edwards family, also hailing from Wales but now in Lambeth working as engineers, and said to be 'for several generations greatly distinguished for their genius and knowledge'.[1] The boy was one of a large family as fifteen Nash children made it to the font at St Mary, Newington. Unfortunately, his father died when John was only seven years old; however, the family 'was possessed of some private fortune'[2] and was able to survive. At the age of fourteen John was then apprenticed to the society sculptor Robert Taylor in Spring Gardens, Westminster. At some point the sculptor turned his hand to architecture and became a fashionable name to reckon with, commissioned to work on some of the more *à la mode* houses in the city as well as revamp the Bank of England and elegant lawyers' chambers, the Stone Buildings, at Lincoln's Inn Fields.

Taylor was a dedicated master who woke at three or four every morning to begin work, and went to bed at nine; he expected his apprentices to be at their draughtsman's desk by five in the morning. One would hope that the eager apprentice Nash, who would later become one of the most famous architects in London's history, might have learnt some of his master's lessons in professionalism, but the opposite was true – Nash was a 'wild, irregular fellow',[3] with an eye for the comforts and outward display of fashionable life.

Nash cultivated this image of himself as a wayward youth. This was the first example of him rewriting his life story to enhance his reputation as a gentleman rather than a professional architect; in later accounts he would claim that, after leaving Taylor's office, he took his small private income and settled in Wales, where he 'led a profligate life for 9 or 10 years but with the character of a gentleman keeping the best company of Bon Vivants and Hunting with the most desperate sportsmen ... during this time Nash never read a book and followed nothing but his pleasure'. It was not until his fellow apprentice Samuel Cockerell came to visit him that he became jealous of his old friend and rekindled his passion for building. As the myth continues, it was only at supper with a Mr Vaughan, who was discussing the design for a bath with Cockerell, that Nash declared he'd 'be damn'd if I do not get before this fellow yet' and offered his own plans for free. Mr Vaughan was so impressed that, as Nash was leaving, he hid a 'rouleau of guineas' in the architect's portmanteau in gratitude.[4]

This false memory offered an idealised version of Nash's rise to fame, obliterating an unfortunate chapter from the autobiography. In fact, he never left London after finishing his apprenticeship and instead, on leaving the Taylor office in 1776, married Jane Elizabeth Kerr, daughter of a Surrey surgeon, who quickly revealed herself to be a woman of expensive tastes. They had a son the following year, who was baptised but not heard of thereafter. That spring, Nash signed contracts for the two plots on Bloomsbury Square and six houses on Great Russell Street, but soon both the marriage and the housing scheme became projects that Nash would prefer to dissemble.

Within a year all eight houses were built and to the highest degree of finish. The large houses on the square pronounced a modern voice, unafraid of making a bold statement; Nash had obviously not completely wasted his time with Taylor. The first floor of No. 17 (today the German Historical Institute) rose as a series of rusticated arches upon which rested eight Corinthian pilasters supporting an entablature; the face was unadorned but it was obvious that this was a building that demanded attention. The whole exterior was then stuccoed, a layer of plaster coating the brickwork of the exterior to give the impression of stone-work. Stucco was cheap, a quarter of the price of stone, but gave a house a finished, even sheen that hid the rough brickwork underneath.

The plaster was probably bought from the firm of Robert Adam, who were developing a new-patented cement, and was one of the first complete cosmetic treatments for a London house. The design thus contained all the flash and personality that would be evident in Nash's later projects; yet in 1778, it was not working for him and Nash could not find a buyer. That year he moved into one of the houses on Great

Russell Street while the other lay unoccupied. He was soon unable to pay his bills to the Adam brothers, which now stood at £688, although he gave a good impression of being 'a solvent man'.[5] The six smaller houses were not taken up until 1781 when Nash moved out. One of the houses remained empty until 1783; the other did not find an owner until the new century.

It was a financial disaster, and there was worse to come. The expensive tastes of Jane Elizabeth drew her husband even further towards the edge, accumulating milliners' bills of over £300. Nash sent her to the countryside 'to work a reformation in her',[6] but there she soon attracted the attentions of a clerk in the local coal yard called Charles Charles. The ensuing divorce offered little succour and in September 1783 Nash was declared bankrupt. He left London and made his way to Carmarthen; it was perhaps here that he gained his first work from John Vaughan. In time he joined the studio of Samuel Simon Saxon and hoped to rebuild his life and his career. He did not work in London for over a decade and it would not be until the next century that he made his mark in the capital.

When Nash returned in 1798, he found a city that had ballooned beyond measure. In 1756 a new road was cut into countryside to cope with the flow of traffic from Hyde Park to the city walls. Until this time all the livestock herded from the south-west had travelled into the metropolis on their way to the abattoirs of Smithfield and Leadenhall; along the fashionable thoroughfares of Piccadilly or Oxford Street the flow of traffic as well as the noisome trouble was intolerable. At its conception the road stood beyond the fringes of the built city but by the dawn of the new century the New Street marked the outer limits of the capital, and already some builders were speculating on the pastureland to the north.

To the south, the new Bedford estate was growing – despite Nash's failures in Bloomsbury Square – to include Russell Square and Tavistock Square as an aristocratic enclave for the well-to-do. To the west, the Adam brothers had transformed the estate of the Duke of Portland on Portland Place while its neighbour, the Harley estate, which included

Portman Square, had now been completed, with Harley Street linking Cavendish Square to the New Street. In the countryside to the west, the exclusive new community of Tyburnia – present-day Paddington and Hyde Park – was beginning to emerge. There were less successful projects too such as Somers Town, shoddily developed by Lord Somers in the 1790s, but even this found a ready market as a refuge for the French community escaping from the Revolution.

In its rapacious growth, the city was caught at a point between the past and the future. The old ways were receding and being replaced by the new urban arts of living. This was made particularly clear in the last few moments of confusion when London's identity seemed unhinged. In 1807 the Berkeley Hounds were removed from Charing Cross, now in the heart of the West End, and sent to the country; there was to be no more hunting in London. However, the boundary between country pursuits and urban culture continued to be tested. As a young man, Grantley F. Berkeley had a reputation as one of the most rapacious sportsmen of his generation. He had been taught to box by Lord Byron's pugilist, John Johnson, and as a huntsman his appetite was insatiable; on a number of occasions his passions blurred the divisions between the city and the countryside.

On one ride, Lord Alvanley drove the stag towards Brentford but had to halt for, after a race through an asparagus field, the beast fell into the Thames. On another day, the animal was chased into Lady Mary Hussey's drawing room in the village of Hillingdon. During a later hunt, the stag made it into the city itself; chased from Harrow, the beast, 'covered with foam and stained with blood, and followed by two couples of hounds', was pursued as far as Marylebone Park. It then passed across the New Street, and continued its panicked escape until it reached Russell Square. Outside No. 1 Montague Street, the animal was seemingly trapped and 'was obliged to stop and turn to bay, backing his haunches against the street door of No. 1; and looking wildly over into the area, into which I could see he had a mind to jump'.[7]

At that moment, two young girls peered out from the window of the dining room above the brouhaha. Berkeley requested that the ladies open the door so that he could capture the stag safely, but before they could answer, another face appeared at the window who took the hunter for a travelling showman with a performing animal and threatened to call the beadle. Finally the aristocrat secured the stag with the help of some butcher boys and a metal tray.

Amid this confusion, Regency London is often dismissed as a time of extremes and paradoxes – a last blast of mischief and pleasure-making before the disapproving matrons of Victorian propriety put an end to the good times. It was a time drunk with consumption, the lifestyles of the rich and famous, the first flashes of celebrity culture. Everything was for sale, and everything had a price. But it was more than that – it was, in the words of one social historian, 'radically untamed',[8] unhinged in its transformation; as the radical conservative Edmund Burke mourned: 'the age of chivalry is gone. That of sophisters, economists, and calculators, has succeeded.'[9] The first decades of the nineteenth century saw London transformed from Jane Austen's metropolis to Dickens's brutal labyrinth, and in time the city would be described simply as the world in microcosm. London was rich beyond compare, and spent the next century not just as the fulcrum of the national economy but as the still centre of the global market.

In previous decades, there had been calls for change. The gulf between high society and the low desperation of the poor ensured that this was a time of hypocrisy and insecurity. Wilkes's cries for reform, which had been such a bone of contention between the Countess of Home and William Beckford in the 1780s, only grew louder. The distant thunder of the American War of Independence in the 1770s and the shadow of the guillotine on the Place de la Concorde gave inspiration to those who wanted change and fortified resolve in those who did not. In 1797, the crew of HMS *Sandwich* mutinied at Nore, at the mouth of the Thames. The action cut London off from all seaborne trade and filled the city with fear of French sedition swamping the Navy. In the end the revolutionary fervour of the rebel leader, Robert Parker, was too much even for his fellows and when he commanded that the captured ships be towed to France, he lost his support. He was swiftly hanged from the yardarm and twenty-nine of his crew were transported to Australia. It was as close as the city came to revolution, only averted by a whisker.

The unrest continued into the new century: in 1800 shots were fired into the royal box at Drury Lane, and a madman, Hadfield, was wrestled to the floor. In 1810 the streets were again filled with the mob, causing the militia to be mustered in the Tower, while artillery was set up in St James's Park, cannon in Berkeley Square and 'all the troops within a hundred miles radius of London were ordered to march on the Metropolis'. In 1812 the Prime Minister, Spencer Perceval, was assassinated in the lobby of the House of Commons. It was initially feared that the murder was the start of a revolution; however, it was soon revealed that John Bellingham was working alone and driven by a personal vendetta against the government. He was later hanged after he refused to enter a plea of insanity.

As well as political and social upheaval, it was a time of war that was felt in the centre of the city. Since the revolution in France in 1789 there had been fears that insurrection might cross the Channel. In 1803 Britain went to battle against Napoleon Bonaparte in a conflict that would continue until 1815. There were bread riots in 1800 as the price of wheat tripled, soup kitchens were established around the city and each family was restricted to one loaf a week. In 1804, Britain stood alone against the might of Napoleon, who had gathered his forces along the French coast in readiness for invasion. It was only the bravery of the British Navy and the swaggering heroism of Admiral Horatio Nelson that saved the nation. In 1805 at Trafalgar, the Admiral cut through the French and Spanish fleets and secured the English dominance of the seas. Yet by 1812 Britain had been at war for nearly a decade with no foreseeable victory, and the hostilities had bled the city dry.

It was the demands of the royal purse, however, that had the greatest impact on the shape of Regency London, and this came about by a sequence of coincidences. In 1811 George, Prince of Wales was named Regent, in response to George III's latest descent into what appeared to be insanity (later diagnosed as porphyria). The Prince Regent was a man of voracious appetites, and not a little taste. He had, however, so far engaged his intellect only rarely in politics and had focused on finding new ways to spend money and chase skirt. For a man who was in constant need of cash, his casual treatment of it was all too telling, for when he died 500 daybooks were found 'of different dates, and in every one of them money' amounting to over £1,000.[10] This was in an age when the average labourer earned £20 a year. He left debts of over £550,000.

George III had done a deal with Parliament that changed the way the Crown was funded. Previously, the revenue from Crown lands, customs and excise and other properties had covered all royal expenses; however, since the Glorious Revolution the Crown was increasingly reliant on taxes granted by Parliament to survive. Parliament, for its part, ensured that the Crown had enough, but avoided excess in order to protect its own interests. In 1760 George III exchanged the complete income from his Crown lands for a civil list paid by Parliament. Suddenly, it was to the nation's benefit that, first, someone actually establish the extent of the Crown property and, second, these estates be run properly. In 1786, a commission was set up to discern the facts, overseen by a Department of Woods and Forests.

One of the first sites that the commission explored was Marylebone Park, which stood beyond the New Street on the northern fringes of the city. Like many of the other parks in London – Hyde Park, Kensington Gardens, St James's – Marylebone Park was royal land once preserved for the regal pursuit of hunting; by the Georgian era, they were public spaces and popular recreation grounds. Marylebone was the last park to remain working farmland as the pasture was controlled by two leases – one was to expire in 1803, the other, owned by the Duke of Portland, in 1811. In preparation, the commission spent the 1790s in discussion over what to do with the land. It was fortuitous that they were led by the far-sighted John Fordyce, who hoped to create something extraordinary on the site that would transform London.

Fordyce had seen how fortunes had already been made from the estates to the south belonging to the Portlands, Grosvenors and Harleys and he had ambitions of his own to exploit the potential of the land. He deflected a scheme to develop some of it and in 1793 suggested a map be drawn of the park and given to 'every architect of eminence in London ... [and] a considerable reward ... be given to the person who should produce such a plan ... as, having been laide before His Majesty and

Your Lordships, should be adopted.'[11] £1,000 was a considerable prize by anyone's standards, yet in response only three plans were produced, and they all came from the same man: John White, the surveyor for the Portlands. On paper he devised a scheme to blend the northern reaches of the Duke's estate into the parkland with an elegant crescent, looping around a monumental church that would have been a dramatic sight at the northern end of Robert Adam's Portland Place. The plans were a stylish attempt to ensure the Duke's interests in the park remained in play, but were not enough to win the prize.

In 1809, Fordyce once again wrote a report to the commission on the potential profits to be made from the park, and stressed that building could commence in two years. In addition he reiterated the golden rule of property speculation: 'distance is best computed by time; and if means could be found to lessen the time of going from Marylebone to the House of Parliament, the value of the ground would be thereby proportionately increased'.[12] In other words, location, location, location. Fordyce was not just envisioning the redevelopment of the park on the outskirts of London but rethinking the shape of the whole city, developing a road that linked the park to the heart of the capital. This report heralded the greatest alteration of London since the rebuilding of the metropolis after the Great Fire by Sir Christopher Wren; unfortunately, the author died two months after publication.

John Nash had learnt a number of lessons in his absence from the city, and by his return in 1798 was a very different architect to the slapdash speculator of Bloomsbury Square. In Carmarthen he started from the bottom again, launching himself as a contractor and supplier of building materials until the commission for John Vaughan's cold bath established Nash's name amongst the local gentry. Soon he was turning his hand to a number of different jobs and styles. He was aided by two gifted draughtsmen – the French émigré Auguste Charles Pugin, later famed for his books of Gothic illustrations, and John Adey Repton, son of the landscape gardener Humphry Repton. Together they worked on a variety of designs for Carmarthen gaol, a number of houses in the town as well as a new front for St David's Cathedral in Pembrokeshire. Here

15. The bust of John Nash
outside All Souls,
Langham Place

he learnt to be flexible and work in both the Gothic and the classical. Nonetheless some of the speculator of old remained; at least one client whispered that his estimates should never be trusted and if possible the patron should 'get some other person to execute his designs'.[13]

Nevertheless, Nash's name was soon being passed amongst the local cognoscenti as an improver of great talent. Most importantly, in 1794 Sir Uvedale Price hired Nash to complete plans for a house at Foxley, situated between the sea and the mountains near Aberystwyth. In a letter, Price set out his requirements: 'I told him however that I must have not only some of the windows but some of the rooms turned to particular points, & that he must arrange it in his best manner: I explained to him the reasons why I built it so close to the rock, showed him the effect of the broken foreground and its varied lines.' Nash would admit that he had 'never thought of it before in the most distant degree',[14] but Price was giving the architect a crash course in the Picturesque.

The Picturesque was a uniquely English reaction to Jean-Jacques Rousseau's sentimental philosophy of Nature. While the eighteenth-century Enlightenment had been obsessed with the cultivation of taste –

a universal rule of beauty and acceptability – the new sensibility encouraged the exploration of individual passions and the imagination. Sir Uvedale Price was fascinated by this subject and had already published a pamphlet, *Essay on the Picturesque: As compared with the Sublime and the Beautiful* (1794), placing the Picturesque as a new aesthetic, somewhere between the awesome sublimity of unregulated Nature and restrained and manicured beauty; it was a stage-managed wilderness. At Foxley, this found its expression in the relationship between the building and the landscape; Price was in no doubt that the architect should 'accommodate his building to the scenery, and not make that give way to the building'.[15]

Following his work at Foxley, Nash established a partnership with Humphry Repton and together they created some of the most emblematic country house landscapes of the era at Corsham Court, Wiltshire and Luscombe, Devon. They also gained a reputation for new suburban projects: villas set within small estates for the newly wealthy on the outskirts of London. At the start of the nineteenth century it was this comparatively modest domestic architecture – built for the city's nouveaux riches, set in an artificially naturalised space between the countryside and the city – that reflected the current aspirations of the capital.

Finally Nash returned to London and set up an office in Dover Street, north of Piccadilly, once again giving off the impression of being a man of repute and taste. It was a house more suited to a flamboyant dandy than a jobbing architect, and it was from here that he launched himself upon the capital. One of the more fortunate relationships Nash struck up in London was with the Prince Regent himself, despite the unusual origins of the friendship: in at least one ballad it was claimed that Nash's second wife was a former royal mistress. It is unclear when they first met, but probably by 1798 Nash had designed a conservatory for the Prince in Brighton, although this was never built. He soon became the favourite architect for a number of the Carlton House set, the Regent's court based south of Piccadilly close to the clubs and shopping arcades of Pall Mall. Nash was unquestionably 'in great favour with the Prince',[16] and one of the hobbies they shared was architecture; so when Nash questioned whether he should go into politics, the Regent made it clear 'he was not ... to be diverted from architecture'.[17]

In 1806 Nash was offered a job in the Department of Woods and Forests as one of two architects, with the 'hideous joint salary of 200 pounds a year',[18] and three years later was tasked with coming up with new plans for Marylebone Park. It is hard to think of a more felicitous sequence of opportunities that, in thirty years, allowed a failed specu-lator to become the man responsible for the greatest project of town planning in London's history. Perhaps the truth was that there was no one else; for, as some critics have argued, Nash's work on Regent's Park and Regent Street was the plan not of an architect but an opportunist of genius.

Nash produced his report for the department in July 1811. The plans promised everything at an unbelievable price; only a man with a reckless regard for figures could make such estimates: on an investment of £12,115 he claimed that the scheme could expect an annual income of £59,429 and a capital valuation of £187,724. His description of the transformation of the park, however, was almost convincing:

> Mary-le-bone Park shall be made to contribute to the healthfulness, beauty, and advantage, of that quarter of the Metropolis: that the houses and Buildings be erected shall be of that useful description, and per-manent construction, and shall possess such local advantages as shall be likely to assure a great augmentation of Revenue to the Crown ... that the attraction of open Space, free air and scenery of Nature, with the means and invitation of exercise on horseback, on foot and in carriages, shall be preserved or created in Mary le Bone Park, as allurements or motives for the wealthy parts of the public to establish themselves there.[19]

It sounded enticing but it was not the description of a picturesque setting on the outskirts of the huddled capital. On the drawn plans, Nash had allowed for the city to encroach into the parkland. At the centre of the pasture was a large circus of houses; there were two further crescents to the north, while around the edges of the park grand terraces of housing were developed, supplied by amenities delivered by water from the planned Regent's Canal that skirted the north of the project.

Here also Nash placed a barracks and artillery ground. Nash convinced the commissioners but not the government: the Prime Minister, Perceval, summoned Nash to Downing Street and ordered him to draw up a new scheme with 'fewer Buildings and a greater extent of open ground'. There was also a fear that the park, which many considered a public space, would be cut off from the rest of the city, 'trenching on the comfort of the poor for the accommodation of the Rich'.[20]

Nash went back to his drawing board and produced a new plan, published in summer 1812. In this overview the barracks had been banished from the designs, the Regent's Canal now curled around the boundary of the park, while the terraces and crescents of housing had been reduced and pushed to the edges; the central double circus was now no more than a scattering of villas, hidden in their own landscapes. The central road that cut across the parkland was replaced by a circular perimeter track. Nash had taken all the lessons of the Picturesque and introduced them into an urban setting, as he explained in a letter he wrote in defence of his radical new gestures: 'The planting of sites of villas is only for the scenery of the park and to screen the villas from each other, the leading object being that of presenting from without one park compleat in unity of character and not an assemblage of villas and shrubberies like Hampstead, Highgate, Clapham Common and other purlieus of the Town.' Yet he was keen to emphasise that these villas in their park settings 'should be considered as Town residences not country houses'.[21]

The design was ready, but there was to be no building for four more years; first the ground had to be made ready. By 1816 the road, fences and individual plots had been prepared. The ornamental lake had been excavated and 14,500 trees planted. Near to where the terraces were meant to rise up, more formal beds were laid. Nash had already spent over £53,000 and yet not a stone was in place. Beyond the park, London was still in the anxious grip of the endgame of the war in Europe, leading up to the Battle of Waterloo in June 1815; as a result the Exchequer, desperately trying to entice investment on government bonds, had few resources to speculate on building projects.

The only place where any progress had occurred was at the Royal

Circus where Portland Place met the park. Here Mr Charles Mayor, who claimed some experience of building in Bloomsbury but in fact had made his fortune 'buying deals, bricks, and other building materials',[22] had taken the lease to build the whole range of houses with a surety of £20,000. It was meant to be the most elegant advertisement for Nash's schemes but within a year Mayor was haemorrhaging money; in 1814 he asked Nash to arrange a government loan, the following year he was declared bankrupt. For the next four years the broken-toothed beginnings of the circus were the punchline to a very expensive joke.

As the criticism and blame game over Mayor's debts spiralled, Nash also lost the chance to place an elegant new church at the centre of his circus, a visually exciting summation of the route before entering the wilderness of the park. Instead, the circus was reduced in scale to a mere crescent that culminated in an ornamental garden and a rather anticlimactic statue of the Regent's brother, the portly Prince Edward, Duke of Kent. Work on the crescent only started again in 1818 when the philanthropist John Farquhar guaranteed to insure the construction and Nash was able to sell the new leases to three builders: Richardson, Baxter and Peto who completed the reduced project to Nash's designs.

Matters were going badly for the Regent's Canal waterway project as well. Digging had started in 1812 to connect the Grand Junction Canal at Paddington with the docks in the East End of the city at Limehouse. It soon stumbled into a catalogue of calamities due to poor planning, over-ambition and lack of experience. Inevitably, it also fell on the rocky ground of economy when in 1816 Nash asked the original subscribers to double their investment; when that did not deliver, he gathered invitations to pitch to a number of banks; when they offered prohibitive terms, he then launched a tontine, a lottery. In desperation he also laid out his own money to secure the leases for the wharves. By 1820, however, the canal was completed and opened with a gala celebration as barges coasted down the waterway to London Bridge, where a dinner was served at the City of London Tavern, and Nash – as architect and chief shareholder – took the seat at the head of the table. Occasions such as this were rare, and they would only get rarer as the project continued.

Nash's Marylebone Park was designed to provide a rural idyll for the rich, an artificial vision of Nature at the edge of London. In his original plans he had densely packed housing around the double circus and along the edges of the park; he also planned a pavilion, a *guinguette*, for the Regent. The royal imprimatur upon the new park should have guaranteed a rush to claim plots and houses. However, in the report of 1819, updating the commission on the slow pace of progress, Nash admitted that none of the original enquiries had borne fruit – Charles Mayor's failures at the Royal Circus had warned off speculators – that only two villas had been built and that plans for the terraces were still a long way off. Nash was therefore forced to assume the role of developer himself.

James Burton purchased the first villa within the inner circle, The Holme. Burton was a speculator himself, having made a fortune developing Brunswick Square in Bloomsbury; but that was not all. As an indication of how London was growing in this period it has been calculated that between 1785 and 1823, Burton built over 1,500 houses, with an estimated value of £1,848,900; he became one of Nash's closest, if not easiest, collaborators. Burton commissioned his own youngest son, Decimus, as architect. The boy had benefited from his father's rise in the world and was educated as a gentleman: he attended lectures at the Royal Academy and was influenced by John Soane's ground-breaking lessons in architecture, but he did not gain his articles, which would have qualified him for the profession. As a result he was a learned amateur in a time of increasing professionalism and the commission to design The Holme was his father's way of ensuring his son had a calling card within the city. The villa was an academic, if rather characterless, study in the fashionable Greek Revival style.

Nearby, work was also under way on St John's Lodge, built for Charles Augustus Tulk, a rather obscure parliamentarian and occultist. The villa itself proves that Nash was willing to work with anyone if the price was right. The architect was the undistinguished John Raffield, who may at some time have worked with Robert Adam.

Work did not start on the outlying terraces until the 1820s, coinciding with the first wave of a building boom that was engulfing the city, five years after the victory at Waterloo. There was now money for investment, and hope returned to Marylebone Park. James and Decimus Burton became major investors, as well as the lesser known William Mountford Nurse, Richard Mott, William Smith and John Mackrell Aitkens. Although the whole scheme was under the control of the Crown Estate, the actual design and building of each terrace was a speculative operation that demanded huge amounts of ready capital, borrowed at good rates from the banks. Having learnt his lesson with Mayor, Nash demanded that each speculator also make a hefty deposit upfront: Aitkens was pressed for £10,000 before he was allowed to build.

Nash commanded his team of architects to come up with a variety of designs to offer visual fascination; while he was in control of how the buildings looked on the outside, the builder could decide on the interior scheme of rooms. This allowed for variety but often created a disparity between the extravagance of the exterior and rather less than generous spaces inside. Like many of Nash's schemes, the terraces offered more from the outside than they actually delivered. Cornwall Terrace was the first to come, in 1820; over the next three years York Terrace to the south, and Sussex Terrace, Clarence Terrace, Park Square and Hanover Terrace towards the west, were completed. Finally, the grandest structures on the east side of the park – Cumberland and Chester Terraces – were finished by the end of the decade. This was a massive undertaking: 1,233 building sites in total, the majority of which were in the hands of eleven major stockholders.

Cumberland Terrace, a massive range of assorted buildings, triumphal arches and blocks that incorporates thirty-two houses, was placed in the hands of William Mountford Nurse. It was originally designed to stand opposite the Regent's *guinguette*, but by 1821 the Prince had become King and once again changed his mind on how his glory should be transformed into architecture, and where. The terrace is unique, an amalgam of conventions and ideas jumbled into an exuberant whole. The facade was designed by Nash, who was never one for subtlety and had no interest in architectural purity: instead he appropriated the front of Somerset House and mixed it with hints of Louis XIV's hunting lodge at Versailles, with a portico that was at least a nod towards the Athenian Acropolis. As Sir John Summerson curtly pointed out: 'it is a Greek order and by all the rules of taste and scholarship Antae should have been introduced as responds. It is doubtful whether Nash knew precisely what anta was.'[23] Once again the whole was slathered with shining stucco that glistened creamily in the suburban sun, disguising the fact that this most resplendent building was nothing more than bog-standard brick.

As James Elmes later pointed out in *Metropolitan Improvements*, the villa was neither a royal palace nor a manor for a nobleman but a retreat for a wealthy man. This was a palace for the bourgeoisie that only proved who was the real power within the new city. However, despite being only the second terrace to be ready for the public, the houses were difficult to shift. In 1828 one solitary name appeared on the rates book, the original leaseholder, Mountford Nurse. It was another eight years before all the houses were taken.

By 1826, Nash had decided that no more new terraces or villas were needed within the park. He was already in danger of losing everything as he was forced to buy up leases on properties that remained empty in order to keep the prices high. At the same time, he had already started work on building the new street that extended from the southern edge of the park into the heart of the city and would, in the end, change the whole shape of the metropolis. Regent Street would bring the Picturesque out of the park setting and into the very centre of London itself.

While work progressed on Cumberland Terrace, Decimus Burton built a Greek temple, the Coliseum, nearby. The building was created to house an entertainment for all the visitors who walked in the park as a respite from the chaos of the city. Entering via the portico, the viewers found themselves under a broad cupola; then, taking a hydraulic lift using the latest steam technology, they were raised to the viewing platform at the centre of the room. There they were transported from the picturesque delights of the park to the top of St Paul's Cathedral in the heart of the industrious city. Painted by E. T. Parris, this panoramic perspective was a wonder to behold, as reported in *Mechanic's Magazine* in 1829: 'the drawing is executed with such a degree of precision ... the most exact geometrical results have been obtained throughout the picture, and to such an extent has this accuracy been carried, that the most minute object to which the range of the view extends may be discerned by the naked eye ... the spectator finds it difficult ... to believe that his eyes are fixed on a plain surface'.[24]

As London was growing, the city was becoming harder to comprehend as a single entity and by 1800 the population was close to a million. For William Wordsworth it was impossible to hear one's own voice amongst the tumult:

> Thou endless stream of men and moving things!
> Thy everyday appearance, as it strikes –
> With wonder heightened, or sublimed by awe –
> Of strangers, of all ages; the quick dance
> Of colours, lights, and forms; the deafening din;
> The comers and the goers face to face;
> Face after face; the string of dazzling wares
> Shop after shop ... [25]

It seemed as if climbing high above the city was the only way to escape the hustle and to look down on the unfathomable bustle below. The Coliseum revealed another truth about the city, for the scene from the viewers' platform was often called the Grand Tour for the middle classes. Unlike the aristocrat's sojourn amongst the temples and ruins of the ancient world, the new Englishman did not need to go abroad – he could have the world come to him. London was the entirety and the pinnacle of civilisation.

Yet thus far the capital had no new monuments to compete with the vainglorious urban replanning of Napoleon's Paris. The French Emperor had raided the treasure houses of Europe and brought the booty back to Paris, new temples were being erected to celebrate his victories; yet his imperial might was not restricted to elegant arches but extended throughout the city. The rue de Rivoli, named after Bonaparte's first victory, created a ceremonial thoroughfare that ran from the Hôtel de Ville to the Place de la Concorde. Although many would concur that 'while Paris is the city of Kings, London is the city of the People', the Prince Regent was determined to build something in his name that would 'quite eclipse Napoleon'.[26] As James Elmes later claimed:

> Augustus made it one of his proudest boasts, that he found Rome of Brick, and left it of marble. The reign and regency of George IV have scarcely done less, for the vast and increasing Metropolis of the British Empire: by increasing its magnificence and its comforts; by forming healthy streets and elegant buildings, instead of pestilential alleys and squalid hovels; by substituting rich and varied architecture and park like scenery, for paltry cabins and monotonous cowlairs ... that bid fair to render London, the Rome of modern history.[27]

Unlike the open pastureland of Marylebone Park, as Nash drafted designs for his Regent Street he was looking at a map of densely built streets and squares, some of the most expensive real estate in London. As set out in the New Street Act of 1813, he searched for a route that linked the new park with St James's and Westminster beyond. The Act itself was a confusing document, containing eighty-seven clauses, but not one of them defined the exact line of the street. As ever, the MPs felt safer poring over balance sheets than architectural projections, and here Nash the developer was able to dazzle them with figures – profit forecasts, estimates of compensation, costs for sewers – that immediately turned out to be fanciful.

In his first three new street plans Nash estimated that 1,280 of the total 1,700 yards to be reclaimed were Crown property and the rest were 'of the meanest description'; this was a long way off the truth. From the park southwards the road took in Portland Place, the jewel in the crown of the Portland estate. Beyond the crossing with Oxford Street, the plans also infringed on Hanover Square, belonging to Lord Scarbrough. Finally the road led to Piccadilly and south across Pall Mall and the St James's estate towards the Regent's palace at Carlton Terrace. Nash was dealing with some of the biggest landowners in England.

The road was not only planned as the great boulevard of the city;

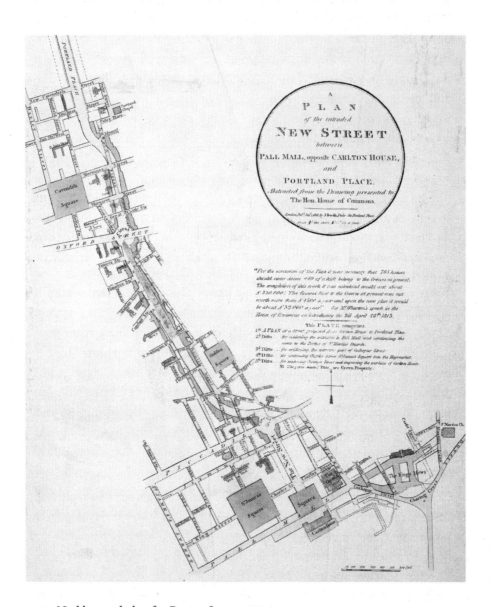

16. Nash's grand plan for Regent Street (*Bridgeman*)

it was also intended as a barrier between the grand enclaves of the
West End and the poor estates to the east. It seemed as if there was a
natural ravine between the declining seventeenth-century development
of Soho – small routes tightly packed with decayed housing that was
now home to craftsmen, small-time traders and French immigrants –
and the grand projects to the west where aristocrats and the new
wealthy conjured up their polite world. The politics of access and
social control was made plain in the street map of 1812; for between
Piccadilly and Oxford Street, while there were a number of main
streets – Hanover Street, Conduit Street, Burlington Street – that
filtered westwards from Regent Street to supply the great estates, the
street was almost impossible to reach from the east, and instead Nash
designed parallel alleys for the hoi polloi: 'thus ... carts and drays
can carry on their traffic by means of back streets without interfering
with the principal street'.[28]

Nash had initially hoped for a straight route between the park and
Carlton Terrace, a rue de Rivoli for the Regent; but this soon proved
impossible and in the final designs Regent Street was picturesque by
necessity, twisting and turning to create a number of vistas and optical
surprises. As is so common in London's story, the grand gesture was
compromised and replaced by something more becoming. Instead Nash
had to negotiate a winding route through the streets, finding the spaces
between commodity and expense, the great estates and cheaper reclaim-
able sites, as well as the financial means to make it happen.

Although Parliament passed an Act in 1813 for the road to begin,
Nash had to find the money elsewhere, and he was forced to found an
insurance company to shore up the project. Sir Theophilus Metcalfe
promised to forward £300,000 on behalf of the Globe Company, against
the guarantee that his new company would benefit from the premiums
of every plot on the new street. Thus work began on purchasing the
land necessary to build, as well as planning the infrastructure – drains
and sewers – to service the venture. Nash was obviously keen to place
as many as possible of the potential sites in the hands of the developers
as soon as he could. In this rush to get going and the inevitable financial
shortfall that appeared, the rise of Regent Street was, predictably, not

the ordered and methodical project envisioned but, in the words of Summerson, 'opportunist, improvisory and rapid'.[29]

The design of the street was originally intended to landscape the Regent's passage from his palace to the *guinguette* in the park, south to north, a voyage that was broken into sections, punctuated with turns, circuses, crescents and squares. At the southern end, work began in front of Carlton House, renamed Waterloo Place to commemorate the victorious battle of 1815. Here Nash planned the grandest houses on either side of Carlton House, like a British Place Vendôme, which was then gated, cutting off a broad, symmetrical open space that had once been a thriving community near to St James's Market. As work began, Nash immediately found that his financial predictions were woeful – his projected compensation package for the tradesmen and residents who clustered around the palace was embarrassingly off-target. One trader was initially offered £600, but eventually received £2,400 in court. A Colonel Stanley was removed from his house on Pall Mall and in exchange was given a brand-new residence in Foley Gardens. Lord Galloway demanded interest on the late payment of his compensation.

Waterloo Place was intended as a royal enclave within the West End for the premier members of London society; here the clubs of Pall Mall and St James's, temples of leisure, lay close to the temptations of the tailors of Jermyn Street and the luxuries of the Burlington Arcade, the first covered retail mall in London, completed in 1819. It was fortunate that James Burton swiftly entered the market in 1815, purchased a plot on the west side of Waterloo Place and built the Athenaeum Club, facing Nash's own United Services Club. The pleasures of the theatre were also close by: the Italian Opera was situated along Pall Mall opposite the United Services Club, with an elegant columned colonnade echoing Carlton House. The Haymarket Theatre was also drawn into the design and given a classical face.

Moving northwards, Waterloo Place turned into Lower Regent Street, which offered living quarters for the well-to-do. At No. 15, Charles Tufton Blicke built a mansion for himself; there was also a hotel, and a set of chambers for wealthy bachelors. On the east side, Nash built his own home and office, designed by himself as part of a large block –

more Florentine palazzo than London terrace – with a row of shops on the ground floor. One unexpected feature of the construction was that Nash shared the building with his cousin, John Edwards, and the two apartments were interconnected by a long gallery that Nash filled with replica art from Italy, worth over £3,000; the decoration was similarly eye-catching in the latest French styles.

It was in this office that Nash conducted the project, meeting the commissioners almost every day from 1815 to 1817, dealing with the rising tide of debts and complaints. The sewers were reviewed and Nash was forced to defend his work. The rich residents of Cavendish Square also began to complain that the backs of their houses were being cut off by the new street. The principal commissioner, Lord Glenbervie, was kicking up a fuss, smarting that 'the project seems to be in a deplorable way ... [and] is held in universal abhorrence except by his royal master and dupe'.[30] Glenbervie was shuffled away, but in 1816 the scheme was forced to beg Parliament for another £600,000 and go cap in hand to the Bank of England, which was still heavily bruised from the wars.

Lower Regent Street led northwards to the crossing with Piccadilly, the royal pathway abruptly coming face to face with the realities of the bustling city. Thus Nash devised a circus to cope with the mass of traffic filling the crossing from four directions. Piccadilly was one of the great streets of the city, developed in the 1660s after the return of the nobles during the Civil Wars who chose this plot of farmland on which to build their grand palaces in the French *hôtel* style. At the same time, nearby St James's Square set the template for the 'look' of modern London. The great houses of the nobles were soon replaced by terraces and squares as the aristocrats went in search of profit and the West End began in clusters of elegant housing.

Over 250 properties were demolished to make way for the new street when work began on creating Piccadilly Circus in 1819, and a price had to be negotiated for every leasehold. On the south side this included a number of inns and coaching houses from where one could get a ride to almost anywhere in the country: the White Bear inn, and the Lemon Tree on the corner of Haymarket, were both reminders of Piccadilly's status as one of the main routes west out of the city. There were also a multitude of small shops and workshops, and on each occasion the owner was given the first offer on the new plot. In many cases the landlords were willing to sell, although they could stay in the property for six months after the deal; others took advantage of the rising prices and stayed: Mr Newman, the stable owner of Swallow Street, turned his hand to building the postmaster's store at No. 121 Regent Street and made a handsome profit. Needless to say, the neighbourhood soon became a quagmire of mud, scaffolding and builders, encouraging the doomsayers in their attacks on the scheme.

Piccadilly was meant to be a dramatic turn in the traveller's voyage along the new street. Seen from Carlton House, Nash wanted it to be one of the great vistas of his new road, 'terminated by a public monument at one end ... every length of street would be terminated by a facade of beautiful architecture'.[31] He had hoped that there would be a statue of William Shakespeare at the centre of the circus and that the view northwards would rise as far as Golden Square, where a great public building, perhaps a theatre, stood facing Carlton House. No statues appeared until the 1880s when the figure of Eros was placed in memory of the philanthropist the Earl of Shaftesbury rather than the Regent. The route never reached as far as Golden Square – the cost of buying up the desirable houses of the well-to-do was to be avoided where possible – and, rather than a public monument, the County Fire Office was built, designed by J. T. Barber Beaumont, a painter more interested in insurance than architecture. As a result Piccadilly Circus has always had a whiff of gaudy magnificence, the compromising meeting place of the princes of pleasure, the bucks and dandies of the West End and the city itself.

To the north, matters were not proving any easier. The route of the new street depended on running through Portland Place. The Duke, however, guarded his own projects jealously and was not willing to let the new road ruin his golden egg without putting up a fight. From the start, the Duke had been keen to gain the contract for developing Marylebone Park and was angered when the prize went to Nash. It was further gnawing that the debacle of Park Crescent was being played out on his doorstep. Now, Nash was requesting that this most elegant thoroughfare be handed over and integrated into Regent Street.

Nash considered Portland Place the 'finest street in London',[32] and it had the advantage of being complete. At that time it was home to no lesser luminaries than the Earls of Mansfield, Sheffield and Stirling, Viscount Boyne, Lord Walsingham and the Dowager Duchess of Richmond. For this reason, the Duke was determined to ensure that house prices on his lands were not adversely affected. In the original scheme the Duke had made certain that his lands were cut off from the rest of the city to the south; there was no direct route from the place to Oxford Street and a resident had to go indirectly via Cavendish Square to the west. Instead Foley House, surrounded by a large garden, stood at the end of the long avenue, leased to Lord Foley, who had only given his permission for the Duke's project if his view northwards was preserved for ever. If the Duke was able to buy back the lease to Foley House, Regent Street could never reach the park along Nash's design.

The Duke was close to a deal when he offered Lord Foley £42,000; yet at the last minute Nash offered £70,000. In addition, the architect had a hold over Lord Foley, who had previously engaged Nash to work on his country estate and had got into some trouble: when the aristocrat borrowed £21,000 from the architect he put his London house as surety. Therefore Nash was able to settle the loan and swiftly set about demolishing the house and selling off the necessary section to the Crown for just over £10,000. It looked close to being one of the worst land deals in London's history until Nash sold off the remaining sliver of land to the Northamptonshire businessman Sir James Langham, including the clause that the new owner had to hire Nash as architect. Nash recouped much of his investment and could finally set out his proposed line for the new street.

Both the situation of Piccadilly Circus to the south and Portland Place to the north determined that the new street would never be a straight line, a rue de Rivoli connecting the many neighbourhoods of London. The southern circus was too much to the east to reach Marylebone Park, while Portland Place headed towards the grand estates of the West End. Nash was therefore compelled to create a series of monuments and twisting picturesque vistas to link the two ends of the route.

Where Portland Place meets Upper Regent Street, the route was forced to bend eastwards in order to follow the straight line of what was once Swallow Street and ran along the boundaries between Soho and the West End. Here, in the words of James Elmes, was 'the isthmus between wealth and commerce'[33] and, for some reason, the appropriate place for a church. Despite the criticism and jokes of his peers, Nash's All Souls, Langham Place, started in 1822, was a brilliant solution to the conundrum. As one looks north from Oxford Street, the building appears in the centre of the road. Broad circular steps in creamy Bath stone lead up to a rounded portico and a simple entrance. This 'pivot vestibule' then led into the main body of the church, which receded towards the east. Above, an unexpected stone spire rose into the air. In its individual parts, little about All Souls seemed to work, but as a dramatic episode on the route to Marylebone Park it was perhaps the closest Nash ever came to architectural glory.

Nash had similar problems to the south, as the road curled away from Piccadilly Circus; Nash's solution on this occasion was extravagantly different. He had already decided that he could not develop the road as far as Golden Square and create a great public space. Instead he had to devise a route that curved around the edge of the square to link up with the new Regent Street. He came up with a grand gesture: a sinuous quadrant, a quarter-slice, emerging from the circus in unbroken uniformity. The problems with building such a structure were manifold. Nash could not risk leasing out plots on the Quadrant to different developers who had their own agenda and timescales: the construction had to be done in one operation to ensure that everything fitted together. On the other hand, no one was willing to invest in the whole scheme apart from Nash himself, and once again the architect was forced to put up his own cash to guarantee his design was completed. He gained promises from the tradesmen, who hoped to profit from the new building, plus a five per cent commission. In total it cost £128,000, of which £60,000 was forwarded by Nash, but it was completed in two years, 1819–20. Nash never saw a profit on his investment.

Nevertheless, the Quadrant itself was soon considered one of the wonders of London. A high colonnade ran along both sides in a continuous arc of 145 columns, protecting the new breed of window shoppers from the rain and the terrors of the road. Above there were three more storeys of houses and apartments. Elmes considered the design to be 'worthy of a Roman Amphitheatre'.[34] The uniform skyline was broken up with a dome, while the curved frontage gave variety and a sense of the unexpected to the traveller as they turned into the street from Piccadilly Circus.

Regent Street itself, a straight line from the top of the Quadrant to All Souls, Langham Place, represented the true heart of the new city as it stumbled into the nineteenth century, a stage set for the drama of mass consumption. Like all scenery, it was less than it appeared; the buildings were stucco and not stone, painted every four years to keep up appearances. In addition the sweep of the street was less impressive than it might have been. Nash had always intended this stretch of the new street to be filled with 'shops appropriate to articles of taste and fashion',[35] but, forgetting the care he put into building, he was keen to pass over the leases to any willing developer. As he would later admit, he often overlooked the quality of design, admitting that 'if a person presents a design for the elevation of a building, and I do not see a material defect, it would be invidious of me to find fault with it'.[36] As a result the street fronts lacked any sense of unity or pattern, mixing styles, materials and features.

Nash was fortunate to sell some of the plots to James Burton, making him the second largest investor in the whole scheme. Samuel Baxter, one of the builders of the Royal Crescent, was also involved and was in charge of creating Oxford Circus, where the new street crossed Oxford Street, which already had a reputation as one of the busiest shopping routes. A number of other architects took their chances here as well: C. R. Cockerell, who had served an apprenticeship alongside Nash in the 1770s, developed Hanover Chapel on Hanover Street; the inestimable Sir John Soane – the visionary architect to Nash's pragmatist – developed one block of houses north of Beak Street for the estate agent J. Robins; Nash's assistant, and son of his old partner George Stanley Repton, handled a number of schemes; J. Carbonell, the wine merchant, also took his chances.

Where Greenwich had been the location for the theatre of royal power, the Crown lands of Regent Street were given over to the new force in the land: retail. By the beginning of the nineteenth century London had already established itself as the emporium of the world; and, despite food shortages and the financial crisis during the Napoleonic Wars, the development of the new street gave a focus to London's consumer power, as the city spent its way out of its problems. Throughout the previous century, fixed shops had replaced the more traditional markets and workshops. It soon became essential that the shops not just supply necessary goods but also attract new customers with glass fronts and intricate and attractive window displays. In 1786 Sophie von La Roche was seduced by the scenes on Oxford Street: 'behind great glass windows absolutely everything one can think of is neatly, attractively displayed, and in such abundance of choice as almost makes one greedy'.[37]

In Regent Street Nash wished to do more than just bring together all the most fashionable and desirable shops in one place; he wanted to create a location that raised the pursuit of shopping into an art, where, according to George Augustus Sala, 'between three and six o'clock every afternoon, celebrities jostle you at every step you take . . . The celebrities of wealth, nobility and the mode, do not disdain to descend from their carriages, and tread the flags like ordinary mortals'.[38] Nash succeeded almost immediately and by 1823 the rates book noted a healthy annual income of £39,000.

In 1838, the printer John Tallis saw that he could turn a profit by commissioning a map that set out the views of Regent Street from Waterloo Place to All Souls. As he noted in his puff, it was a 'noble street . . . [that] consists chiefly of palace like shops, in whose broad showy windows are displayed articles of the most splendid description, such as the neighbouring world of wealth and fashion are daily in want of . . . it should be visited on a summer's day in the afternoon, when the splendid carriages, and elegantly attired pedestrians evince the opulence and taste of our magnificent metropolis'.[39] On the map itself Tallis was careful to note the names of the major retailers. On Piccadilly Circus a number of tradesmen advertised their royal patronage, such as Ponsonby and Sons, carvers to the Queen; the demolished old coaching inns were replaced by travel agents like the Bull and Mouth Coach Office. Regent Street itself offered almost everything for sale: wine, stuffed animals, Carrara marble from Italy, coach repairs, guns, hats, sheet music, antique lace and gold. At No. 232 stood Dickins, Smith and Stevens, which later became Dickins & Jones. Nearby, overlooking Cavendish Square, William Debenham opened his first store to provide for the rich denizens.

Today Regent Street and the West End claim to be the largest retail quarter in Europe and boast over 600 shops in which, according to the London Retail Consortium, £4.5 billion is spent every year by 50 million visitors. Architecturally the street continued to develop after Nash, with a number of the leading architects of the Victorian and Edwardian era playing their part, such as Richard Norman Shaw and Sir Reginald Blomfield. The Quadrant was dismantled in the 1840s, ridiculed as a 'haunt for vice and immorality' and an inconvenience for traffic.[40] Despite the fact that every store front is now listed, renovation continues on the street. The Apple Store, still leased from the Crown Estate, now

17. Regent Street in 1900, the shopping Mecca

dominates two floors of the Venetian palazzo, Regent House, which was built to replace the Hanover Chapel in the 1890s, with lavish mosaics advertising the glories of Paris, New York, Berlin and St Petersburg.

After eight years of working on Marylebone Park and the new street, Nash's grand project was once again put in jeopardy by the whim of the Prince Regent. In 1820, the Prince finally became King and decided that Carlton House was no longer fit for his purpose; as George IV, he needed a new royal palace for his so-called glorious reign and Nash was forced to rethink the entire scheme of the West End to accommodate the caprice of his patron. By this time the architect and the King were old men: Nash was nearly in his seventies, George IV fifty-eight, no longer the flamboyant centre of London society but a painted and bloated remnant of a past era. The King could not tolerate the bustle of Waterloo Place and sought to retire to his mother's residence, Buckingham House, in nearby St James's Park. Work was to start on converting it into a palace, while Nash also had to think about how to integrate the royal residence into his West End scheme.

The original Buckingham House was built in 1703 for the Duke of Buckingham, yet in 1763 was purchased by George III for his wife, Queen Charlotte, as a royal retreat, just a few hundred yards away from the official residence at St James's Palace; it was there that fourteen of Charlotte's fifteen children were born. Surrounded by parkland, the house was anything but ideal; situated in a bowl of land, it suffered constantly from damp caused by nearby marshes in Pimlico, which was soon to be drained and developed into an exclusive new enclave. As the city continued to grow westwards, the land surrounding Buckingham House also started to be built up, consuming the parkland and restricting the vistas. There was little the King or architect could do about this, and they soon found that they had less money than they had hoped even to improve the palace itself.

George needed a new house to contain the vast collections he had gathered as Regent. There was almost nothing that he did not hoard and, despite being considered a man of exquisite taste, perhaps one of the greatest royal patrons of the arts, he was criticised for his voracious appetites. There were over 250 paintings in the attic of Carlton House, as well as voluminous clusters of French furniture rescued from the revolution, chandeliers, candelabras, porcelain and clocks that had to go into storage.

In 1819 Nash put forward a figure of £450,000 for the cost of renovating Buckingham House, but Parliament offered £150,000; by June 1825 this had risen only to £200,000. Work began and *The Times* reported: 'The centre building will ostensibly remain, but the interior of it will be entirely renovated. Two magnificent and tasteful wings, which have been projected by his Majesty himself, upon a very large scale will be added to the centre ... The workmen have already commenced their labours; the whole will be finished in 18 months.'[41] As with all London projects, it seems, this was overly hopeful, and far from the truth; in fact Buckingham Palace would prove the downfall of John Nash.

Nash had not shown Parliament his complete plans for the palace; nor, it soon appeared, had he discussed them in full with the King. As work commenced on the interiors, Nash thought he was building a pied-à-terre, a minor royal residence; yet George was so impressed with the work that he started to dream of it as the centre of his government, with the state rooms being converted into his court. In addition, George began to think of his new home as a monument to the recent national victory at Waterloo, and commanded his architect to devise a triumphal arch to compete with anything in Paris to stand in front of the house. The arcadian idyll, *rus in urbe*, was slowly transforming into another of the old Prince Regent's *folies de grandeur*.

At the same time, Nash was adapting the palace into the Regent Street scheme. The demolition of Carlton House brought Waterloo Place to the edge of St James's Park. In place of the Prince's old home, Nash designed a series of new terraces to run along the edge of the park, mirroring the designs than encircled Marylebone Park, with the hope that rents from the new terraces would subsidise the growing costs of the palace. Carlton House Terrace was a set of three long ranges that faced southwards towards the park, thirty-one bays each, with columns based on the Pantheon in Rome. Between the two main blocks, leading from Waterloo Place, Nash placed a broad set of stone stairs, topped with a tall column, modelled on Trajan's triumphal pillar, upon which stood a bronze statue of the King's brother, the Duke of York. The terrace almost instantly became one of the premier addresses in the city – and therefore one of Nash's most profitable speculations.

The grand old Duke looked out over the massive work that was transforming St James's Park itself. The landscape had originally been converted by James I for his hunting ground and speculations in silk-making; it was made more formal by Charles II in the Restoration to include ornamental lakes and flower beds. In the 1760s Capability Brown was commanded by George III to update the scenery, but it was not until the 1820s that Nash asked George Stanley Repton to convert the ground to something more picturesque, from 'a meadow with a formal dingy canal ... into a cheerful ... pleasure ground'.[42]

Carlton House Terrace had the effect of broadening out the Regent Street scheme. The new terraces that lined the widened Pall Mall hugged the north side of St James's Park from Buckingham House in the west towards Whitehall in the east. The plans now penetrated into the heart of the West End and reached as far as the outer fringes of the city; just as it seemed that his project was complete, Nash was now compelled to turn his attention to new plans. Until recently, Charing Cross had been the site of the Royal Mews, Crown stables and other utilitarian outhouses. When, in 1820, it was decided to bring all the mews to Buckingham Palace, this region of rundown and ignored buildings, sometimes known as 'porridge island', was torn down to make way for the new scheme. In 1826, Nash laid down plans for an enlarged square, but it would take another thirty years, long after the death of the King and his architect, before the open public space was fully completed. In 1835, after Nash's death, it was finally dedicated to Horatio Nelson's victory at Trafalgar, and the column in the admiral's memory was not finished until 1843.

In 1829, there were rumblings in Parliament concerning the work at Charing Cross; once again the issue revolved around Nash's weak grasp of finance. In the 1826 Charing Cross Act, £400,000 was set aside to pay for the scheme; three years later the bill stood at £851,213 0s 10d. This anger only fuelled the resentment that was now brewing over Buckingham Palace. The previous year Nash had visited the Prime Minister, the Duke of Wellington, to tell him that the King was planning to demolish the two grand wings that he had only just recently completed; the Duke was furious, replying with the blast: 'if you expect me to put my hand to any additional expense, I'll be damned if I will'.[43]

What was happening inside the palace was even more startling. Nash had never been an interior decorator but was now commissioned to furnish an endless range of state rooms, in every style imaginable. He hired the finest craftsmen to help him redesign living spaces fit for a king, and there were rarely less than 120 carpenters on site. Each room had its own theme, all created with an eye for rich detail: every pillar in the state rooms was individually painted to appear like coloured marble; a dome was created in the music room solely for the purpose of variety. In the end, while Nash could protect himself against his critics on questions of taste, he had no defence against complaints about the extravagant cost.

In 1829, things came to a head. In May Colonel Davies, an MP from Worcester with an eye to making a name for himself, grumbled about the costs of the palace and ended up accusing Nash of fraud. This was a charge that Parliament had to investigate, and a select committee was set up; the hearing would last ten days and interview twenty-five key witnesses. Nash himself was not called and was forced to follow the proceedings in the pages of *The Times*. It was claimed that he made an illegitimate profit from the Regent's Canal scheme; that he paid below the open market rate for plots of land along Regent Street; and that he was open to bribes. In the end, he was acquitted without censure but the architect felt compelled to defend himself. In a line-by-line rebuttal of Davies's charges, Nash retold the story of his extraordinary vision for London and how, on so many occasions, he risked his own fortune in order for his plans to be fulfilled.

For Nash, it was all too much. He had risen on the exquisitely cut coat-tails of the Prince Regent, but following the King's death in 1830, and with Buckingham House still a botched building site in the middle of St James's Park, his hours were numbered. The creation of the West End had drained the old man of all energy, the failures of Buckingham

Palace left him defenceless from attack, and his pursuers had been waiting a long time to exact their revenge. By 1830, London was now a more sober and serious place; Nash represented the old way of doing things, the untamed, speculative mode of the Age of Cant.

Nash was cleared, but had lost the argument. In June the King wrote to Wellington asking him to make Nash a baronet, in recognition of his services to London. Wellington refused, stating that honours were only deserved once the palace had been completed. After the King's death, the world started to collapse for his architect. He suffered a stroke aged seventy-eight but he nonetheless rallied to defend himself once more against grumbles about the burgeoning expenses at the palace. On this occasion, the Treasury were unsatisfied and on 15 September decided to suspend Nash from the board, stop work at Buckingham Palace and pay off the workmen. In the following year there was a new committee that damned Nash even further for 'inexcusable irregularity and great negligence'.[44] There was also time for a critique of the architecture, one visitor claiming that 'instead of being called Buckingham Palace, it should be the Brunswick Hotel'.[45]

In one swift movement the man who had recast the whole of the West End of London was judged not by his lifetime's achievement but by his last failure. Nash was condemned both by the public and by the select committee of MPs, and could do little else but retire to his house in the Isle of Wight, where he died, in debt, in 1835. The *Annual Register* summed up this animosity in its obituary: 'as a speculative builder, this gentleman amassed a large fortune; but as an architect, he did not achieve anything that will confer upon him lasting reputation'.[46] Yet few architects have ever had such a profound impact on London, shaping not just the physical city but also using design to engineer the everyday lives of Londoners. His deep, instinctive understanding of the Picturesque, his development of the inner city as a place of visual surprises and fascination, were the perfect representation of the complex transition between the polite Georgian century and the Victorian era.

Nash knew that London was a public space and the scenery for this social theatre was flashy and skin-deep, stucco rather than marble, flamboyant on the exterior, functional inside. In Regent Street and in laying the foundations for Trafalgar Square, the two most popular meeting places in the city were formed. By establishing these new centres, Nash not only shaped the modern city's public places but also gave the West End an identity that still holds today.

CHAPTER 8

THE HOUSES OF PARLIAMENT

Sir Charles Barry, A. W. N. Pugin
and the Rewriting of History

The echoes of its vaults are eloquent. The stones have voices and the walls do live: it is the house of memory.

C. R. Maturin

The palace was empty, the MPs and the Lords had not sat in either the chamber of the House of Lords or the Commons for nearly three weeks; yet there was much work to be done. On the afternoon of 16 October 1834, two workmen, one later accused of being a jailbird, the other an Irish papist, set about their task to clear out the Tally Office, a defunct part of the Exchequer, in order to make room for the new Court of Bankruptcy. The Clerk of Works, Richard Whibley, had originally ordered that the old lengths of stick once used as a system of accounting be gathered in the Exchequer yard and burnt. However, he changed his mind when he considered that such a bonfire might cause a stir and instead he told the two men to chuck everything into the House of Lords furnace. Work started at 7 a.m. and continued all day into the afternoon when both men, exhausted, retreated to the tavern.

The regular caretaker of the House of Lords was away that day, but her mother-in-law, Mrs Wright, was on hand and, as was usual, was making a bit of cash on the side by showing a couple of visitors, a Mr Snell and a Mr Shuter, around the chamber while the members were away. Both commented on the heat inside the main room, and later Mrs

Wright stated that she could also smell burning, but at the same time she dismissed the sweltering temperature as normal. It was not until 6 o'clock when Mrs Mullencamp, the Doorkeeper's wife, came rushing to her door that Mrs Wright started to fret and bustled out 'without bonnet and shawl'[1] to find Mr Whibley. Smoke and flames were seen coming from the back of the Lords chamber. By 7.30 the fire, fanned by a brisk south-westerly wind, was spreading towards the Commons chamber and into the warren of connected buildings and corridors that made up the complex plan of the palace. The fire brigade were finally called, but it was too late to save the Lords.

Soon a gawping crowd began to gather in front of the palace, watching the conflagration in stunned silence. As the mob grew a few amongst the throng were bold enough to shout their feelings. One old man asked whether it was possible that the recently debated Poor Law could be burnt alongside all the rest of the buildings, cursing 'worst luck to them that save it, and I wish as them that made it and them that saved it was burnt themselves'.[2] A coal heaver, a little worse for wear, tried to push

18. The fire at Westminster, 1834 (*Bridgeman*)

his way through the crowd and complained when he was halted by the
soldiers mustered in front of the scene, 'Well, then, my fine lobster, so
you really mean for to say as you won't by no manner of means let me
go and see my own property a-burning?'[3]

Was it arson? Could the inferno have been caused by some modern-
day Guy Fawkes wanting to do away with the Mother of all Parliaments
for good? Were the instigators protesting against the failure of the recent
Reform Act to widen the franchise, or was someone fearful that too
much had been given away? Surely this was no accident; even as the
buildings blazed, the fire was interpreted as a woeful reflection of the
deep divisions within the nation itself. The crowd stirred in excitement,
while others attempted to save what they could.

The Prime Minister, Lord Melbourne, co-ordinated a fleet of hackney
cabs to carry valuable books and documents that were being thrown
out of the window of the House of Commons library. Down below in
the yard, treasures were covered with tarpaulins and carpets before they
were carted off. Inside the building, there were other acts of heroism: in
the library, the Earl of Munster narrowly missed being brained by a
falling rafter when a labourer called McCallum pulled him to safety.
The team were forced to climb up to the western turret and be helped
down by the firemen. Lord Duncannon was also driven onto the roof
in his escape, refusing to come down until all his men had been rescued
safely, and 'in two minutes after he stepped from the ladder, the roof
descended to the floor'.[4]

Amongst those who watched the ancient stones crumble were the
painters John Constable and J. M. W. Turner. Turner hurried home that
morning and tried to capture his memories in watercolour. The fire was
a subject that he would return to on a number of occasions as if it were
a visual representation of violent forces of Nature and the city. Also
there, the journalist Charles Dickens noted the chaos of the gathering
with amusement as the fire station dog barked and corralled the crowd.
The architect Charles Barry was travelling back from Brighton and after
spying 'a red glare on the London side of the horizon', rushed to the
scene where, alongside the mob, he 'was absorbed in the grandeur and
terror of the sight'.[5] His son would later report that 'the thought of the

LEFT The west front of Westminster Abbey: the towers were built by Nicholas Hawksmoor in the eighteenth century. (*Bridgeman*)

BELOW The Royal Exchange today: although rebuilt twice since Gresham's time, the Golden Grasshopper still reigns above the city.

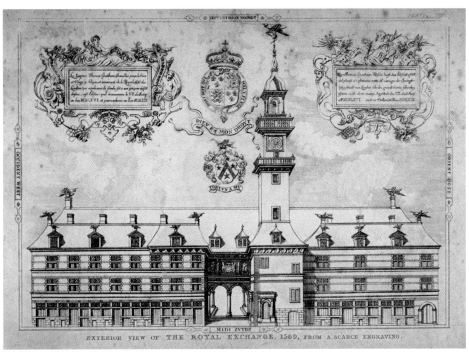

EXTERIOR VIEW OF THE ROYAL EXCHANGE, 1569, FROM A SCARCE ENGRAVING.

The exterior of Gresham's Royal Exchange, a new cathedral to capital. (*Guildhall*)

ABOVE Greenwich Hospital seen from the river, with the Queen's House as the focal point of the vista.

LEFT Inside the Great Hall, the artwork by James Thornhill shows the benevolent reign of George I enjoying the fruits of his Stuart forebears. (*Bridgeman*)

FACING PAGE

TOP Adam's plan for the interior of Home House. (*Bridgeman*)

BELOW LEFT A pattern by Anna Maria Garthwaite, the leading silk designer who lived in Spitalfields. (*Bridgeman*)

BELOW RIGHT A. W. N. Pugin's detailed design for the tiling in the new palace at Westminster, shows a rage for the Gothic. (*Bridgeman*)

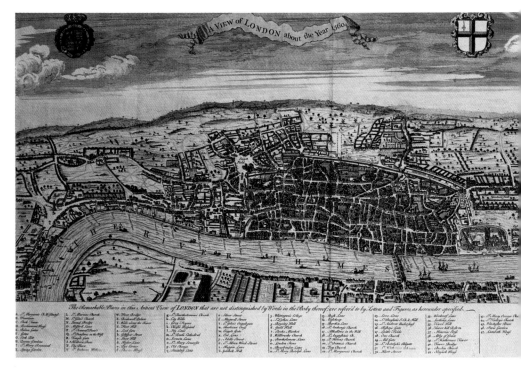

One of the first maps of London from the sixteenth century, before the growth of the suburbs that John Stow so lamented. Westminster can be seen on the left. (*Bridgeman*)

An early Victorian panorama, taken from a similar point as above, south of the river. The metropolis is now beyond calculation. (*Bridgeman*)

The apex of the Gherkin with Canary Wharf beyond.
Is this the future of the city? (*RIBA*)

John Nash's Quadrant, which allowed Regent Street to curve northwards from Piccadilly towards Oxford Circus. (*Bridgeman*)

Ancient and modern: the Houses of Parliament today. The Norman Westminster Hall is in the foreground, with Barry's Clock Tower, 'Big Ben', behind.

Inside the Victoria Embankment: roadway, sewers and subterranean railway line in one design. (*Getty*)

The towers of Wembley Stadium under construction in 1923. Completed in reinforced concrete, they were inspired by Lutyen's Palace in New Delhi, transplanted into a north London suburb. (*Getty*)

Keeling House today, seen alongside a traditional Bethnal Green street. (*RIBA*)

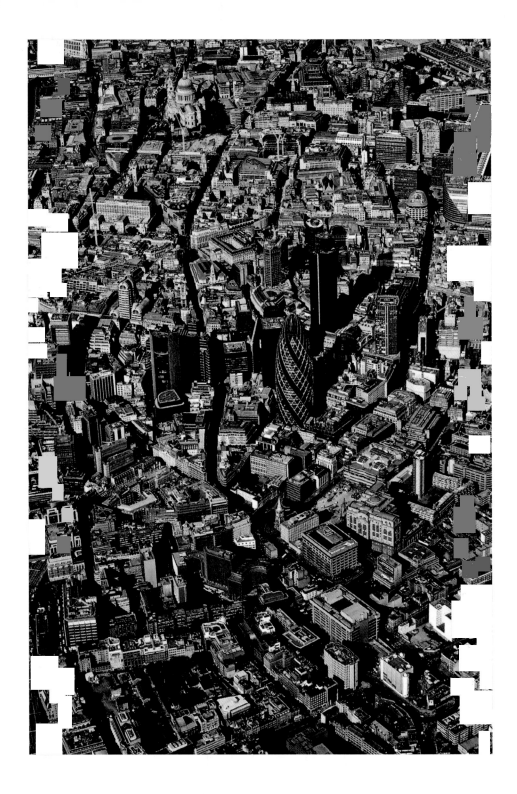

The contemporary skyline: the city of transformation. Many of these streets were first built by the Romans two thousand years ago. (*Getty*)

great opportunity, and the conception of designs for the future, mingled in Mr Barry's mind, as in the minds of many other spectators'.[6]

Also in the crowd was the designer Auguste W. N. Pugin, who had started the evening at his family house in Bloomsbury. His comments were more pointed, but in front of the flames he also dreamt of what would rise out of the ashes: 'I was fortunate enough to witness it from almost the beginning till the termination of all danger as the hall had been saved which is to me almost miraculous as it was surrounded by fire.' He was less complimentary of the modern additions: 'there is nothing much to regret ... turrets were smoking like so many manufacturing chiminies while the heat shivered them into a thousand pieces'.[7] Little did either man know that the future of the palace would soon be in their hands and that it would absorb the rest of their lives, for better or worse, risking their reputations and sanity.

The following morning, the porter of the Royal Academy library announced to the room of students: 'Now gentlemen, now you young architects, there's a fine chance for you.'[8] Once the flames had died down, the debate as to what to do next began in earnest. That same day *The Times* offered its thoughts that 'we may be allowed to utter a wish that the restoration of the dilapidated parts may be made in a style harmonizing with the original building, instead of exhibiting a heterogeneous mass of architectural erections in which taste, chronology, and convenience, are equally set at nought'.[9] Soon the whole nation would have an opinion about how the new palace should look.

In the meantime, a survey of burnt ground was needed to see what remained. On 22 October, John Rickman, the Second Clerk Assistant in the House of Commons, offered his preliminary findings and on a map of the original site he scratched out the extent of the fire, leaving little untouched. At the heart of the complex, now mostly debris and ash, stood the broken medieval structures that once formed the royal palace: Westminster Hall built by William II, as well as the other royal buildings created by later monarchs: the Chapel of St Stephen's, the White Hall and Henry III's elegant Painted Chamber, the state room that he had filled with wall paintings of Edward the Confessor.

Since the thirteenth century, the Painted Chamber had been the location of the Royal Council as well as Parliament. It was not until the 1530s, when Henry VIII moved his palace to nearby York Palace, renaming it Whitehall, that Westminster became dedicated to the business of Parliament and the law courts. Rather than creating new buildings for the development of the Houses of Commons and Lords, a make-do-and-mend attitude oversaw the haphazard expansion and management of the ancient site for the next three centuries. St Stephen's Chapel was adopted as the Commons chamber, while the Painted Chamber became the Lords; the White Hall was transformed into the Court of Requests.

Thus the royal palace was transformed into the English senate, and the burgeoning complex of buildings and structures took on a mixture of meanings. Westminster Hall, the ancient site of royal banquets, became the law courts – it was here that Charles I was tried by the Parliamentary faction in 1649 – but in 1834 it was still referred to by its old name by Tories and radicals alike for different reasons; as the fire engulfed the House on 16 October, the leading reforming peer, Lord Althorp, cried 'Damn the House of Commons, let it blaze away: but save, oh save the Hall.'[10] The chambers themselves had also gained historical resonance when, after the Glorious Revolution of 1688, a constitutional monarchy was negotiated in which Parliament was guaranteed. The relationship between ideas and stones, the evolution of democracy and the way it was organized within its various institutional spaces was felt in every brick of the building, however uncomfortable.

By the eighteenth century, however, the palace was ageing and beyond repair; a network of timber additions had mushroomed around the edges of the old buildings to accommodate the ever-burgeoning offices of government. This deleterious state was further emphasised in the 1750s when work started on the nearby Westminster Bridge that broke into the palace grounds and cleared up some of the slum streets surrounding the complex. It was now made starkly clear that the current situation could not be tolerated – Britain was the greatest country in the world but was run from a dangerous pigsty. What was needed was a new vision of Parliament, a Neoclassical senate house to confirm

London as the new Rome, and many of the finest designers of the century turned their hand to converting it from a jumble of medieval buildings into a classical whole: William Kent, John Vardy, James and Robert Adam all sought to refashion this national icon.

Little work was actually done to the fabric of the building. It was Parliament itself that decided how it should look and, as has often been seen, politicians rarely have opinions on architecture; it was not until the 1780s that any hopes of renovation were made real. The first phase of rebuilding was initiated by the Prime Minister, William Pitt, who, following the failures of the American War of Independence, desired to clean up Parliament for the new era. John Soane envisioned sealing the ancient buildings under one roof, constructing a single Neoclassical building with Corinthian columns, domes and plinths. At the centre of the design was a scala regia, a grand entrance for royal visits, reminding the nation that while the rational order of a democratic Parliament was powerful, the Crown remained at the heart of government.

At the time Soane was Professor of Architecture at the Royal Academy of Art, the leading voice in the attempt to preserve the classical language of design in the confused modern world. He had been born the seventh son of a bricklayer near Reading, had travelled to Europe on the Grand Tour yet, as he later confessed, he believed that 'architecture speaks a language of its own ... and above all, a building, like an historical picture, must tell its own tale'.[11] Soane had just begun his designs for the Bank of England, opposite the Royal Exchange, which became the most emphatic example of his purist's architectural vision. Where Nash was an exuberant chancer, Soane sought correctness in form, and as a result his buildings have a melancholy air.

None more so than his own house on Lincoln's Inn Fields, an idio-syncratic mixture of rooms and his voluminous cabinet of curiosities; as one later critic commented on his unique vision, 'there was but one man, the late Sir John Soane, who dared to be positively original. All others were mad in some particular foreign fashion; but he alone was mad in his own way ... [but] there was a method in the old knight's madness'.[12] At Westminster Soane wanted to deploy his immense learning to bring a rational order to the mess; it was never going to work.

Yet in the 1790s Soane could not account for events far away in France. Following the revolution of 1789, when classical architecture was adopted as the style of the new republic, the use of the Roman ideal back in England became entwined with the image of a murdered king and the spectre of a hated emperor, Napoleon. In response, English designers started to retreat from their classical fantasies and embraced the Picturesque, and, in particular, the Gothic style that had been ignored for some decades. At Westminster Palace, James Wyatt – the first architect hired by Elizabeth Home on Portman Square – announced in 1799 that his design should 'assume the appearance of a large Gothic edifice'.[13] Wyatt's aspirations had little impact on the fabric of the palace as a whole, however: between 1799 and 1815, while Britain was at war, the Westminster Improvements Commission spent £250,000; but rather than on decorations and architecture, it was spent on slum clearance around the palace grounds in fear of the uncontrollable mob. Wyatt was only allowed to tweak the Speaker's House and make changes to the Old Palace Yard, which was later compared to a gentlemen's toilet.

The wars with Napoleonic France put paid to any large-scale building plans and it was only in the 1820s that there were further attempts to improve the palace; once again John Soane was called upon to reflect the latest change in the political landscape through the buildings at Westminster. Liberal Toryism, overseen by the Prime Minister, Lord Liverpool, but put into practice in the policies of George Canning, Sir Robert Peel and others who wished to benefit from a period of economic stability by a raft of reforms, rationalised finance, law and the penal code hoped to appeal to the new middle classes. Soane began work on Westminster Hall, at the centre of the palace complex; the law courts were removed from the ancient institution and rehoused in specially built rooms running along the exterior wall. The project was partly a recognition of the splendour of the Gothic hall; it was also a realisation that the business of law-making now needed more space and specialisation.

The question of law itself was soon to become a dangerous issue and came to a head in the years just before the fire at Westminster. The reasons for the deep divisions within Parliament were complex and focused on the role of the economy, reform of the law, the rights and wrongs of free trade, the position of the king within the constitution, which foreign powers to befriend and whom to be wary of, the natural authority of the aristocracy to rule – yet nothing made the divisions clearer than the 1832 Reform Bill. The Bill was a recognition of the shifting power within the nation, the rise of the industrial centres and cities and the inevitable decline of rural communities. It was also an acknowledgement of the changing shape of society, particularly the ascendancy of the urban middle class, as has been seen in the story of both Home House and Regent Street. Thus where once eligibility to vote was based upon the ownership of land, there was now a need to manage the political aspirations of the vast swathes of urban pro-fessionals – educated, wealthy, politically engaged – who perhaps leased a large town house rather than owned a freehold. In short, it was the realisation that England had become an urban society.

The impetus for reform was much closer to home: corruption within the election system. For decades, many seats within the House of Commons were not won through free elections but were in the pockets of local grandees, who took advantage of the changing situation in 'rotten boroughs' where the rural population had dwindled. Thus before the Act the cotton capital of Manchester had no representative MP and London elected only four MPs, while Old Sarum in Wiltshire consisted of only three houses but still sent a member to Parliament every election.

The Act therefore planned to wipe fifty-three rotten boroughs off the electoral map. Needless to say, the task of reform was in the hands of the parliamentarians themselves, a clique who have never been keen to self-prescribe strong medicine; the journey to the final Act was arduous and unpleasant, splintering the body politic into factions. The Act itself, once it was passed, of course, satisfied no one. While historians have often made 1832 a key moment in the nation's story, a moment of closure of one world and the fresh dawn of a new era, it was nothing of the sort.

In London the debate spilled out into the streets, and almost seemed to threaten revolution. In summer 1830, the French King Charles X was forced out of Paris and fled to London, reminding everyone of the dangers of doing nothing; in the countryside Captain Swing riots,

protests by the poor agricultural workers against low wages and industrialisation, added to the spectre of class war. In September the first
Reform Bill was introduced into the House by the historian Thomas
Babington Macaulay, who urged the House to forgo 'a hopeless struggle
against the spirit of the age',[14] or expect a fate worse than France. The
House of Lords, who were concerned that the extension of the franchise
would weaken their inherited right to rule, were not quite ready for
change and blocked the Bill. Apsley House, with the unique address of
No. 1 London, the home of the leader of the Ultra-Tory faction, the
Duke of Wellington, who had been such a hero on the battlefield, was
stoned until every glass window was smashed.

The Bill floundered twice as it reached the Lords, only making its
proponents more determined, and radical. Soon there were calls for the
abolition of the House of Lords; there was a run on the Bank of England
in fear that the economy might collapse in the tumult; many protesters
refused to pay their taxes, while also suggesting that money should be
cut off from the government until they acquiesced. In their stub-
bornness, the Lords whipped up just the kind of radicalism of which
they were so afraid. In the end, King William IV threatened to create a
raft of new Whig peers who would vote the Bill through. The Tories
were defeated but decided to abstain. The Bill gained royal approval on
7 June 1834.

Once the Act had been passed the reactions of the various factions
were just as telling as the vociferous opinions expressed within the battle
itself. The Whigs were happy with the improvements but saw the Act as
the first gradual step towards political liberty. The Tories were glad that
the whole debacle was over; they regretted that concessions had been
made but were certain that they could not give another inch. The
radicals, on the other hand, bemoaned a missed opportunity and were
eager to push the process forward towards glorious republicanism.
While the Act itself in fact changed little in the country beyond Westminster – expanding the franchise by 1.5 per cent from a measly 3.2 per
cent of the population to only 4.7 per cent – some were in a 'handshaking,
bowel-disturbing passion of fear'[15] in case the Act failed, while others
claimed that success would bring the House of Lords to its knees.

Thus when the crowd started to call out on the evening of 16 October, as they stood before the flames engulfing the Palace of Westminster, there was a storm of emotions: was this ancient monument to privilege no longer fit for its purpose? Or was the loss of tradition and history to be mourned? Did the fire represent a resolute break with the past or the opportunity for a new beginning? Would a new building unite the nation that had so clearly fragmented into so many shards? As the philosopher John Stuart Mill had said about the Act, 'the old doctrines have gone out, but the new ones have not yet come in'.[16] Could the revived palace set the new constitution in stone?

In the days after the fire it was presumed that Melbourne would commission the Surveyor of Woods, Sir Robert Smirke, to provide a plan for the new building. Smirke was also ordered to make an assessment of the ruins of the palace, see what was left and find new accommodation for both Houses as swiftly as possible. Smirke had worked alongside Nash and Sir John Soane within the Office of Works, yet by 1834, after the disaster of Buckingham Palace, Nash's reputation was trashed and the whole Office of Works was treated with suspicion. Therefore there was instant muttering of disapproval when it became clear that Smirke had won the prize as an act of privilege.

This was not the only reason for raised voices in the chamber. The design of the palace was not just an issue of architecture but a maelstrom of interests and factions that collided amongst the burnt ruins. In December 1834, the Whig Lord Melbourne was forced to dissolve Parliament and call a new election; his rival, Sir Robert Peel, then became the Leader of the House of Commons. Fortunately for Smirke, the new PM was an old friend and patron, and the architect kept his job. Yet Peel was soon embroiled in controversy that once again demanded a new election, in January 1835. The country voted in a hung Parliament; this was not enough to oust Peel but neither did it give him the means to make government work. In the stalemate, individual policies were slowly undermined, and eventually, when the press began to criticise Smirke's designs as a way of attacking the government, Peel could do little to defend his friend.

On 31 January, many of these fears were summed up in a pamphlet published by Lt-Col. Sir Edward Cust, former equerry to Leopold, King of the Belgians, a former ex-Tory MP who had lost his seat in the shuffle of the 1832 Reform Act, and 'an amateur delighting in the pursuit of architecture'.[17] The paper called for a public competition, and soon gained the backing of much of the popular press. Some later suggested that Cust's stance had ulterior motives, and that he was surreptitiously promoting the interests of his friend, Charles Barry, whom he had got to know while the architect was designing the Travellers' Club in Pall Mall in 1829. Others mooted that Cust's outcry was a protest against the new palace falling into the hands of a Neoclassical artificer. This placed the choice of style for the designs at the heart of a stormy debate.

When Parliament finally met in February, the members found themselves in the new temporary chambers that Smirke had devised for the short term, the Lords huddled in the patched-up Painted Chamber while the Commons made do in the Court of Requests; it was never going to be a comfortable session. Peel, with only minority support, moved cautiously on all fronts and on 2 March set up a committee of experts to consider the matter of the new palace. The gathering reflected all the major groups within the House of Commons: the Ultra-Tories, Tories, Derbyites, Canningites, Whigs, Radicals, Repealers and one token Independent. How were they ever going to agree on the design of the new Parliament when they rarely agreed on what Parliament stood for in the first place?

The first item on the agenda was the discussion about whether to move the palace. The old building had been born out of happenstance, growing out of the ancient royal hall situated on the low-lying and marshy Thorney Island. Now Westminster was a cramped neighbourhood, on the edge of the metropolis. Surely, this was an opportunity to do something better. One of the committee members, the radical Joseph Hume, had already raised the issue in 1833, before the fire, and now he suggested that both Houses move either to St James's or to the centre of Nash's metropolitan improvements, Trafalgar Square. William IV played his part and offered Nash's disastrous Buckingham Palace. There were also plans for a renovated Covent Garden, or Leicester Square. But the debate confirmed the historical importance of Westminster as a place of collective memory, and that 'the genius of place' should not be disturbed. The new palace would be built upon and around the ruins of the past; there was to be no blank slate upon which to redraft the constitution.

The committee looked at Smirke's Italianate first designs and voted fourteen to two in favour; however, big politics got in the way of architecture once again and on 8 April Peel resigned and was replaced by Melbourne, who inherited the same set of problems – a hung Parliament and little chance of getting anything done. Melbourne's thin majority rested on a Whig–Radical alliance, and matters such as the design of the new palace were part of the compromise. As the press stirred up the debate, a public competition looked increasingly like the best option and on 3 June it was announced that entries had to be submitted by 1 December, that a judging panel had been set up, 'and that the style of the building be either Gothic or Elizabethan'.[18]

The selection of style was no accident. It was firstly a means to reject Smirke's Italianate plans, but it was also a compromise between the factions within the committee who could not agree on anything; as the historian W. J. Rorabaugh suggests, it was 'an ingenious Whig device to maintain Melbourne's government by splitting Tories and Radicals. While the Gothic style delighted the Tories but not the Radicals, the overthrow of Smirke pleased the Radicals but not the Tories.'[19] There were two prizes of £500 for the best designs, but only one would eventually be transformed into stone. Despite the short-term nature of the deal, the decision would have lasting consequences.

Charles Barry did not relish the limitations of style stipulated by the committee; he would have much preferred to have been allowed to dream up an Italianate plan. But he was a versatile thinker and had already shown that he could turn his hand to most styles. Thus, as his son later noted, 'the original idea of his plan was sketched out on the back of a letter ... [and] this contained the germ of all that was to follow'.[20]

Born in Westminster, the son of a stationer, Barry had been in the design business since the age of fifteen. After an apprenticeship he gained his inheritance and went to Europe, where taste drew him towards the classical wonders of Italy and even as far as Athens, Egypt and Syria. Returning to London in the 1820s, Barry saw that the capital was in the middle of a building boom, and he made his way both by acquiring rich patrons – such as the Holland House group – as well as winning competitions. He was a student of the Picturesque, an eclecticism of styles that reflected the many different faces of society, and turned his hand to a contemporary Gothic church near Manchester; another early English church in Brighton; an Italianate villa for a south-coast solicitor; and renovations to the home of the Duke and Duchess of Sutherland at Trentham. In time the commissions became bigger and in 1824 he produced bold Grecian plans for the Manchester Institution (today Manchester City Galleries). He also gained fame in London for his Florentine palazzo, the Travellers' Club, which established Barry as the leading exponent of the Renaissance revival.

Barry's next major commission, in 1833, was for King Edward's Grammar School, Birmingham, which drew upon his latest interests in perpendicular Gothic. Although the style was not determined in the rules of the competition, Barry felt that the Tudor origins of the school demanded this treatment. Thus he explored the Gothic as a means of balancing space and function in a brand-new way. It was in the summer of 1835, as Barry was thinking about the finishing touches to the designs as well as his first drawings for the Houses of Parliament, that he was introduced, perhaps by Cust, to Auguste Welby Northmore Pugin.

Barry was well aware of Pugin's father, Auguste, illustrator of the popular *Examples of Gothic Architecture*, who had also worked as John Nash's sidekick in Wales and London. His son was almost exclusively educated in his father's drawing school, which filled the family home in Bloomsbury, and he soon became obsessed with ancient architecture. However, rather than working in stone, Auguste began his career in the trade as a furniture designer and decorator; his first break came when he was discovered in the reading room of the British Museum copying a Dürer drawing. As a teenager he advised on some renovations at Windsor Castle; later, like Inigo Jones, he learnt much of his craft as a set designer at Covent Garden Theatre.

Despite his exhaustive study of old books and his experience of the wonders of the Gothic world at the side of his father, he did not set himself up as an architect until 1833–4 when he began to design a series of medieval fantasies in a set of iconic drawings, living stage sets with names such as the Hospital of St John, the Deanery, St Marie's College. In 1835, when he met Barry, he was working on his first house, St Marie's Grange, for his family. Many aspects of Barry's designs at Birmingham were already indebted to *Examples*, but the son added some of his own special touches to the decoration as well as devising all the furniture. It was the first time he could display in public 'the embodiment of his daydreams for years'.[21]

In the summer of 1835, as Barry turned his attention to the competition for the Houses of Parliament, he was keen to engage Pugin's eye for Gothic detail to complete his designs. From Barry's initial sketch on the back of a letter, the architect had swiftly imagined the schema for the new palace. He conceived his building according to what was left from the fire, the history of Westminster, and Henry III's abbey nearby. He studied Henry VII's Lady Chapel, renowned for its extraordinary fan vaulting, as well as the elegant exterior in which glass and stone seem to melt into each other. The survival of Westminster Hall also dictated the revival of this Neo-Gothic style, and encouraged Barry to think of how to integrate the ancient hall into the body of the new palace.

The designs needed to fit into the cramped circumstances of the old ruins. When Barry made suggestions that the palace spread out across neighbouring streets, the cost of purchasing the land was considered too great. Instead, he had only eight acres in which to pack the many different parts of the palace, offering light, air and ease of circulation through an ordered pattern of courts and yards. The extent of the task was phenomenal and would set the mysteries of the British constitution in stone, making real what did not exist on paper:

Fourteen halls, galleries, vestibules, and other apartments of great capacity and noble proportion ... it comprises eight official residences, each first rate mansions; twenty corridors and lobbies are required to serve as the great road-ways through this aggregation of edifices; two and thirty noble apartments, facing the river will be used as Committee-Rooms; libraries; Waiting Rooms, Dining Rooms, and Clerk's offices.[22]

Traditionally, the ancient royal palace was approached from the Thames, so consideration had to be given to the river front. From the yard, there needed to be entrances for the general public through the hall as well as separate entry points for the Lords and Commons. Barry's plans, despite the necessity to appeal to Melbourne's Whiggish Parliament, were deeply conservative, harking back to the ancient constitution of Crown, Lords and Commons rather than the political reality of the Reform Act. In particular it was designed around a royal entrance, a scala regia, that laid bare the true identity of power within the nation. This was made manifest on the two days of the year that the monarch entered the palace – the opening of the new sessions of Parliament. The King's Tower, at the north-west corner, was to be the most impressive structure, 150 feet wide, from which the royal entourage descended from carriages into the building. The royal passage through the palace then determined Barry's design: from the Robing Room into the House of Lords. Inside the chamber the monarch sat in ceremony, the whole building transformed into a microcosmic fantasy of the ideal polity.

In addition to this, Barry had to think of the modern needs for the functioning Houses of Parliament: libraries for each House, a range of committee rooms to accommodate the increase of business conducted behind closed doors; there were also refreshment rooms to ensure the members did not retreat to their clubs at any opportunity. Finally he had to decide the relationship between government and the general public; the size of the public galleries, the elegance of the central lobby, dictated the effective transparency of the processes of power.

To find a design that brought the different aspects of the nation together, Barry looked for native precedent and found little of help. As an ecclesiastical style, Perpendicular Gothic offered few examples to copy; there were no Gothic palaces, yet he could hardly set his plans on a cathedral or even an abbey. He looked at some of the town halls of the Low Countries as potential templates, and the examples he found in

Brussels and Louvain encouraged him to add a tower to the main body of the building, where the members met guests and constituents; but Barry wanted a regal palace, not a civic hall.

If the past offered few answers, could the imagination of the present be more productive? His previous experience of building a school and a gentlemen's club was perhaps the best, albeit unexpected, preparation for designing the new palace. Barry devised a plan for the main body of the building that owed more to classical plans than Gothic; without a native template he found safety in a classical structure, then giving it a Gothic face, knowing that he needed the advice of an expert on such a vast project. Once more he called on Pugin to draft the designs for the decoration of his Italianate creation. Pugin was already working on the palace designs for the Scottish architect James Gillespie Graham, but was happy to accept the brief: Barry offered him 400 guineas, Graham 300. Pugin was able to transform every inch of Barry's designs in readiness for the competition deadline of 1 December 1835.

Ninety-seven entries were considered by the commissioners, all anonymously submitted and each given a number. The competition seemed impartial but, of course, many of the leading Neoclassical architects did not even bother to enter. It was not until March the following year that the judges' decision was announced, and four designs were given special praise. The greatest exhortations, however, were reserved for no. 64, and in their presentation to the King the judges boasted, 'it is impossible to examine the minute drawings of this design and not feel confident in the author's skill in Gothic architecture.'[23] The Houses of Parliament committee was more circumspect; the choice was confirmed but questions were raised about possible alterations. Thus began the painful process, from paper projections to building site, that would take three years and involve a debate about the very nature of English architecture.

It was decided that Barry's design was to be put on display at the new National Gallery for everyone to see. Rather than being a celebration, this allowed every architectural rival, antiquarian, man of taste and political adversary to have their say about the value of the plans and the rightness of Gothic architecture as the national style. While Barry was consumed by the debate over the costs of the building, Pugin was more than happy to jump into the thick of the controversy. Just as the nation was at the centre of a political storm about representational democracy, so there was a sea change in the way in which society wished to portray itself. In the face of the mayhem, many began to believe that Britain was on the verge of fragmentation; the cleric Thomas Mozley wrote that 'the whole fabric of English society ... was trembling to its foundation'.[24] He later observed that 'few changes in our history can be more sudden, more rapid, and more complete than that from the Greek and Roman styles in church building to ... the medieval'.[25] The connection between the fear of social breakdown and the rise of the Gothic sensibility was no accident.

As a response to the tumult, thinkers sought an ideal model for society and many hoped that the brutal industrialisation of the nation that sapped the spirit of the people would be combated by the peace and consolation of the idyll of a bygone England. The rising middle class was undermining the ancient order of things. This was summed up by the philosopher Thomas Carlyle, nicknamed the Sage of Chelsea, who bemoaned the loss of national spirit in the age of the machine. Carlyle saw that society had been reduced to transaction and reason, fearing that 'we have profoundly forgotten everywhere that cash payment is not the sole relation of human beings'.[26]

The revival of the Church was one way to re-establish unity, but how were the new churches to look? In the 1830s William Cobbett stood in front of the majestic Salisbury Cathedral and sighed that it 'could never be built now'.[27] The answer was found in a new interest in the native treasures of the past and an increased fascination with medieval institutions, chivalry, documents – all vividly brought to life in the novels of Sir Walter Scott, which were devoured in drawing rooms throughout the country. This was reflected in the suburbs of the city, where Gothic villas had been created by Nash and his contemporaries in picturesque riposte to the mercantilist realities of the city. The most famous of these was Horace Walpole's Strawberry Hill, ten miles west of London, the exquisite arcadian redoubt for a man of refined taste and a rebuke to the posturing of the classical stately home.

The passion for Gothic architecture was soon becoming widespread, yet lacked a singular philosophy to establish it as the universal native style. As he was working on his designs for Barry, Pugin began *Contrasts*, which he published in 1836, a call to arms for the 'Young Englanders' with the rallying cry: 'On comparing the architectural works of the present century with those from the Middle Ages, the wonderful superiority of the latter must strike every attentive observer.'[28] He then went on, with a series of drawings in his own hand, to compare and contrast the rotten nature of modern society and how this was reflected in contemporary buildings. Architecture should have a function, he argued, and its meaning should be expressed in ornamentation. Rather than an abundance of styles there should be one standard of beauty. A revival in craftsmanship would deliver a reformed social order. Gothic architecture, he concluded, could make modern society whole and reverent again. The uncompromising book was incendiary, and turned the Gothic Revival into a national religion.

This new style was not without critics, however, and was, according to some, barbaric. W. R. Hamilton wrote in a published letter to the Earl of Elgin of his fury 'that Gothic Barbarism is again to be allowed to triumph over the master pieces of Italy and Greece, and that Britons are henceforth to look for the model of what is sublime and beautiful in art, to the age of ignorance and superstition'.[29]

Thus, as the plans stood in the National Gallery, Barry's new palace became the whipping-boy of the whole heated debate. The radical MP Joseph Hume once again made a bid for a more rational building at Westminster, a vision of Utilitarian philosophy. This was echoed in the *Westminster Review*, the mouthpiece of the philosopher Jeremy Bentham, which pointed out that Gothic was a French style, and that a design based upon function rather than history was in order. Near the Westminster site, Millbank prison had been built to Bentham's notions of the panopticon, the acme of Utilitarian architecture; could these same principles be applied to the palace?

By January 1837 Barry and Pugin submitted a new set of plans, responding to some of the comments made by the MPs, while the official surveyors came up with an estimate of £865,000 and a timetable of six years. In these revised designs, an embankment had been added to enhance the river frontage of the building. The entrance by Westminster Hall for the general public was enlarged, while the royal entrance was reduced. The roof of the House of Lords was increased, and there were many changes to the Commons as a result of consultations with the members concerning acoustics: a full House needed to seat over 600 members, but on an average day accommodated only a handful. Needless to say, the designs continued to change, both from Barry's own desires as well as alterations forced upon him, which in time led the architect into trouble. Pugin would not revisit the site for another seven years, while Barry began a project that would continue for the rest of his life.

Work began in 1838 on the river embankment with large coffer-dams driven into the Thames riverbed, which were then filled with cement. As Barry planned some parts of the building to rise up from the river, this was a complicated process. The riverbed itself was found to be unstable, 'like quicksand', and a solid core was needed on which to set the foundations. Upon this Barry poured between five and fifteen feet of concrete the whole 1,200-foot length of the site, and then layers of brickwork in preparation for the first stones.

The first stones of the palace were laid on 27 April 1840, by Mrs Barry; but it was already clear that things were taking too long. In the intervening years the government had set up a committee to decide on what stone to use, with the prescription that the new palace deserved only the best. Endless trips were made to quarries to test out the durability and suitability of certain stones. They chose the magnesium limestone from Bolsover Moor, only to discover that it could only be quarried in small pieces, so they had to make do with Anston stone from the Duke of Leeds's quarry; Painswick stone was selected for the interiors as well as Caen stone from France. As the building began Barry must have hoped that the MPs remained patient as the new palace was completed, or that events would not overtake the project.

Two months after work began, eighteen-year-old Victoria, niece of William IV, was crowned in a ceremony at Westminster Abbey, heralding a new era. The 1840s were a dangerous decade, of uncertainty and hunger. At home it was the age of Chartism and the Corn Laws, when the streets were often filled with desperation and protest. Nearby there was also the threat of insurrection. In 1848 there were revolutions in Italy, Germany and France. Once more there was a fear that the violence could cross the Channel.

Through this turmoil work on the palace continued, as Barry was forced to work around the members and officers who remained on the site throughout the building period. The architect would be caught between his vision of a Gothic palace and the realities of the practice of government within the building, as it attempted to steer the nation. Barry's original plans were deeply conservative, steeped in the history of Westminster and the ancient hierarchical order of society: the Crown, the Lords, the Commons – a chivalric fantasy that perhaps never existed, rewriting the story of Henry III's struggle against the barons and the birth of Parliament. Meanwhile, members of the two Houses were still cramped in their temporary arrangements, and were growing impatient at the constant delays.

The first challenge that Barry faced was the river-front facade. With the increased length of the range, reaching 940 feet in total, Barry had to reconsider how to offer variety and movement to the frontage. Taste dictated that he could not design a single-height, monotonous face to the building, yet he would have to disguise the Italianate devices with which he was most comfortable; he decided to draw the front into three sections divided by towers, the central section rising to the third floor like a classical portico. With the exterior of nearby Henry VII's chapel as inspiration, he devised a system of turrets rising from the towers. He also reconsidered his original plan for a crenellated roofline by opposing the flat, horizontal face with a scheme of pinnacles that ascended above the level of the steep lead roofs, offering a sense of verticality to disguise the length of the front.

There was a strict hierarchy of decoration on the facade. He worked on numerous plans for windows on each storey in order to add to the sense of lightness. The windows of the first floor were solid and plain, indicating the use of the rooms behind – vaults for public records and papers. The second and third floors housed the many committee rooms, waiting rooms and libraries where much of the business of government was now being conducted. In 1835 Barry had been asked to provide thirty-two committee-rooms, libraries, waiting rooms, dining rooms and a clerk's office, but by the mid-1840s these spaces were gaining more power as the place where new laws and Acts, especially the numerous Railways Acts, were debated before the formal vote in the House. This increased importance was reflected in the design of the windows.

The river-front facade was devised to tell a very particular history lesson and in 1843 Barry hired the stone carver John Thomas, with whom he had worked in Birmingham, and started to plan intricate stone sculptures along the whole face. Barry decided to face the front of the royal palace with the coat of arms of every monarch from William the Conqueror, which were placed on the window sills along the first floor. Where the kings before Richard II had no arms, Barry simply invented them, so that William II had Westminster Hall upon his shield and Edward II George and the dragon. In between, the surface was emblazoned with angels bearing shields, Tudor characters, the initials of the Queen, V. R., as well as suitable mottos: *Dieu et Mon Droit*, *Victoria Regina feliciter regnans*, and so on. There were also emblems, crowns, foliage and flowers symbolic of the three nations of the Union, ribands and shields ensuring that not a single inch of the surface was left without the weight of national grace and meaning.

The issue of decoration, both inside and out, was at the heart of the new palace; it was the surface of the stones rather than the overall structure of the machine that was important. Yet, as Prime Minister Melbourne noted, the marriage of politics and fine art was bound to be stormy: 'God help the minister who meddles in art',[30] and so, in 1841, as the architect was starting to build, a committee was set up to discuss what paintings and sculptures should be chosen. The Fine Arts Commission was chaired by the Queen's Consort, Prince Albert, who had arrived in Britain that year. It was thought that, like architecture, fine art, and in particular the pinnacle of achievement, historical heroic painting, had a moral effect on the viewer, and, like building, was enduring a period of crisis. Despite the nation's predominance, where was the English Jacques-Louis David or Eugène Delacroix to record Britain's triumphs? Thus twenty distinguished men, alongside the Prince, debated the subjects for the wall paintings of the new palace.

By 1844, the commission were well on their way to devising a scheme that redrafted the myths and history of Britain. Just as Barry wished to carve the nation's dynastic story into the exterior of the building, so the commission looked to images and decorations that set out the glories of England's past. Barry, bizarrely not on the committee, was determined that the selection of paintings and sculpture should work in concert with his symbolic division of space. Where Barry's advice was asked he hoped that the paintings would be frescoes, an allusion to the greatest of the Renaissance artists as well as being contemporaneous with the pseudo-dating of the palace to the age of the early Tudors; he also suggested modestly that 'the paintings be wholly free from gloss on the surface, so that they may be perfectly seen and fully understood from all points of view'.[31]

Rumours soon began to stir that Prince Albert was lobbying for German painters to be hired. The Munich school of painters, the Nazarenes, were greatly admired for their skill, and undoubtedly the Prince showed plans for the palace to their leading proponent, Peter Cornelius. Swift action was taken and foreigners were banned from applying, but there was a strong case for the British artists to learn from their German counterparts and a number travelled to Munich. Albert himself hoped to encourage new techniques and was instrumental in translating a pamphlet on the new method of water-glass painting, which he then sent to all leading young British artists. Another competition called for cartoons in chalk or charcoal, 'not less than ten nor more than fifteen feet in their longest dimension; the figures to be not less than the size of life, illustrating subjects from British History, or from the works of Spenser, Shakespeare or Milton'.[32]

The Queen herself came to see all 140 exhibits that hung in Westminster Hall for public judgement. The exhibition caused some sensation as one painting, 'St George after the Death of the Dragon', was by Richard Dadd, who had recently returned from Egypt with sunstroke and had murdered his father in Cobham Park. He soon became one of the most famous inmates of Bedlam Hospital. The prizes were won by previously unknown artists, caustically described by a rival as 'an assistant painter of panoramas ... [and] a surgeon now become artist'.[33]

In September 1844, *The Times* surveyed the progress at Westminster for its readers. The river front was now close to completion, the exterior 'a rich display ... which, whilst they strike astonishment to the beholder, must raise in his heart a high admiration for native genius'.[34] Work on the King's Tower (now renamed Victoria Tower) and the Clock Tower was no more than thirty-five feet high; the north front was no further along than the foundations, but the House of Lords at the heart of the complex was close to the roofline.

Nonetheless, the peers were beginning to get agitated; it had been over ten years since they had been forced to conduct their business in the inadequate Painted Chamber. Barry had promised that everything would be completed by the following year – this now looked like a bad dream. It was compounded by a conflict brewing over the safety of the building itself. As he pushed the work forward, he continued to adapt his designs to suit the changing conditions and improvements he had in mind. Now, his focus also returned to the decoration of the surface of the building and, once again, Barry called for Pugin to bring his Gothic vision to Westminster.

In the previous seven years Pugin had been consolidating his reputation as 'the virtual pope or chief pontiff'[35] of the Gothic Revival. In his writings, including *The True Principles of Pointed or Christian Architecture, On the Present State of Ecclesiastical Architecture in England* and *An Apology for the Revival of Christian Architecture in England*, he had become the beacon, and acknowledged expert, of Gothic theory; Barry was now asking him to transform the surface of the most important public work in the country.

The impact and range of Pugin's designs over the next eight years would be vast, and would in time lead many to question whether it was the architect or the decorator who deserved the acclaim as creative genius behind the palace. In December, Barry ensured that his colleague was given an official title, Superintendent of Woodcarving, and a salary of £200 a year, excluding travel expenses. Pugin began his work immediately, devising a new scheme for the window panes, transforming the arched windows into long vertical lozenges of sparkling glass.

Over the following years Pugin would have a direct influence on the design of every aspect of the building. His attention to detail was astonishing and he worked closely with manufacturers and craftsmen – both native and foreign. He also gathered a vast library of artefacts and models, medieval salvage and rare treasures to guide his designs and ensure authenticity. His vision can be found in every aspect of the palace, from wallpaper and carpets to the carving upon the exterior, as well as the final designs of the Clock Tower (soon to be famed for its largest bell, Big Ben), metalwork and tiling, furniture, draperies and lighting fixtures. Nothing was beneath his attention, from the lavatory doors to the elegant gilt and carved canopy that rose behind the throne in the House of Lords.

His close working relationship with Barry was occasionally stormy as they conferred on everything. For example, here is Barry commenting on the minute details of the design for a door: 'they look too large. I should like them to be reduced and modified in design ... Amongst the screws in the parcel I have sent is one that we have in town which I prefer to yours as the head is regularly punched and not burred as yours is to the risk of injury to knuckles.'[36]

This attention to detail was in contrast to the rising complaints about the progress of the project from the people who saw the palace as their place of work. In 1844, the House of Lords were becoming anxious on the slow progress of their chamber and a Committee of Enquiry was set up to see what was happening on the ground. It soon became clear that Barry had departed on several occasions from the agreed designs. Many saw this as an opportunity to chide the architect for his tardiness. However, Barry had his defenders; the London popular press were swift to offer their support, ever eager to annoy the members, as were the professional trade magazines. When it was proved that few of these alterations incurred any additional costs and were the result of timely reconsiderations of the plans, Barry may have hoped that he was in the clear once again, with the simple stricture to complete the House of

19. A detail from Charles Barry's design. Together with Pugin, the architect created thousands of similar plans in intricate detail. (*Bridgeman*)

Lords 'with the greatest possible speed'.[37] However, the rumpus was only about to begin.

There had been discussions and debates about the heating and ventilation of the new palace since the very first suggestion of a competition in 1835. In 1839, as building commenced, Barry had asked the committee to hire an engineer to oversee the practical aspects of the project and had been offered the assistance of an Edinburgh chemistry teacher, Dr David Reid. Despite his lack of experience of building Reid soon ensured that he had full power to execute his own plans, with the only reservation that his work did not endanger 'either the solidity or the architectural character of the building'.[38] By 1842, he was demanding a central tower to act as a chimney for the whole palace and in response Barry started to develop some plans and ideas.

Out of adversity, the architect searched for a solution and there is some evidence that in his quest Barry may have looked at plans of William Beckford's Fonthill. Before his evening with Elizabeth, Countess of Home, Beckford had fled England as the result of a homosexual scandal and spent many years travelling through Europe, voraciously collecting art and books. He returned and began to focus his attention on rebuilding the family estate in Wiltshire, converting it from a classical villa into an awesome Gothic fantasy. Designed by James Wyatt, this extravagant romantic folly was based around a central atrium, above which a ninety-foot Gothic tower reigned. The tower, cheaply constructed from timber and concrete, soon fell in a storm, and Fonthill became a picturesque ruin, symbolic of its fanciful patron. As Barry considered how the body of the new palace was to be formed, the idea of a tower disguising the necessary chimney, rising above the central lobby, was born.

But by the beginning of 1845, as Barry and Pugin's plans for the Lords were being settled, Reid's demands became increasingly impossible, and the architect and engineer were no longer on speaking terms. Barry claimed that Reid, called by *The Builder* 'an aerial Guy Fawkes',[39] had demanded so many flues and pipes – taking up one third of the entire space – that the whole chamber was rendered unsafe. Reid countered that without Barry's precise plans he could only guess at the job in hand.

An arbiter, Joseph Gwilt, was appointed to smooth the divisions, and he suggested that two directors working together was impossible and that Barry alone should be in charge. Thus, as Parliament was consumed with the violent debate on the repeal of the Corn Laws, it was finally decided that Barry should have complete control of the design of the House of Lords. In response, and in thanks, Barry promised that he would complete the interior of the river-front rooms with the libraries, refreshment rooms and committee rooms by the following summer. Having been given the benefit of the doubt, the architect was now under pressure to deliver on his promise.

Two years later, on 14 April 1847, Queen Victoria noted in her diary: 'Another cold day. The children's coughs and colds much better. Again went to the riding school. At twelve we went to see the New House of Lords, which is unfortunately to be opened without the House of Commons, as the Lords are so impatient to get into it.'[40] The Queen had been coming to the State Opening of Parliament since 1833, while still a princess, but this was a special day. The chamber was not complete – only one mural was on the wall and one stained-glass window in place – but the rest of it was in order.

On such occasions, the royal coaches left St James's Palace and arrived at the base of the Victoria Tower, where the royal party – the Queen, Prince Albert, Gold Stick (the ceremonial commander of the Forces), the Master of the Robes, the Lord-in-Waiting, Master of the Horse, Groom of the Stole et al. – descended amidst pageantry and 'bands of the Scots Fusilier Guards playing "the Garb of Gaul",[41] and were met by the Prime Minister, Black Rod and the Garter King of Arms. Through the royal entrance into the Robing Room, the party prepared to process into the House of Lords via the royal stairs leading to the royal gallery; the Queen was led by pursuivants and heralds, officers carrying the sword of state, the cap of maintenance and the crown and was followed by gentleman ushers, household officers and the ranks of nobility and parliamentary officers in order of precedent. The whole operation was a delicate reminder of the traditional stations of society from the highest down. Finally entering Barry's chamber, decked with Pugin's exquisitely detailed re-imagining of a medieval court, one could imagine that the room modelled an idealised state, a dream vision of a perfect Britain.

The Queen sat on the throne facing the chamber, a ninety-foot-long double cube with six large pointed windows on either side. Upon this bare stage the two architects had concocted a magnificent political drama: the Queen's throne was raised upon a dais, surrounded by a richly carved canopy, heraldic coats of arms, the Garter and crests of the nations of the Union, devised in every detail by Pugin, and gilded. The canopy itself was a lesson in the mythology of royal power. Above, the ceiling was divided into eighteen panels that were then festooned with paintings and carving, the initials V. R. at the centre of each one. Each wall was similarly filled with neatly sculpted panelling and pillars that rose to intricate busts of English kings; 'God Save the Queen' was also festooned between each bust. On the ground, every inch of space had been weighted with the symbolism of power.

Above the throne were three recessed panels upon which the first of the magnificent frescoes depicting the history of Britain were placed: 'The Baptism of St Ethelbert' by William Dyce, 'Edward III conferring the Order of the Garter on the Black Prince' and 'Committal of Prince Henry by Judge Gascoigne', both by C. W. Cope. On the corresponding southern end, above the public gallery were three more paintings, chosen to exemplify the three constituencies of the aristocracy: 'Chivalry' for the Lords Temporal, 'Religion' for the bishops, 'Justice' for the judiciary.

On the day of the opening, the chamber was packed. As the Queen took her throne and Prince Albert sat on her right, the Bishop of St Asaph read the formal prayers. Then the Lord Chancellor, the leader of the House of Lords, was requested to take his official seat on the red-draped Woolsack at the centre of the room. He then rose to start his address, but before he could commence Black Rod arrived with an announcement from the House of Commons, followed by a phalanx of MPs who wished to present a Bill. The ceremony proved two things: firstly, that the acoustics within the chamber were terrible and secondly, that despite the weight and power of ornamentation, it was now the Commons, not the Lords, that were to be the masters of the new palace.

Nevertheless, the chamber would soon be acclaimed as the highest example of the Gothic Revival in the country; Victoria, not known as a great architectural critic, noted: 'the building is indeed magnificent ... very elaborate and gorgeous. Perhaps there is a little too much brass and gold in the decorations, but the whole effect is very dignified and fine.'[42] Barry himself was not completely satisfied with the result but would have been happy with the encouragement. Needless to say, it did not last long and in 1848 the architect was faced with a crisis that nearly destroyed his career.

The Lords were finally gruntled, but this only left room for the growing disgruntlement of the MPs in the House of Commons; for by 1848 there was still very little sign of the new chamber. Money was also in short supply as Barry's budget had been reduced from £150,000 to £100,000, the insult made more livid by the committee chairman, Lord Morpeth, suggesting that Barry could make savings on the orna-mentation. The complete building had thus far cost over £1.4 million, almost double the original estimate, and was now two years overdue. As with almost every public works project in London's history, the blame was placed upon the architect rather than the accountants. Barry was to be punished and it was decided that he should no longer expect a salary for his work, and that a committee be set up to monitor his every move.

Barry was devastated, and threatened resignation. But there was little that any side could change; as one commissioner, Lord de Grey, observed: 'though nothing is completed; everything was begun; and so far advanced that all attempts to diminish the expense or control the architect were perfectly futile'.[43] For the meantime, architect and client were stuck with each other and made to find a way to work together. This was not helped by a long, hot summer in which there was little for the MPs to debate except their own discomfort.

Barry hoped that this swarm of criticism would be calmed by the House of Commons finally opening on 3 May 1850. The members should have been pleased that after fifteen years they could return to a chamber designed for their purpose, but they found strange ways to show their appreciation. There were instant complaints about the proportions and the acoustics and, inevitably, a new committee was set up to deal with the problems, packed with men who had long wanted to cut Barry down to size. It was open season against the architect: Joseph Hume claimed that so much money had been spent that the seats ought to have been made of gold, while the up-and-coming Benjamin Disraeli wondered whether the works constituted a crime grave enough to convict the architect to hang. The response was a tortuous process that offered few results: a new roof was installed, and the division lobbies outside the chamber were improved. It was said that, after the second opening in 1851, the frustrated Barry refused ever to enter the chamber again.

Meanwhile work continued on the completion of the rest of the building and in particular the gallery of artworks that retold the nation's story upon the palace's fabric. It had been decided that the walls should recount the story of Britain from the Saxons to the victories of the most recent era, the Battle of Waterloo and the discovery of Australia by Captain Cook in 1770. However, the location of each image was carefully selected by the Fine Arts Commission in order to offer instruction. The first works to be green-lit were the six frescoes in the House of Lords that intended to show chivalry, religion and justice as well as three historical scenes that were taken from the earliest accounts of the Saxon past. In the Robing Room, William Dyce also completed seven paintings depicting the legends of another Saxon monarch, King Arthur, high-lighting the virtues of religion, courtesy, mercy, generosity and hos-pitality.

The story of Britain's victories was more straightforward, and the Royal Gallery that linked the Robing Room to the House of Lords was given over to 'the military history and glory of the country'.[44] It was originally intended to include images of Boudicca inciting her army against the Romans, King Alfred in the Danes' camp, Queen Edith finding the dead body of King Harold after the Battle of Hastings, Richard the Lionheart advancing on Jerusalem, various noble sorties against the French, Elizabeth I at Tilbury spurring on her men before the Armada, and on to the campaigns that established the British Empire: the Parliamentary Admiral Robert Blake at Tunis, whose racked body was laid out at the Queen's House at Greenwich; the death of James

Wolfe at Quebec; Lord Cornwallis accepting the sons of Sultan Tipoo as hostages. The only frescoes that were completed, however, were a long painting of the death of Horatio Nelson at the Battle of Trafalgar, which took Dyce eight years to finish between 1857 and 1865, and the meeting of the Duke of Wellington and Blücher at the Battle of Waterloo.

Parliament was also able to redraft its own history, at times in contrast to Barry's expressed aim to create a royal palace. Thomas Babington Macaulay had been an MP between 1830 and 1857, and in his first year he had been the first member to speak in favour of reform; he was also on the Fine Arts Commission. In 1848 he published two volumes of his masterwork, *The History of England from the Accession of James the Second*, which promoted a decidedly one-sided view of Britain that saw the perfection of the nation through the evolution of the Westminster Parliament. In particular, the stories of the English Civil War and the Glorious Revolution were recast to recount not the destruction of royal power but the rightness of the bourgeois ascendancy and the constitution. Where conflict might arise, such as the picture of 4 January 1642 when Charles I entered Parliament with a troop of men to arrest five errant MPs, there were attempts to 'do justice to the heroic virtues which were displayed on both sides'.[45] The King's subsequent execution was avoided altogether in favour of a touching and intimate scene of a royal burial at Windsor.

There were plans for almost every free surface in the palace: the Upper Waiting Room was renamed the Poets' Hall and decorated with scenes from Shakespeare, Chaucer, Spenser and Byron; paintings and bas-relief of the Tudor dynasty were created for the Prince's Chamber; the central lobby was given over to images and sculptures dedicated to the union of the four nations; the peers' Robing Room was intended to promote 'the idea of justice on earth and its development in law and judgement viz. Moses bringing down the tablets of the law to the Israelites'.[46] Not all the projects were a success, and it was quickly discovered that working in frescoes was difficult in the damp conditions of the palace, so close to the Thames. The paint soon began to deteriorate and here also London dirt accumulated, with the unfortunate result that, in an official report on the picture of King Lear dividing up his nation amongst his three daughters, it could not be decided whether the damage had obscured Cordelia's face or Regan's ear.

In February 1852, the Queen made another formal visit and this time was able to enter using the royal approach; now both Houses were in session and, although much was left to be done, it was acknowledged that the palace was, if not a complete triumph, 'the most difficult and most magnificent work ever attempted'.[47] A few days later, Barry was knighted.

For Pugin, fortune was less kind. The previous year he had been in charge of the medieval court of the Great Exhibition at Hyde Park, housed in Sir Joseph Paxton's extraordinary crystal palace. Of course, Pugin disapproved of the engineer's designs and the intention of the committee to fill the space with the wonders of the modern industrial world, and he secretly hoped that the palace would leak. The exhibition, however, was a huge success and Pugin's court, displaying a wooden rood screen, crucifixes and hand-carved cabinets, gained praise as a counterpoint to the heavy machinery elsewhere. Pugin's belief in crafts-manship and ornamentation was being raised high as one of the most compelling of the age. Yet it could not last; that same year John Ruskin published *The Stones of Venice*, which argued for a new Venetian para-digm of architectural perfection. Also, Pugin started to behave errat-ically. As Barry demanded new designs, Pugin's daughter Jane had to write in November 1851, 'the truth is he has worked too hard lately and unless he has more rest and less anxiety I am very much afraid he will be very ill'.[48] He began to have visions; despite trying to keep on working, travelling and writing, the condition got worse and his nightmares began to disturb him during the day.

When Pugin travelled up to London on 25 February 1852 for a routine meeting with Barry, the architect was so concerned by his friend's behav-iour that he called a doctor and Pugin was taken first to a private clinic in Kensington and then to Bedlam Hospital. The admitting doctors noted that he suffered from mania and a 'general confusion of ideas'[49] and could not stop moving, as if constantly agitated. He was then transferred to a private house in Hammersmith but he did not improve, so his daughter brought him home to Ramsgate. On the first evening back they visited the local church, which he had designed, sat in the garden and then went to bed, where he slipped into a coma and died a week later.

Without his partner Barry was left to complete the palace on his own; thankfully most of the designs were already on paper and he and Pugin had drafted over 800 plans and schemes for every detail. The work on the ground, however, was not so straightforward; in particular, as the offices, libraries, chambers and committee rooms were slowly opening for business there was still much to be done on the two towers that dominated the skyline.

When it was completed in 1860, the Victoria Tower on the north-west corner of the building was the 'largest and highest square tower in the world', reaching 331 feet, and a fitting monument to Barry's plans for the new palace as a royal building. It rose eleven storeys and contained the parliamentary archives, previously stored in various buildings around the capital. Because of its royal significance the tower was high-carved, with an octagonal turret and pinnacles that echoed the west front of Westminster Abbey which had been added to Edward I's original in the eighteenth century by Nicholas Hawksmoor.

20. Houses of Parliament as seen from the river front, the overpowering Victoria Tower on the left

The Clock Tower on the north-east side of the palace was a more troublesome creation. From the outset Barry wanted a structure that would stand tall besides the Gothic palace, yet no such Gothic towers existed on which to model his plans. Nonetheless the commission in 1836 approved plans for a campanile with a fine clock with faces on four sides, each thirty feet in diameter, an hour bell weighing sixteen tons and eight smaller quarter bells. When the designs were shown at the Royal Academy there was not universal approval and some baulked at the expense, when 'almost every mechanic carries a watch in his pocket'.[50]

Barry was fortunate that Pugin had worked on a similar design on a smaller scale at Scarisbrick Hall in Lancashire. Thus he projected his tower as an Italianate campanile and then allowed Pugin to add his Gothic surface. Work began on building soon after. At the same time, Barry wanted to commission the clock itself and the bells, and he asked B. L. Vulliamy, the royal clockmaker, to estimate the costs for an impressive clock. Another rival, E. J. Dent, got wind of this and demanded that he be allowed to tender his estimate, promptly proffering a far cheaper option. Thus it was necessary to call for a competition that was presided over by the Astronomer Royal, George Airy. Vulliamy's bid fell on stony ground, with Airy commenting, 'such a clock would be a village clock of a very superior character but would not have the accuracy of an astronomical clock'.[51] The prize went to Dent.

The clock was completed in 1855 at a cost of £1,600, but it could not be hoisted into place as the bells were still missing. Since 1846 Barry had gone in search of a foundry that could cast an eight-ton bell. Here once again a so-called expert got in the way of Barry's wishes: E. B. Denison, QC inveigled himself into a position of authority on the approval committee and started to make the architect's life intolerable, to the extent of insulting his adversary in the pages of *The Times*, criticising 'the stupidity of Sir C. Barry and his crew of hand makers and certificate writers'.[52] Denison's first recommendation was to use a new technique promoted by the Warners Foundry of Cripplegate. 'Big Ben', named after the commissioner Sir Benjamin Hall, was delivered to London the following year, in November 1856, for testing. Within eleven months it had cracked and had to be recast, hoisted in place once more and retested. Again it cracked, and Denison began a campaign of blame against everyone except himself. The bell was finally repaired in 1862, and turned slightly so that the clapper did not repeatedly strike the damaged area. The following year an electromagnetic link was made between the Clock Tower and the Royal Observatory at Greenwich. The chiming of Big Ben from then on became the official timepiece of the nation.

Sir Charles Barry died in May 1860, and did not see the completion of his life's work. There was much left to do but Barry would have been reassured that the major projects were in hand or near completion. The work on the history paintings would continue into the next century; the Speaker's House was habitable, if not finished; and the detailing and carving were coming to an end. The task of overseeing these final parts was given to Barry's son, E. M. Barry, the Professor of Architecture at the Royal Academy. As before, the MPs aired their grievances about the state of their accommodation and the architect would do what he could to adapt to the changing desires of the clients. When the members then complained about the expense, the architect was forced to accept the censure. Both sides needed each other, and both wanted to be in charge. There was no official date for the completion of the new palace; like its neighbour, Westminster Abbey, it was the site of continuous development, and is still today coping with problems of an ever-evolving institution located in a very limited space.

The whole of the new palace takes up eight acres, on low-lying ground facing out towards the Thames. The scope and cost of the project to revive the structure in the aftermath of the fire of 1834 were unprecedented. Looking at it today, it is impossible not to be impressed by the scale of work, the attention to decorative detail and the sense of historical power within the site. Since the 1860s Barry's palace has influenced senate houses and parliamentary buildings throughout the world and offers some architectural qualification for the place to be termed the 'mother of all Parliaments'.

In the end, the rebuilding of the Palace of Westminster never successfully developed a relationship with London. The House was not the political centre of the city, despite coming to represent more of the metropolis between the decades of rebuilding. It is ironic that when, in 1855, the young German refugee Karl Marx went in search of revolution in the capital, he went not to Westminster but to Hyde Park. Until summer 2010, on the green in front of the palace, clusters of tents made a permanent home for protesters, routinely cleared away by the Metropolitan Police when the Queen came to open Parliament and on other official occasions. Here Brian Haw holds his campaign against the latest atrocities in Iraq and Afghanistan. The ramshackle canvas and posters are a sharp rebuke to Barry's vision of the nation.

CHAPTER 9

VICTORIA EMBANKMENT

Sir Joseph Bazalgette and the
Formation of the Modern City

Could we imagine that this great capital of capitals should ever be
what Babylon is – its very site forgotten – one could not but almost
envy the delight with which the antiquaries of that future time would
hear of some discovery of a *London below the soil* still remaining.

Charles Knight, *London*

On the morning of Friday, 8 September 1854, a few hundred yards from
the glamour and elegance of Regent Street, a group of parish officials
gathered at the corner of Broad (now Broadwick) Street, in the heart of
Soho. Despite its proximity to the leading boulevard of the nation, Soho
was by now a warren of dilapidated housing. It was also in the grip of
the most terrible pandemic: cholera. The previous year, over 10,000
had died throughout London; since the beginning of that summer, the
disease had decimated parishes south of the river. It was not until 31
August that the devastation entered Soho, and in the next three days 127
people in the Broad Street area died. Within a week over eighty per cent
of the population had fled, leaving behind only the sick and the poor to
their fate.

One of the officials who were meeting that day was Dr John Snow.
The previous evening at a parish council meeting he had presented his
unlikely prognostication of the epidemic and had urged the meeting
to trust his remedy. Snow's diagnosis went against the vast weight of
conventional opinion and powerful vested interest; and while the news-

papers were reporting that cholera was spread by foul and pestilent miasma that transmitted the disease through the air, Snow had studied the spread of previous deadly outbreaks, charting its movement through the packed city streets and dark corners. He had discerned that, rather than by the air, cholera was carried through the metropolis's water system. Thus he urged the parish committee to join him at the Broad Street pump and break off its handle to ensure that no one was able to draw water from its fetid and infected well.

Snow was not a Londoner, but was born in York in 1813 and had first encountered the sickening effects of cholera while studying medicine in his home town. The disease had first been reported in India when, while on a sortie in 1817, the Marquess of Hastings had stationed his men near Bundelkhand, near Calcutta, where it was said that he lost over 5,000 to a strange disease. Soon, the scourge began to spread, following the military trains and trade routes, and by 1818 the disease had captured the whole of India. Then it began to follow the merchants' trail; the following year it had reached Mauritius; within a decade it had engulfed Afghanistan and Persia and in 1831 it crossed the Channel and found its first victim in the port of Sunderland, and swiftly entered York. By 1834 it had reached London, sneaking aboard the hospital ship, the *Dreadnought*, that was tied up outside Limehouse. The fear and numbers were so great that the local Woolwich vicar only conducted his funeral service when enough bodies had been gathered; he gave the benediction a distance away from the graveside, dropping a white handkerchief as the signal to lower the dead to their resting place. The disease, which at first symbolised the rapacious greed of empire, became a damning verdict on the state of the modern city.

John Snow arrived in London in 1836 and continued his studies at the Great Windmill Street School of Medicine, only two streets away from Broad Street; two years later he set up his surgery in nearby Frith Street, where he became a pioneer in the use of ether and anaesthesia. From here he observed the major cholera outbreaks that shocked the city in 1849, arriving via the German steamer, the *Elbe*, the previous September. A crewman, John Harnold, had contracted the disease abroad and, having rented a room in Horsleydown, south of the river, died in his bed. The next occupant in the unkempt lodging house, a Mr Blenkinsopp, also contracted the disease, and within weeks it had spread throughout London. Snow noted this progress in his first report on the pandemic, *On the Mode of Communication of Cholera*. By conducting a systematic study of the course of the disease, noting the houses, timings and location of each report, he slowly formulated a deathly map of the city.

In his study Snow noted that Harnold had fallen in a house on Thomas Street, and within days twelve more residents of the slum dwellings had died. Visiting the site, he observed that the row, Surrey Buildings, all shared a well and that an open drain ran along the front of the buildings into the water supply, which was further polluted by being near to the open cesspool. Surely, Snow argued, these were the perfect conditions for the proliferation of a waterborne disease. The doctor therefore developed the controversial theory that cholera was not airborne, but transmitted via some form of contact with the waste material of a previous victim – most probably by drinking contaminated water. He pressed his new theory into the hands of the leading civic planners and authorities, but they were too convinced by the miasma theory to listen. It would take another five years, and the devastating resurgence of death, until Snow was able to test his prognosis.

The pump handle at Broad Street was removed after the disease had been rampaging for a week, and the death toll continued to rise for a week. By 10 September, the number of dead stood at 500, despite the *Globe* newspaper reporting, in total belief of the miasma theory, 'owing to the favourable change in the weather, the pestilence which has raged with such a frightful severity in the district has abated'.[1] The following day, the journalist had to eat his words. By the end of the outbreak over 700 people who lived near the pump had died; throughout London, the Bill of Mortality noted 10,738 deaths in all.

Even in the darkest days of the pandemic, John Snow had continued his work and made a statistical study of the spread of the disease on his doorstep, finding some startling facts to support his own theory. As he went from house to house, he made certain to discover where the family sourced their water, learning that nearly all the deaths had taken place within a short distance of the Broad Street pump. He studied the water under a microscope and discovered 'white, flocculent particles'; he was also able to unpick some anomalies, such as deducing that the deaths of an old woman in Hampstead and her niece in Islington were caused by the same source: the woman previously lived in Soho and liked the Broad Street water so much that a servant visited the pump every day; the niece had been infected on a weekend visit to her aunt's. He also worked out why some who lived near the pump were not contaminated, establishing that a local workhouse that suffered only five deaths out of 530 inmates had their own private well, while many who worked at the nearby brewery rarely touched the water and preferred to stick with small beer.

Snow published his new findings in a second edition of *On the Mode of Communication of Cholera*. In addition to the pathological causes of the spread of the disease, he also highlighted the social consequences of the epidemic. The rich need not fear disease in the same way as the poor, for when it enters 'into the better kind of houses ... it hardly ever spreads from one member of the family to another'.[2] The living conditions of the poor, however, made the spread of such misery almost inevitable. One could hardly find a more damning indictment of what was then considered the greatest city in the world.

Foreign visitors marvelled at the vastness of the city at the height of its mid-Victorian pomp, and were informed by a rash of guidebooks to help the hapless tourist make sense of the metropolis. In *Mogg's New Picture of London and Visitor's Guide to its Sights* of 1844, the new arrival was given a route map to visit every necessary monument and place of interest, a task so arduous that the whole tour was spread out over eight days. The city was the emporium of all the world's goods and sparkled with shop fronts; Charles Knight's *Cyclopaedia of London* informed the reader that, from Whitechapel onwards, 'commerce has taken such complete possession of the leading thoroughfares, that almost every house is a shop until we reach the western ends of Piccadilly and Oxford Street'.[3] The metropolis was a hive of bustle and business, the streets packed all day, as Knight's description of Oxford Street showed: 'goods, wagons, and private carriages, omnibuses and men and women on horseback, men of business, fashionable loungers, and curious strangers ... legions of costermongers and shoals of advertising vans'.[4]

Yet beneath this surface of superlatives, London was a city of extremes and, as one German visitor noted in 1851, it was 'the world city of the present age', but also warning that 'things have been conducted here to the utmost limits of the present social system'.[5] London was testing the very notion of urban life and, if it was to survive, a brand-new civic philosophy was needed to sustain its progress. Since the beginning of the 1800s, the metropolis's population had spiralled: at the start of the century, the population was near one million; in 1841 the census reported 1.9 million souls; a decade later this had risen to 2,362,236, reaching 3,254,260 by 1871. This was three times the size of Birmingham, Manchester and Bradford combined, or the entire populations of Australia and New Zealand. The journalist Henry Mayhew estimated that if the population of the city were to line up in pairs and march at a reasonable pace, it would still take nine days for it to pass the line.

Many had come to London to find their fortune, but only a few had succeeded. And as this flood arrived, the urban landscape, stretched to its limits, began to fragment: while the suburbs rose with new housing serviced by the latest transport links, the inner city was abandoned and soon became an unworkable and decaying insult to civilisation, a breeding ground for crime and disease. As happened in the silk weavers' enclave at Spitalfields, rather than building new tenements for the rising population, it became more profitable to divide up once-elegant terraces into lodging houses that swiftly descended into slums. This was now happening all over the capital and whole neighbourhoods were declining into rookeries. While many compared the metropolis to Imperial Rome, one could as easily damn it with reflections of a modern Babylon. In his *Ragged London* (1861), John Hollingshead describes a visit to Berwick Street, only a hundred yards or so from the Broad Street pump:

> The small yard seemed rotting with damp and dirt. The narrow window
> of the lower back room was too caked with mud to be seen through, and
> the kitchen was one of those black-holes, filled with untold filth and

rubbish, which the inspector had condemned a twelvemonth before. The stench throughout the house, although the front and back doors were wide open, was almost sickening; and when a room-door was opened this stench came out in gusts. In one apartment I found a family of six persons, flanked by another apartment containing five.[6]

The city was straining at the seams. In the age of Henry III the capital had been imagined as a body, with each part given its function and significance: thus the King was at the head, and every station had its role and place within the organism. In the time of Sir Christopher Wren and the rebuilding of the capital after the devastations of the Great Fire, the metropolis had been transformed into a new symbol: the human body had been anatomised and found to be a circulatory system. Now the veins and arteries of that body had become clogged and damaged; the lungs were filling up with smoke and disease, the liver and kidneys were finding themselves overworked to the point of exhaustion. The city could no longer cope with the undertow of humanity that moved through it every day.

Instead, the Victorians were forced to find a new way of thinking about the city. Rather than a body, the metropolis had transformed into a machine, a mass of movable, interlocking parts. In the 1820s Charles Babbage, who lived in Dorset Street, Marylebone, was devising a Difference Engine, the first calculating machine, to tabulate logarithms and trigonometry. In 1837 he proposed an improved edition, the Analytic Engine, which could be programmed for various functions, remembering 1,000 figures to fifty decimal points. The engine was so complex that it never saw the light of day, yet it was the perfect reflection of the city in which it was dreamt up. London was now the city of engineers.

Yet there was still no end to the speculation as to why London was not working. For some, the solution was to be found in the air. If, as many believed, disease was spread through miasma, then the cleansing of the atmosphere was paramount. One method promoted was to enclose the city in glass, and in 1845 Frederick Gye proposed a glass arcade built on a series of arches above the ordinary streets from the

Bank of England to Trafalgar Square, which would combine ease of traffic with 'reading rooms, exhibition-rooms, concert rooms, large apartments for public buildings, baths, cafés on the Paris plan etc as well as shops of every variety of trade'.[7]

Gye was not a solitary fantasist. In 1855 William Mobrary and Joseph Paxton, after his success with the Great Exhibition, proposed the Great Victorian Way, a 'crystal girdle' to ring the whole city, linking together the major train termini as well as the Royal Exchange, Cheapside and Southwark south of the Thames, crossing once more at Westminster to include the Houses of Parliament, Kensington Gardens, Oxford Street and Holborn. Paxton devised a glass viaduct seventy feet high with a large central covered roadway lined with columned loggia on either side. The internal space would be temperature-controlled and serviced by a ventilation system. Each section of the Way would be divided into zones, so that there was a shopping mall between the city and Regent Street, and a residential section from Westminster to Kensington. Paxton's plans were presented to the Select Committee on Metropolitan Communication and gained widespread approval, but such a radical re-engineering of the city came at a price that not even London could afford.

Yet something had to be done, as was made painfully clear three years after Paxton's presentation when, in the summer of 1858, the River Thames became so infested with sewage that it almost came to a halt. The Great Stink was an environmental catastrophe that signalled the failures of the metropolis and commanded that the city not only respond to the problems of the basic services that made it work – sewers, water, housing, communications, transport – but also delivered a fundamental revolution in its very identity.

The solution would need to be radical, and change the mechanics of the capital, both in its organisation and the creation of a civic government that was able to treat the city as a whole. Where Sir Charles Barry's Houses of Parliament were a triumph of the Gothic Revival, drawing on an idealised, imagined past as a way to transform the nation, the city beyond Westminster needed more than the healing power of ornamentation to cure its ills.

Many offered solutions, but this is the story of two men who did most to rethink and redesign the city. Sir Edwin Chadwick was a disciple of the philosopher Jeremy Bentham and his life is perhaps the clearest expression of the Utilitarian philosophy of the greatest good for the greatest number. From the 1830s he was central to the campaign for improving the sanitary conditions of London and the organisation of a governing body that could oversee the transformation of the capital. Unwavering in his determination as he attempted to create a centralised civic government, he had a knack of making enemies as he was unafraid to face up to vested interest and inset prejudice. Eventually, he would push through the creation of the Metropolitan Commission of Sewers, which became the Metropolitan Board of Works in 1855. This proposed a governmental structure that unified the many neighbourhoods, parishes and vested interests of London for the first time in its history. Only once London was treated as a single entity could any effective solutions be offered.

The board was fortunate enough, in the year of its inauguration, to hire the talents of a young engineer, Joseph Bazalgette, who has a right to stand alongside Sir Christopher Wren and John Nash as one of the great men who transformed the city. Rather than constructing monuments, Bazalgette's contribution is almost invisible: the river embankments that redrew the flow of the Thames, as well as a new infrastructure – sewers, roads, railways – that would prove that a city should not just be judged by the grandeur of its stones and its palaces, but also by the spaces in between and beneath. The embankment was one of the greatest public works in London's history, and a fitting improvement to the imperial capital at the height of its power.

In 1854 it was estimated that over 200,000 people walked into the city to work every morning. On top of this, 1,000 carts and horses crossed London Bridge every hour and omnibuses from the four corners of the suburbs brought in hordes of middle-class office workers. Cattle were still being driven into the markets and abattoirs and nearly 37,000 tons of dung were collected in the streets every year. For some this was a vision of hell, with no traffic regulations; and certain crossings, such as the Strand

and at the north end of London Bridge, were at a constant standstill.

The River Thames was not much better, and had become the sorriest victim of London's rapid expansion. In 1855 the leading scientist Michael Faraday took a boat ride on the river and discovered, as reported in a letter to *The Times*, that the water was 'an opaque, pale brown fluid'; following an experiment in which he dropped pieces of white paper into the stream, he discerned that the water was so thick with waste that the card disappeared an inch below the surface. The river by this time had become the main conduit of all the sewage of the city, the outlet for every factory and workshop and home.

In the intense heat of the summer of 1858, the River Thames became 'a stream of death instead of a river of life and beauty'.[8] Only in the 1820s Samuel Leigh had claimed that the quality of the water 'must also have an excellent effect on the cleanliness and consequently on the health of the inhabitants of London',[9] yet things were about to change and it was reported that the last fresh salmon was caught in the Thames in 1833; by 1858, in a *Punch* cartoon, a gruesome Father Thames was depicted introducing his children – diphtheria, cholera and scrofula – to London,

21. Thames water under the microscope, from a *Punch* cartoon of the 1850s
(*Bridgeman*)

pushing forward the sorriest trio of deathly ghouls the caricaturist could imagine. For anyone who had the misfortune to walk alongside the river, the truth was plain to the eye and nose: at low tide, a thick layer of dark ooze formed upon the exposed riverbanks that moved with an infestation of bright red worms; as the waters rose this vile sludge was then churned up by the riverboats, turning the Thames into a foul quagmire.

That summer, the stench was so great that in the Houses of Parliament Benjamin Disraeli was seen with a handkerchief clasped to his face. While the more fortitudinous members were obliged to place curtains soaked in chloride of lime across the windows of the new Westminster Palace, many members campaigned to move the session outside the city. Commentators noted that, just as in the Great Plague of 1665, the rich and powerful were abandoning the city, leaving the poor and needy to their fate. Of those members who remained, some proposed to take a boat and observe the problem, the advice of one of their fellows echoing in their ears: 'take a good supply of brandy and other condiments ... for the purpose of obtaining relief for the sickening sensations they must experience'.[10] The city press was more clear in its condemnation: 'it stinks; and whoso once inhales the stink can never forget it and can count himself lucky if he live to remember it'.[11]

Parliament had done nothing to remedy the situation until it had become intolerable, and so suffered the consequences that summer. Yet, having been so assailed by the stench, they now demanded immediate action. Ironically, the Great Stink was in part caused by a new innovation in sanitation: the flushing toilet. In 1801 there were approximately 136,000 new houses in London, each with a toilet; by 1851, this had increased to 306,000 which spilt 80.8 million gallons of waste into the river through seventy-one sewage outlets each day.

As a physical space, London was expanding faster than the cartographers could chart it, and it was all still reliant on the same antiquated infrastructure; those without the latest water closet depended on the nearly 200,000 cesspools that collected human waste and were cleared by an army of night-soil men, who for one shilling emptied and sold the waste to many of the farms on the outskirts of the city. By the 1840s, however, this was considered unsanitary, and the system could no longer cope with the volume of waste as housing became cramped and many of the poorer enclaves of the inner city swam upon a lake of shit. As one commissioner to St Giles reported: 'upon passing through the passage of the first house, I found the yard covered in night soil, from the overflowing of the privy to the depth of nearly six inches and bricks were placed to enable inmates to get across dryshod'.[12]

The Thames had always been the city's conduit for surface sewage – waste carried by rainwater from the street to the riverbank – but until 1815 it was illegal to discharge any effluent from buildings into the sewers. Ditches and drains had been used within the city since the time of the Romans, most of them constructed out of the old natural watercourses – rivers and brooks that ran from springs in the outlying neighbourhoods to the Thames. This was not a perfect system of drainage and the deleterious state of the River Fleet, which went from Highgate towards the river on the western fringes of the city walls, had been the subject of barbs for centuries. The elegant eighteenth-century poet Alexander Pope jibed that the river was a stream of dead dogs and detritus, while in 1846 an accumulation of combustible gases, trapped in a covered section of the ditch, exploded, creating a tsunami of sewage that swept away three houses in Clerkenwell.

In addition to the state of the cesspools, their maintenance was a grave concern. Controlled locally, on a parish or ward level, with local commissions and councils to oversee their condition and upkeep, there was no central administration responsible for the whole city. This meant that some neighbourhoods were better managed than others, and there was no 'joined-up' governance between vested interests. Since the beginning of the century, it had become clear that the old way of doing things needed a radical overhaul.

The city was first jolted into action following the first cholera epidemic of 1832, when it was obvious that the disease struck the poor more than the rich. At that time Edwin Chadwick was a clerk on the Royal Commission on the Poor Laws. Born in Manchester to a radical journalist father who had spent his youth in Paris alongside Tom Paine, Edwin Chadwick started his career as a lawyer but also dabbled in political writing. On arrival in London, he took lodgings at the Inner

Temple but was drawn into the circle of radical thinkers that buzzed around Jeremy Bentham. By 1831 he had moved into Bentham's house in Queen Square, Bloomsbury, and on his master's death the following year swiftly secured a place on the committee, which was looking at the issues of poverty within the city. Inspired by his mentor, he was determined not just to talk about the betterment of society but to do something about it.

Until this time, the definition and care of the poor had been a local affair, as set out in a series of Poor Laws that stretched back to the Elizabethan period. It divided up the helpless into four groups: the impotent poor, who could do nothing about their condition; the able-bodied, who lacked skills or were victims of economic forces; the idle poor, who were unwilling to work; and vagrants. All types were controlled by their local authorities, which collected a local tax to pay for relief. By 1832, as the slums of London began to fill up and were ravaged by disease, this was no longer enforceable.

Instead, Chadwick encouraged the commission to collect reams of data on the extent of the crisis, and recommended that, as parishes could no longer cope on their own, they should form unions. He also suggested that all outdoor relief, assistance payments, should cease and workhouses be built to house all those who truly needed help. The workhouse was based on the 'less eligibility principle' – a deterrent against idleness, and the very last possible resort. The commission's conclusions were passed to Parliament and became the 1834 Poor Law Amendment Act, naming Chadwick as secretary to the Poor Law Commission that oversaw the construction and nationwide management of the new workhouses. In effect, the governance of the poor was taken out of the hands of the parish and centralised, with Chadwick as its unelected welfare tsar.

Chadwick was also convinced that there was a relationship between poverty and disease. More research was called for on the costs of the outbreaks and whether there was any way to prevent such dangers. This came perilously into focus in the 1837–8 typhus pandemic in the East End which proved that the environment had a direct influence on health and poverty. In 1838 Chadwick produced a short report that suggested that 'the causes of fever in the metropolis ... might be removed by proper sanitary measures'.[13] In 1842 he followed this up with a fully scientific study: *Inquiry into the Sanitary Conditions of the Labouring Population of Great Britain.* It was an instant bestseller with 20,000 copies sold in the first year.

Chadwick proposed that there was a salubrious relationship between living conditions and disease. As a staunch apostle of the miasma theory he was convinced that 'all smell is, if it is intense, immediate acute disease; and eventually we may say that, by depressing the system and rendering it susceptible to the actions of other causes, all smell is disease'.[14] The results were economic and long-term so that sickness, poor diet, and deleterious housing suppressed the poor and made it impossible for them to pull themselves out of the slums. Terrible living conditions, cramped rooms and poor hygiene also had a social and moral impact on individuals – encouraging drunkenness, promiscuity and violence. In the age of Samuel Smiles's bible of Victorian positive psychology, *Self-Help*, which held that an individual could overcome any circumstance with character and courage, Chadwick suggested that the city itself was not just a victim of pollution but also its agent. London made people sick.

One peculiarity of the miasma theory was the belief that human and animal waste could be made safe by being immersed in water. Thus Chadwick campaigned for a new way for the waste of the city to be flushed away and, in the Building Act of 1844, it was required that all new buildings be connected to the common sewer and that a sewerage network be built so that no new houses were ever more than thirty feet away from a pipe. All of London's 200,000 cesspools were to be abolished in view of this new hygienic infrastructure and the city's waste was to be washed out into the Thames, courtesy of Joseph Bramah's hydraulic press. This was given an added boost in 1861 by the new designs showcased in Thomas Crapper's Chelsea emporium, promising 'a certain flush with every pull'.

Chadwick then took on the challenge of engineering a system of connected sewers to carry the waste from every neighbourhood to the Thames and in 1847 the Metropolitan Commission of Sewers was established, with Chadwick as its the guiding light. He was unafraid to put noses out of joint as he ensured that his Utilitarian vision was not to be derailed by local tradition or vested interest. Since the reign of Henry VIII the sewers had been overseen by seven different local commissions, each with their own Act of Parliament, committee and obligations. Chadwick was determined to sweep this aside and thus 1,065 local commissioners were replaced by twenty-three members of the Metropolitan board.

For many, this rabid desire to centralise power into the hands of unelected officials was, if not downright European, then nonetheless dangerous. As revolution was breaking out once more on the Continent it was un-English to govern in this way, and threatened absolutism by the back door. Was this not exactly the kind of thing that the parliamentary system, symbolised by Barry's Gothic palace, was built to combat? As a result, while Chadwick argued that the state of the city was a result of 'the experiences of evils arising from the want of unity in the metropolis',[15] *The Times* reported the proud popular response that 'we prefer to take our chance of cholera and the rest than be bullied into health'.[16]

Unsurprisingly, the commission made little headway. It measured the amount of waste that was now flowing out of the 76,386 feet of sewers built in the previous decades and devised a highly detailed ordnance survey map of the whole region of London and the suburbs on which to plan its new system. The map would take ten years to complete and cost £23,000. There was also debate about the nature of the task; the temperature rose as Chadwick took on the engineers over the ideal construction of the new sewerage network, if it were ever to come.

The 'sewer pipe wars' discussed the shape and manufacture of drainage pipes but were really a conflict between Chadwick's opinion that the engineers were self-interested jobbers and the commission's determination to impose new standards of sanitary policy. The engineers, like the rest of the city, did not enjoy being lectured on how to do their job by this unelected bureaucrat. The current designs, however, were haphazard and often shoddy. As Henry Mayhew reported, at the boundary between two parishes the work was often incomplete and uneven, patched-up with boards rather than brick, and many areas of the walls had collapsed. It was even worse in Soho, where the sizes of the pipes were utterly random; he saw one chamber, 'from the roof of which hangings of putrid matter like stalactites descend three feet in length'.[17] He noted, with some surprise, that the sewers of the rich were no better than those of the slums. Chadwick was determined to create a single network of sewers and promote a uniform design of pipe, an upside-down egg that increased flow in all weathers.

In the meantime cholera returned in 1848–9, claiming the highest death toll so far: 14,137. Little did anyone know that the business of the Metropolitan Commission of Sewers was making matters worse rather than better. By flushing the infected water into the Thames, the disease spread throughout the city. It also became clear that many of the private companies that supplied fresh water to the city were sourcing their supply from the riverbanks. The Lambeth and Southwark Company, started in 1845, as reported by Charles Dickens actually took their water from between Waterloo and Hungerford bridges at the heart of the West End. As a result, when the epidemic struck it ripped through the poor communities on the southern riverbanks. Powerless to stop the pandemic, Chadwick was rapidly losing support for his radical plans. He was also getting too ambitious in the face of private interest. When he suggested that all water companies should be banned from sourcing their water from the Thames and rather pipe from Surrey, the businessmen were up in arms. Chadwick then proposed to merge the eight companies supplying the capital 'under one and the same management'.[18] This was a step too far.

Nonetheless, a year after the Great Stink the commission was forced to admit that it had no cure and launched a competition for any engineer who could find a solution to the problems that were engulfing the city, echoed in plaintive tones by *The Times*: 'London dock is black as Acheron ... where are ye, ye civil engineers? Ye can remove mountains, bridges, seas and fill rivers ... can ye not purify the Thames, and so render your own city habitable.'[19] As it happens, in the same month the engineer Joseph Bazalgette was hired by the commission as assistant surveyor, and so began a career that would transform the stones of London and solve the lethal issues of the Thames, and in doing so, according to the historian John Doxat, save more lives than any other Victorian public official.

Bazalgette was the archetypal Victorian engineer: a stickler for detail, determined and dedicated to the task, almost to a fault. He would sometimes work himself to nervous exhaustion, driven by a desire to do the job to the best of his ability, coupled with an abiding sense of duty. He was born the grandson of a French tailor who had migrated to London and in his lifetime built up such a successful business that he not only clothed the Prince Regent but also lent the spendthrift over £22,000. His father had served with Nelson at Trafalgar but retired wounded soon after to work for the Naval and Military Bible Society. Privately educated until the age of seventeen, Bazalgette then entered the service of Sir John MacNeill, a leading engineer who was in charge of a series of government projects in drainage and land reclamation in Northern Ireland. By 1838 he had returned to London and was accepted into the Institution of Civil Engineers, four years later setting up his own offices nearby on Great George Street and beginning his own practice. He soon became recognised as a rising star, his curriculum vitae containing glowing references from the Stephensons, Isambard Kingdom Brunel and Sir William Cubitt.

Bazalgette was not the only engineer on the commission looking for a technological solution to the problem of the capital's sewers: Robert Stephenson was on the board, while the head engineer was Frank Forster, who had considerable experience working on the railways. Together they sifted through the 137 entrants to the competition, later reporting that many 'may for the main part be described as vague, speculative, disquisitous or colaterial ... few of which can be said to possess any practical value'.[20] The task inevitably returned to Forster and his team to offer a proper proposal.

Forster, alongside Bazalgette, came up with a preliminary plan to build intercepting sewerage pipes that carried the city's waste beyond the metropolis and, through a system of embankments on either side of the Thames, ensured that it was not mixed with the water supply. The proposals were radical and gave the commission much to chew over. Work had already begun on a similar project between Victoria and

Westminster on the northern riverbank and was soon a financial disaster as the plotted land was beset by quicksand, poor workmanship and an ugly debate over materials. The final bill came in at £54,866, over four times more than planned. No wonder that for the next two years Forster's grand designs would be ceaselessly scrutinised and costed, resulting in his premature death in 1852 from 'harassing fatigues and the anxieties of official duties'.[21] In his place Bazalgette was named the new head engineer of the commission, and immediately began to alter and improve Forster's plans.

The idea of building a series of embankments along the Thames had been a continual subject of speculation. After the Great Fire in 1666, Christopher Wren, Surveyor General of the King's Works, proposed an elegant quay to run from the Tower to the Temple. After initial surveys, Wren and his friend, the city surveyor Robert Hooke, soon found that the project was unfeasible – vested interest and private property owners were immovable obstacles. Yet the idea did not disappear: in the eighteenth century, John Gwynn, author of *London and Westminster Improved*, revived and bettered Wren's plans with quays along both sides from London Bridge to the newly completed Westminster Bridge – but with the same result. In 1824 the MP Sir Frederick Trench had proposed a sequence of new walkways, built to control the flow of the river. Trench's scheme was aimed at the improvement of the road system and the creation of handsome steps and jetties; 'its beauty and magnificence will eminently contribute to the embellishment of the metropolis'.[22] Again, to no avail.

Ten years later the painter John Martin suggested that the river front could be improved by replacing the unsightly wharves with a stone embankment. Martin's plans were more practical and were the first to look at the issue of waste; the embankments could be integrated into a larger intercepting sewerage system, in which the waste then flowed into large reservoirs along the riverside, whence it could be transported to the outskirts of London by canal. In 1842 Thomas Cubitt made a more palatable proposal in *Suggestions for Improving the State of the River Thames and the Drainage of London*: rather than allowing the waste to gather in reservoirs, 'the best means of obviating this evil would be to conduct the sewer drainage at once from west and north parts of London, by the shortest and straightest lines that can be found, to a place to the east of town'.[23] Later that year the chief engineer of the City of London Corporation also proposed his own set of embankments, but was attacked from all quarters – Parliament, private companies, parish authorities and even the Chancery, who informed him that the riverbed actually belonged to the Crown. However, as the work in Victoria had proved, without the complete ordnance survey map of the city it was a dangerous guessing game.

Bazalgette's plan was inspired by those who came before him: to dig a series of main drains from west to east on both sides of the Thames in order to intercept the existing rivers and brooks that had carried much of the city's waste and rainfall to the river. Yet the technical task at hand was not necessarily as complex as the chicanery needed to get the plan approved. Building sewers was not the problem; being allowed to build them was. Bazalgette not only needed to find 'the shortest and straightest lines', he also had to work through the vexed issues of vested interest, local bureaucracy and property rights. Even before the first ditch was to be dug, a government revolution was necessary to make it possible. This inevitably came to the fore over the painful issue of money.

In 1853 it was pointed out that, while the Metropolitan Commission of Sewers only raised £200,000 a year from the sewerage rate, Forster and Bazalgette's first set of plans came in at £1,080,000, excluding the heavy extra costs of compulsory purchase of any building that was needed. Parliament was not unsympathetic, but wanted to find an alternative solution and, rather than promising to underwrite the project, they sought to find a means that addressed not just the problem of the sewers but that of the whole city. As a result, in 1855, they debated and passed the Metropolis Management Act and in August the Metropolitan Board of Works was created.

The Metropolitan Board of Works (MBW) was set up to tackle the changing face of the city, its main task being 'the better management of the Metropolis in respect of the sewerage and drainage and the paving, cleansing, lighting and improvements thereof'.[24] But the Act was even more radical than that because, for the first time in the city's history, the numerous parishes, local interests, wards, liberties, corporations and boroughs of London were united under one governmental body. The board had power to work within both the city and Westminster, and on both sides of the Thames. The new institution did away with much of the local infrastructure and vested interest and replaced it with a single power base to tackle the challenges of life in the modern city; where the Metropolitan Commission of Sewers had failed, perhaps the Board of Works could make the machine of London work again.

The MBW represented Edwin Chadwick's hopes of uniting the city, yet the man himself was absent. He had gained too many enemies on the way up to share any of the praise once he had been proved right. Instead, the leading figure in the establishment of the board was the MP for Marylebone, Chadwick's rival and often the defender of vested interest, Sir Benjamin Hall, after whom the Big Ben bell in the Westminster Palace clock tower was named. Hall told Parliament that a city of two million could no longer be governed by ninety different local bodies and, instead, an overarching board of forty-six members should be voted in by the smaller groups. There was also a team of official experts to be employed by the board – a clerk, architect and engineer – to deliver solutions to the problems of the day. Without much surprise, Joseph Bazalgette was named Chief Engineer and was commanded to push forward his plans for a new sewerage system. He would also be forced to turn his attention to work on schemes for road widening, slum clearances, the Metropolitan Railway and bridges. Inevitably, things did not start smoothly.

The first problem was found in the small print of the parliamentary Act; clause 136 stated that all plans had to be submitted to another Royal Commission and 'no such plan shall be carried into effect until the same has been approved by such commissioners'.[25] There were also financial limitations on what the board could borrow and Parliament had the final say on any project over £100,000. Bazalgette was effectively powerless in the hands of larger organisations that checked and restrained his every move. When he handed in his first plans on 23 May 1856, he meekly hoped that he had not developed anything new but worked on the previous plans of others 'to the peculiar wants and features of different

22. Joseph Bazalgette, the
    urban engineer
    (*Bridgeman*)

districts, with which my position has made me familiar'.[26] The plans
were rejected by Sir Benjamin Hall, who did not believe that the waste
was discharged far enough out into the Thames estuary, east of the city.

Bazalgette was forced to rethink his plans. He knew that to build
longer sewers was costly and he also saw that the further east he dug the
more complicated the operation would be; on the south bank, just
outside Greenwich, he was faced with laying pipes across a river and
marshy ground. Nonetheless he soon found a new map for the intercepting sewers, as he later reported to the Institute of Civil Engineers:

> ... three lines of sewers have been constructed on each side of the river,
> termed respectively the High Level, the Middle Level, and the Low Level.
> The High and Middle Level Sewers discharge by gravitation, and the Low
> Level Sewers discharge only by the aid of pumping. The three lines of
> sewers north of the Thames converge and unite at Abbey Mills, east of
> London, where the contents of the Low Level will be pumped into the
> Upper Level Sewer, and their aggregate stream will flow through the

Northern Outfall Sewer, which is carried on a concrete embankment across the marshes to Barking Creek, and there discharges into the river by gravitation.

On the south side the three intercepting lines unite at Deptford Creek, and the contents of the Low Level Sewer are there pumped to the Upper Level, and the united streams of all three flow in one channel through Woolwich to Crossness Point in Erith Marshes. Here the full volume of sewage can flow into the Thames at low water, but will ordinarily be raised by pumping into the reservoir.[27]

Bazalgette was not concerned solely with the position of the new network of sewers but also with their function, and he had to think about the shape and manufacture of the pipes, conducting experiments on such matters as 'As to the Velocity and Flow of the Minimum Fall', 'As to the Quantity of Sewerage to be Intercepted' and 'How to Dispose of Rainfall'. He saw London's infrastructure as a large industrial machine that needed to be calibrated, measured and quantified. Perhaps the most difficult problem to solve was that of gravity.

The sewers worked on the basis that waste and water ran down pipes at an average of three miles an hour. This was possible for the High Level and Middle Level Sewers on the north bank that drained downhill from Hampstead and Kensal Rise to Hackney, but in the Low Level which ran from Chiswick alongside the river, there were stretches of riverbank where he could not find the right gradient to ensure a steady flow. Similarly, on the southern shore there were long stretches of ground where no inclines could be found. Therefore he had to create them, planning for a sequence of pumping stations at various points on both sides of the Thames to drag up sewage and then push it eastwards.

This new plan was submitted on 31 December 1856 and Hall handed it to a team of engineers who jealously scoured it for mistakes, producing a 500-page report seven months later with a plethora of improvements. The 'Referees' plans', however, were soon scrutinised by the board and while Bazalgette's scheme was costed at just under £2.5 million, the new plans came in at a massive £5.4 million. He had also factored in the rise in levels of waste based on predictions of a forty per cent gradual increase in population. Thus the project was stuck at the crossroads and it would take the pestilence of the Great Stink the following summer to shake the MPs into action – for, as *The Times* reported that June, 'Parliament was all but forced to legislate upon the great London nuisance by the force of sheer stench.'[28]

On 15 July 1858 the Metropolis Management Amendment Act was passed, which asked the Board of Works to start whatever scheme they had with 'all convenient speed'. In addition the parliamentary veto was swept aside and the board was permitted to borrow up to £3 million guaranteed by the Treasury, to be repaid by a coal and wine levy, the very same that had paid for the rebuilding of St Paul's and the city churches after the Great Fire. On 11 August the board then approved Bazalgette's plans and the project was set to start in January 1859.

In the meantime, each sewer was tendered out to contract, and the board, as was to be expected, accepted the lowest bids on almost all occasions. For the High Level Sewer that was to run from Hampstead to Old Ford, a distance of about nine miles, intercepting the water from the Fleet, Kentish Town, Highgate, Hackney, Clapton, Stoke Newington and Holloway, a Mr Moxon of Cannon Street and Dover claimed the tender with a promise to complete the task for £152,430. Much of the work was then subcontracted down to other teams. Large ditches were to be dug, at least twenty-seven feet deep, and then the pipe completed in brick before it was covered over again. As Bazalgette reported, his plans were very precise, with a width varying in size: 'from 4 feet in diameter to 9 feet 6 inches by 12 feet; its fall is rapid, ranging at the upper end from 1 in 71 to 1 in 376, and from 4 to 5 feet per mile at the lower end. It is constructed of stock brickwork, varying in thickness from 9 inches to 2 feet 3 inches, and the invert is lined with Staffordshire blue brick'.[29] Where they were not able to dig, such as crossing the Union Canal, they used tunnels; in the circumstance of going underneath property, such as in Hackney, the pipes were 'underpinned and placed upon iron girders'.[30] The High Level Sewer was completed by 1861.

As work began on all three intercepting sewers on the north side of the river, it seemed as if the whole of London was being dug up. The Middle Level Sewer followed a line that went through the heart of the city; where only five years previously Joseph Paxton had proposed his crystal arcades, now the roads of Notting Hill, Bayswater, Oxford Street and Holborn were muddy, unpassable quagmires. It also had a number of branch lines that flowed off it, including one that ran all the way up Piccadilly. The Middle Level pipe made its way to Old Ford, where it connected with the High Level Sewer at the Penstock Chamber. Here there was machinery to steer the combined waste further eastwards or, in emergencies, into the nearby River Lea.

In 1861 the journalist John Hollingshead ventured down into the new sewers 'as if going into a wine cellar'. He wandered from St John's Wood to Piccadilly, coming up for air at Green Park. At one point his guide asked him to guess where they were; when told he was beneath Buckingham Palace, Hollingshead 'taking off my fan-tailed cap, ... led the way with the National Anthem, insisting that my guides should join in the chorus'.[31] That same year the board invited 1,500 members of the local boards and vestries to inspect the work alongside the Chief Engineer; the afternoon was a huge success apart from two injuries, one man falling off a plank into the waste below.

The Low Level Sewer was by far the longest, at eleven and a half miles, and most complex construction. The western division ran from Chiswick to Pimlico, with a number of branches and feeding pipes. At Pimlico the land was so low-lying that it was impossible to construct the drains on a gradient. Bazalgette had originally planned for a reservoir on Fulham Fields that was chemically treated and then discharged into the Thames, north of Chelsea Bridge, as this was still a lightly populated area. It was not until 1862 that the Fulham medical officer, Dr Burge, complained and a pumping station was planned to raise the waste nineteen feet so that it could then continue its journey eastwards along the new works on the embankment.

Bazalgette planned four pumping stations in total, the only visible evidence above ground of his great scheme: the pump at Chelsea, two stations south of the river at Deptford and Crossness, and Abbey Mills in West Ham along the eastern stretch of the northern pipeline. The stations were dazzling in their ornate decoration and ornamentation, perhaps the most outrageous manifestation of Victorian historicism

23. Building the sewers

applied to such an impolite task. Abbey Mills was designed to lift the Low Level Sewer thirty-six feet to meet the two other pipes before spilling out through the outfall sewer. Work began in 1865 under the direction of the architect, Charles Driver, who, while influenced by the architectural criticism of John Ruskin, was tasked to build his monument in the least meaningful (Ruskin would even say deceitful) material – cast iron. The station was a strange hybrid between ornamentation and Utilitarianism – where the sensibility of the new palace at Westminster collided with the age of the engineer.

Driver concocted an oriental fantasy of coloured stone combining a medieval Venetian tower, a French mansard roof, Moorish chimneys and a Norman arch circling the entrance. Inside, the vast central room was filled with industrial machinery – eight enormous cast-iron beam engines, each of 142 horsepower with thirty-seven-foot beams and cylinders of four feet six inches in diameter – pumping and churning throughout the day; the roof was held up by thin columns, spandrels and brackets in cast iron, yet one could also imagine oneself – noise aside – in a Byzantine temple. The station was opened with great fanfare in 1865 by the Prince of Wales, in lieu of the Queen, alongside Members of Parliament, archbishops and members of the board. If any event summed up the many heady contradictions, conflicting interests and notions of the Victorian era, it was this.

By 1862, there had been successes as well as criticism. A handful of the contractors who offered their lowest bids to gain the work had gone bankrupt in the process. There was also a sense within the city that, despite the upheaval and the mountains of mud, the metropolis was changing. The newspapers marvelled at the news when two tunnel systems burrowing under Woolwich were so well devised that they met without an inch's deviation. Bazalgette still hoped to complete the task by the end of that year and under £3 million, but work on the embankments along the Thames, the conduit for the northern Low Level Sewer, had not yet even begun.

In 1864, Charles Dickens started to produce the monthly instalments of his final, and perhaps darkest, novel, *Our Mutual Friend*. It is a story obsessed with the Thames from the very first scene when the body of the young heir is dragged out of the water. For Dickens the Thames was a bringer of life and rebirth, as well as death; it could destroy well-laid plans in an instant while also providing a good living for those willing to scavenge amongst the dust heaps and mudbanks. Dickens wrote most of the book while living off the Strand, a few yards away from the waterfront. As he was writing the very world he was describing was disappearing.

In 1861, Parliament started to debate the future of the river front and the last section of Bazalgette's main drainage scheme. In the previous three years the Chief Engineer of the MBW had overseen nearly 1,200 miles of intercepting sewers, rain outfill pipes, subways and tunnels, the equivalent of four times the distance from London to Glasgow. The system was now capable of dealing with an annual flow of 31,650 million gallons of waste, industrial spill, rainwater and sludge. However, it still ran into the Thames. To catch this waste and funnel it out of the city, Bazalgette proposed that three sections of the riverbanks be built into embankments – in Chelsea, between Battersea Bridge and Millbank; the Albert Embankment that ran along the southern shore between Vauxhall Bridge and Westminster Bridge; and the Victoria Embankment from Westminster to Blackfriars. Combined, all three schemes would reclaim fifty-two acres of land from the the river and would improve navigation by increasing the flow of Thames water and therefore clearing the riverbed of silt, also creating new roadways to unblock the almost permanent congestion of the city centre.

Yet this did not make the operation a foregone certainty; there were still many obstacles, vested interests and technical issues to overcome. To begin with, the whole scheme was considered too big for the MBW to handle by themselves and so a Royal Commission headed by Sir Joseph Paxton was set up; this allowed for a flood of plans and schemes to swamp the committee. One Thomas Weller proposed a long garden the full length of the Thames disguising a two-level viaduct for road traffic and a railway; meanwhile Londoner Edward Walmsley developed a crystal arcade filled with shops and galleries. Detailed and professional plans were also sent in from the leading engineering firms of the day, proving that this was indeed a contract worth fighting for. In most schemes considerable thought had gone into the question of how the work was to pay for itself, and many came up with methods for the rents and sale of freeholds to fund the effort. These were not ideas to be cast aside, and each plan was scrutinised by the committee.

It was not until late in the deliberations that Bazalgette proved to the committee that he was the man and his plans were the scheme for the stretch between Westminster and Blackfriars. On the afternoon of 13 May 1861, in front of the parliamentary committee, Bazalgette was asked whether it was possible to replace the wharves that ran along the river's edge, and at that moment the Chief Engineer stood in front of his map and drew a line with red ink that curved around the northern shore. Bazalgette's scheme was nothing new – perhaps his genius was in combining the best bits of all previous plans rather than reinvention – yet his preparation was so assiduous, comprising thirty-four detailed plans and drafts, and fifty-six pages of technical specifications, that they are still used today by maintenance staff. For the Victoria Embankment he would reclaim a thirty-two-acre section of the river and in the 'fill' he would place both a new roadway as well as the intercepting pipelines. This was affirmed in the 1862 Thames Embankment (North) Act. Parliamentary Acts for the two other embankments were passed in 1864 and 1865.

Work did not start straightaway. Firstly Bazalgette had to advertise for a contractor; he also had to ensure that when it was time to start there would be no delays or interference. The Act specified that, despite the upheaval, the work could not disturb steamboat traffic on the Thames and temporary wharves had been built at Westminster and Hungerford bridges. He also needed supplies: tons of gravel – a million cubic yards – that was to be dredged up from the riverbed, and the finest Scottish granite to construct his elegant river wall.

Most problematic was the rising tide of complaints against property rights infringements. The stretch of river from Hungerford to Blackfriars was home to numerous wharves that were in constant use bringing goods into the West End; there was also a mechanical engineering firm and the City of London Gas Works which received nearly 400 barges laden with coal every day to light the city streets at night. All these needed to be removed and paid off. In addition, the Duke of Buccleuch, whose Montagu House looked out over Whitehall, kicked up a stink concerning the potential loss of value of his newly decorated residence. Such powerful opposition could have stopped proceedings in their tracks, but the press and eventually the Prime Minister came down on the side of progress. It was by no means a coincidence that, on 6 September 1862, *The Times* reported the commencement of works with the first pile being driven into the riverbed directly outside Montagu House.

The technical process of building the embankment was, in the words of Bazalgette, 'child's play ... I get most credit for the Thames Embankment, but it wasn't anything like such a job as the Drainage'.[32] To begin with, wooden piles were driven into the riverbed following the line drawn in red ink upon the Chief Engineer's map. The gaps between the piles were then filled in with gravel and clay, making it watertight. Only then was the water pumped out, leaving a dry area for the construction of the embankment. When there were concerns that steam-driven pile drivers were causing damage to nearby housing, metal caissons were used instead and were then sealed with wooden pegs. Nevertheless the process was dangerous and there were numerous injuries; one man was chopped in half as a badly laid caisson tumbled, while another man fell into a coffer-dam and drowned as it was filled with concrete. The river wall was constructed with brick and concrete to twenty feet below the riverbed and then faced with granite, rather than iron that was thought to rust too quickly, reaching eight feet into the mud.

While there was progress, Bazalgette's plans were dealt a blow in 1864 when the Metropolitan District Railway was incorporated with a new railway line along the river front from Westminster. The embankment was no longer concerned solely with the traffic of waste but also the latest technology – the subterranean railway. The idea of bringing railways into the heart of the city had been debated for some time. By the 1850s there were stations situated at the edges of the metropolis on the south side of London Bridge, Fenchurch Street inside the city, Shoreditch to the east, King's Cross and Euston to the north, Paddington to the west and Waterloo, south of Westminster.

The new technology was heralded as a remedy for the excruciating conditions of trying to travel by road as the hordes entered the city by omnibus, private carriage, and by foot every morning. As the Royal Commission of 1854 reported: 'the overcrowding of the city is caused, first by the natural increase in the population and area of the surrounding district; secondly, by the influx of provincial passengers by the great railways North of London, and the obstruction experienced in the streets by omnibuses and cabs coming from their distant stations, to bring the provincial travellers to and from the heart of the city'.[33] The first line proposed by the Metropolitan Railway Company was to connect Paddington with the city via King's Cross to Farringdon, near where the city walls once stood. Thus, alongside the upheaval of the digging of the sewers, Euston Road (previously New Street, once the boundary between the suburbs of Marylebone and Regent's Park), was also excavated with an eighty-foot-wide ditch. The operation was completed by January 1863 and within months over 26,000 Londoners had experienced their first trip on the new subway.

This was speculative business rather than civic works, and soon the Railway Company saw profits to be made by extending the line further, drawing more commuters into the service. The first extension was to the west from Paddington, towards the outer fringes of the city at Hammersmith. They also sought to monopolise the West End traffic and made plans to dig underground, from Paddington in the west and Farringdon in the east, towards the river, delivering commuters into the centre of the city. By 1868, they were looking for a way to connect the two ends by running a line along the northern bank of the Thames from Aldgate to South Kensington; Bazalgette's embankment, growing out of the Thames riverbed, was the perfect solution by building a tunnel alongside the sewer. Also, four stations were devised at Westminster, Embankment, the Temple and Blackfriars.

These new plans delayed Bazalgette's progress, as he had to rethink his embankment and integrate the railway tunnel into his designs. This was not helped by the failure of the Railway Company to find investment, and it was not until 1869 that they got their hands on the necessary £1.5 million. After that the task was straightforward and the rail line was built using the cut-and-cover method, with the two tracks covered with elegant stone barrel ceilings. Steam engines pulled the carriages along the tracks; most carriages were about forty feet long, divided into six compartments. There were three classes of compartment; first class, in the words of Henry Mayhew, had 'extremely handsome and roomy vehicles', with plenty of room for ordinary citizens who were now able to travel into the city.

Yet the embankment had a third function: the modernisation of the machinery of the city as a road for above-ground traffic, offering a new route in and out of the metropolis. The problems of the nearby Strand, as the main thoroughfare between Westminster and the City, were all too apparent. It was impossible to widen these ancient streets without great expense. It was not until 1873 that the Temple Bar, the elegant stone gateway designed by Sir Christopher Wren in the 1670s to straddle the northern end of Fleet Street, was removed. The revered structure was a dreadful bottleneck that allowed only one coach or horse-drawn omnibus to pass at any time. The new embankment offered an alternative road to unclog the city and make it work once more.

While most of the work was being conducted underground, the ornamentation and design of the new embankment that could be seen above ground was debated. How was such a structure to look? It was undoubtedly 'the most extensive and wonderful work of modern times', but should it be finished in a classical style, or given Gothic tones? Perhaps, given the location, it could appear Venetian. In 1863 Bazalgette had displayed four different sets of plans for the site at the Royal Academy, to almost universal approval (but, needless to say, none saw the light of day). The quay was to be clad in shining granite. It would combine classicism with modernity, and Bazalgette devised a series of gaslights made from cast iron, with twinned dolphins curled around the base. These were complemented by bronze lion-head mooring rings on the face of the river wall. Tree-planting began, forming an avenue of planes on the other side of the broad roadway, and from 30 July 1868 people were able to stroll along the river front for the first time.

The embankment would be a destination as well as a place of transit. After 1877 visitors also came here to see the distinctive shard of stone nicknamed Cleopatra's Needle, which was placed between Hungerford Bridge and the Temple. The ancient monument, dating from 1460 BC, was intended as a memorial to the British victory over Napoleon after the Battle of the Nile and was given to Nelson by the Egyptian ruler Muhammad Ali.

Bazalgette was also thinking about a garden to run from Hungerford Bridge to Somerset House. Initially he planned an ornate series of terraces, fountains and staircases linking the embankment to the furiously congested Strand to 'afford the most valuable building frontages, and form one of the finest features of London'.[34] However the plans encroached on lands belonging to the Marquess of Salisbury who, it was claimed, was prone to 'instances of quite exceptional stupidity' and who would have none of it. Instead a more modest Victoria Embankment Gardens was planted, with a bandstand as well as an array of statues, including one of Bazalgette himself with the claim: *Flumini Vincula Posuit*, 'he placed chains on the river'.

The Victoria Embankment was officially opened on 13 July 1870. As the Queen was in her most reclusive mood, the Prince of Wales, with five other royals, twenty-four ambassadors, almost the full House of MPs and 10,000 ticket holders, gathered for the formal celebration. The mood was almost ruined when a horde of roughs, ready to celebrate in their own way, began to push to the front of the crowd only to be confronted by a line of Metropolitan policemen. Nonetheless the ugly elements of the mob could not disguise the elegance of the occasion. Bazalgette's achievements were not technical, nor were they especially architecturally impressive; however, the work on all three embankments – the Albert Embankment being completed in 1869 and the Chelsea Embankment in 1874 – was a significant task of organisation and planning. Victoria Embankment included 650,000 cubic feet of granite; 80,000 cubic feet of brick; 140,000 cubic yards of concrete; 500,000 cubic feet of timber; 2,500 tons of caissons and one million cubic feet of filling and gravel, eventually costing £1,156,981.

Part of Bazalgette's achievement in transforming the river front was

24. Victoria Embankment in 1901, with Cleopatra's Needle at the centre point of
the new promenade

controlling Nature for the purpose of the modern city, reclaiming land
in order to ease congestion. The process that defined this transformation
began in the debates over the nature of disease, the conditions of the
poor and the morality of poverty as well as the very identity of London
itself as a modern capital under one government rather than a fragmented corporation of municipalities, vested interests and ancient traditions. The testament to this could be found in the quality of the Thames
water itself. The horrors of the Victorian city would never disappear,
but Joseph Bazalgette, perhaps more than any man of his generation,
helped to construct and to protect the modern city.

Bazalgette's Victoria Embankment symbolised a revolution in government but also in the everyday lives of ordinary Londoners. It was no
longer necessary to live and work in the same neighbourhood; as Henry
Mayhew made his way on the subterranean railway he interviewed
workmen who worked inside the city; they all agreed that 'the cheap and
early trains were a great benefit to the operative classes'. One workman
expounded the advantage: 'he saved at least 2 shillings a week by them
in matters of rent alone. He lived in Notting Hill and would have to

walk six miles to and from his work every day if it were not for the convenience of the railway.'[35] The railways opened up the fringes of the city to new ways of urban living and also offered the potential to convert the hinterland into the new suburbia.

Bazalgette continued to develop London as a machine, applying his engineering know-how to Chadwick's Utilitarian philosophy of the sanitary metropolis. As Chief Engineer of the MBW he was also focused on how to change the roadways, searching for an integrated approach that saw the city as a whole. In the 1860s, London looked jealously at Baron Haussmann's reconfiguration of Paris into a system of wide boulevards and streets, even if it feared the absolutism of the centralised power of Napoleon III. Bazalgette could never alter the complete plan, but he was determined to find a way to build new roads as well as clear away some of the more unsightly neighbourhoods and rookeries. In 1866, while work was starting on the embankment, the MBW approached the Duke of Northumberland, who owned the land between Trafalgar Square and the river, in order to create a large thoroughfare. The Duke refused but, after his death in 1867, the board asked his heir with more success, albeit at a cost of £500,000.

The board also looked into the heart of the city and Bazalgette drew up plans for three new arteries: Charing Cross Road that ran north of Trafalgar Square, Shaftesbury Avenue that started at Piccadilly, breaking through the ancient rookery of St Giles, and New Oxford Street that connected the West End with Holborn. The 1877 Street Improvements Act was one of the most heavy-handed, if necessary, reforms in the city's history, displacing over 10,000 tenants from squalid housing. The new scheme invented the modern West End. Bazalgette also turned his hand to designing a number of bridges to improve the cross-river traffic, finally putting the dominance of London Bridge to rest. The MBW stopped the use of tolls and looked at new ways of widening the existing bridges at Battersea, Putney and Hammersmith. Bazalgette began to collate designs for a bridge near the port. In 1878, the City accepted that this was necessary but refused to adopt the engineer's plans and instead began work on Sir Horace Jones' and Sir John Barry's iconic 'bascule' design that was opened in 1894. Tower Bridge immediately became a symbol for the new capital, the industrial descendant of that first wooden bridge created nearly 1,900 years earlier.

Undoubtedly, London's health improved as a result of Bazalgette's sewers. The rise in life expectancy, which in the 1830s was as low as thirty-four in a suburb like Clapham and even lower in the rookeries and slums, was the result of many factors, but clean water was certainly an important one. The cleaning of the Thames did not occur overnight and cesspools lingered throughout the worst parts of the city. In 1866 cholera returned to the capital, but the disease was contained within those neighbourhoods that drew their water from the Old Ford reservoirs, which were owned by the East London Waterworks Company. By the 1890s, it had almost disappeared, although the memory of its devastation still haunted the streets. When, in August 1892, a young girl, Ida Samyan, newly arrived from Hamburg, was rushed to hospital with symptoms, the newspapers were keen to point out that 'a post-mortem examination showed that her death was not due to cholera'.[36] Nonetheless, hospitals were put on full alert and inspectors were instructed to visit lodging houses, while health authorities also descended on Covent Garden fruit market to ensure that no rotten goods – considered to be a contagion of the disease – were on sale, confiscating many tons of the stuff.

Today there is a new focus on the Thames and the acknowledgement that after 140 years Bazalgette's 1,800 miles of tunnels cannot cope with the waste of the twenty-first-century city. In 2007 Thames Water, the private company that manages the capital's water and sewerage, announced a major new initiative, the Thames Tunnel, which will extend twenty miles under the riverbed from Hammersmith eastwards beyond Tower Bridge, connecting the thirty-four most polluting overflows that still pour into the river on average fifty times a year. The scheme hopes to conclude its public consultation in 2011 and start work two years later.

CHAPTER 10

WEMBLEY STADIUM

Suburbia and Empire

Dear realm of rest from London's weary ways, My Metro-Land
Brightly beam beyond the City's haze, My Metro-Land
My Town-tried nerves, when work-a-day is o'er,
Where comes no echo of the City's roar,
You brace to health and calm content restore, My Metro-Land.

'My Metro-Land', George R. Sims

On Saturday, 2 February 1901, the world came to London to follow the coffin of Queen Victoria as it made its way through the city from Victoria Station via the Mall, St James's Street and Marble Arch towards Paddington, and onwards to Windsor Castle. The Queen had made it clear that she disliked black mourning and so the entire city was draped in purple and white; she had also wished the event to be 'as simple as that of a daughter of a soldier', but it was never going to be that restrained. The horde had been delivered into the heart of the city by a specially organised night tram service that began even before dawn and a million bystanders gazed in complete silence as her hearse rolled past. Victoria had been the symbol of continuity and stability; *The Daily Telegraph* was compelled to ask, 'Who can think of the nation and the race without her?'[1]

Her coffin was followed by her family and representatives of her wider brood – the Kaiser, the Romanovs – and any number of European royals who were joined to the Crown by blood. There were also members of the leading families from throughout the empire, while across the seas, the Dominions themselves stood still in mourning: in India there were services in Anglican chapels, Muslim mosques and Hindu temples; in South Africa, Cape Town was draped in black while General Kitchener and his staff held a service in Pretoria. Montreal and Toronto were also clothed in mourning. Even in far-off trading ports of the globe, the passing was marked: in Tien-sin the expat community marched in the rain, while the Stock Exchange in New York was closed for the day. On 2 February, as had come to be expected, the rest of the world followed London.

The end of the sixty-three years of the Victorian era was a benchmark of how much the capital had changed, and how its standing within the world had transformed. The young monarch had taken the throne as the first stones of the Houses of Parliament were being laid; the new palace at Westminster was now complete, although the painting of historical scenes inside continued for another twenty years. The role of government had radically changed in that time: the House of Commons had now usurped the Lords as the powerhouse within the palace. This was also reflected in the expansion of the franchise in the Second and Third Reform Acts of 1867 and 1884, which gave the vote first to the 'respectable middle class' and then to the workers.

Victoria also left her throne an empress. Britain controlled lands in every continent and commanded over 400 million people across the globe; the Navy ruled the oceans and London was at the very heart of this empire. The docks, which continued to be filled with steamboats and sail rigs transporting the cargo of the world to the capital, now occupied twenty-six square miles of riverbank to the east of the city; there were in addition 320 wharves on both sides of the Thames which in 1899 landed 7.5 million tons of goods.

The bustle of the docks was reflected on the trading floor of the exchange and banking companies that invested in opportunities around the globe. In 1850 there had been 864 members of the Stock Exchange; in 1900 there were 4,227, and all were located within the ancient square mile once ringed by the Roman walls. This was the financial powerhouse of the world, raising capital, trading stocks and speculating on everything from new railway schemes in Asia to guano from Peru to factory building in Yorkshire. Every morning trains arrived at the stations on the edge of the city, disgorging tens of thousands of eager salary men to their offices. In 1898 Bank Station was built in front of the Royal Exchange, connecting with Waterloo Station south of the river and delivering this endless flow of bodies into the metropolis's heart – bursting forth 'at the foot of the staircase ... The young men spring forward ... they are not just going to business! They are rushing there.'[2]

London was also the government office of the empire: the Colonial Office was close to Downing Street, while individual bureaus for each Dominion jostled to be as close to Whitehall and the corridors of power as possible. Empire could be found on every advertising hoarding; every public space had statues to remind the citizens of their imperial destiny; pageants, exhibitions and parades reaffirmed the benefits of being British. Schoolbooks drummed a preternatural superiority into a generation of young minds. When new members were elected to the London County Council (LCC), they were reminded that they were 'trustees of the metropolis of the empire'.[3]

Yet there was also a sense of foreboding at the dawn of the new century. There were murmurs that Britain no longer held sway in the world's trade without opposition; in 1900 the LCC warned, 'London is losing its share of the import trade'.[4] In the words of the editor of the *Illustrated London News*, L. F. Austin: 'the world does not grieve over an imperceptible point of time. But at the end of the Victorian era, who is not conscious of a great blank?'[5]

Architecture went some way to fill the gap between the city's perception of itself and reality as the balance between the centre and its colonies was changing. The Edwardian era, the first decade of the century, was often seen as the high-water mark of empire, but it was in fact the time of ebbing, and the attempt to dam the receding tide. The road to independence for the white colonies had already begun: Canada had been granted Dominion status in 1867, Australia followed suit in 1901, New Zealand in 1907 and South Africa, once the Boer War was concluded, in 1910. In 1900, this mood for self-determination was brought to bear at home with the Pan African meeting in London. Organised by the West Indian solicitor Henry Sylvester-Williams, head of the newly formed African Association, the meeting attracted Caribbean, African and American campaigners and anti-colonialists. Amongst the delegates was the American intellectual W. E. B. Du Bois, who vehemently debated the importance of unity of experience as well as complaints amongst the colonised. Thus the very idea of the empire was being slowly undermined. London was still the greatest city in the world by a long chalk, but its journey through the twentieth century was clearly not going to be straightforward.

This apparent questioning of power was balanced by an increase in imperial architecture within London, for as the reign of Edward VII began there was a desire to find a new way to express the grandeur of the metropolis. The Arts and Crafts movement of William Morris was fine for the suburbs but lacked magnificence; the Victorian Gothic was also giving way to a new English Baroque, a Wrenaissance, harking back to the perceived glories of the late seventeenth century when the first seeds of modern London were sown, a classical city more magnificent than Paris or Rome.

In 1900, there were plans to widen further the Strand and to create a new route to meet it from Holborn. Kingsway was much needed, and where the two streets met, the Aldwych, site of the Saxon settlement Lundenwic, was to be built into a dramatic crescent. There were debates about whether to place here a pantheon, a 'hall for heroes', but in the end it was given over to India House, the administrative centre of the jewel of the empire. The boulevard would be a Regent Street for the twentieth century and also had the benefit of continuing Bazalgette's policy of slum clearances with the rolling-over of the ramshackle rookery Clare Market. Regent Street itself was changed and Nash's Quadrant that ran northwards was knocked down to help the congested traffic, while along Piccadilly the old houses were replaced with impressive offices and hotels, such as the luxuriously opulent Ritz.

The centre was no longer a place for private architecture; the majority of new buildings in the first decade of the century were offices, hotels, shops and government departments. The variety of purposes reflected the diversity of the city: the white classicism of the Admiralty and the Board of Trade in Whitehall, the terracotta castle of the Prudential building on Holborn, Harry Gordon Selfridges's temple to retail on

Oxford Street. There were also new methods of construction: the Ritz was first built as a steel frame and then filled in with stone cladding. These monumental buildings were intended to give London an imperial swagger – in the words of William Emerson, the 1899 President of the Royal Institute of British Architects, they represented 'an architecture that may enhance the glory of this great Empire'.[6] But there was a sense of emptiness within the heart of the capital: the buildings had lost their human scale and become monumental; nobody lived here any more.

The city had become a centre of business and retail, while the grand public spaces were reduced to places for beetling office workers to cross on the way to their desks in such a hurry that, in the words of Oscar Wilde, everyone looked as if they were late for a train. London was now the domain of white-collar workers, who, in the words of C. F. G. Masterman, author of *The Condition of England* in 1909, constituted a new class of Englishman: 'They are the creation not of industrial, but of commercial and business activities of London . . . Its male population is engaged in all its working hours in small, crowded offices, under artificial light, doing immense sums, adding up other men's accounts, writing other men's letters.'[7]

The exponential rise of the ordinary office clerk created fresh desires and aspirations, and as their economic power increased they slowly demanded a different way of urban living. This tribe found its own world within the suburbs, the latest ring of urban growth, and because they arrived in such numbers they formed not just new neighbourhoods but a social revolution. It was calculated that by sheer numbers alone they were powerful: 250,000 moved from the city centre to the new suburbs in the 1880s; by the 1900s this had risen to over 1,400,000.

Suburbia was made possible by a transport revolution that had begun even before the Victorian era and continued to develop in the following century. In the 1820s a programme of road building opened up neigh-bourhoods like Battersea, Wandsworth and Brixton to the south-west; Dulwich, Lewisham and New Cross to the south-east; Kilburn, Kentish Town and Crouch End creating an arc across the north. Yet with the development of the railways, these regions soon came to be considered part of the inner suburbs. The first Metropolitan line from Baker Street to Farringdon revolutionised the possibilities of transport inside the city in the 1840s; this was improved by the extension of the line, into what is today the District and Circle line, along the Thames and through the Victoria Embankment in the 1860s. New lines went to Hammersmith and Richmond in the 1870s, and further to Wimbledon in the 1880s.

The rise of the suburbs and the decline of the empire met in unexpected ways. In 1923, following the devastations of the First World War, it was decided to revive the spirit of empire with an exposition. The location for this exhibition was not in the centre of the city but at Wembley, to the north-west of the metropolis, on the virtual edge of the capital. There was a certain absurdity in the relationship between the high seriousness of the event and the reality of its suburban pleasures that reveals a significant turning point in the city's history. In the official guide, the purpose of the show was 'to foster inter-Imperial trade and open fresh markets for dominion and home products. To make the different races of the British Empire better known to each other, and to demonstrate to the people of Britain the almost illimitable possibilities of the Dominions, Colonies and Dependencies together.'[8] The truth was perhaps more pithily summed up by Noël Coward: 'I've brought you here to see the wonders of the Empire, and all you want to do is go to the dodgems.'[9]

'As quiet and retired at seven miles distance as if it could have been seventy',[10] wrote the landscape designer and sometime colleague of John Nash, Humphry Repton, in 1795. He was working at Wembley Park, situated to the north-west of the city, belonging to Sir Richard Page. The picturesque villa was the height of fashion for the wealthy estate owner who wanted to indulge his whimsical love of beauty; it was only a few hours' ride from the capital but in the hands of a master like Repton, the surroundings were tweaked and improved to give the impression of complete isolation. Wembley Park nestled by a small village of about 160 houses, surrounded by enclosed fields and wasteland; the community had a windmill and a tavern, the Green Man. To the west stood the larger settlement of Harrow on the Hill with its distinguished school for the sons of city grandees.

Civilisation began to creep towards Wembley six years later when the Harrow Road that led westwards from the Edgware Road towards the small villages along the route was improved. Previously there had only been one daily coach leaving Harrow for the Bell Inn, Holborn; by 1826, there were two coaches which could go and return to the city in a day. The settlement was further disturbed when the first line of the London–Birmingham railway was built through the landscape, creating a level crossing where Wembley Central Station stands today; a halt was added to the line in 1842, called Sudbury but later renamed. Slowly the village began to grow: it gained its own parish church, designed by Sir George Gilbert Scott, the architect of both St Pancras Station and the renovations at Westminster Abbey.

By the mid-century it was advertised as the perfect rural spot for a weekend trip out of town, the local inn being recommended as 'a commodious tavern, a favourite resort for a respectable class of person at the West End',[11] while the villagers, on the whole, still made their money from agriculture, supplying vegetables and fruit to the London markets. In 1871 the population stood at 444, consisting of labourers, railwaymen and a handful of professionals; the record also noted the presence of Rajah Rampal Singh, temporary resident of the Dairy Farm.

Nevertheless, Wembley still remained a bit too far, and too rural, for city commuters who were looking closer to the centre for their idyllic refuge. Elsewhere, the railway was already having a huge impact on the shape of the city. In 1864, the Metropolitan Railway Company extended their line from Baker Street two and a quarter miles northwards to Swiss Cottage, with plans to stretch towards the hilltop village of Hampstead. This new line offered a twenty-minute service between Finchley Road and Moorgate, ideal for any worker within the Square Mile. It was hoped that, while the menfolk would buy lucrative season tickets, preferably first-class, for their daily commute, the company coffers would also be filled with day tickets bought by wives popping into the city for amusement.

By the 1880s, this new class of Londoner was already a subject for the satirist's barbed wit. The middle-ranking bank clerk, Henry Pooter, immortalised in George and Weedon Grossmith's *Diary of a Nobody*, serialised in *Punch* magazine between 1888 and 1889, was proud to bursting of his suburban castle at The Laurels, Brickfield Terrace, Upper Holloway. He was so well drawn that even today it is almost impossible not to cringe as his creators show him to be a man of inordinate social aspirations and limited connections. His love of his new suburban status is palpable:

> 'Home, Sweet Home,' that's my motto. I am always in of an evening ... Carrie and I can manage to pass our evenings together without friends. There is always something to be done: a tin-tack here, a Venetian blind to put straight, a fan to nail up, or part of a carpet to nail down – all of which I can do with my pipe in my mouth; while Carrie is not above putting a button on a shirt, mending a pillow-case, or practising the 'Sylvia Gavotte' on our new cottage piano (on the three years' system) . . .[12]

Pooter's experience was felt beyond Upper Holloway, and had become the essence of urban living throughout the outer ring of the capital that swept from Greenwich, Clapham and Tooting in the south, Ealing and Belsize Park to Hackney, north of the river. Like Nicholas Barbon two hundred years earlier, the new suburban speculators knew that their customers wished to improve their station, and suburbia was growing from private companies who took their designs from the burgeoning trade in pattern books. These estates were carefully developed with both eyes on the market, but delivering exactly what the new city worker wanted: the anti-city, a refuge from the capital, the myth of *rus in urbe* at an affordable price.

In 1881 William Clarke published *The Suburban Homes of London*, a survey of the new neighbourhoods outside the city, many that within living memory had been villages. The handbook was designed as an aid to 'narrow the search which bewilders even an experienced householder when circumstances compel him to take a fresh outlook'.[13] Wembley itself did not yet appear except as a village outside Harrow. Nearby, Hendon is reached 'from a thickly wooded lane that connects Hampstead and Edgware, and turns by a short path into the always open God's

Acre',[14] yet the railway developed new colonies such as Cricklewood, Mill Hill and Winchmore Hill that had little or no connection with the rural community. The new arrivals had 'their own churches and chapels, their own set of friends and local acquaintances with due and proper exclusiveness, having one feature in common, that they all depend on London for their incomes'.[15] Houses were rented from £40 to £100 a year, while to the north leases rose to £150, with a few mansions available for the rich. Harlesden, to the south, was aimed at a lower level of income but with the same aspirations; it was well served by omnibus and trains, and by this time the old 'ill reputed wayside congregation of cheerless cottages' were being replaced by 'good houses of various values from £30 to £80 a year'.[16]

This idyll was about to change once more. Thus far the Metropolitan Railway Company's tracks only reached as far as Swiss Cottage, north of Baker Street Station. The venture was an unfortunate disaster, and between morning and afternoon rush hours the trains were more than half empty. The business soon reached a crisis point: should they build more tracks, or had London reached its limit?

It was at this point, as the result of a boardroom coup, that Sir Edward Watkin was made president of the company. Watkin had been born in Salford in 1819 and trained in the cotton trade, but in the 1840s became involved in the boom enterprise of railways. He was secretary of the Trent Valley Railway, which was sold for £438,000 to the London and North Western Railway (LNWR). He then moved on to become general manager of the Manchester, Sheffield and Lincolnshire Railway, later the Great Central. He even had time to set up the Grand Trunk Railway of Canada before returning to Britain and proposing a Channel Tunnel, starting excavations at Dover, only to be halted when it was proved that the foreshore was the exclusive property of the Crown. In 1872, he agreed to run the Metropolitan as a means to profit from linking his newest venture with his existing interests in the north – in his words, using the suburban line to '[get] out into the country and shak[e] hands with any new or old neighbours who wanted to get their traffic through to London'.[17]

Watkin was certain that expanding the railway beyond the city and connecting it to the rest of the country would bring more traffic into the capital; the Swiss Cottage line should be extended northwards towards Harrow and beyond. He also believed that the railway company needed to provide incentives and attractions to draw passengers to the line from inside the city, so as they started construction, they purchased large parcels of meadow on either side of the track to develop housing. Work started in March 1879 with a tunnel from Swiss Cottage to Finchley Road Station and then cuttings into the landscape as the line curled towards West Hampstead, Kilburn and Brondesbury. Watkin hoped that the line would be ready to take passengers to the Royal Agricultural Society show at Queen's Park that summer but the weather was against them. Nevertheless, by 2 August 1880 trains were running between Baker Street and Harrow over thirty times a day, with the added weekend special of a 6d return to West Hampstead.

Yet Watkin was not satisfied; he wanted to extend the line further towards Rickmansworth; he also planned an intermediate station between Harrow and Willesden – Neasden – and prepared to transfer all his railway workshops and facilities here. This meant he also had to move all his workers as well, so he bought up another 377 acres and built a new workers' community of 102 cottages 'with gardens and convenient back premises'[18] as well as shops. By 1904 there was an off-licence and beer shop, a grocery, haberdashery, a post office and confectioners, a bread shop and coffee house; there were also over 200 children living here and land was given to the local Wesleyan chapel to build a school-room.

At the same time, the company sought more sensational means to draw the public to use their line. In 1889 the world had been stunned at the Paris World Fair by the 1,000-foot steel tower built by the engineer Gustave Eiffel. While William Morris, who was in Paris attending a socialist conference, unsurprisingly called it 'a hellish piece of ugliness',[19] other visitors were awed by its magnificence. Watkin was also impressed by the fact that, although the tower had been built with a subsidy of one and a half million francs, it had more than paid for itself even before the exposition closed, with queues at the ticket booths snaking around the massive steel feet of the edifice for many hours. Watkin was

25. Watkin's folly, an Eiffel Tower for suburbia, never completed (*Brent Archives*)

determined to have a tower for himself that would be the showpiece of an entertainment complex, situated on the new Metropolitan line at Wembley; he called for a competition in October 1889, demanding that his tower be taller than Eiffel's effort.

In 1890, Watkin spent £32,000 buying up the Wembley Park estate and set about promoting the Tower Park. As work began on dismantling the 1790s villa and making the ground ready for the new tower which would, according to the plans, sit on a base 300 feet in diameter upon eight legs and reach over 1,200 feet into the air, Watkin also set out a pleasure garden with an eight-acre boating lake, a variety hall and a bandstand, a cricket ground and athletics track, tea rooms and restaurants. To complete the scene, Wembley Park Station was also added to the Metropolitan line between Neasden and Harrow. 120,000 visitors came out of curiosity in the opening season of 1895, but few returned. By the following year the tower had reached the first platform level at 155 feet, and sat like a giant broken machine in the open countryside.

By 1899 the tower company was facing bankruptcy and went into voluntary liquidation. Three years later the tower, which had begun to list slightly, was declared unsafe and demolition began. Watkin had gambled and lost: the Metropolitan line company now had a rail track that led into the countryside; they also owned large tranches of land with nothing on it. As the company entered the new century, it faced the same 'blank space' of uncertainty as the rest of the nation.

In the new century London continued to expand as suburbs grew, supplied by transport links and newly completed neighbourhoods in the latest designs. In 1901 the population of Greater London was 6,600,000; this increased to 7,300,000 in 1911 and 8,200,000 in 1931, yet the figure for the inner city showed a decline. Between 1891 and 1911 the population of the new suburbs doubled from 1,374,000, to 2,718,000. This growth could also be measured by the number of journeys taken on the trams, buses and trains: from 850 million in 1901 (an annual average of 130 per person) to 2,255 million in 1913. It was also reflected in the churning-up of suburban pastures into terraces and semi-detached homes: between the wars, an estimated 700,000 private houses were built within approximately twelve miles from Charing Cross, the equivalent of a large provincial city every year.

The rapid growth of a new community like Golders Green, north of Hampstead, was astonishing. In 1902 Parliament passed an Act to extend the Charing Cross, Euston and Hampstead Railway (later the Northern line), to be dug 100 feet under Hampstead Hill and surface beside the Finchley Road; work on the line was completed by 1907. From 1906 speculative builders set up offices in two wooden huts on the edge of the countryside and started to lease out their plots. Soon, land that was initially priced at £250 rose to be worth £1,000; retail space near to the station claimed £5,500. Housing began with the larger family homes close to the station, advertising a bath and upstairs WC. The streets were soon filled and cheaper dwellings were laid out further from the centre. Elsewhere, a similar rate of growth saw farms and woodland disappearing in a matter of years as the population of new suburbs ballooned; between 1901 and 1911 Acton grew by fifty-two per cent,

Chingford by eighty-six per cent and Morden by a hundred and fifty-six per cent. Soon some social commentators began to wonder whether the old notion of a city had any future?

In 1899, Ebenezer Howard, a stenographer in the Houses of Parliament, published his book *Tomorrow: A Peaceful Path to Real Reform*, which launched the influential garden city movement. Howard had been influenced by Edward Bellamy's utopia novel *Looking Backward*, in which a young Bostonian, Julian West, wakes up to find that he has been asleep for 113 years and it is AD 2000. West is guided around this new society by Doctor Leete and discovers a perfectly run state in which the goods of the world are equally distributed. Howard was determined to find a new balance between industry, Nature and town planning in the Victorian present. Like so many before him he feared that London was growing too large without a master plan, while also understanding the magnetic draw of the city. He proposed that technology should be used to enhance people's quality of life, not degrade and destroy families as it had done throughout the nineteenth century. The town should promote the merits of the countryside – the suburban ethos – in contrast to the horrors of the city centre. The new garden city would combine the best of the town and the countryside:

> But neither the Town Magnet nor the Country Magnet represents the full plan and purpose of Nature. Human society and the beauty of Nature are meant to be enjoyed together. The two magnets must be made one. As man and woman by their varied gifts and faculties supplement each other so should town and country ... Town and Country must be married, and out of this joyous union will spring a new hope, a new life, a new civilization.[20]

Howard prepared a well-audited scheme to launch the first garden city. He put a plan together to purchase a plot of approximately 6,000 acres on the edge of the city, which was to be run by a board of managers who controlled it on behalf of the investors. A sixth of the land was given over to building a town, while the rest was returned to agriculture. The new town itself offered all the latest amenities, and was planned on a concentric grid with a library, town hall, museum, concert hall and hospital, all gathered into the centre and set in parkland. This civic heart was ringed by the main shopping zone, designed as a glass arcade, similar to Paxton's Great Victorian Way. Moving out from the centre were rings of housing, based around a 420-foot grand avenue, which also enclosed a school. After that, outer zones of factories, dairies and services. There was to be no smoke or industrial pollution in the garden city and every machine was to be driven by electricity.

Work began in 1903 at Letchworth, with the purchase of 6.1 square miles of land outside the Hertfordshire town of Hitchin, thirty-four miles from London. The railway platform was the first thing to be built, and later a station was developed. Under the supervision of the architects Barry Parker and Raymond Unwin, who had become famous as the leading campaigners for the Arts and Crafts movement, new designs for houses were assembled. The pair had already had some experience of building model housing: in 1902 they had created the village of New Earswick on behalf of the Yorkshire philanthropist Benjamin Rowntree. As the community began to rise, it was famously reported that only one tree needed to be felled to make way for the city. Howard advertised his new creation at the 1905 and 1907 Cheap Houses Exhibition, when over 80,000 curious visitors came to see the progress at Letchworth, exploring the new houses that showed off the latest innovations – prefabricated materials, front and back gardens, hand-powered brick machines, the latest ventilation solutions. Factories also began to arrive: in 1912 the corset manufacturers Spirella, which later made parachutes during the Second World War, set up works on the outskirts. By 1917 Letchworth Garden City was recognised with its own urban district council. The following year, it paid a two and a half per cent dividend to all its shareholders, although Howard himself, who had no interest in money, never made his fortune.

In 1906 Unwin and Parker were also involved in another suburban revolution at Hampstead Garden Suburb, which sought to offer an alternative way of living on the outskirts of the city. The new suburb was the idea of the philanthropist and reformer Henrietta Barnett, who was already famous for her work in improving the East End. In the 1870s, alongside her husband the cleric Samuel Barnett, Henrietta had moved into the slums of Whitechapel and there established the Metropolitan Association for Befriending Young Servants, to prevent young girls from falling into dangers; as well as the Children's Country Holiday Fund. Barnett was convinced that education was the key to defeating poverty and with her husband campaigned to set up Toynbee Hall on Commercial Road as a university for working men, and the Whitechapel Gallery to bring the benefits of fine art to the masses.

Hampstead Garden Suburb, north of Golders Green, was intended to be a new mixed community of rich and poor, in the hope of reintegrating the classes and reforming society. Housing was to be planned for all levels of income, but in each case there needed to be care for design and comfort; the roads should be wide and lined with trees. There were parks and gardens and in the central square, Barnett asked the leading architect Sir Edwin Lutyens to plan an Anglican church, St Jude's, a Quaker meeting house and a Free Church. There were educational facilities for all: two primary schools, a girls' grammar school and an institute for adult learning.

Both Letchworth and the garden suburb offered a revolution in urban living. In the main, however, the suburbs were growing as fast as the speculators could raise the investment and convert the once rural vales and hills into terraces and back gardens. Profit, not social reform, created suburbia, while the railways advertised the enticements of an imagined Garden of Eden only a few minutes down the line. In the economic boom of the Edwardian era, as the docks continued to unload the bounty of the empire and industrialisation unleashed a new wave of social mobility, suburbia became the obtainable ideal for almost everyone.

The Metropolitan Railway Company were not slow in promoting the pleasures of Wembley and the other stations along its railway line. The failures of Wembley Park were just a minor hindrance; the company were determined to attract the new middle classes with a hugely successful publicity campaign that began in 1903 and continued for decades. *The Illustrated Guide to the Metropolitan Railway Extension* (1903) contained all the wonders of the countryside within reach of the city; this was slowly transformed into the iconic *Metro-Land* booklet, started in 1915, that created the image of a rural idyll a few miles from Baker Street. Through the clever thinking of the copywriter, James Garland, Metroland was born, that fantasy world offering a better life: the thatched cottage eternally bathed in sunlight; the Edwardian beauty gathering the first flowers of spring; the warm glow of sunset upon the front garden of a Tudorbethan 'homestead'; a picnic under a large oak. In 1923, the company produced a brochure explaining its particular virtues: 'London is at your very doorstep, if your needs must keep in touch with London, but it is always pure country at the corner of the lane beyond your garden fence ... Metroland is a strip of England at its fairest, a gracious district formed by nature for the homes of a healthy, happy race.'[21]

The Metropolitan Railway Company developed a finely tuned image of the anti-city, yet it was firmly based in the realities of the market. They needed to attract builders to grow the communities, but they also wanted to draw the office workers out of the city for country pursuits: sport was considered one of the best ways to lure day trippers. North of Wembley, Preston Road was sold to the Oxford Street store Marshall & Snelgrove as playing fields for the staff; this was later sold to Selfridges and a pavilion and tea rooms were added. Nearby there were also fields for W. H. Smith, the stationers, Debenhams and Lloyds Bank. More significantly, the company also encouraged the development of golf courses as the ultimate suburban landscape. In 1907 the tower at Wembley was temporarily given over to the Wembley Park Golf Company at £600 per acre. Other courses began to cluster alongside the rail line and by 1920 there were advertisements for fifteen courses in that year's *Metro-Land* booklet.

Around the edges of the golf course the Wembley Park Estate Company aimed to build housing for the better class of aspirant commuter, and plots were sold to builders in an auction at £650–£750 an acre. Very quickly large detached villas began to spring up along Park Drive, Oakington Avenue and Raglan Gardens, designed and planned 'with the greatest care and its picturesque layout is further advanced by skilful building of varying types of houses'.[22] By 1915 there were 105 houses and, most importantly, the revenue from Wembley Park Station had risen from £3,807 in 1906 to £6,150 eight years later; in 1918, houses were selling on average at £1,610 an acre. Nearby the once tranquil 123-acre Chalk Hill estate was also being churned up by the company for the benefit of commuters with more modest hopes of the arcadian dream, set within either a full acre or half-acre space at an average price of £600 per acre.

As the plots began to be bought up and the speculators sensed profits, instead of building each house surrounded by its own land, they started to develop streets of a new style of dwelling: in the post-war period the semi-detached house replaced the urban terrace as the signature look of the city. The latest innovation was an eclectic mixture of styles devised to house the modern nuclear family. From the outside, a fence or wall divided the two connected houses; there was a front garden with a path that led to the door, usually at the far end of each dwelling so that there was no unnecessary neighbourliness. The house was arranged over two floors with a hipped, steep roof. A bay window rose across both floors; the ground floor was left with exposed brick while the upper floor was often clad in rough paste or pebble-dash. Entering into the hallway, there was a front parlour, a sitting room, a small toilet room and a kitchen on the ground floor; upstairs led to a landing off which ran three bedrooms and a bathroom.

For many in the inter-war years, the semi-detached house offered a respite from the horrors of the city. The rise of the Mock Tudor or Tudorbethan style summed up many of the attitudes and aspirations of suburbia. Unlike early developments, there was no interest in the Arts and Crafts philosophy of workmanship and decoration. 'Stockbroker Tudor' was inherently conservative and backwards-looking after the horrors of the first mechanical war. In the words of the 1930s critic Anthony Bertram: 'probably the popular love for the Tudor, whether genuine or bogus, is based on fear and a wish to escape … These are insecure and frightening times, and I believe that economic depression and the fear of war are the chief promoter of the Tudoresque.'[23] The age of Elizabeth was seen as a time of tranquillity and stability – a golden age – while the additions of timbering and leaded windows allowed the bank manager, returning from a day at the office, momentarily to consider himself lord of the manor.

As monotonous streets of these faux-historical semis began to replace what was once pleasant pastureland, the only rural notions left were the mournful street names that looked nothing like the front of the *Metro-Land* brochure. Suburbia soon became a byword for a modern malaise. In poems, novels and plays the suburbs became the enemy of progress, liberty and creativity, summed up in the cutting wit of John Betjeman or the sketches of Osbert Lancaster. They are more dreadfully measured by George Orwell's novel *Coming Up for Air*, which tells the life of George Bowling, a forty-five-year-old insurance clerk who decides on a whim to visit the places of his childhood with disastrous consequences when he realises that time ravages all. The suburbs no longer offered escape but stifling conformity – was this the brave future that Britain had to offer? It was an unlikely setting indeed for what was intended as an exhibition of the great British Empire.

While suburbia was created as a response to the deleterious nature of the city, it was never a refuge from the wider world, and this was made starkly clear by the Great War. In 1914, on the news of the declaration, there was panic-buying at the shops in Harrow, while others concentrated on organising the Voluntary Aid Detachment (VAD), nurses and special constables in case of attack. The local territorial unit, the 9th Middlesex Regiment, was mustered ready to be shipped out to Mesopotamia to take on the Sultan's Ottoman forces, and encountered fierce fighting at Nadaf and Mosul. A unit called the Foreign Legion was stationed at the East Lane Sports Ground, North Wembley, probably made up from foreign volunteers, mostly Belgian refugees, who arrived in the first months of war. It is estimated that fifty-nine refugees settled in Wembley, a large addition to the small community, and at least three houses, Sheepcote Farm, Amble Cottage and 33 Clifton Avenue, were given over to relief.

The first local casualty was Private H. G. Leek, the postman, at the First Battle of Ypres, on 11 November 1914. After that the *Willesden Chronicle* and *Wembley Observer* marked the passing of each local with remorse, and in time a corner of the cemetery was developed into a 'Heroes' Corner'; in total 169 names were recorded on the memorial at St John's Church. Wembley was not targeted by air raids and the Zeppelins that began to cruise over London from autumn 1915, although a three-inch anti-aircraft gun was stationed at nearby Kenton. However, a local man was injured after a bombing raid when the floor of his central London office collapsed. In the months after the war, the community was rocked by the Spanish flu epidemic that arrived in summer 1918, killing just under fifty locals. Wembley was certainly far from the front line, but it had shared the deprivations of the war.

The end of the war was greeted with triumphalism and pride, but it soon subsided to reveal a more anxious condition; the war had changed the world, and Britain was likely to pay the dearest price by holding on too tightly to the past. In addition, the glorious advantages of imperial power were beginning to appear hollow. Where once, in the words of the economist John Maynard Keynes in 1919, the inhabitant of London 'could order by telephone, sipping his morning tea in bed, the various products of the whole world in such a quantity as he might see fit, and reasonably expect their early delivery upon his doorstep',[24] this all ended in the trenches of Flanders. In 1918 trade barriers rose in the hope of stimulating home markets back into life. The old policies no longer seemed to work as the national debt rose tenfold. The empire had made Britain rich; perhaps now, however, it was becoming too expensive to maintain.

The Great War was a reminder to many that Britain was not a great power on its own. The colonies had sent almost a third of all troops during 1914–18: more than a million Indians served on the Western Front, while New Zealand sent 100,000 men and nurses, a tenth of its entire population. Despite the impression that the conflict was a European affair, the war was indeed global; in Africa there were 100,000 Allied casualties, of whom only 1,300 were native-born English. In that theatre the Camel Corps perhaps summed up the diversity of the volunteers: three-quarters were recruited from Australasia and there were also troops from Hong Kong, Singapore, Rhodesia, South Africa and even the Canadian Rockies. While the global conflict was ended by the war of attrition in Western Europe, the contribution of the empire was unquestioned.

The idea of an empire exhibition had been mooted since before the war. In 1908 there was a Franco-British exhibition organised at Shepherd's Bush, to the west of the city, on the site of what became known as White City after the colour of the exhibition buildings, to celebrate the recently signed 'Entente Cordiale'. Eight million visitors found their way to the fair, which spread out over 140 acres, including exhibits from around the world and a collection of reconstructed villages displaying local crafts and architectural styles. That summer the Fourth Olympiad was staged at a stadium within the park; twenty-two nations competed in twenty-four disciplines including, for the first time, figure skating. The length of the marathon was changed twice: to begin with it was altered from twenty-five miles to twenty-six so that Windsor Castle could be made the starting line; yet when the future Queen Mary requested that the start be outside her nursery window, the race was duly increased by a further 385 feet. It was perhaps this extension that deprived the Italian runner Dorando Pietri of his gold medal as he collapsed when he entered the stadium and had to be carried over the finishing line.

Following the success of the White City fair, the imperialist Lord Strathcona suggested that London host another exhibition to celebrate the empire. It was not until after the Great War, however, that dreams turned into serious planning. In May 1919 Lord Morris was named chairman of a new committee, with the support of the Prime Minister, Lloyd George, and the Prince of Wales. The following year Parliament decided to guarantee the enterprise to the sum of £1 million, and Wembley was selected as the ideal site. It was later that year that the Prince of Wales, at the annual dinner for the Royal Colonial Institute, also declared that the site would be a 'great national sports ground'.[25] That summer 216 acres of land were bought up despite the complaints of the Wembley Urban Council, who wanted to develop the plots as a garden suburb. It was then planned that a new national stadium was to be built on the site of Watkin's Folly, while Wembley Park itself was transformed into an exhibition unlike any built before.

Speed was everything and on 10 January 1922 the Duke of York cut the ceremonial turf to announce the commencement of work. They had little more than a year to build a new city that would be the envy of the world and started on the stadium immediately; dynamite was used to blow out the original foundations of the tower, while workmen dug out the clay hill upon which it once stood. The contract for the building had been won by Robert McAlpine, with the promise that he would hire ex-Servicemen to complete the job, alongside the architects, Sir John Simpson and Maxwell Ayrton. The final member of the design team was Owen Williams, the civil engineer, who was the most experienced in the group in the use of reinforced concrete. Williams would be knighted for his work at Wembley and later diverse projects such as the Dorchester Hotel and the M1 motorway.

It was decided early on that the whole of the Empire Exhibition, for the benefit of time and cost, was to be made in concrete – even the lamp-posts, water fountains and bins; however, a project on this scale had never been contemplated before. In a publicity brochure produced for the exhibition by the Concrete Utilities Bureau, reinforced concrete would be the latest material for a modern London: 'Wembley as we see it now, the expression of a great empire, would never have been built but for concrete ... Concrete is the economic material of the age.' Wembley was to be celebrated not just as a vision of the imperial future but also as the first city of concrete, the shape of the urban future.

For the stadium alone the structure needed 1,400 tons of steel work, half a million rivets and 25,000 tons of concrete; and it was completed in 300 days. For some, the use of reinforced concrete only heralded the future stability of the empire: 'no longer the hidden source of strength, it was a visible source of beauty. Its infinite versatility had been adapted perfectly to its purpose, to give architectural symbolism of the majesty and splendour of the British Empire.'[26] For others it was the height of ugliness, the bland face of industrialised functionalism, for which there was little to praise except its utility.

The stadium itself offered little of architectural interest, but provided forty miles of terraces that were tested assiduously by a battalion of Guards before opening day. The sole architectural features of note were the two 125-foot white towers to be found on the north side of the building, facing the route from Wembley Park Station. These had been devised by Williams and were created with a concrete shell only three inches thick. Above the suburban skyline the designs were certainly eye-catching, and had been influenced by styles a long way from Metroland.

In 1911 it was decided that the capital city of India was to be shifted from Calcutta to Delhi and the leading architect of the day and designer of the Hampstead Garden Suburb's central green, Sir Edwin Lutyens, was commissioned to construct a new government centre, New Delhi. Lutyens devised a new classical order with which to build his metropolis, with pillars, columns and domes that were as Mughal as they were Roman. At Wembley Owen Williams reintroduced this new empire style – in concrete rather than stone – into the towers of his stadium, creating allusions to ancient palaces and the hopeful reconnection with the empire.

Until this moment, the Football Association had no permanent fixture for their annual competition, the FA Cup, but it was agreed that the Empire Stadium was the ideal site for the gala event and it was made ready for the contest on 28 April 1923. With a capacity of 127,000 the organisers thought it was safe to sell entry at the gate rather than allow pre-booked tickets; however, the London team, West Ham, were due to play Bolton Wanderers and were chasing after the double of a League win and the Cup. By 1 p.m., two hours before kick-off, the stadium was full. At 1.45 the gates were closed, but still crowds poured out of the railway station while inside the mob began to push their way onto the terraces. By the time George V arrived at the royal box, the crowd had burst onto the pitch, singing the national anthem and giving three cheers. At this point a single mounted policeman, George Scorey, and his white horse, Billie, attempted to push them behind the goalposts and off the pitch, at least as far as the touchline. Only then could the two teams come out and, despite another pitch invasion after ten minutes, a full game was played with Bolton inching a 2–0 victory. The official attendance was 126,047, but there were estimates that at least another 90,000 got in to see some part of the match.

The following year only 92,000 came to watch the 1924 FA Cup,

26. The White Horse FA Cup Final, 1923 (*Getty*)

but nonetheless four new stair towers had been added to help with congestion. Three days before this match the Empire Exhibition itself was opened with great pageantry by George V. He had first travelled by car from Windsor Palace to Alperton and then changed to a horse-drawn coach, crowds lining both sides of the route to the stadium, while 110,000 waited patiently inside. Under a royal dais at the eastern end of the field the King gave his speech, reminding his audience that 'this exhibition will enable us to take stock of the resources, actual and potential, of the Empire as a whole; to consider where these exist and how they can best be developed and utilized; to take counsel together how the peoples can cooperate to supply one another's needs, and to promote national well-being'.[27]

The opening was one of the first global media events: despite its blandness and pleasantries, the royal speech was then telegraphed around the world from the stadium post office and a young post boy was able to deliver congratulations from the far corners of the empire to the royal party within eighty seconds. Thousands listened to the speech for the first time over the wireless and a recording was made at the HMV studios in nearby Hayes; the record was on sale within thirty-six hours. The opening was also filmed and broadcast throughout the empire.

Unlikely to miss a golden opportunity like this, the copywriters at *Metro-Land* had produced their own special pamphlet to tempt the many thousands who would use the Baker Street line to Wembley Park. The station itself had been widened to six platforms, with nineteen booking windows, advertising 3s 6d for a first-class ticket and 2s 6d for second-class. It was also here that you could catch the 'never-stop' service that circled the exhibition. (The pamphlet made no mention of the car parks, tramways or London Omnibus service that were also available.) On disembarking from the station the visitor was confronted by the vastness of the project. The organisers claimed that the show was 'unparalleled in the history of mankind ... [offering] a hundred gates to the Empire. They gave access to the five continents and all the seas, from the mystic east, the stirring west, the sterner north, and the romantic south.'[28]

The exhibition itself was spread out over 216 acres, a new shining metropolis in concrete. Rudyard Kipling, the unofficial chronicler of imperialism, had been invited to name the thoroughfares that spread throughout the complex: Empire Way, Drake's Way, Commonwealth Way, Chitta Gong Road. The main axis, the King's Way, connected Wembley Park Station with the stadium, leading between the vast Palace of Industry and Palace of Engineering. The vista then opened up to a wide landscaped lake area around which the major Dominions had their pavilions: Australia, New Zealand, Canada, India. While the richer and whiter nations congregated around the ornamental lakes, the rest lined secondary streets. Running off this central plaza were the pavilions of the lesser colonies: Malaya, Sarawak, Burma, South Africa. The many regions of Nigeria, Gold Coast and Sierra Leone were all gathered together into a West African village near the funfair. The empire, it seemed, had been transformed into a suburb of London with its richer

27. The Wembley exhibition (*Getty*)

houses and villas set within gardens and the smaller side streets of semi-detached domains tucked away behind.

The two palaces to Industry and Engineering were lessons in the power of empire and the promotion of the latest inventions of the industrial world. Hidden within defiantly classical facades, each concrete palace gave the impression of being a temple rather than a factory. Inside the Palace of Industry, numerous manufacturers showed off their wares, exhibits including everything from explosives to a reconstruction of Sir Ernest Rutherford's Cavendish Laboratories in Cambridge where he split the atom. There were sections on coal and gas, the emerging chemical industries, and the pharmacological trades, with stalls displaying new wonders such as Vitamin A, extracted from cod liver oil, insulin, as well as a fully stocked Boots pharmacist. Nearby, in the tobacco section, housed in a replica old Virginia house, a machine packed 350,000 cigarettes a day. The Lever Brothers showed off their soaps and dyes; Thomas Lipton displayed his tea-making operation and sold a commemorative Exhibition tea caddy. The Courtaulds, descendants of Louisa Perina Ogier who had returned to silk weaving and developed factories in Essex, also showed their wares, including their latest innovation, rayon, a synthetic silk.

The Palace of Industry was faced by the Palace of Engineering, for as the guidebook reminded the reader, 'The romance of Empire is very largely a story of engineering'.[29] When the vast showroom was being built the floors were reinforced and tracks were run into the building from the train lines, so that vast pieces of machinery – some over 150 tons – could be wheeled into position. Everything was on show, from historic trains – such as the Rocket and the Flying Scotsman – to the latest innovations in automobiles from Austin, Wolseley and Morris. Marconi had a stand displaying the future of the wireless telegraph. A complete power station was levered into place, while the electrical section tempted the visitor with the latest home gadgetry.

In the Palace of Arts, set behind the Palace of Industry, the cultural highlights of British endeavour were on show. For an extra 6d, 2.1 million people walked through a series of rooms designed to appear from a different age: 1750, the age of William Hogarth; a Regency room from 1815; a reconstruction of the 1851 Great Exhibition; the Arts and Crafts style of William Morris and a contemporary room selected by the readers of *Country Life* magazine. Most popular, however, was the Queen's Doll's House, designed and built by Sir Edwin Lutyens for the Princess Marie Louise. At five feet high and eight and a half feet wide, the house was perfect in every detail: the entrance hall was carved in marble and lapis lazuli, with a miniature wall painting by William Nicholson. The basement kitchen was stocked with everything a chef desired and even the bottles in the wine cellar had been carefully carved and painted. Elsewhere, water ran through the taps and electricity worked the lifts and light fittings. Unsurprisingly, this gained far more attention than the sculpture halls or the displays of paintings from the Dominions.

The official guide suggested that 'you can "do" Wembley in a day in the same sense as an indefatigable globe-trotter can "do" Europe in a week'.[30] Most visitors, however, avoided the empire shows altogether, making a beeline for the forty acres of pleasure park behind the Indian Pavilion. Costing over £1 million to build, it included a Hall of Laughter, with its room of mirrors, and motorcycle displays on a 'Wall of Death', dodgems, helter-skelters, a water chute and a menagerie; this was more to the taste of many London pleasure seekers. The gardens themselves were elegantly laid out with over 5,000 delphiniums and 100,000 Darwin tulips, formal lakes with rowing boats, pedal boats and motor launches. There was always a café nearby and Lyons catering provided 175,000 meals a day, served by 7,000 staff. P. G. Wodehouse's Bertie Wooster sums up the attitude of many on his fictional visit.

> By the time we had tottered out of the Gold Coast and were working towards the Palace of Machinery, everything pointed to my shortly executing a quiet sneak in the direction of the rather jolly Planter's Bar in the West Indian Section ... I have never been in the West Indies, but I am in a position to state that in certain of the fundamentals of life they are streets ahead of our European Civilizations.[31]

There were also constant entertainments at the stadium: the FA Cup was played three days after the opening ceremony and Aston Villa took on Newcastle. There were evening concerts by the 10,000-strong Imperial Choir, the largest choral troop in history. In June 1924 the International Rodeo took over and representatives from America, Canada, Australia and Argentina showed off their skills, much to the protests of the Royal Society for the Prevention of Cruelty to Animals. With two performances every day, and prizes up to £20,000, more than two million came to watch the show. Over the summer ran the Pageant of Empire, in which 12,000 performers re-enacted key moments of the nation's story including the settling of Newfoundland by John Cabot, the victories of Nelson and the memories of Flanders Field. Before the exhibition closed down in November, there was also time for a military tattoo and a series of baseball matches.

The exhibition was considered a huge success; between April and November 1924, 17,403,267 passed through the gates, the greatest daily attendance figure being on Whitsunday – 321,000. The exhibition was everything the Metropolitan Railway Company could have hoped for, with a record 10.75 million train journeys as well as the added income from 1.2 million meals consumed in the dining cars. It was therefore decided to open the exhibition again in 1925 from May to October, in which time a further 9.7 million visitors came. Nonetheless, the exhibition lost money: despite a £2.2 million government subsidy, the enterprise accrued debts of £1.5 million. Thus in October 1925 the land was quickly sold to the demolition millionaire Sir Arthur Elvin.

Elvin had been a flying ace, shot down over the trenches during the war. In 1924 he got a job in a cigarette kiosk at the exhibition and had invested in eight more, making £1,000 by the end of the first year. The following year, after the park had been closed he began to buy up the pavilions and sell them for scrap. He also made an offer of £127,000 for the stadium which was now considered, like Watkin's Folly before it, a white elephant. Once the offer was accepted Elvin had to find a way to make the site pay for itself. The stadium would remain the location for the FA Cup and soon became the home of the England national team, but this hardly ensured the future. Instead, Elvin devised new attractions; in 1927 he replaced the cinder racetrack that ran around the edge of the pitch with a dog-racing track. On the first night of racing, 10 December 1927, over 50,000 came to watch; soon the average attendance was about 9,000. Two years later he also attempted to introduce the Australian sport of speedway motorcycle racing. That same year he proposed the Rugby League Challenge Cup, bringing a traditionally northern sport to the capital.

The stadium was used as the main site for the 1948 Olympics, known as the 'Austerity Games', in the aftermath of the Second World War and conducted under ration conditions. Whereas in 1908 Britain had been top of the medal table, they could now only reach twelfth position, while America was far ahead of the rest of the field, gaining over twice as many gold medals as the second-placed nation, Sweden. The stadium was finally demolished and a new one built in its place, designed by Norman Foster, which retained Owen Williams's original twin towers.

Beyond the site of the 1924 exhibition, Wembley itself was transformed. Road-widening and other improvements had increased access to and from the centre of London. During 1924, arrivals at Wembley Park Station would have noticed work on the Haymills Barns estate, soon to be joined by new housing on Barn Rise, Barn Hill, Grendon Gardens and Eversley Avenue, where a three-bedroom detached house could be bought for £1,275. There was also the development of a street of shops along Forty Avenue, leading away from the station. Nearby a three-bedroom semi-detached house was selling for £750–£1,000. The last remains of the rural origins of the community were disappearing; by 1933 it was reported: 'the Barn Hill Estate from the Wembley side is reaching up to the road between the station [Preston Road] and the old Hamlet of Preston . . . new rows of villas stretch towards Forty Farm and invade the fields towards Harrow. The slopes of Woodcock Hill are also filling up. The old farm house is almost lost amongst the crowd of newcomers.'[32]

By the beginning of the Second World War in 1939, Middlesex had lost all but 0.9 per cent of its woodland to development, fifty per cent of its grassland disappeared and the number of cattle was reduced by seventy-five per cent. Suburbia, which had developed out of a distaste for the inner city, inspiring the publicity posters of an arcadian idyll, had turned the Elysian Fields into monotonous streets of uniform speculative housing. In 1938 the London County Council became so disturbed by the exponential expansion of the city that they promoted the notion of a green belt to encircle it, and limit the sprawl. The war itself would change London's needs, and once again force many to reconsider not just what it had been but also demand a new response to the issue of the shape of the city of the future. The conflict itself would also herald the end of empire.

Metroland no longer exists; however, like many thousands, I take the same rail line that Sir Edward Watkin extended beyond Swiss Cottage to the northern suburbs of London to work every day. Today, eighty-four per cent of people in the UK live in suburbs and therefore not just the history of London but also the history of the nation can been seen as a suburban story; yet this narrative is rarely taken seriously. The suburbs are often seen as non-places, but they are where most of us spend much of our lives. They also form much of our taste: in 2002, to coincide with the prestigious Stirling Prize organised by the Royal Institute of British Architects, a MORI poll was taken of 1,000 random respondents from all over the country to comment on their favourite type of housing. To the RIBA's chagrin, the bungalow was chosen by thirty per cent, while most others selected a 1930s semi and a modern semi.

The city has continued to grow and now covers over sixty square miles, reaching from the Forest of Epping in the east to beyond Richmond in the west. This is managed by an ever-evolving transport system that had its origins in the first Metropolitan line in the 1840s. In 2008–9 there were over 1.1 billion journeys made on the Tube, with a total of over 70 million miles travelled, as well as 2.2 billion trips on the bus network. Over 3.5 million travel into the city every day by public transport. The most ambitious plans are currently in hand to prepare for the 2012 Olympics as well as Crossrail, a new link under the city from Chelsea to Hackney which will then connect at both ends to the wider rail network. It is planned to be completed in 2017.

The history of the suburbs is a dominant chapter in the story of modern London, but the majority of the commentary has come from its critics. From the age of Henry Pooter, writers, artists and poets have all agreed with Lewis Mumford, who wrote in the influential *The City in History* that the shift to the suburbs 'from the centre carries no hope or promise of life at a higher level'.[33] But the majority of people move away from the mêlée and bustle of the city centre for many other reasons. The appeal of new housing, the latest gadgets and the sense of owning a plot of one's own cannot be forgotten, despite the way those streets look today; as J. B. Priestley wrote in the 1930s, 'a great deal is to be said for the suburbs: nearly all Englishmen are at heart country gentlemen. The suburban villa enables the salesman or the clerk out of hours, to be almost a country gentleman.'[34] And that is an aspiration not to be ridiculed, even though, as the classic series of the 1980s, *The Good Life*, proved, the gulf between the desire and the reality is a constant source of comedy.

We can no longer write about the city of London without looking at the complex relationship between the centre and the outskirts. In the Roman era, citizenship to Rome defined belonging; it was not until the formation of the walls in AD 190 that the delineation of physical space came to offer the limits of London, which became further entrenched within the medieval era. Today, the administrative region of Greater London includes a population of over 7.5 million. A sense of belonging to a city of this scale is more difficult to divine when now the majority of Londoners work within the city but live outside it. Will we have to redefine the terms of citizenship in the future once again?

Since the Second World War, many communities made their way to London. In 2001 it was reported by the Office for National Statistics that Wembley is now the most diverse location in Britain, if not Europe, with communities from across the Commonwealth – India, Sri Lanka and the West Indies – as well as from Eastern Europe. London has transformed from the world's capital to the world city. In 2007, it was estimated that over forty per cent of London's population were from non-British ethnic groups, nearly three-quarters of these from former colonial nations. While many immigrants once arrived from the docks and made their way to the edge of the city in locations such as Spital-fields, immigrant communities now make their homes in many of the outlying suburbs of the metropolis. Suburbia has now become the world.

Wembley today is a different place to when it was first built. In the post-war period it gained popularity as a main shopping area for north-west London, yet this declined by the 1970s as large shopping malls and industrial units along the North Circular Road started to open. There are currently attempts to make Wembley a destination again, alongside the stadium. 'Wembley City' is planned to be London's latest, and biggest, leisure complex, incorporating the stadium and the Arena concert hall with swimming pools, multiplex, exclusive hotels and shops. London, perhaps, is no longer a centre surrounded by concentric circles of suburbs; the suburbs have become their own cities. London, which began as one city and then, with the rise of Westminster, became two, is today a conglomeration of metropolises, an endless city of many centres.

CHAPTER 11
_____

KEELING HOUSE

Sir Denys Lasdun and the New Jerusalem

On this ground so recently a derelict and bomb scarred wilderness, has arisen not a town of jerry built and pokey dwellings, but a new urban landscape in which buildings are growing together as a community.

Festival of Britain Official Guidebook, 1951

By 1993, Keeling House had fallen into disrepair and Tower Hamlets Council were ready to have the whole project demolished, condemning it as 'a running sore'.[1] Mould had begun to attack all fifteen floors, while safety nets were strung around the cluster structure in order to catch falling masonry. The lift could be accessed from outside the main body of the building and was therefore open to anyone who wanted to get in. George and Irene Harrold, the only family who had resided in the block for the thirty-four years of its life, lived in fear of vandalism, while the structure began to show the strains of its poor construction.

As the residents were rehoused, however, the debate began on what was to be done with the place. A spokesman for the council confirmed their opposition to any kind of redevelopment: 'the building has little validity in terms of social housing needs. We have to consider the form of housing that people require and want and not the architectural merit.' It would cost at least £8 million to repair, and every week it stood empty it lost the council £2,000; it had to go. The architect was keen to blame the caretakers rather than the building itself, claiming, 'It's in a ropey condition but the basic structure is sound.'[2] For others, the edifice was far too important even to consider its destruction. Keeling House, fifteen floors of concrete, dwarfing the surrounding neighbourhoods of two-storey Victorian workmen's cottages, broken and empty, was a national treasure and needed to be preserved.

As the borough council expedited a demolition order in November 1993, English Heritage came to the rescue and gave the structure a Grade II listing, hailing it 'an architecturally outstanding example of 1950s public housing',[3] thus halting any hopes to bring it to the ground. Yet, what was to be done? English Heritage could stop demolition but had no plan for redevelopment and for the next six years Keeling House stood empty and alone; some of the flats were burnt out, others were blocked in with bricks. In 1995 the housing charity the Peabody Trust offered to buy the building for £1 and convert it into new housing, with the help of a £9 million grant from the National Lottery Fund. But the offer was rejected and once again the council applied for permission to knock it down. In a series of letters to the editor of *The Times*, the architect complained that, while the architecture of the recent past was allowed to wither, money was wasted on old buildings just because of their age. In response the chairman of the Lottery Fund remarked that the issue was money and not architecture.

And it was about money: the question was not how to revive Keeling House but how to make it pay. In 1999 house prices in Bethnal Green were rising: the rebirth of the City as a financial capital made this local neighbourhood, only a mile to the east, attractive to the yuppies in search of modern urban living. A new tribe of fashion-conscious and wealthy modernists, 'who are fed up with Victorian conversions', were beginning to seek out the high-rise concrete towers that their parents had spurned.[4] In 1999 alone demand for ex-council blocks rose by twenty-five per cent, especially within the more severe Brutalist icons of the era, and as a result developers Lincoln Holdings saw a golden opportunity in Keeling House. By 2000, sixty-four flats had been refurbished and cleaned. A new glass entrance hall with a twenty-four-hour concierge was added, locked behind gates and high railings disguised by herb bushes. Each flat had white wooden floors and an Italian kitchen. On its debut in July 2000, forty-five two-bedroom flats were for sale, starting at £185,000, seven one-bedroom flats at £127,500 and seven penthouses at £375,000, all with safe parking.

Keeling House, in its day, heralded a new design in social housing. It had been built in 1959 from an emerging idea of the purpose of architecture in the post-war world, and in the desperate situation of London following the Blitz. The original designs had been formulated in response to the hopes of creating a New Jerusalem out of the horrors of war, a hope of reforming community through architecture. Keeling House is where the long history of poverty meets the rise of the scientific study of society; the ensuing theories of what a community could be found their expression in the severe creations of Modernist architecture. It is the story of how London was rebuilt out of the rubble of the Blitz, a dream that soured, and the rise and fall and eventual rebirth of a building and its neighbourhood.

The first bombs did not come until the evening of Thursday, 7 September 1940, when 300 Luftwaffe planes filled the night skies over the docks, setting the wharves alight with incendiary devices. Within a couple of weeks, over ninety-five high-explosive bombs, some as large as 1,000 kg, two parachute mines and thousands of incendiaries had fallen on Bethnal Green, an East End neighbourhood north of Spitalfields. Many of the children had been evacuated from the area the previous winter when war was declared, but they had returned when the threat of attack seemed to dissolve; now they huddled in Anderson shelters, dug into the back gardens and squares of the neighbourhood. On 25 September, the Queen Elizabeth Hospital for Children on nearby Hackney Road took a direct hit.

Families sought refuge where they could – inside the cellars of the Royal Oak pub on Columbia Road, in the railway arches at the top of Bethnal Green Road near the Salmon and Ball inn where the Spitalfields martyrs had been executed, down in the basement of the Columbia Road Market, a vast Gothic building paid for by the philanthropist millionairess Angela Burdett-Coutts as a hall for local traders. By chance a German bomber dropped an explosive down the air shaft of the building directly into the shelter, killing fifty-three outright. Over the next eight months, each evening would be disturbed by the whirr of the air raid siren and the cold damp of the shelter. The booming sound of the anti-aircraft artillery in nearby Victoria Park was the only sign that one was not helpless under the onslaught of a relentless enemy. On one evening, Isabella Wilkinson was in a shelter that had been poorly fastened close by her home in Columbia Road, when a near blast ripped off the corrugated iron covering to reveal a scene of horror beyond:

> it was like night gone to day. Blood red the sky was with flames. Bits of people I knew lay scattered around, an arm here a leg there, even a head in the middle of it. We were all paralysed with shock, so was the air raid warden. I'll never forget he leant down, picked up an arm and shook it over his head, blood and all running down his face: 'Forget the dead' he screamed out. 'For Christ sake help me with the living'.[5]

The Blitz, which lasted from September 1940 to May 1941, was an attempt by the Nazi regime to pummel Churchill's Britain into submission. In the previous year, Hitler's Blitzkrieg had rolled from Germany to the English Channel, forcing the BEF's desperate flight from the beaches of Dunkirk. Since the summer the German generals had prepared for the invasion of the island, Operation Sea Lion, first hoping to disable the RAF in a campaign of aerial combat in the skies above the south-eastern counties. When this proved to be indecisive, the war was taken to the cities; if Hitler could reduce London to rubble victory was possible. It was the people of London themselves who now stood on the front line. The Luftwaffe wished to crush morale but also key military locations, and targeted not just the metropolis but also naval and industrial centres across the country. Lying close to the docks, Bethnal Green was the victim of much of the collateral damage and stray bombs dropped by the Germans; the impact was devastating.

For decades Bethnal Green had been a huddle of small workers' cottages, slum housing and the occasional row of social housing built in the Victorian era in response to some of the worst living conditions encountered in the city. There had been numerous attempts since the Great War to improve the area, but the still-cramped housing was some of the densest and most precarious in London. In 1933, when seeking government help, a local MP stated that forty-three per cent of the population lived in an overcrowded huddle, seventeen per cent survived below the poverty line, and twenty-three per cent of the male population were unemployed. The quality of the housing stock was so poor that it offered little defence against the bombs.

In March 1941, a raid dropped its load on Ion Square, a small quarter of thirty-eight cottages built in 1845 set around a square to the north of Columbia Road. At two in the morning Ernie Walkerdine was woken in his shelter, where he was sleeping with his wife and two sons, by a whoosh and a bang; little did he know that he was in the epicentre of an explosion that wiped out all but five of the cottages. It took until midday the next day to dig out the bodies buried under the rubble; between seventeen and twenty-four people were said to have been killed that night.

The last night of the Blitz, 10 May 1941, was the most vicious and tore through the whole city. It was a full moon, so the Luftwaffe were able to navigate their way up the Thames; more than that, there were no clouds in the sky. Five hundred and fifteen planes were packed with explosives and given orders to attack London. As fires raged throughout the dark, it was only in the morning that the extent of the assault could be calculated: 1,486 people were killed and 1,616 seriously injured, 11,000 houses were burnt or pummelled into the ground. The Houses of Parliament were devastated, the chamber of the Commons reduced to ash, as well as St James's Palace, Waterloo Station and the Queen's Hall on Langham Place; it soon became known as 'the longest night'.

Yet the bombing was not over and 3 March 1943 saw the worst atrocity to strike Bethnal Green during the conflict. On that night, in retaliation for long-distance raids on Berlin by the RAF two days previously, the Luftwaffe flew over the East End. At 8.17 p.m. the siren sounded and many made their way towards the new shelter within the Bethnal Green Underground Station. In the first months of the Blitz the station had been closed as a shelter, but soon the Ministry realised that it was the safest place in the borough; by 1943 there was sleeping space for 10,000 with a canteen and a sickbay staffed by nurses and a doctor, a concert room that could hold 300, as well as a library of 4,000 books. Ten minutes later the anti-aircraft guns on Victoria Park started to aim into the sky, making the crowd queueing at the top of the station's stairs jumpy. In panic, people at the back started to push. Reg Baker, a schoolboy at the time, remembered what happened next:

> ... once some fell, the others pushing in just kept pushing and pushing, and people were crushed to death. My sister was fortunate because she was on top of all the bodies so they had to pull her out ... Some of the sights the wardens saw were unbelievable. Most men wore boots then so there were hobnail bootmarks on children's faces. There were whole families wiped out ... when we came out we stood with a school friend of mine and all the ambulances were coming up and going away, and we thought it was about fifteen killed. It wasn't until later, when people had died in hospital that it came out that 178 had died.[6]

The Prime Minister, Winston Churchill, demanded that neither the location nor the number of casualties be made official, fearful that news of the catastrophe might destroy morale.

During the Blitz itself it was estimated that 20,000 tons of bombs were dropped on the whole of London, from Richmond in the west to the docklands in the east. While King George VI rallied his subjects by exhorting, 'The walls of London may be battered but the spirit of the Londoner stands resolute and undismayed',[7] the toll of the damage was enormous. Approximately there were 50,000 casualties, with 20,000 deaths within the city; 130,000 houses and nine million square feet of office space were destroyed, while 750,000 homes were patched up and the owners forced to make do. In Bethnal Green alone the bombing killed 555 and seriously injured 400; 21,700 houses were hit – 2,233 destroyed, 893 uninhabitable, and 2,457 seriously damaged. London had been sorely tested; how was it ever to recover from such an attack?

Yet even before the end of the Blitz, there were schemes to create a new city. The New Jerusalem was, for the very first time, to be planned and organised, it was to be divided and measured and revived to reflect the latest ideas of what a city was, and how it worked. This revolutionary urban philosophy promised a new street grid for the better circulation of traffic; the cramped centre was to be cleared up to complete the work started in the 1860s; industry was to be located in designated zones close to the fringes of London, dividing the city into spaces for work and living; finally, it hoped to chase away poverty and deprivation, using the latest materials and ideas in architecture to reform the very fabric of society itself. It was undoubtedly the greatest human experiment, never attempted before, in the capital's history.

Since the 1860s the efforts of the city governments – the MBW until the 1880s and the LCC thereafter – at social housing had been piecemeal and reactive. In November 1887, a riot broke out on Trafalgar Square, Nash's elegant civic space, as 10,000 marchers were halted by a troop of police, infantry and cavalry who attacked them with fists and truncheons, hospitalising over 200. 'Bloody Sunday' was a protest in favour of Irish Home Rule; however it was also a cause adopted by the East End poor, who were desperate and becoming politicised by the socialists, Fabians and anarchists streaming into Whitechapel to foment revolution. The riot sparked the creation in the popular imagination of the East End as a lost world, which was soon perceived, in the words of Jack London, as a social abyss. This image only grew darker in April 1888 with the first news of the serial killer Jack the Ripper; this was followed by the match girls' strike in Bow that revealed the horrific working conditions in the Bryant and May factory; in 1889, workers began to strike on the docks for the right to form unions. Fear of social dilapidation, tabloid fascination and puritanical sentimentality combined in calls for action: state intervention and private philanthropy both attempted to act as doctor, both with mixed results.

In 1896 Arthur Morrison published *A Child of the Jago* which became an instant bestseller, revealing a thinly fictionalised life and crimes of the Old Nichol estate, west of Bethnal Green, garishly confirming the shocking statistics of Charles Booth's systematic 1889 survey of London's poverty, *Life and Labour of the People*. Booth had commissioned a team of researchers to study every street in the city and colour-code it according to living conditions and income. The map for Bethnal Green went from black at Old Nichol to indicate the 'lowest class. Vicious, semi-criminal', through dark blue 'Very poor, causal. Chronic want' to light blue 'poor. 18s to 21s a week for a moderate family'. While Booth's statistics displayed the true extent of hardship in numbers, Morrison's novel turned the worst slum in London into a tourist site, a modern-day Bedlam where the rich came to gawp at the extremes of human endurance. The LCC was forced to react.[8]

The old tenements of the Jago, the broken remnants of the speculative housing booms of the seventeenth and eighteenth centuries, were razed to the ground, heaped into a mound and turned into the central garden and bandstand of Arnold Circus, which sat in the middle of the renamed Boundary estate. A new system of tenement buildings was designed with the hope of 'raising the character of the neighbouring occupants by improving their surroundings, in planting trees in the street and the central open space'.[9] Each tenement block was named after a Thames village and designed in the latest Arts and Crafts style, bringing the ideas of Ruskin, William Morris and Norman Shaw to the East End; as with so many similar high-minded projects, local residents were never asked their preference.

The Boundary estate was the first major LCC rehousing project of the twentieth century. Elsewhere private philanthropy was hoping to reform the slums. The Peabody Trust was started in the 1860s by the American banker George Peabody, to provide housing for those who could pay a small regular rent; the first project was on Commercial Road, Spitalfields. There were also a number of housing trusts set up – the Guinness Trust, the Industrial Dwellings Company, the Samuel Lewis Housing Trust – with charity and profit in mind, providing housing for the respectable poor but also enticing investors with the promise of a five per cent return on their money. The Rothschild Buildings, founded by the fabulously rich banking family for poor Jewish immigrants, also imposed strict rules on behaviour. Many of these new schemes improved the lots of those in regular work, who could organise their lives; but the lowest of society were left to the worst conditions, irregular work and an early death.

On Columbia Road, at the centre of Bethnal Green, there was a mixture of trust housing and old cottages from the time when the neighbourhood was a farming community outside the city walls, famed for its watercress. The Jesus Hospital estate was built in the 1840s, partly as a charitable trust, but by the 1860s John Hollingshead, the journalist who walked along Bazalgette's sewers singing 'God Save the Queen' under Buckingham Palace, wrote that Bethnal Green was home to 'mainly poor Dock labourers, poor costermongers, poor silk weavers, clinging hopelessly to a withering handicraft, the lowest kind of thieves, the most ill-disguised class of swell mobsmen'.[10] In the 1870s the Gothic Columbia Road Market, built under the patronage of Angela Burdett-Coutts, was generally ignored by the locals, who preferred to trade in the open air without the strictures and rules imposed upon them.

In the years following the Great War, housing policy went hand in hand with the bourgeois taste of the suburbans. 'Houses for Heroes' meant moving communities out of the inner cities to new cottage estates in the hinterlands. These new communities were inspired by Ebenezer Howard's vision of garden cities, and by the late 1930s there were large estates in all directions, housing 258,000 in total; by far the biggest was Becontree in Essex, transplanting many of the East End families to a ready-built community of 25,766 new houses, 400 shops, thirty schools, churches, pubs and cinemas. Each cottage conformed to a set of regulations, the Tudor Walters Standards: a minimum of 760 square feet of floor space, with six good-sized rooms and large windows, set within a patch of garden and following one of three designs set out by the architect of Hampstead Garden Suburb and Letchworth, Raymond Unwin.

Yet the policy was not only centrifugal and in Bethnal Green there was a concerted effort to develop estates of tenements without moving communities away from the area. In 1936 the LCC cleared thirty-six acres of slums north of the Old Bethnal Green Road which they romantically renamed Bethnal Green No. 1 Redevelopment Area. In place of squalid houses and cottages, new, sturdy, brick three- or four-storey blocks were built. The flats were organised along balconies that ran the length of the building, connected by a central staircase. By 1945 the LCC had built 2,170 new flats and had plans for another 1,830; however, the slum clearance was not met with universal approval. Despite the horrors of the old system and the crumbling fabric of the slums, many residents were disgruntled by being forced into flats; in a survey conducted by Mass Observation there were ceaseless complaints that this vertical living had banished the old ways.

In 1946, a year after the end of the war, the sociologist Ruth Glass was in Bethnal Green working for the Association for Planning and Regional Reconstruction; as she looked for ways to redevelop the neighbourhood she noted: '89 per cent of all households have no bathroom. The only source of hot water for 78 per cent of all households is boiling a kettle on the kitchen range or stove . . . whole streets were knocked out. Everywhere there are derelict sites which already seem to be part of this scene of urban decay.'[11] She seemed to be implying that the Blitz was no more than the latest layer of degradation that the area had endured in a long history of brutality, neglect and muddle-headed attempts at charity. The neighbourhood had long been one of the poorest and worst managed in London and now had also suffered one of the most vicious batterings of the Second World War. The region needed to be rebuilt, not just physically but also as a modern community.

Even as the bombs rained down, plans were already in place to rebuild the metropolis. Central to these schemes was the idea of the welfare state, that government should intervene and improve the lives of all those who had survived the war. These ideas had their gestation in the East End, for the leading architect of the new state, William Beveridge, had spent his formative years as sub-warden at Toynbee Hall, Henrietta Barnett's learning centre for the East End poor. Here he had absorbed many of the ideas that would form the bedrock of his 1942 report *Social Insurance and Allied Services*, a very dry 300-page document that became a huge bestseller, with 600,000 copies purchased during wartime. Beveridge had been asked by the government to look at ways to revitalise society with the directive 'Go and discover why, with so much wealth in Britain, there continues to be so much poverty, and how poverty can be cured',[12] and in the most memorable image of the report he sought to banish the giants of Want, Disease, Ignorance, Squalor and Idleness. The Beveridge Report, as it later became known, was the blueprint for a new Britain.

However, it was another document, the Abercrombie Plan, that converted Beveridge's abstract values into a proposal for the physical transformation of London. In his 1943 *County of London Plan*, Patrick Abercrombie, alongside J. H. Forshaw, saw five key problem areas that were suffocating London: traffic congestion, poor housing, lack of industrial planning – meaning that factories and neighbourhoods huddled against each other – a lack of open spaces and the continued sprawl of the suburbs. Abercrombie was bringing Ebenezer Howard's vision of the city of tomorrow up-to-date, except that, while the original garden cities were built for profit, the new communities were to be constructed by the state. In 1943 the population of the inner city was 2,482,000 and Abercrombie wanted to reduce the density by at least 600,000, in particular diminishing by fifty per cent the crowded and Blitz-damaged easterly boroughs of Stepney, Shoreditch, Southwark and Bethnal Green.

Since the 1920s Abercrombie had been at the head of the Campaign to Protect Rural England, promoting the cause of areas of outstanding natural beauty and national parks. He was also passionate about the creation of a green belt, a no-build zone, around the capital, which he placed at the heart of his new plans. It seemed that he had laid himself a trap, however, for how could he reduce the density of the inner city while also restricting the growth of the suburbs? The solution was a series of new towns built beyond the preserved strip encircling the city: Stevenage, Hatfield, Basildon, Welwyn and Bracknell. The 1946 New Towns Act hoped to create a socially mixed, economically contained community providing new industries to the locale so that it did not become a commuter dormitory for the capital. It was all done with the best intentions, as MP Lewis Silkin announced to Parliament: 'Our aim must be to combine in the new town the friendly spirit of the former slum with the vastly improved health conditions of the new estate, but it must be a broadened spirit embracing all classes of society.'[13]

In 1957 the social researchers Michael Young and Peter Willmott published *Family and Kinship in East London*, the result of an extensive survey of the changing attitudes and circumstances in Bethnal Green since the war. One of the key areas of the study was the displacement of many of the locals to 'Greenleigh', twenty miles outside the city. To begin with the change of environment was traumatic: 'When I first came,' said Mrs Sandeman, 'I cried for weeks, it was so lonely.'[14] Many who were brought up in a close community of relatives, all living within walking distance, were forced to leave their families behind; yet in time the advantages of having a house and regular visits often encouraged other family members to move out. Many others claimed that they had left the old neighbourhood for the sake of the children, Mrs Ames reporting, 'We came to Greenleigh for Bill's sake. He was very ill with diphtheria. He got it by drinking the drain water from the sinks of two families living above us.'[15] In time, the old ties to Bethnal Green receded and were replaced by a new sense of community within the new towns.

Housing remained a political hot potato, however; the battleground not just for local issues but also for national policy. The outflow from the inner boroughs into the countryside was strongly contested between the urban Labour councils, who were nervous that they were losing rates and votes, and the rural Conservative boroughs, who did not want an influx of working-class socialists muddying their safe constituencies. When Silkin went to sell the idea to the 6,000 residents of the village of Stevenage, which was to expand by a thousand per cent in the following years, the response was predictable and he was forced to tell the meeting that 'the project will go forward, because it must go forward. It will do so more surely and more smoothly, and more successfully, with your help and co-operation,' before he was shouted down with cries of 'Gestapo!' and 'Dictator!'.[16]

There was also a political divide on the fundamental purpose of social housing itself. In 1945 a new Labour government was elected with Aneurin Bevan, the firebrand Welsh socialist, as Minister of Health, who believed that rehousing was at the centre of the welfare nation. Despite the scarcity of materials and labour in the austerity years following the war, Bevan was passionate about providing the highest standard of social housing and refused to sacrifice quality for quantity, despite the desperate need for new homes. In his opinion, dropping the Tudor Walters Standards was 'the coward's way out ... if we wait a little longer that will be far better than doing ugly things now and regretting them for the rest of our lives'.[17]

This caused huge problems inside London, where the need for new houses was at its greatest; to make matters worse, between 1945 and 1950 the metropolis's population rose by a further 800,000, all requiring new homes. Housing riots occurred throughout the city and in 1947 the Communist Party organised a squatting campaign in Kensington. Unscrupulous landlords like Peter Rachman in Notting Hill took advantage of the high demand by buying up cheap and damaged housing and then filling it with tenants. The government's short-term response was desperate: many of the unnecessary Army camps and open spaces were given over to 15,000 prefab temporary bungalows, which were hastily constructed by redundant wartime aircraft factories. They were created to have a life expectancy of only ten years, although some still are in use today. Larger properties were also compulsorily purchased and converted into smaller units with the hope that better housing would soon be available.

Nonetheless, Bevan struggled to do the best he could for the nation, providing long-term housing that would offer pride and dignity to the working man and his family. In 1947 alone 227,000 houses were completed, but this was nowhere near enough. In Bethnal Green 830 dwellings were built by the LCC between 1945 and 1951; yet while Bevan hoped that each family was offered a house of their own with an indoor toilet, hot water and a patch of garden, the reality was a flat on a new estate.

In 1951 it was decided that a Festival of Britain was to be staged, an altogether different event to the Empire Exhibition at Wembley. Its official purpose was to 'demonstrate to the world the recovery of the United Kingdom from the effects of the war in moral, cultural, spiritual fields',[18] but it was more – in the words of Herbert Morrison, the former head of the LCC and then a Labour MP, a 'tonic for the nation'. A location was chosen on the south bank of the Thames, opposite Bazalgette's Victoria Embankment, a shambles of wharves, old factories and working-class houses, hardly the image of a bright, new future city. In their place was to be built, as cheaply and fast as possible, a display of the latest architectural designs, 'a new urban landscape'.[19]

At the centre of the site was the Festival Hall, a new concert space for London designed by the LCC Chief Architect, Robert Matthew. Because of the cramped site and the desire to create not just a place for music but also a cultural centre – a people's palace – with bars, restaurants, rehearsal space and a gallery, he was forced to push the hall itself into the air, suspended over the main hall, and build all the rest underneath and around. From the outside, the poet of Metroland, John Betjeman, thought it looked like the Tote, the state-run bookmakers; but the interior, despite being 'modishly modernist', was a triumph.[20] To the west of the hall stood Ralph Tubbs's Dome of Discovery, at 356 feet wide the largest aluminium structure in the world. Nearby the Skylon, a 90-foot visual joke in steel and wire, rose seemingly unsuspended into the sky.

Yet the Festival was not only to be found on the South Bank; as well as the temporary pavilions, events and shows were organised throughout the country. Over 86,000 people went to visit the Lansbury estate in Poplar, a few miles down the Thames in the East End. Here was an example of a new system of social housing, a modern council estate built out of the squalor of the working-class slum and rising from the rubble of the Blitz. That June, Sir John Summerson also went to visit the estate and described what he saw: 'the general idea is the redevelopment of a neighbourhood ... the old street pattern is wiped out and a new pattern, with fewer streets, imposed; houses and flats are loosely and agreeably mixed, there is a fluent adequacy of open space and churches and schools are well-sited'.[21] The old terraced streets of squalid brick houses had been torn down and replaced by a new configuration of what a community could be – mixed and ordered, wide open spaces, flats organised vertically alongside traditional dwellings. This was the future.

The estate had been named after George Lansbury, a popular East End Labour MP, who had long campaigned for social justice in this most deprived region of the city. Architectural critics were lukewarm about the design, worried that it lacked purist principles, yet for the people who were about to move in it was a blessing from the government beyond their expectations: 'Our new place is just a housewife's dream,' reported Alice Snoddy, a part-time paper sorter who lived with her husband, two children and mother-in-law,' 'there are fitted cupboards and one to air clothes in, a stainless steel sink, hot water tanks, it's the sort of home to be proud of.'[22]

The work at the Lansbury estate and the hopes for the birth of modern Britain within the Festival grounds were expressions of a deep transformation within London and the nation. The Second World War had changed pretty much everything, and everything had to be reformed to survive in the new post-war world. As the architect H. T. Cadbury-Brown noted, 'There was a real sense in which the Festival marked an upturn in people's lives … it was an event for a new dawn, for enjoying life on modern terms, with modern technology.'[23]

But by 1951, the nation became tired of Bevan's exhortations to wait and a new Conservative government was elected with Harold Macmillan named as the Housing Minister, campaigning on the promise to build 300,000 new houses a year. It was a promise to deliver quantity with little reference to quality for, unlike Bevan, Macmillan believed state housing was there for the short term, a stepping stone for the working man to drag himself out of poverty on the journey towards self-suffi-ciency. As a result, while the number of homes rose, the quality of the 'people's house' declined: the floor space of the Tudor Walters Standards was reduced by thirty per cent, poor materials were used such as plas-terboard instead of brick, there were fewer windows and smaller gardens. In addition, under Macmillan London saw the increase of high-rise blocks, reaching into the city sky like new cathedrals of the modern age. It was here that the design of the city met the latest ideas in architecture, where the ultra-Modernist dreams of the Festival collided with the political realities of 1950s Britain.

The year after the Festival, the architect Denys Lasdun wrote an essay on housing in London for the *Architects' Year Book*. Despite the best efforts of the Labour government, there was a crisis: demand for houses was increasing, yet to rush any project was to jeopardise quality. Where once the administration had called for houses and cottages to improve

28. Denys Lasdun, a Modernist in search of a new language of building (*Getty*)

the life of the honest working family, they were now looking to the skies and naming the tower block as the solution to the many problems of population explosion and community engineering. Lasdun himself was at a crossroads in his career and in his thinking about the purpose and form of modern architecture. What was the relationship between the building and the city? In the pursuit of a new philosophy of building, how was the modern architect meant to treat the past? What was the social function of building?

Denys Lasdun was born in 1914 in London, to a Jewish-Russian father and an Australian mother. He studied at Rugby School and, after a brief stint at the Royal Academy of Music, moved to the Architectural Association (AA) in Bedford Square, Bloomsbury, because, in his words, he did not know what else to do. Until this moment the graduate student had only the briefest architectural education. His mother had been a keen musician and had introduced him to the key ideas of the Modernist movement, and he had already developed an interest in Cubism, which questioned the relationship between movement and space. He was also fascinated by postcards his father had sent him from New York, yet he had thought little about what architecture was: 'I went to school and prayed every day, and twice on Sundays, in a Butterfield chapel ... The only other memories are of a sketch done at the age of eight of Waterhouse's Natural History Museum; of being taken to the Wembley Empire Exhibition whose concrete buildings Russell Hitchcock described as "scraped academic".'[24] At the AA he was thrown into a melting pot of new ideas that would transform architecture over the next decades.

Here he was tutored by E. A. A. Rowse, who taught that architecture 'was above all a social art'.[25] This concept was further cemented in Lasdun's developing ideas when he was given a copy of Le Corbusier's *Vers une Architecture*, which he devoured with a passion, as a birthday present. The manifesto by the leading Swiss-French Modernist dismissed everything that went before it and demanded an architecture for the machine age with a fresh emphasis on efficiency and function, developing new materials, the abandonment of ornamentation and a commitment to an integral response to construction. As he wrote these essays Le Corbusier had also been working on city planning and in 1935 produced a second revolutionary call for action, *La Ville radieuse*, that sought to rationalise and reorganise society through architecture.

Outside the library, Lasdun was fortunate to absorb ideas from many of the eminent European theorists who were coming to London from Germany as political refugees from Stalin and the early days of Nazism: the leading thinker of the Bauhaus movement, Walter Gropius; Erich Mendelsohn, who had worked with Gropius and Ludwig Mies van der Rohe, and Serge Chermayeff, who worked with Mendelsohn on the influential De La Warr Pavilion in Bexhill-on-Sea in 1935. There was also Ernö Goldfinger, the Hungarian designer who arrived at this time, as well as the Russian Berthold Lubetkin, who formed his influential architectural firm, Tecton, in 1932 with six graduates from the AA. They brought the latest ideas from the Continent and in 1933 were central to the foundation of the MARS (Modern Architectural Research) Group that was started in London as the English wing of Le Corbusier's International Congresses of Modern Architecture, which sought to reduce modern architecture and social planning to a set of axioms.

While still a student, Lasdun travelled to France to experience Le Corbusier's work at first hand, in particular the Pavillon Suisse, a hostel for Swiss students in Paris; he was won over by the power and clarity of the master's vision, later writing: 'this building presaged a vision of the city and how to deal with mass housing. It was antithetical to the obsolescent slums of the nineteenth century.'[26] He was now an ardent convert to Modernism but in his third year, unexpectedly, he chose to measure out the Orangery in Kensington Gardens, built by Nicholas Hawksmoor in 1704, as his final project. The detailed study of the English Baroque building haunted him and 'started a life long interest in an architect so singular and so profoundly concerned with the roots of architecture and the nature of space'.[27] In a lecture on Hawksmoor in the 1990s, Lasdun noted that it was Hawksmoor, not Le Corbusier, who seeded in him the 'paradox between desire of renewal and a deep attachment to [the] past' that would begin to germinate in the 1950s.[28]

After graduating from the AA Lasdun took on a number of small projects including an unapologetically Le Corbusier town house in Paddington, which became the home of the cartoonist Ronald Searle. He then worked for Wells Coates, a Canadian founder member of the MARS group and a passionate disciple of Le Corbusier's notion that buildings were 'machines for living'. This was emphatically displayed in his 1934 set of flats in Hampstead, the Isokon Building, which promoted a new model for communal living with a shared kitchen and services such as a laundry and a shoe-shine. Lasdun then moved on, working for Tecton under the powerful influence of Berthold Lubetkin, who since 1928 had designed some of the most forceful examples of Modernist architecture in London. For Lubetkin, architecture was 'three-dimensional philosophy', reason set in stone informed by a deep under-standing of materials and a dogmatic desire to provide not what people wanted but what they needed, without recourse to history, feeling or a study of place.

When he was commissioned to build a new enclosure at Regent's Park Zoo, situated inside Nash's picturesque landscape, Lubetkin aimed to tame Nature 'not with a fist, but with a smile',[29] best seen in the iconic geometric shapes of the penguin pool, two spiralling walkways descending into the water. His Modernist vision was tested on a larger scale in the creation of Highpoint I, a block of flats in Highgate, that explored Le Corbusier's ideas of dense communal living – geometric, functional, with every aspect of the building scrutinised, from the bath taps to the arrangement of the retractable windows – set within a sculpted landscape. Like the Isokon building, Highpoint I was social housing for 'left-wing intellectuals' who had the luxury of choosing their innovative way of life.

In 1938, the year that Lasdun joined the office, Lubetkin was also involved in the first Modernist project commissioned by a municipal authority: Finsbury Health Centre, which set the Modernist social agenda in concrete and glass bricks. The centre was intended to rationalise the local council health provision even before the National Health Service had been invented. The open spaces of the communal areas created a welcoming atmosphere, instilling access and inclusion, breaking down the traditional barriers between doctor and patient, the state and the people.

Modernist architecture had a clear social agenda to improve the lives of the masses; at the same time, the MARS group were also looking at the condition of London as a whole. They began with an attempt to develop a 'general housing scheme' for Bethnal Green, but the results floundered in bickering and theoretical differences; thus they concluded that if they could not decide on how to revive a neighbourhood, they would perhaps impose their axioms upon the entire metropolis. In 1937 they produced a new plan, '"The Theory of Contacts" and its Application to the Future of London', based on a scientific 'study of patterns of human interaction'[30] and the expectation that between 1935 and 1950 London would double in population.

For the Modernists, garden cities were anathema, new towns were to be abhorred and the idea of a green belt was a noose: the city should be allowed to grow under strict controls based on functionality and the concept of 'contacts', the rational root of social harmony. Thirteen ribbons were to be constructed running out of the city, serviced by a new transport system and governed by a fascination with speed: so that the whole was organised by human traffic walking at ten km/h; local traffic at under 100 km/h; long-distance highway traffic at over 100 km/h, and finally air travel. The new society that lived, worked and died along these new contacts was divided into social sections (producers – working class; distributors – middle class; consumers – upper class), with different kinds of housing: flats, rows and villas. The dwellings were to be mixed so that each 'contact unit' of 30,000 people comprised 480 flats formed from eight multi-storey blocks, designed in line with Highpoint I by Tecton, alongside 380 conventional homes, spread out in an ordered plan with schools and services.

When the plans were shown in the Architecture Exhibition of 1938 at the AA, they did not meet with universal approval, even from within the MARS group. One faction, led by the planner Arthur Ling, who had studied under Abercrombie, thought that London should be planned within 'neighbourhood units', cells of 6,000 people only, based around a grid system. All classes were to share living spaces within the blocks that were set in an ordered landscape, and there was little interest in transport, because everything was provided by the unit.

The start of the war made such speculation void. Many of the key members of the MARS group enlisted, while some of the Continental figures were interned as foreign aliens. Lasdun joined the Royal Artillery but was soon seconded to the Royal Engineers. There is an extraordinary photograph of the architect on the beaches of Normandy following D-Day, standing in front of a blackboard giving instructions to a corps of men; here he was mainly occupied with the repair of damaged airstrips and even designed a fighter station in Holland; he would later remember the pleasures of commanding bulldozers as they sculpted the landscape, sweeping the ground into platforms.

After the war he returned to London and began work once again with Lubetkin, and while the master turned his attention to the creation of

Peterlee, one of Abercrombie's beloved new towns, Lasdun was put in charge of a new project in social housing in Paddington, Hallfield, an inner suburb to the west of the city. From the start, Lasdun began to feel an aversion to the old doctrines and theories of pre-war Modernism, as he later recalled:

> What modern architecture itself needed was some kind of reorientation, I certainly felt myself firmly in that tradition descending from the pioneer masters of the Modern Movement ... but for all this I was fundamentally averse to Le Corbusier's utopian idea ... I knew that there was no future in the sort of abstract urbanism which caused architects to work without a sense of place or the past.[31]

Lasdun would break with the past by going back to history; he would also return to the idea of designing a building in relation to the city, creating a philosophy of urban landscape, not solely as a means of transforming it. Hallfield was a social housing estate based upon Le Corbusier's *Ville radieuse*, a community of fifteen blocks, ranging in size and height, set within a landscape of seventeen acres. Replacing a community of bombed-out cottages surrounded by large nineteenth-century stucco houses, Lasdun wanted the new blocks to contrast and engage with the neighbourhood, to recognise the city's historical process, as he would later write: 'I cannot separate my ideas about architecture from the nature of cities which are there in time, have to change and have to grow and I really see architecture as a microcosm of the city.'[32]

This emerging philosophy in the urban landscape was seen in the particular attention paid to the elevations of the blocks. Le Corbusier believed that the whole was more important than the individual parts, and in Lubetkin's designs individual apartments were set within a united pattern. Yet as work progressed Lubetkin and his associate began to argue: the Russian was spending too much of his time working on the Peterlee New Town in the north of England, and Lasdun was left to work at Hallfield; he would later reveal that this was the moment he decided that he had to 'unlearn some of the lessons Lubetkin had taught'.[33]

In 1948 Tecton was dissolved as a partnership in some acrimony and Lasdun continued at Hallfield. Although much of the main work had been completed on the mass of the blocks, he was still able to adapt a few features, such as the curving geometric balconies. The estate hoped to achieve four aims: to develop an urban rather than a suburban space; to set high-density housing within a planted garden to give a sense of an urban landscape; to build the estate of blocks away from the road and orientate the dwellings to enhance a sense of community; finally, to offer visual diversity of buildings and decorations and a sense of variety. Lasdun hoped to create a 'humane, geometric space'.[34]

Lasdun also went on to design a primary school to serve the estate, and here he began from scratch, developing his ideas on the ground. He was resolved that architecture should respond to the environment surrounding it and that it needed to engage with the principal users. Lasdun wanted the school to feel like a protected space, with the sense of a second home. The many parts of the school were to be connected, the infant classes placed at the centre of a sinuous sweep of buildings. He also modelled this curve on more 'biological' shapes and drew a diagram of the school as a plant clipping, the leaves as the classrooms, the flower as the assembly hall, the dining room as a seedpod, administration offices running along the branches. Different materials, heights of building, light and shade, set within a series of gardens and terraces, created something of a safe, fantasy world, 'a wealth of interesting possibilities around every corner'.[35] It was instantly recognised as a hugely successful building.

In 1952 Lasdun, now working in his own practice alongside Lindsey Drake, turned his attention to a new housing project in Bethnal Green and, as if setting out his manifesto before beginning work, wrote his article 'Second Thoughts on Housing in London' in the *Architects' Year Book*. He warned that the current policy of Housing Minister Harold Macmillan was driven by the need to be seen doing something, clocking up a cricket score, and was heading towards an 'architecture of statistics – unimaginative and lifeless'. Instead he demanded that architects re-evaluate the purposes of social housing: 'we are dealing with people – old, young, single and married'; secondly, to deal with the problem solely in terms of providing quantity would be unforgivable: 'density control should now shift its focus from an overall plan which cannot be realised to a more human and practical one'.[36] Finally, acknowledging that the creation of a tower block was in part the development of a new community, he argued that something more than the provision of services was needed to create the new society: 'the architecture and the layout would begin to express the pattern of life for which it was designed. This pattern is not only concerned with physical habitation but with the broader concept of life.'[37]

Lasdun was not alone in his concerns over the rigid axiomatic nature of Modernism. This new generation, who wished to replace strict aesthetic regulations with a flexible set of principles, would by 1953 be called the New Brutalists, an in-joke that for some reason stuck. The movement, such as it was, emerged from the writing of the critic Reyner Banham and the work of Alison and Peter Smithson, and was first seen in the competition for the Golden Lane estate in 1951. The Smithsons believed that sociologists had nothing to teach architects and that community was the heart of their own practice. In their designs for the new estate, they planned to build 'street decks' in the sky to recreate the sense of the old East End neighbourhood within a housing block, with a communal space outside the individual flats, replacing the traditional working-class lane. They did not win the competition but their ideas were soon turned into reality in the hands of other architects, such as Jack Lynn and Ivor Smith at Park Hill, Sheffield, who saw their 'streets in the sky' as expressions of 'our national independence of character and at the same time with community structure'.[38]

Lasdun was unhappy to be called a Brutalist – a style that was never enshrined in a manifesto or conference paper – but accepted many of the key ideas. He later wrote: 'In spite of everything, I think there is more virtue in Brutalism than in 90 per cent of the architectural theorising that is going on at present. But . . . the three Brutalist "dogmas": A-formalism, truth to structure, materials as found, only touch the fringes of architecture and leave the real problem of creating specific buildings almost exactly where they are.'[39] A-Formalism was the attempt to turn away from a priori solutions to architectural problems; all issues were site- and time-specific. 'Truth to structure' was concerned with the treatment of decoration, reducing a building to its structural core without ornamentation, the building material itself transformed into the effect – hence, for some, the worship of rough concrete above all other surfaces. It was also a desire to display the function of the building and its parts. Finally, 'Materials as found' was a very formal way of discussing how a building might interact with its environment, so that it did not stand alone but within a physical and historical landscape. Lasdun would try to adopt all these lessons as he sought to find a new model for social housing in Bethnal Green.

Since 1945, Bethnal Green had become the laboratory for 'virtually every English experiment in public housing',[40] and Lasdun did not wish to add another formalist estate block, a symmetrical concrete behemoth within a neighbourhood of dilapidated cottages; he could not transplant the work he had just completed at Hallfield into this very different environment. Instead, he sought a new style that would understand the particular geographical, historical and social concerns of the place and he began to study the work of Bill Brandt, the German-born artist who had photographed the families of the East End in the 1930s. In the haunting images of poverty, despite the deprivations, a strong sense of community emerges. In his book of the period, *Observing the English*, he juxtaposed the life of privilege with that of Stepney and Bethnal Green, young students in their Eton uniform, tails and shiny top hats, standing next to ragged boys; last orders in the pub; maids waiting timorously in a Lyons Tea Room; a young girl washing her front door-step; a children's birthday party in Kensington with balloons and hats.

The strong communal ties of the East End were the subject of Young and Willmott's *Family and Kinship in East London*, written as Lasdun was developing his plans. For those who did not exit the neighbourhood to 'Greenleigh', the generations within a family remained closely knit, helping each other with the upkeep of the house or childcare, uncles, aunts and cousins living nearby. Daughters moved close to the husband's family, but this was often within the same neighbourhood. Many people stayed in dire conditions rather than move to the new towns because 'they are attached to Mum and Dad, to the markets, to the pub and settlements, to Club Row and the London Hospital'.[41]

The coming of the tower blocks and the immigration out to the suburbs from the 1940s onwards threatened to break these old ways of living, however; being shuffled into a flat rather than a house was considered to be a stain on a family, despite the advantages it offered. As Young and Willmott pleaded in their conclusions: 'The sense of loyalty to each other amongst the inhabitants of a place like Bethnal Green is not due to buildings ... In such a district community spirit does not have to be fostered, it is already there.'[42] Lasdun understood these lessons and as he began to formulate his designs he hoped to find a form of architecture that could enhance and preserve this spirit where most previous attempts had failed. In 1957 he wrote to the editor of *The Times*, 'Architects have only one function: to produce surroundings for a decent life.'[43] But what was the shape of decency? What materials provided the good life?

While Lasdun was considering these questions he was also reading the work of the American Professor of City Planning at MIT, Kevin Lynch, who wrote an article in *Scientific American* in 1954 on the form of cities, dividing the civic space into 'grains' or 'clusters', so for example a single pre-war East End street was a unified community. Lasdun believed that new housing needed to acknowledge these pre-existing 'grains' and find a way to enhance the internal cohesion, improving its conditions rather than attempting to break it up and reform it. Modernist architecture, therefore, had a duty to provide cluster housing rather than 'machines for living'.

Lasdun had already started to put his thinking into an eight-storey block in Usk Road, east of Bethnal Green Station, alongside the Roman Road, that involved two wings running along from a central lift block, so that the living spaces were separated from the services. In 1954 he began work on developing more ambitious designs for a plot on Claredale Street, at the east end of the Columbia Road, a few hundred yards from Ion Square which had been obliterated by the Blitz. He started with the concept of recreating a traditional East End street, a cluster, but turning it onto its end, so that the street rose into the city sky.

Rather than flats on a single storey, Lasdun developed a system of

29. Lasdun's plans for a vertical street – privacy, clean air and a new kind of
    neighbourhood (*RIBA*)

four blocks, each with fourteen maisonettes, recreating the 'two-up,
two-down' design of a traditional cottage with bedrooms and bathroom
on the second floor and living space below. Entering through the lift in
the central service tower, walkways connected to the front door that
were exposed to the open air to offer a sense of a 'street in the sky', and
here too provisions were made for hanging washing and socialising. The
ground floor was given over to stores and heating; this offered the
advantage that even the owners of the lowest level of maisonettes would
not be lost in gloom, but benefit from fresh air and light.

   In one of the most intriguing plans for the building, Lasdun charted
the effect of the sun moving across the sky and the shadow that the
block would cast upon the surrounding area, like a vast sundial. He was
adamant that each maisonette should offer a sense of privacy for the
occupants and that it would be impossible to see inside one dwelling

from another. Thus the four blocks stood at unexpected angles, so from above the whole structure appeared like a concrete butterfly. He also calculated how each flat could receive the maximum natural light throughout the day.

As the block was rising into the sky, Lasdun started to put his new philosophy of design into words in a series of articles and interviews with John H. V. Davies, 'Thoughts in Progress', in the journal *Architectural Design*. The articles ranged from his thoughts on the New Brutalism to the 'Truth to Structure' as well as more technical considerations such as the efficacy of the curtain wall. In particular, the writing emphasised the relationship between the advantages of new technology to bring improvements to people's lives and the necessity to temper this with history or a sense of place:

> An architect is subjected to many influences, scientific, technological, social, economic, cultural, architectural; out of his response to them, when he is faced with the specific problems of specific situations, architecture comes. An architect must study and take a view of everything that can possibly affect his building. He must always question, never accept a solution that has worked somewhere else just because it has worked somewhere else.[44]

Residents began to move into Keeling House in 1959, and by this time Lasdun was already working on new projects, a set of exclusive flats on Piccadilly that looked out onto St James's Park. In the 1960s he was acknowledged as one of the leading Modernist architects in Britain: in 1960 he created a new Royal College of Physicians in Regent's Park alongside Nash's stucco terraces. This was followed by a number of commissions to create new university buildings, including the whole complex of the University of East Anglia, Norwich, science buildings and a museum at Cambridge and the Institute of Education and other additions to the University of London.

By this time, Lasdun had distilled his many ideas that had begun to emerge as he worked on Keeling House, shown to dramatic effect in the new commission for the National Theatre, close by the Royal Festival Hall, the original site of the 1951 Festival of Britain. The building today still commands violent opinions; in the 1980s Prince Charles claimed that it was proof that the Modernist city planners successfully smuggled a nuclear reactor into the heart of the city without anyone noticing. In 2009 the *Daily Mail* journalist Quentin Letts included Lasdun as one of '50 People who Buggered up Britain'. In the heat of the Prince Charles debate of 1989 that split the architectural community between trad-itionalists and Modernists, however, Lasdun disagreed with a certain fury. He viewed himself not as a disruption with the past but as part of a long succession of London architects that included Sir Christopher Wren, and Nicholas Hawksmoor in particular. As he was building Keeling House he would have studied with interest the nearby Christ Church, Spitalfields, built by Hawksmoor to offer the new community a place of worship. Just as Hawksmoor regarded his building as a medi-tation on the history of architecture, so Lasdun considered his work as part of a continuing discussion between the physical city and its inhabitants. As his notes for a 1991 lecture show, Lasdun saw his concrete creation in dialogue with the English Baroque master: 'although [Hawksmoor] broke all strict classical rules, HE NEVER IGNORES BASIC ARCHITECTURAL PRINCIPLES WHICH LIE BEHIND THE RULES OF CLASSICISM – MASS, SPACE, LINE, SURFACE, PROPORTION, COHERENCE, ETC. This is the secret of all good architecture.'[45]

In an interview in 1990, Lasdun revealed that he kept stuck on the inside back cover of his pocket diary a quote from Edmund Burke: 'those who carry out great public schemes must be proof against the worst delays, the most mortifying disappointments, the most shocking insults, and what is worst of all, the presumptuous judgement of the ignorant upon their designs.'[46] He was to be disappointed by what followed: as Keeling House was nearing completion, the high-rise housing boom was at its peak. In 1953, seventy-seven per cent of social building was houses for individual families, twenty per cent low-rise flats and only three per cent were tower blocks, but this changed radically. In 1955, the government announced that, due to the impossible demand for homes, their con-struction would be opened up to private contractors. A subsidy was also offered based not upon the number of houses built or the size of the plot, but on the number of storeys a building would have, encouraging the development of high-rise blocks: a six-storey block would be offered 2.3 times the basic subsidy, rising to 3.4 times at twenty storeys and over.

The combination of government payouts and private profits had an instant impact on the number of blocks planned: in 1953 6,730 tenders were approved by local authorities, which rose to 35,454 by 1964. This was also reflected in the scale of the blocks: towers ten to fourteen storeys high accounted for only 0.7 per cent of all building in 1955, but this was to rise to 8.4 per cent by 1963. London was at the heart of the construction boom, accounting for sixty-seven per cent of all high-rise building in 1971. In 1965 the LCC was transformed into the Greater London Council and within ten years had built 384 tower blocks of ten storeys or higher, offering a total of 68,500 new flats.

30. Living at Keeling House, a young girl in the 1950s. Social engineering without any grass to play on (*RIBA*)

Building on such an industrial scale also had an impact on the design and fabric of the tower blocks, for the worse. Construction companies such as G. Wimpey, J. Laing, Taylor Woodrow and Wates, rather than architects, began to dominate the process, often utilising standardised designs as well as industrially produced materials, pre-cast panels, which needed the lowest possible labour costs to fit. In 1965 the subsidy was taken away and replaced by 'housing cost yardsticks' that sent quality of fabric to an all-time low.

By this time, opposition to the wholesale demolition of the old neighbourhoods for new estates was growing. Despite the fact that, in 1965, the Milner Holland Report announced that 200,000 Londoners were still without adequate housing, another survey two years later estimated that sixty-seven per cent of the old housing stock being destroyed was structurally sound and could be renovated. This was repeated in the comments of those who had been forced from their former terraced dwellings into the supposedly improved blocks.

In 1993 the Fabian researcher Paul Thompson visited Keeling House and reported that, while a hundred per cent of the tenants had enough privacy, only twenty-six per cent felt the building encouraged neighbourhood relations, while another forty-seven per cent feared that the design restricted interaction. He went on to conclude:

> It is difficult for a visitor, seeing the communal drying spaces perched high in the wind with slatted wooden sides and masses of exposed piping, or standing in the well of the entrance, the coarse base concrete pencilled with obscenities, looking up at the criss-cross pattern of galleries above ... not to feel the architect's real intention (and achievement) was to combine in one building the aesthetic effects of an East End backyard or a Neopolitan tenement.

However, in the end, the results were to be found lacking: 'it was a sculptural triumph but a social failure'.[47]

The same story was heard across the city and was made all the more vocal in 1968 when part of the Ronan Point Tower, a newly built block completed only two months earlier by Taylor Woodrow Anglian, collapsed. On the morning of 16 May a fifty-six-year-old cake decorator,

Ivy Hodge, went to the kitchen in her eighteenth-floor home; lighting her gas stove, an explosion occurred which blew out one of the wall panels that held the weight of four of the flats above. Like a set of lethal dominoes, the floor slabs began to crumble until the whole south-west corner of the building had folded. Four people were killed instantly and seventeen injured, including a woman who was stuck on a thin ledge as her front room fell away before her. For many, the explosion only confirmed the case against tower blocks, and local councils began to wind up their plans for high-rise estates.

Yet this still left thousands of Londoners living their lives far above the ground, in blocks that were quickly displaying the results of cheap construction. In the East End the decline of London was shown in stark extremes. 'The London factor' was repeatedly used by manufacturers who wanted to move their factories outside the city; it was impossible to grow, as modern technology demanded single-storey buildings spread out over a large area, when land was so expensive. Between 1966 and 1974 about 390,000 jobs were lost due to closures or government restrictions on development. In addition, the docks, which had for so long been the centre of the community and the workplace for generations of labourers, were coming to the end of their near-2,000-year existence. The increased usage of containers to carry cargo around the world meant that the port needed an extensive road and rail service to transport goods away; the densely populated neighbourhoods that had huddled near the wharves and warehouses for centuries made any improvements impossible. In the mid-1960s Tilbury Dock in Essex, east of the city along the Thames estuary, was converted to cope with the new traffic and could turn round an ocean-going ship in thirty-six hours. Despite protests, by 1973 the number of registered dockers had been reduced from 23,000 to 12,000.

Immigration continued to rise in the East End, despite the shortage of jobs and new housing. Following in the footsteps of the Huguenots in the seventeenth century, the refugee Russian Jews and the Irish fleeing the famine in the nineteenth century, from the 1970s a Bangladeshi community came to Spitalfields and Bethnal Green to escape poverty and persecution at home. Just as in the 1680s, reaction to the arrivals was extreme and violent, as young white men saw the new community as a dangerous threat to the scant resources of the area. Many of the most recent arrivals were housed in the unpopular council houses and tower blocks, further isolating them from the rest of the city.

The demand for new housing continues to define London politics. In February 2010 the Mayor, Boris Johnson, delivered the 'London Housing Strategy' with the promise to build 50,000 affordable homes by 2012 and end rough sleeping in London, as well as to halve severe overcrowding by 2016. In the face of the global recession, which had its origins in the housing market, this is no small ambition. Estimates predict that over the next twenty years the metropolis will grow to 8.9 million, driven by increased life expectancy of residents rather than a rise in immigration. Household numbers will drop in response to smaller family sizes, later marriages and divorce, and therefore 750,000 of the 850,000 new homes to be built by 2031 will need to be single-person occupancies.

As house prices rise throughout the 2000s the demand for affordable housing has become ever more urgent; the cost of an average house within the city is now far beyond the income of most key public-sector workers. Johnson promises to build 13,200 affordable houses every year (reduced from the previous Labour Mayor's promise of fifty per cent of all housing) and to integrate them within other building schemes, creating mixed communities. According to the Mayor, 'accessibility, adaptability and flexibility ... [to] meet the needs of London's diverse population, [and] address the challenges of climate change'[48] are the key to happy neighbourhoods. For existing houses, reinvestment rather than demolition is essential to reduce carbon emissions; green spaces should be planted 'in which residents can escape from the stresses and strains of high density urban living',[49] and those estates that have become inaccessible and dangerous sinks must be reconnected.

Yet, in the attempt to balance the nation's books in the aftermath of the recession, social housing will suffer the same cuts as all other sectors and the aspirations for preparing the future homes of London for the twenty-first century will be open to the market place and private speculation as never before. In October 2010, following the spending review, the *Independent* reported that the actual number of social houses being built had been reduced to one a week. At the same time, the government planned to reduce housing benefits, provoking local councils to block-book bed and breakfast rooms outside the capital. On BBC Radio Mayor Johnson expressed his determination to ensure that these cuts would not effect a 'Kosovo'-style exodus by the poor from London.

CHAPTER 12

30 ST MARY AXE

Planning the Future City

London is the whole world in one city.

Ken Livingstone, July 2006

We cannot avoid being part of London's history. My family and I moved into our new flat when the property boom was at its height. The house sits a short walk away from Watkin's Metropolitan Railway line, built in the 1870s to open up the north-west suburbs of the city towards Wembley and beyond. Over the next decades, the pastureland to the north of the station was filled in with standardised terraces, a mixture of housing for office clerks to bank managers, jammed in between the workers' neighbourhood of Cricklewood and the larger mansions of Hampstead and Frognal. Our street had long been a small settlement of village houses around the country estate of West End House, which was owned by a number of merchants from the seventeenth century onwards and in the 1790s was in the hands of Maria Beckford, a relation of the more scandalous William.

Building on the street was slow. In the 1860s the land was sold by the Beckfords for development, but only a few houses were built alongside the Field Lane Industrial School for Boys, now replaced by a police station. By the first decades of the twentieth century the development of the suburbs from the south engulfed the hamlet, turning an old orchard into two parallel rows of large houses, built by various building companies; some of the ancient apple and pear trees remain randomly planted in the back gardens of the houses on the northern end, the last remnant of its rural past. The big house was demolished and replaced by a mansion block ranged on four sides around an enclosed garden. The neighbourhood suffered some bomb damage during the Second World War, and on various streets the modern replacements stand out starkly from the uniform frontages.

Yet even the house itself tells a story of how London has changed in the last decades of the twentieth century, connecting the domestic scene with the larger changes within the metropolis. It was built in the 1860s by the Land Company of London, just as Bazalgette was working on the embankment which enabled the subterranean railway to deliver the first home owner from West Hampstead Station to the city, with a change at Baker Street Station. Solid, practical and unassuming, the house would not look out of place in most parts of London. From the street a gate leads into a front garden, a stone path running straight to three steps and the front door. The large window of the front room barrels outwards; there are minimal decorations on the facade, the red London brick is unadorned.

At some point, our four-storey house, built by speculators with a large family and at least one servant in mind, was divided up into flats; the rising price of property, changing attitudes to housing density, the reduction in the size of families all combined to convince the former freeholder that profit could be made in subdividing the space. In certain rooms, this process can be seen where the mouldings on the ceilings have been cut by partition walls; the floor paving in the main hall, a mosaic of mass-produced Puginism, ends abruptly before the front room. In many houses on the street, the wall between the ground-floor front room and the back parlour has been opened up to create a large living space, reflecting the increased informalisation of modern life. Many people have added new, large kitchens onto the back of the building so that one can eat and cook in the same area, another current fashion. While the fronts of the houses are uniform, the back ends are a myriad of catalogue conservatories and side returns.

These innovations seem to suggest that we want to create a Modernist space – Lasdun's vision of a bright, open, clean space – inside a historic skin; the Victorian exterior hides a twentieth-century idea of home. These features of modern living are as reflective of our own times and tastes as the Countess of Home's devices at Home House were to hers. This is the place we call home and it has a deep impact on how we feel about the city beyond.

At its beginning, the DNA of London could be defined by five foundation stones: the bridge that brought the people together at a crossing place, the walls that defined citizenship, the forum that regulated the relationship between trade and law, the temple that sanctified the civic space and the London Stone that transformed mythology – the stories we tell of ourselves – into the reality of the city. These genetic origins can still be found today throughout the metropolis in numerous forms, despite London's evolution from a scattering of barns and workshops to the modern-day megalopolis.

The idea of the city itself has also evolved. Where once the medieval capital was two cities, fixed between the Manichean dualities of the spiritual domain and the mundane, the struggle between the Crown and the people, Westminster versus the City, it then became an integrated whole – the human body. This body took on a life of its own and in the seventeenth century was reconfigured as a circulatory system, concerned with the flow of things, just as the New Philosophers like Robert Hooke and Sir Christopher Wren explored the wonders of the passage of blood through the veins of the body. In the age of Bazalgette this metaphor no longer worked; the body had become sick and the veins had collapsed. Instead London became an engineer's city, a difference engine of interconnected cogs and wheels, driven by technology. Today, the city is something new: a computer.

Technology has always dictated the way we interact with the city, and the contemporary capital is intelligent, a mainframe computer hardwired with stone but liberated by information. Once, money and goods travelled through the streets, now they move through electronic pulses along a network of wires. Our bodies have also become packets of information as we move around – our whereabouts collected from the 10,000 CCTV cameras, our every transaction offering data, GPRS on Smartphones identifying our position by satellite. We leave traces of ourselves wherever we go. While this raises questions of liberty, the same technology has the potential to set us free.

Now, with SatNav, one can no longer get lost within the metropolis's streets. Mobile computing allows us to mobilise flashmobs such as the chaotic mass pillow fight in front of St Paul's Cathedral on 3 April 2010; euphoric mass dancing events, such as the one organised to promote mobile phone networks at Liverpool Street Station; or protests such as the G20 marches in 2009. The Grindr app can tell us where our next intimate liaison could be. Facebook Places allows us to see where our friends are and share our own location with others. We can now be alone but part of a virtual crowd, radically changing our definition of what a community or citizenship can be.

The recent innovation of augmented reality software, such as Layar, changes our relationship with the city: we can now find information on all manner of local knowledge, from the best pizza, the nearest tube station, to average house prices; and this is just the beginning. Social networking sites are starting to use locators so we navigate the streets in new ways. This technology is also beginning to change our perceptions of the history of the city: in May 2010, the Museum of London launched Streetmuseum app, which allows us to point the phone at a particular historical site and see a photograph from the museum collection layered on top of the contemporary view.

In time, technology will break down the walls between the library, archive or depository and the city, so that one can read it, hear it and map it in new ways. One day, to lose oneself inside London, one of its great pleasures, will become an act of defiance; citizenship soon may not be defined by birthplace or heritage but by access to bandwidth.

Yet this new technology creates a divide between the solid form of the metropolis – the stones, streets and spaces in between – and an invisible city of information. Information wants to be beyond geography, while the capital is restricted by its physical nature. In the November 2009 UK edition of *Wired*, a section was dedicated to 'Unlocking the Digital City', which explored the potential for new technology to transform the future. Real-time information networks can help to drive an efficient traffic infrastructure – so that the Underground railway or the street lights control system can respond to traffic flow. In Incheon, South Korea, Cisco are already working with local planners to develop a 'high-tech, globally competitive and environmentally sustainable smart connected city';[1] this will soon arrive in London. Technology personalises the city, making it infinitely adaptable and flexible for individual needs or desires.

This future urban reality has to be built and planned out of the present city, genetically engineered from the foundation stones, to address the pressing issue of the relationship between the past and the future, as well as provide the hardware for the software of the future. It must be a bridge to connect communities, not alienate them; it should redefine citizenship; regulate and promote trade and good relations within itself and beyond; it should add meaning to general well-being – adding 'spirit', to use Thomas Carlyle's word; finally, it must integrate with the past not destroy it, so that the story of London continues. Technology will be used to store our memories, and access them in different ways than before. The preservation of the past is as much an act of forgetting as it is a process of renewal. What should remain goes hand in hand with a decision on what should be lost; once a building has been demolished it can never be rebuilt.

This intelligent city is already being planned and built and can be told through the story of one of London's most recent icons, 30 St Mary, Axe, better known as the Gherkin, designed by Foster + Partners in the first years of the new century. Norman Foster has a greater claim than most of the current world architects to be the Christopher Wren or Denys Lasdun of the contemporary city, with work across the capital including domestic houses, museums, bridges, government buildings, office blocks and, just outside the perimeter, the super-national descendant of the first London Bridge, airports.

The story of 30 St Mary Axe begins in ruins and violence, the IRA terrorist bombing of Bishopsgate in April 1992 and the debate about how to revive the damaged building. At the same time, this story entwines with the narrative of the transformation of the area – the Big Bang of the financial markets and London's ascent to the world's banking capital. Foster's unique designs, his concentration on the most modern methods and materials, make the Gherkin a symbol of the future world city, as much as Wren's St Paul's Cathedral was in its day.

But what is a world city? In the first years of the new century, terrorism made us question its purpose and future. Following the attacks on New York in September 2001, there were already some who questioned its function: now that technology allowed us to communicate in new ways which no longer demanded proximity, business no longer needed to be transacted in the traditional market places. In July 2005, terror re-emerged in London with the suicide bombing on the London Underground and a bus in Tavistock Square, killing fifty-two people and injuring another 700. Beyond the human cost, the event had a deep impact on London: the public transport system ground to a halt and people were forced to walk, inspiring *The New Yorker*'s Adam Gopnik to marvel at the city's resilience:

> ... hundreds of thousands of people went trudging in the bright sun-light – across Westminster Bridge and in front of Westminster Abbey and down Birdcage Walk ... No one ran, or cried, or even talked much about what had happened. Businessmen walked side by side from the City to the South Bank, still doing business, jiggling their cell phones impatiently in a futile attempt to make them work.[2]

There was even relative calm in the City. The pound fell 0.89 cent against the American dollar, and the FTSE 100 juddered downwards forcing the Stock Exchange to issue special measures against panic selling. This sent ripples through international markets, with losses registered in France, Germany, the Netherlands and Spain, while the US showed a small rise.

In the aftermath of the bombing the Mayor, Ken Livingstone, addressed the terrorists: 'In the days that follow look at our airports, look at our sea ports, and look at our railway stations, and even after your cowardly attack, you will see that people from the rest of Britain, people from around the world, will arrive in London to become Londoners and to fulfil their dreams and achieve their potential.'[3] In numerous articles and speeches, Londoners were reminded that they were united and that, as Livingstone later wrote in *Time Out*: 'London is the whole world in one city.'[4]

This diversity was confirmed in the 2001 national census; at the beginning of the new century London was now over 7 million strong, a five per cent rise in the last decade. In terms of ethnicity, 72.9 per cent had been born in the UK, 5.3 per cent within the European Union and 21.8 per cent outside the EU. Twenty years beforehand, in the 1981 census, the percentages were eighty per cent born in Britain, three per cent in the EEC and only nine per cent from the rest of the world. This put into bare statistics what was already the living experience of many over the previous decades; London had long been established as a port, a haven and home to the world. The government policy of multi-culturalism had emphasised the need for tolerance of difference rather than integration, giving the city a global sense of place, breaking down traditional definitions of citizenship. Now, on the high street there was a plethora of hyphenate citizens.

In reflection, London is now also a city of many different centres, a spatial as well as social diversification. As seen in the redevelopment of Wembley Central, offering a new cultural/entertainment focus along-side modern housing, London is no longer a series of concentric rings around a single centre point. Instead the metropolis has transformed into a cluster of mini-cities. Some of this has become essential because of the changing nature of work or retail – the rise of Canary Wharf succeeded because of the technological needs for banking and trading. In the same way, the vast Westfield Shopping Centre in Shepherd's Bush which opened in October 2008 has transformed its neighbourhood, creating a novel destination with new train stations and car parking for 4,500 vehicles. Initial reports suggest that suburban shopping centres defied the recession and had a deep impact on other shopping areas such as Oxford Street and High Street Kensington; nonetheless the new mall also showed a rapid spike in local crime rates. The Millennium Dome, built by Richard Rogers for the year 2000, was initially a disaster of hubristic proportion, but within a decade has become Europe's largest live music venue, the O2 centre.

Most significant of all is the development of the city towards the east, altering the patterns of growth westwards traditional since the seventeenth century. The day before the 7/7 bomb, the Olympic Committee in Singapore announced that London was to be the home of the 2012 Games, and work started immediately on building a new quarter for the city. The project has attracted some of the major names in world architecture as well as led to a concerted effort to improve transportation and services to the Stratford site in the East End. Much of the discussion concerning the dream of the 2012 Olympic Village is about legacy – what remains after the three weeks of the Games. The site has therefore been integrated into a longer-term project, the Thames Gateway, which aims to provide for the continuing demand for living space. The plans are huge in scope and ambition, bursting beyond the current boundaries, stretching the metropolis forty miles along both sides of the Thames all the way to the Channel, engulfing the seaside towns of Southend in Essex and Sheerness in Kent. In the next twenty years, half of all new homes built will be in these eastern boroughs, which in turn are being promoted as new enterprise zones.

With such radical changes to its dimensions – a metropolis without walls, a capital without its centre point – can London remain as a single narrative? Do we need to find new foundation stones – the bridge, the temple, the forum, the walls, the stone – to refresh our story, now that the old definitions of a city are being challenged? London is no longer defined by geography, a shared space, a moment of arrival. Undoubtedly, it must continue to grow if it is not to die, however traumatic this might be. Yet the bridge can now be found outside, at Heathrow, Gatwick, Luton, Stansted and City airports, making London a crossing place to the rest of the world; the physical walls may have been replaced but the question of what defines citizenship is even more important now; the temple is not just a place of religion but a place that symbolises the organising principles of the community; the London Stone still stands on Cannon Street and will not be removed.

However, it is London's role as a forum – a place of trade and law – that is central to its identity as a world city. By 2008, London was the largest banking capital in the world, outstripping Wall Street and fending off the threat of the growing strength of the Pacific Rim. Its return to pre-eminence was by no means predictable, and connects London's story with the rises and falls of the global market. Few would have held out much hope for the City, which had become run-down and insular. By the beginning of the 1980s it was clear that the global financial arrangement set up in the aftermath of the Second World War, the Bretton Woods Agreement, no longer worked. The system organised how nations traded with each other, but also had a powerful impact on economic possibilities within the states themselves. As the world was attempting to get back to work after six years of conflict, it was thought that the flexible exchange rates of the inter-war years were partly to blame for the era of anxiety, and so a fixed rate of exchange was negotiated, based around the power of the American dollar. It meant that, alongside a commitment to full employment – encouraged by William Beveridge's 1942 report – Britain's main economic focus was on balancing the trade deficit, ensuring that not too much currency left the country in exchange for foreign goods. This was kept in check by the government's manipulation of the interest rates that controlled the rates of borrowing.

By the mid-seventies, this policy started to look shaky: governments around the world kept interest rates low, but this in turn led to high inflation – imports began to get more expensive as more money began to chase too few goods. In addition, America's involvement in the Vietnam War made the dollar weak. At home, in an attempt to support full employment, the government over-invested in dying heavy industries to the detriment of supporting the new. The Bretton Woods Agreement eventually fell apart in 1979.

In the Square Mile of London, this revolution tolled the death of what author Philip Augar called 'gentlemanly capitalism'. Under the old system, London banking had been a very clubbable affair, a protected business dominated by long-established small firms. The traders of that era would have recognised the world of Walter Bagehot, who wrote in his classic portrait of high-Victorian finance, *Lombard Street* (1873): 'Lombard Street is thus a perpetual agent between the two great divisions of England – between the rapidly-growing districts, where almost any money can be well and easily employed, and the stationary and declining districts, where there is more money than can be used.'[5]

Suddenly, however, the London market was opened up to the rest of the world. This was further encouraged by the prevailing economic policies in Britain and the US, influenced by the Chicago economist Milton Friedman, who campaigned against state control and intervention of any stripe: the market, not the bureaucrat, knew best. The stalwart English banker was therefore no longer restricted to investing in home-grown companies but could trade in any company around the world; and foreign companies could start to trade in new ways in London as well. The first sign was seen in the launch of LIFFE, set up close to the Royal Exchange in 1982; of the first 373 seats allocated, nearly 100 came from overseas funds. As Michael Lewis wryly noted in his classic account of banking life in the 1980s, *Liar's Poker*, London was very attractive: 'London became the key link in this drive for world domination. Its time zone, its history, its language, its relative political stability, its large pool of dollar-hungry capital and Harrods (don't underestimate the importance of shopping opportunities in all this) made London central to the plans of all American investment bankers'.[6]

The liberalisation of the markets demanded a systematic dismantling of the old laws and traditions – and it was decided that it would occur on one day, 27 October 1986, named the Big Bang, an allusion to the recent theory of the instantaneous creation of the universe. Formerly, there had been a division between jobbers, who traded shares on the Stock Exchange on behalf of clients, and brokers, who managed the clients and advised investors. Under the new rules, brokers could trade for themselves. Secondly, it was decided that brokers working for a bank or fund could invest their own assets as well as those of their clients, putting their money where their mouths were. It also broke the old cartel of fixed commission rates, so each investment firm could compete on what they charged to clients.

Finally, it heralded the end of 'open outcry' trading, where jobbers stood in a pit or on the trading floor and did their deals in person; when the market had just become globalised, there was no point in face-to-face trading, and the business of business was translated to large trading floors, telephone trading and flashing computer screens blinking prices from around the world. This saw the end of the Royal Exchange in 1991, which was swiftly converted into a European-style café/bistro rather than being the centre of the financial world.

The Big Bang blew the cobwebs out of the City, as well as the old boys' network that had maintained it as a private club for decades. The opening-up of the globalised market meant that a company needed deep pockets to invest and profit, or lose their clients. Clients themselves were no longer judged by loyalty or the long-term relationship – which soon lasted only as long as the deal – but on the 'size of wallet'. Almost all the big banks, who once were involved solely in the management of savings, converted into investment banks; while many of the small firms refused to put up a fight. The arrival of large American banks with limitless funds demanded the consolidation, merger and winding-up of their parochial rivals. By 2006, there were 251 foreign banks in London and over 550 foreign companies listed on the Stock Exchange. In 2008, it was estimated that at least ten to fifteen per cent of the City workforce were non-domiciled, foreign workers; over a third of all employees of the major investment banks were non-British nationals.

Michael Lewis started work on the bond desk at Salomon Brothers, the most successful and aggressive investment bank in London. His starting salary was $48,000 with a bonus of $6,000 after the first six months, twice as much as his professor at the LSE, where he had previously been studying for a Master's. He found a world split between the old ways and the new; the American arrivals were 'off the social scale, beneath the social scale, and frankly pretty much untouchable',[7] but their ruthless quest for profit soon became the norm; 'you want loyalty, hire a cocker spaniel'[8] boasted one gilt trader. Yet not even the masters of the universe at Salomons were safe; in the pursuit of security and market position, by 1981 Salomons was already part of the Phibro Corporation, but was then bought up by Travelers Group in 1998, only to be merged with Citigroup later that year.

The Big Bang injected perpetual volatility into the global market and, as a result, the City was to be exposed to both highs and lows. There was a crash in 1987, almost immediately after the blood-rush of deregulation. In September 1992, on a day known as Black Wednesday, the

Conservative government was forced to withdraw British sterling from the ERM, the European Exchange Rate Mechanism, following a sustained attack upon it by currency market investors who saw profit in deflating the value of the pound, despite the Chancellor, Norman Lamont, pumping in £27 billion to prop it up. Yet in 2006, on the twentieth anniversary of the deregulation laws, the *Financial Times*, in a special report on the new City, commented: 'the self-congratulation has been epic. In newspaper articles, in lectures and in private meetings with Cabinet ministers, extremely rich men have reminded us how the Big Bang ushered in 20 glorious years of success.'[9] It was this very volatility – the assumption that the complex market would somehow balance itself – that drove the irrational exuberance to the edge in 2008.

This boom time in the Square Mile had a huge impact on the stones of London. This new-found power demanded a new architecture. Firstly, ways of working changed with the rise of vast trading floors. Within the cramped confines of the City, with its vast rents, it was difficult to find the right kind of building. In 1985 the estate agent Savills surveyed 251 City firms and found that two-thirds were currently looking for large, open-plan offices of at least 10,000 square feet. Citicorp were the first to jump out of the Square Mile, firstly commissioning Richard Rogers to convert the old fish market, Billingsgate, and eventually deciding to build a new tower from scratch at Canary Wharf. Salomons were soon to follow with new offices above Victoria Station.

There was also a temptation to built prestige skyscrapers. Developers saw the advantages of thrusting new towers into the sky as the demand for office space became insatiable. In particular, Canary Wharf revived the dilapidated dockland region of the city that had died in the 1970s into a new kind of port: where once shipping from around the world unloaded its cargoes upon the miles of quays and warehouses, now the new, gleaming office towers traded currency and bonds, connected to the global financial markets through phone wires and trading screens, creating a banking centre that challenged the Square Mile.

The idea began in 1979 when Michael Heseltine, Secretary of State for the Environment in Margaret Thatcher's Conservative government, flew over the East End in a small plane and was shocked by 'the immense tracts of dereliction ... rotting docks ... crumbling infrastructure ... vast expanses of polluted land left behind by modern technology'.[10] In 1981 he formed the London Docklands Development Corporation with the mandate to override local planning controls and offer tax breaks to any developer who wished to build on the wasteland. In the following year three American banks expressed interest in moving their operation out of the Square Mile.

How was the old City to compete against these new enterprise zones? Would the Square Mile, the centre of trade for the last 1,700 years, be allowed to wither? Would it, like Paris, be held back by history and slowly become a museum while Canary Wharf and La Défense became the new business hubs? London needed to find a way to build the future from the foundation stones of the past.

One of the first things that Ken Livingstone did when he took office as Mayor of London in 2000 was to develop a set of planning rules that defined the city not by its buildings but by its vistas. Rather than draw up a register of sites that had to be preserved, he created a series of sightlines that were to be protected. This was further developed in May 2009 with Mayor Boris Johnson's 'London View Management Framework', which identified the panoramas, linear views, river prospects and townscape views, with an added appendix on the earth's curvature and the refraction of light in case any developer used this as an excuse to build too high. This 'visual management' of the capital was an attempt to combat the rise of random skyscrapers and protect the historic skyline. But it is the sheer verticality of the modern megalopolis that gives it its visual power; unlike the social housing tower block of the sixties and seventies which grew out of thrift, the skyscraper announced its prominence and power through its engineering and size. In magnificence and architectural potency, the skyscraper is the cathedral of the modern era.

In the 2009 document there was a sense of conflict between the old and the new – not because of the fear of demolition but that the city's past could be blocked out or overshadowed by the future. St Paul's Cathedral, the Hospital at Greenwich, the Tower of London and Barry's Palace of Westminster were designated London's most important buildings, 'protected silhouettes'. These were to be shielded from 'poor or unresolved town scapes' or 'unsightly and overly prominent elements ... such as intrusive block sizes, building heights, roof design, material and colour as they could disrupt the viewing experience'.[11] The largest group of protected views were those along the riverside from every bridge, from Tower Bridge in the east to Bazalgette's Albert Embankment opposite the Houses of Parliament.

Yet the Mayor was keen to state that he was not against tall buildings, insisting that there needed to be a balance between the thrusting new and the smaller-scale past. The 2009 London Plan pointed out that: 'Well-designed tall buildings can also be landmarks and can contribute to regeneration and improve London's skyline';[12] but they 'need to be flexible and adaptable, and of exemplary design'.[13] Nonetheless, almost on the same page of the report, the concern that ravenous modernity might crush the city of the past is clear to see:

> Two thousand years of building have left layers of history, illuminating London's social, political and economic heritage. Today London has a great wealth of fine historic buildings, spaces and archaeology ... The Mayor wishes to see the sensitive management of London's extraordinary historic assets planned in tandem with the promotion of the very best modern architecture and urban design.[14]

How do we find this delicate balance between the past and the future?

The Victorian city began with dreams of crystal palaces and ended in underground passages; in contrast, that of the twenty-first century starts beneath the surface and reveals itself in steel and glass towers. Both reflect the changing shape of the city – the infrastructure allows for communities to emerge, linking them with the old centre, while mega-buildings are built to fit new ways of working and living with bold architecture that defines the sites of power.

In 1990, the Jubilee line extension was authorised to link the centre of the city with the new development at Canary Wharf to the east. Originally, the line was built as a continuation of Watkin's original Metropolitan line into the West End ending at Charing Cross, and was named after the Queen's Silver Jubilee year of 1977. There had been a number of plans to extend it during the 1980s, linking the West End with the City and then eastwards across the Thames to Lewisham and the new development of Thamesmead to the south-east. It was not until the redevelopment of Canary Wharf on the Isle of Dogs, built out of the ruins of the old docks and transformed into a modern business centre, that hopes for the extension of the rail link were revived. It was decided that the new line should cross the Thames at Westminster and travel along its southern side, reviving the neighbourhoods of Southwark, Bermondsey, Rotherhithe and Deptford towards Greenwich and then crossing over once more and ending at Stratford. Work started in 1993 and was expected to take fifty-three months, but continued until 22 December 1999.

Canary Wharf was already being called a 'Wall Street on Water', centred around César Pelli's monolithic glass tower, 1 Canada Square. Nearby City Airport was developed in 1987 to link the new 'enterprise zone' with the rest of the world and the Docklands Light Railway, a futuristic monorail system, was also completed in 1987 to carry workers from Tower Bridge. Yet, as Canary Wharf became increasingly popular as a business district, the infrastructure looked decidedly thin, especially in terms of getting people from the centre of London; the Jubilee line, therefore, was planned to carry passengers on thirty-six trains per hour from the heart of the capital to their desks in twenty minutes. Yet this aspiration of the hyper-modern city could not fail to unearth the many layers of the past, and as the new line was dug – providing new ticket halls, escalators, ventilation and escape shafts and buildings – the archaeologists from the Museum of London were never far behind.

Like Professor William Grimes, who found the Temple of Mithras in the ruins of Bucklersbury House in 1954, the extension line revealed unexpected treasures. At Westminster, beside Barry's Houses of Parliament, they found two thirteenth-century water gates and a series of medieval houses. At London Bridge, fragments of Neolithic pottery from 4500 BC were uncovered, as well as enough evidence for historians to rethink their assumptions on the shape of Roman London, discovering a large community at the southern end of the bridge as well as a layer of ashes dated to 60–70 AD, further proof of Boudicca's violent destruction of the protean city. Nearby there was more ghoulish quarry: a mass of bones in unholy ground, which indicated a burial site for prostitutes from the local 'stews' or brothels, confirmed in the *Annals of St Mary Overy*: 'the women inhabiting these houses are said not to be allowed Christian burial ... there is an unconsecrated burial ground known as the Cross Bones at the corner of Redcross Street'.[15] At Stratford, the new station was planned on top of the ruins of a vast medieval Benedictine monastery.

Preserving the past slowed the development of the extension line by months; it was opened only just in time to deliver crowds to the Millennium Dome by North Greenwich Station. On that night the royal family, leaders of the New Labour government and ordinary Londoners gathered to watched the dawn of the new century. Nearby Greenwich itself, as embodied in the structure of Christopher Wren and Robert Hooke's Royal Observatory that still stands above the Queen's House and Hospital, marked the line of 0° latitude.

The Jubilee line extension itself was a herald of the new century, as well as an acknowledgement of the way in which the city had already transformed, especially the expansion towards the new business zones to the east. It highlighted the fact that the geography of the metropolis was moving once more and that the infrastructure had to adapt to provide for the latest communities. The development of the rail link was an indication of this new direction and was reflected in the plans of Canary Wharf Station itself, placed in the hands of Norman Foster. It was designed with its function in mind, utilising the latest hard-wearing materials to cope with an estimated 40 million users a year. For some the new stations along the Jubilee line were as graceful and elegant as St Paul's Cathedral, and perhaps as important as civic symbols. London no longer proclaimed itself as a spiritual capital but was the world's altar to Mammon.

Foster + Partners were also the architects of the HSBC Tower that rose above the curved glass canopy of the tube station, started in 1999, the year that the Jubilee line was opened, and completed in 2001. The seventy-metre tower is the joint second largest skyscraper in London, and the sister to Foster's HSBC Tower in Hong Kong, connecting London to the rising financial cities of the East. Next door he was close to completing the Citicorp building, with two 3,000-square-metre trading floors to accommodate the new demands of modern banking. Both these buildings were projected to impose on the London skyline; it was also intended that their long shadows be felt across the world.

At the turn of the century, Foster + Partners were working throughout the city, effecting what the architectural critic Jonathan Glancey called 'the Fosterisation of London'.[16] The projects took a number of different manifestations: individual buildings – banks, offices, government departments, museums, university libraries, bridges – as well as reconfigurations of the public spaces of the city. At the British Museum Foster reimagined the Great Hall with an impressive glass canopy that covered a garden surrounding the cylindrical Reading Room, creating Europe's largest enclosed public space from a former dumping ground with a minimum of intervention. The Millennium Bridge, which spanned the river in front of St Paul's Cathedral, used the latest technology and innovative design to link the two sides of the city.

Work had also started on the new Wembley Stadium, which was planned to be ready for the new century. Foster transformed the reinforced concrete hulk that had been created in under 300 days for the 1923 Empire Exhibition to make it the home of football, preserving the two Mughal domes to reign above a new vision of steel and glass.

There were new office blocks in Holborn, as well as the redevelopment of Her Majesty's Treasury Building in Westminster, completed in 2002; the Sir Alexander Fleming Building at Imperial College in South Kensington; and the GLA building, the home for the Mayor of London on the southern bank of Tower Bridge, designed to reflect the new politics of the city: transparent and ecologically sustainable – a self-ventilating, virtually non-polluting building.

Through the projects scattered alongside the Thames, Foster was expressing his own urban philosophy – what the city of the future should look like, how the idea of community could be re-engineered for the twenty-first century. He promoted the use of the latest techniques that imagined buildings, which could never have been conceived of a decade earlier, a passion to explore the limits of new materials to aid sustainability and versatility, and a determination to create flexible buildings that could be adapted for the future. He was also looking at the question of public space within London – the spaces in between – and how these made up the fabric of the capital. In 1999, in his description of the 'World Squares for All' master plan that aimed to redevelop the West End from Trafalgar Square along Whitehall towards Parliament Square – donning the mantle not just of Christopher Wren but also John Nash – Foster set out his vision of London as a world city.

Foster planned to redefine the city away from the dominance of carbon-emitting cars, which had informed most planning decisions since the Second World War, and give it back to the pedestrian, making London a living city on a human scale. 'London', he wrote, 'is a compact and relatively well managed, humanistic city and the potential model for sustainability, particularly because of its high density ... the key is to focus on what makes a city sustainable.'[17] Access to public spaces, the potential for communal meeting points within the dense urban environment, was at the heart of his new metropolis, and London could lead the world:

> ... improving the urban fabric and achieving a better balance between people and traffic is one of the keys of the future ... where Londoners can enjoy their monuments and open spaces together with visitors from across the nation and abroad. A century ago, the Victorians transformed a city of slums, pollution and congestion into a model of civilized urban life ... we should be ready to take up that challenge.[18]

Norman Foster was not born in London. His story is that of many outsiders who arrive in the city to transform it. He was born in Stockport, Greater Manchester, and left school at sixteen despite showing talent in art and mathematics; he went to work at the Manchester Council treasury office. By this time he was already interested in architecture, having discovered Le Corbusier's *Vers une Architecture* in the local library. After National Service, he paid his own way through architecture school as he was not eligible for a government grant. Like many of his forebears, he completed his education with travel, but unlike the

Grand Tourists of previous generations he chose America rather than Europe and gained a scholarship to study for his Master's at Yale.

At New Haven he discovered the difference between American and European attitudes to architecture. He was one of a handful of British architects on the course, including Richard Rogers and the sisters Georgie and Wendy Cheesman. The head of the faculty was the American Paul Rudolph, who was a key influence in encouraging Foster to experiment, with a strong emphasis on the practice of design. The gulf between the two traditions is illustrated by a well-told tale that, at some point, the American faculty put a banner over the corner of the room where the English group did their work, saying, 'START DRAWING'. The English response was typical: they replaced the banner with one of their own, 'START THINKING'. Yet the English clique also had much to learn from their companions, and on one holiday they all bundled into a car together to tour the Midwest and study every design by Frank Lloyd Wright.

This balance between practice and theory would dominate Foster's career. He was a risk-taker and an explorer; his first wife, Wendy Cheesman, later described him as a juggler who would throw the ball higher than anyone else and catch it lower than was thought possible. Part of this fascination with pushing the limits of the possible could be found in the first designs of Team 4, the company Foster set up with Rogers, Wendy and Georgie Cheesman in London. All the commissions were on a small scale, most notably a glass boathouse for Rogers's in-laws in Cornwall, as well as a hi-tech warehouse for Reliance Controls Electronics in Swindon. Both designs were breathtakingly simple – the factory used prefabricated parts that could be easily replaced to create a single 3,200-square-metre space. This was a radical restructuring of the office, replacing the hierarchical divisions between departments, management and shop floor with an open plan that could (except for the fixed services) be reconfigured at any time.

Team 4 disbanded but Foster and his wife opened Foster Associates from their house in Hampstead. It was during this period that Foster became close to the American thinker and designer, Buckminster Fuller. 'Bucky' soon became one of the greatest influences on Foster, forcing him to think about the relationship between building, technology and the environment. To Fuller the legacy of Modernism – from Le Corbusier to Lasdun – was only skin-deep, and missed the point: 'they only looked at problems of modification of the surface of end products, which end products were inherently sub functions of a technically obsolete world'.[19] This was symbolised by Fuller's most famous invention, the geodesic dome, which attempted to create the largest possible space with the minimum of material. For Fuller, the architecture of the future had to engage with a world that was running out of resources, addressing the problems of ever-increasing population density within rapidly shrinking urban spaces by adopting the mantra 'doing more with less'.

Foster absorbed these ideas with relish, and also saw a way to explore his own fascination with the limits of technology in three buildings he constructed outside London. As he drew up designs for the Willis Faber & Dumas headquarters in Ipswich (1971–5) he set out to democratise the office space, with the aim of engendering a sense of community. In 1974 he started work on the Sainsbury Centre for Visual Arts to stand alongside Denys Lasdun's main campus of the University of East Anglia, Norwich. Where Lasdun's 1960s concrete buildings melted into the landscape, with a continual wall of interlinked structures including innovative ziggurats for student accommodation, Foster designed a metal and glass box only connected to the campus by a single walkway, seeming to hover above the landscape. Internally, he reconceived the traditional idea of a museum and university faculty as a series of discrete divisions by creating large open spaces, divided by glass walls and offices, so that the art collection, seminar rooms and administration areas appeared a single whole.

These many ideas came together with Foster's first commission to build a skyscraper, the HSBC Tower in Hong Kong. As an English architect he had no experience of building impressive urban towers, yet his designs reinvented the idea of a skyscraper that had previously been conceived as a steel frame set around a solid concrete core that held the services, lifts and stairs. Instead, he sought new ways of creating 93,000 square metres of office space within the dense city centre of Hong Kong. There were many issues at stake and Foster's ability to juggle was tested to its limits. The building was more than just a functional place of work: the client wished to project its power through architecture at a politically sensitive time. The bank itself was in the midst of radical transformation as it expanded into a worldwide operation. Foster also had to manage the different traditions between East and West, and had the building painstakingly configured in order to have 'good Feng Shui'.

In the new projections he did away with the standard skyscraper design, and tried to reconsider the purpose of the tower as a series of bridges layered on top of each other, shaped like a chevron, with the central core and lift shaft missing. Again, the office spaces were open-planned; this was made possible by the services being located on the outside of the building. Thus it expressed itself through its structure, the skeleton outside the skin of plate-glass windows. The technology that was used to build it followed the mantra that the architect should be 'sceptical of all architecture in which the very nature, the spirit of the building can be tidily isolated from its technology: how can a Gothic cathedral, a Classical Temple or a medieval manor house be perceived except by their spaces and the state of the art technology that made them possible?'[20]

After the HSBC bank was opened in 1986, Foster was fêted as a new pioneer; and despite remaining in London, he was in demand across the globe, developing into an architectural brand that added power to any job he turned his hand to, directing his vision for modern design beyond the traditional boundaries of geography or place. As a result his body of work projected a global urban philosophy promoting technology, new materials, sustainability. It is this radical approach to building that he brought to bear at the start of the new millennium when work began at 30 St Mary Axe, changing the identity of the historic Square Mile and offering a vision of the city of the future.

By 2000 there were changes inside the Square Mile as a result of the upheaval of the Big Bang, the rise of electronic trading floors and need for larger office spaces. In 1986, the new Lloyd's of London Building was opened behind Leadenhall Market. The insurance giant was designed by Norman Foster's old partner Richard Rogers, who would also become one of the world architects who defined the new London experience. After Team 4, Rogers had set up his own company and started on a number of striking domestic projects. It was not until 1971 when, alongside the Italian designer Renzo Piano, he won the competition to create the Pompidou Centre, Paris, that he formulated his 'design strategy' that would also be the guiding principle behind the Lloyd's Building. Rogers turned the idea of a museum inside out, putting all the services outside the main structure. Thus he was able to create a flexible open-plan space within, while also devising a system in which the services could be replaced and altered as the function and density of the building changed:

> The days of the fortress, and the glass box are over. Both are inflexible straitjackets for their users, suppressing self-expression and technologically indefensible for different reasons. We propose a free and open-ended framework where the ever-changing performance is a dynamic expression of the architecture of the building ... a place where ever-changing activities overlap in flexible well-serviced spaces.[21]

The Lloyd's Building was a clarion call for change within the Square Mile. Modernity, however, did not gain unanimous approval; as one underwriter noted, 'Poor old Lloyd's. After three hundred years ... we started off in a coffee house and finished up on a coffee percolator.'[22] Worse opprobrium was heaped upon the 1 Poultry building that was created to face the Royal Exchange, a marble Postmodern tanker designed by James Stirling who was teaching at Yale at the same time as Foster and Rogers. Postmodern architecture evolved as a reaction to the severe Modernism of the previous era and sought to restore a sense of community by raiding the historical dressing-up box, scattering ornamentation without order, replacing a solid philosophy of architecture with a recourse to 'wit' and fancy. Thankfully for the City, it was a very short-lived joke; instead, the key issue for the future of the Square Mile was the changing demands of the big banks to find space for their expanding electronic trading floors.

In February 1986, when Salomon Brothers moved westwards to Victoria Station, the Corporation of London delivered a plan to create an extra 185,000 square metres of offices with the hope of retaining business within the Square Mile. In particular, this saw development moving east: in 1986, work started at Broadgate, replacing the old Victorian train station with glass and steel, new offices for Warburg, Shearson Lehman/American Express, Security Pacific, Lloyds Merchant Bank and USB. Expansion continued at the turn of the century when Norman Foster designed new offices to wrap around the old Spitalfields Market, including space for the ill-fated ABN/AMRO bank, which was bought by the Royal Bank of Scotland in the wake of the 2008 recession. This was joined in 2010 by the Heron Tower at 110 Bishopsgate, the largest skyscraper in London. This new chapter, however, started in devastation: on 10 April 1992 an IRA bomb, 100 pounds of semtex wrapped in fertiliser, was detonated outside the Baltic Exchange on St Mary Axe, close to Leadenhall. Three people were killed, but business soon continued; within three days the Exchange was moved to Lloyd's and was trading in under a week.

Like Lloyd's, the Exchange was first founded in the eighteenth century in a coffee house, with a particular interest in maritime trade. It was housed in an elegant Edwardian building of red granite, coloured marble and Portland stone, that echoed the glories of the former age, created to promote the wealth and power of the empire, as seen in the finely decorated ceiling of the main trading hall that was used until the 1980s, detailed with mermaids and splashing dolphins. After the bomb, there were instant calls for the preservation of this most elegant institution.

There was another bomb in April the following year. On the 23rd, a truck filled with a ton of fertiliser and explosives was parked outside the HSBC building in Bishopsgate and was detonated before the police could evacuate the area. The ancient church of St Ethelburga was flattened, while the windows of the surrounding high-rise banks were shattered; £1 billion of damage was calculated. The restoration work that had started on the Baltic Exchange was halted.

There was a widespread outcry following the bombs. The first concern was for security and 'the ring of steel' was devised to monitor all transport going in and out of the Square Mile. There was also the issue of restoration, particularly of the Exchange. English Heritage were determined to preserve the building, or at least the classical facade that looked out onto St Mary Axe. In 1993, the head of the Exchange encouraged his partners to dig into their own pockets to pay for the preservation of the building, but two years later it was recognised that its only future was a new scheme that kept some of the details of the old within a new groundscraper. Soon it became clear that the plans were going nowhere; despite some innovative design, no one wanted this kind of office space and a buyer could not be found. The following year the owners of the site, Trafalgar House, were taken over by the international Kvaerner, and more ambitious ideas were required.

The arrival of Norman Foster's first set of designs for a Millennium Tower, a skyscraper that would dominate the London horizon, coincided with the New Labour government sweeping into power with a landslide in 1997. The new regime, for the first time, extended a hand to the financial capital, handing over regulation to the Bank of England and encouraging the light-touch controls of the newly formed Financial Services Authority, while Chancellor Gordon Brown vowed to end the cycle of boom-and-bust economics. The City, it seemed, knew best how to balance the books, and was left to its own devices.

The government was also in thrall to 'newness', in a reaction to what could have been perceived as the heritage culture of the previous Conservative regime. Foster's Millennium Tower was certainly new: it was a vertical city, 120 metres high with over 158,000 square metres of space to be divided into offices, retail, apartments, 'sky gardens', an innovative environmentally concerned ventilation system, as well as a public observation deck with unparalleled views over the city. The scale was impressive, dominating the nearby NatWest Tower, the highest building in the City, but was considered to be just too big.

Nonetheless the tower raised the issue of the balance between preserving the old and the advantages of developing something iconic and contemporary. By 1997 English Heritage, long seen as the enemy of change, unexpectedly announced 'it would be willing to consider, in principle, the loss of the remains of the Baltic Exchange in the context of a scheme which provided a new building of architectural quality'.[23]

The tower was not feasible, despite Foster's claims that it could have been built; but something else might be agreed upon, and Foster and his team returned to their office in Battersea to rethink the designs.

Such a vast project demanded a huge wealth of talent and the designs were handed to a team led by Robin Partington, who worked on sketches originated by both Norman Foster and his co-director, Ken Shuttleworth. Both men came up with reams of ideas. (Shuttleworth, it was later revealed, was central to the designs for many of Foster + Partners' most emblematic buildings on the London skyline, including City Hall, the GLA building, and the scheme beside the Tower of London.)

Initially they looked at ways of reducing the size of the Millennium Tower in response to the criticism that the skyscraper was too tall. When this new tower was passed over, they sought a number of smaller-scale ideas which soon gained nicknames such as the 'glorified beehive', 'the loaf of bread', the 'cosmic dome'. Yet by the end of 1997, there were still no final plans. At that time a new client, the reinsurance company Swiss Re, bought the Baltic Exchange site and added new energy to the project. Swiss Re were world leaders in their business and London was the centre of their life and health division; they were looking to set up their headquarters in the Square Mile and needed at least 37,000 square metres of office space. They bought the land with the understanding that planning permission would be forthcoming and were determined to see results, creating an internal team to work through the process of getting the building completed; they swiftly agreed to continue with Foster + Partners as architects.

Foster and Shuttleworth knew that they had to find a new design that was lower in height but offered more office space. From February 1998, they began work on an oval form rising from the ground, bulging out in the middle and then rising to a peak. Despite being a radical new form for a skyscraper, Robin Partington later admitted that the process was one of hard work rather than computer wizardry: 'the building was not, as many imagine, designed using computer programs. This was an analogue building, you could say. There was no "eureka" moment, no blinding flash of inspiration when the form of the building suddenly became fixed. It was more a matter of bloody hard work.'[24] Over the

31. A cross section of Foster's
    design for St Mary Axe
    (*RIBA*)

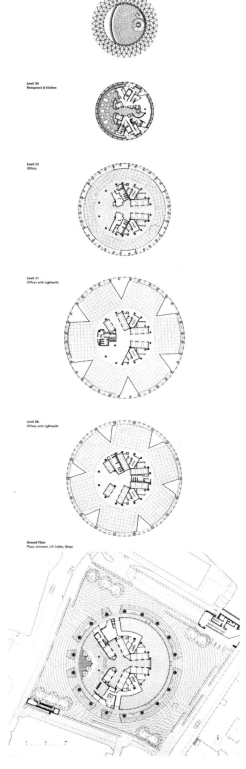

32. The ground floor showing the distinctive structure of 'the Gherkin'

next two years the team produced seven new ideas that worked around the concept of the oval, so that the 'beehive' was transformed into an 'erotic gherkin' as the oval became tapered, streamlined and taller, rising from 154 to 180 metres.

Meanwhile, the job of gaining support for the new plans was in hand; 'We did a lot of schmoozing,' admitted Swiss Re's Carla Picardi, as they hoped to gain permission to build.[25] The sale to Swiss Re was a wake-up call to many who thought that the old Exchange was saved and just waiting to be restored, and the reinsurers hired an army of publicists, consultants and lawyers to fight their cause. English Heritage had already decreed that they would contemplate a new building, but others were not so open-minded. The project also needed the approval of the City Corporation, and as the head officer, Peter Rees, revealed, he 'warmed to the Swiss Re scheme as it developed – the enthusiasm of Swiss Re was very impressive, and infectious'.[26] Elsewhere, the Exchange itself allied with a number of conservation organisations in defiance of any suggestion of replacing the existing building, even if dilapidated. However, it was the Deputy Prime Minister, John Prescott, who had the final say on whether the Grade II listing of the old Exchange could be lifted and demolition allowed.

By February 1999, the new designs had developed to create a revolutionary building, unlike any seen in London before. The penultimate plans were for a structure 166 metres tall, 54.4 metres at its widest point on the seventeenth floor, and 49 metres on the ground. The impact of the building began in the creation of a public plaza which was open to all the streets surrounding it. A detailed analysis of pedestrian traffic was commissioned to show that the new space could create a 'city within a city'; the ground floor would also offer cafés and shops to integrate the building with the living city. From the outside, one would also notice its unique external curved structure. Unlike most skyscrapers, which were created out of a solid service core and a facade of cladding that offered no structural significance, a network of 360 exterior diagrids, a series of A-frame steel rods, was developed by the engineering company Arup to hold up the whole edifice. This curved shape allowed for twenty-five per cent less external surface with no great loss of internal space.

Computer studies on fluid dynamics, more often used for the design of sports cars than architecture, modelled how this would have an impact on windflow around the building and found that it could be used in new ways for environmental purposes.

The building had a circular steel core containing lifts, washrooms and services from which, on each floor, six 'fingers of space' radiated out to the external skeleton. It was also decided to make these fingers spiral, so that each floor was rotated 5° from the one below. This left a spiralling gap between the fingers that curled alongside the inside and offered not just a dynamism to the interior but also a series of innovative functions. In case of fire, the spiral of atria allowed for the escape of smoke through windows that could open; there was also the environmental advantage of creating a low-energy ventilation system. Environmental considerations were applied to other parts of the building too. Rather than being in the apex of the tower, the heavy service plants like water tanks, chiller and electrical services were located in the basement. A new structure was designed on the plaza to house the necessary cooling towers, while each floor was planned with its own air conditioning plant. Thus the internal space remained flexible and adaptable for any future use.

When the designs were presented to the many interested parties in February 1999, it was decided by English Heritage that the tower was in fact too small, and that it should be extended from 166 to 180 metres. The final plans were submitted and accepted in July 2000 by the Secretary of State for the Environment, English Heritage, the City Corporation and the Royal Fine Art Commission. Just as work was starting there was a last-ditch legal challenge from SAVE, a conservation trust, to demand a public enquiry into the planning process and calls for a new environmental impact assessment study. In the end SAVE withdrew the complaint, despite widespread media support.

Before work could begin, however, the old Exchange had to be dismantled. English Heritage had originally campaigned that the Victorian stained-glass windows should be preserved and integrated into the new design, but this was soon put to one side and the glass was transported to the National Maritime Museum in Greenwich for safe-keeping. As it was demolished, each part of the building was photographed, delicately packed away into wooden crates, stored outside Canterbury and put up for sale. It was not until 2007 that two Estonian businessmen paid £800,000 and shipped the parts to Tallinn, where it was faithfully reconstructed.

Meanwhile, work began on the site. The first task was piling, creating 333 deep bores into the London soil which were then filled with concrete down to the level of the London clay beneath the line of the Thames riverbed. By July 2001, a reinforcing cage was laid on top of these piles to create the base foundations, a main pile cap, of the building. Because the site was so tightly packed within the heart of the City the workers had to wait until the following weekend for 290 trucks to deliver over 1,800 cubic metres of concrete in under eleven hours, so as not to reduce the Square Mile to a noisy standstill. The first external diagrid was ceremoniously installed on 12 October, despite the recent tragic news of 9/11, which briefly raised the question of whether tall buildings should be built at all. From then on, the outer skeleton of the building began to rise at an average of a floor a week.

Installing the glass exterior, the cladding, was the most expensive and tricky aspect of construction. The glass had to be fitted into steel frames but needed to be flexible enough to withstand the building's movement in the wind, so a diamond frame was devised by the Swiss company Schmidlin, who built the frames and shipped them to be assembled on site. The diamonds were installed by a team working inside the body of the structure, levered out by robots with suction pads and then lowered into position. It was also decided that different coloured glass was to be used to emphasise the spiralling nature of the internal space, giving the building its distinctive twist. Each pane was to be treated to combat solar glare.

By January 2003, when the final shape was emerging and the cladding had already reached close to the apex of the tower, work began on completing the dome that encased the final three storeys, floors 38–40, which would contain private dining rooms, a restaurant and a bar with panoramic views across the city. This final section demanded a different construction, as the cladding was attached directly to the steel frame which had to be raised to the tip by crane and welded together into place. Rather than installing the glass from the inside, it was winched into place by a team of expert abseilers working in difficult conditions, the wind rising to above thirty miles an hour. The work was complex and it was calculated that only fifteen panels would be fixed each day. The apex was completed by a single 2.42-metre dome of curved glass. On the first attempt, a bolt was tightened too fast and a crack appeared across the glass; on 20 June 2003 a new dome was placed and successfully fitted.

While the work on the exterior was completed, Foster + Partners were also working on the interior. Norman Foster had originally hoped to create garden spaces surrounding the spiralling atria, but this was deemed impossible when it was decided that many of the floors were to be rented out by Swiss Re. Nonetheless, it was hoped that the internal decoration would bring unity of design yet also flexibility of function. Open-plan offices were encouraged for a sense of community. Technology was also paramount, with video conference rooms and A/V facilities to cut down the need for expensive, and environmentally damaging, business travel. The simplicity of the decoration echoed the openness of the building itself; the use of natural light and the visibility of the city through the windows were highlighted.

The first Swiss Re staff began work just before Christmas 2003 while the lobby was still a work site, but as Sara Fox, the company project director, noted, the building itself was morale-boosting: 'People were pleased to leave it in the evening and see tourists staring up at it and taking pictures – suddenly they were working in a building that was as much a sight as St Paul's or the Tower of London.'[27]

In the words of Peter Rees of the City Corporation, the Swiss Re building 'single-handedly changed the perception of tall buildings in London'.[28] On the official launch in April 2004, the press were almost unanimous in their praise, despite confirming the popular nickname for the building, 'the Gherkin', a term of endearment that has proved permanent. In September 2004, as part of the London Open House weekend, over 8,000 Londoners queued to see inside the offices for the first time. The following month it won the prestigious RIBA Stirling Prize for 'Building of the Year'. Since then it has been adopted as a symbol for London in films, cartoons, advertising for the 2012 Olympics and TV, as well as being a more general signifier on magazine covers and papers for the thrusting, modern Square Mile – the world's leading financial capital.

Without the success of the Gherkin, there would be few arguments concerning the changing shape of the City, but Foster's tower is only the start of this discussion. One of the first victims of the 2008 global recession was the London skyline. Where once the horizon was filled with the sight of cranes within the dense hub of the Square Mile, the machines halted as if in the middle of a game of 'What's the time, Mister Wolf?'. There were plans for fifteen skyscrapers within London with comic names such as the 'Cheesegrater', the 'Walkie Talkie', the 'Shard', all floating on a tsunami of foreign money coming into the capital markets.

Their arrival inspired widespread condemnation from different parties: Ed Vaizey, Shadow Culture Minister, complained, in a speech to the Heritage of London Trust, that the New Labour government and the Mayor, Ken Livingstone, were 'in thrall to the skyscraper',[29] while the architectural critic Rowan Moore decreed that 'tower proposals are bad for London's economy and environment, and it's up to developers to prove otherwise'.[30] Architectural commentator and Chairman of the National Trust, Simon Jenkins, simply called it 'urban anarchy'. In his words, London, 'essentially a street-based, intimate urban landscape', was to be transformed into 'a series of point blocks set in piazzas'; the view along the Thames was to become 'a wall of glass'.[31] The powers within the metropolis had succumbed to a strange 'edifice complex', a desperate need to proclaim the power of the capital through towering steel and glass.

This is in stark contrast to the opinion of those who see London as a place of work rather than just a theatre in which the drama of the city is set. London needs to continue to grow, mindful of the past but with bold ambitions for the future. In August 2010, Stuart Fraser, policy director of the Corporation of London, wrote about plans for the Swiss financial house UBS to build a new tower inside the city, the largest office within the Square Mile. Fraser pointed out that 'there is no doubt that the City will be home to another iconic building and, more importantly ... this sends out a very positive message about the City's future as an international financial hub'.[32]

The approval of plans for the Shard and the Cheesegrater was only possible because of the acclaim for the Swiss Re Tower. The lion's share of this success is due to Norman Foster and his team, as well as the determination of Swiss Re itself. But it says something about London, the city that continues to flow around the base of the iconic tower. The building stands within a neighbourhood that has worked and transformed for nearly 2,000 years, from its origins at the two ends of the first rudimentary wooden bridge constructed by the Romans in the AD 50s.

The argument for the new city is by no means concluded – the Gherkin was just one step in developing a new urban philosophy. The twenty-first century has brought with it new demands and opportunities. Technology continues to test the boundaries of what should be and is possible. As the urban population continues to rise, the question of density comes to the fore: what are the physical limits of the capital? Will the experiments in sprawl of the twentieth century be replaced by a new vertical city, or will London continue to grow outwards until it reaches the sea? The planning of the sustainable city is essential. Our instinct to assume that cities are bad for the environment compared to the countryside is only just starting to be questioned. Could London, in fact, be 'greener' than its rural hinterlands? New ways of shopping, working and home life may change the way we use the city – will the corner shop soon fade away? How often will we have to travel to the centrally located office if we can work more efficiently at home? As more of us live alone, will a sense of community be less about life on the street and more about online social networks?

We are living through an exciting moment in London's history, as profound as any of the turning points that have been covered within this book, and the consequences of the choices we make now will have as lasting effects on the future as they have on us today. We must appreciate that history is as much an agent for change as an archive. Cities evolve, and must be allowed to do so in order to respond to the changing demands of any particular moment. New technology alters the way we navigate, work and build. The spirit of London, encapsulated in its buildings, should not be considered so precious that it needs to be bottled, kept safe or preserved as a museum – it has survived the roughest of times and been reborn in adversity; it thrives on change. The stones of London are not chapters of the past but essential parts of the living metropolis, markers to remind us of how we got here; they are the genetic material with which we will modify the future.

NOTES

CHAPTER I
WORDS AND STONES

1 Grimes, W. F. (1947), p.379
2 Shepherd, J., ed. (1998), p.49
3 Mattingly, D. (2007), p.47
4 Dio, trans. Cary, E. (1914), ch. LX, p.23
5 ibid., p.24
6 ibid., p.25
7 ibid., ch. LXI, p.33
8 http://vindolanda.csad.ox.ac.uk Vindolanda tablet 310
9 Tacitus, trans. Ogilvie, R. & Richmond, I. (1961), p.31
10 Watson, B. et al., eds. (2001), p.43
11 Tacitus, trans. Ogilvie, R. & Richmond, I. (1961), p.31
12 ibid
13 Mattingly, D. (2007), pp.277–8
14 Tacitus, trans. Ogilvie, R. & Richmond, I. (1961), BK. XXX
15 Stow, J., ed. Kingsford, C. L. (1908), pp.19–20
16 ibid., p.1
17 Monmouth, Geoffrey of (1976), p.14
18 Nennius, ed. Morris, J. (1980), p.9
19 Monmouth, Geoffrey of (1976), p.65
20 ibid., p.73
21 ibid., p.75
22 ibid., p.106
23 Shakespeare, *Henry VI*, Part 2, Act 4, Scene 2

CHAPTER 2
WESTMINSTER ABBEY

1 Baron, X., vol. 1 (1997), p.102
2 Augustine, ed. Dyson, R.W. (1998), ch. 1, book XV
3 Mason, E. (1996), p.12
4 Inwood, S. (1998), p.49
5 Barlow, F., ed. (1962), pp.44–6
6 Sheppard, F. (1998) p.68
7 Gerhold, D. (1999), p.13
8 ibid., p.11
9 Sheppard, F. (1998), p.79
10 Inwood, S. (1998), p.54
11 http://www.bl.uk/treasures/magna carta/translation/mc_trans.html. (clause 13)
12 Field, J. (1996), p.27
13 Baron, X., vol. 1 (1997), p.102
14 Nuttgens, P. (1972), p.42
15 Swaan, W., (1969), p.48
16 ibid., p.4
17 Lethaby (1909), p.9
18 Ball, P. (2008), p.46
19 Recht, R. (2008), p.306
20 Colvin, H. M., ed. (1971), p.229
21 Baron, X. (1997), pp.103–4
22 Lethaby (1909), p.129
23 Carpenter, D. A., 'Ware, Richard of (d. 1283)', *Oxford Dictionary of National Biography* (Oxford University Press, Oct. 2006); online edn

24 Colvin, H. M., ed. (1971), p.144
25 Carpenter, D. A. (1991), p.188
26 Carpenter, D. A. (2004), p.328
27 Lethaby (1909), p.66
28 ibid., p.15
29 Grant, L. & Mortimer, R., eds (2002), p.50
30 Jordan, W. C. (2009), p.109

CHAPTER 3
THE ROYAL EXCHANGE

1 Stow, J., ed. Kingsford, C. L. (1908), p.1
2 ibid.
3 Inwood, S. (1998), p.155
4 Keene, D.; Burns, A.; Saint, A., eds (2004), p.80
5 Baron, X. (1997), p.57
6 Arrighi, G. (1994), p.107
7 Wilson, E. (1884), p.11
8 Stow, J., ed. Kingsford, C. L. (1908), p.232
9 Burgeon, J. W. (1839), vol 2, p.485
10 Blanchard, Ian, 'Gresham, Sir Thomas (c.1518–79)', *Oxford Dictionary of National Biography* (Oxford University Press, Sept. 2004); online edn
11 Guicciardini, L. (1976), p.28
12 Burgeon, J. W. (1839), vol. 1, p.60
13 Guicciardini, L. (1976), p.29
14 ibid.
15 Marnef, G., from audio talk at Gresham College
16 Guicciardini, L. (1976), p.38
17 Burgeon, J. W. (1839), vol. 2, p.477
18 Feltwell, J. (1990), p.145
19 Bryson, A., from audio talk given at Gresham College
20 Ramsay, R. D. (1975), p.115
21 ibid., p.128
22 Anon., Memoir: BL 1082.d.16. p.6

23 Saunders, A. (1997), p.26
24 Burgeon, J. W. (1839), vol. 2, pp.410–11
25 Saunders, A. (1997), p.26
26 ibid, p.27
27 Thornbury, W. (1876), vol. 1, pp.494–513
28 Hanson, N. (2002), p.164
29 Thornbury, N. (1876), vol. 1, pp.494–513
30 Stow, J., ed. Kingsford, C. L. (1908), pp.187–200
31 Bindoff, S. T. (1973), p.18
32 Mitchell, R. J. & Leys, M. D. R. (1963), p.110
33 Anon., Memoir: BL 1082.d.16. p.7
34 Gascoigne, G. (1872), p.28
35 Ronald, S. (2007), p.46
36 Hollis, L. (2007), p.8

CHAPTER 4
GREENWICH

1 Jonson, B. (1816), p.261
2 ibid., p.265
3 ibid., p.269
4 From facsimile Jones, I., intro. by Piggott, S. (1971)
5 Summerson, J. (1966), p.xx
6 Leapman, M. (2003), p.23
7 Aslet, C. (1999), p.62
8 ibid., p.83
9 Hollis, L. (2008), p.xx
10 Oman, C. (1976), p.39
11 Sharpe, K. (1992), p.171
12 Summerson, J. (1966), p.48
13 Bold, J. (2000), p.60
14 Brotton, J. (2006), p.12
15 Aslet, C. (1999), p.101
16 Bold, J. (2000), p.61
17 Roy, I. (1984–5), p.17
18 Brotton, J. (2006), p.17
19 Leggett, D. (1972), p.198

20 Hollis, L. (2008), p.26
21 ibid., p.85
22 Bold, J. (2000), pp.80–81
23 http://www.pepysdiary.com/archive/ 1664/03/04/
24 Hollis, L. (2008), p. xx
25 Wren Society, vol. XIX (1942), p.114
26 ibid.
27 ibid., p.113
28 ibid.
29 Newell, P. (1984), p.6
30 Aslet, C. (1999), p.159
31 Hollis, L. (2007), p.278
32 Wren Society, vol. VI (1929), p.7
33 Bold, J. (2000), p.108
34 ibid., p.116
35 Downes, Kerry, 'Hawksmoor, Nicholas (1662?–1736)', *Oxford Dictionary of National Biography* (Oxford University Press, Sept. 2004); online edn
36 Aslet, C. (1999), p.162
37 ibid., p.164
38 Barber, Tabitha, 'Thornhill, Sir James (1675/6–1734)', *Oxford Dictionary of National Biography* (Oxford University Press, Sept. 2004); online edn
39 Thornhill, J. (1726), p.8

CHAPTER 5
19 PRINCELET STREET

1 From Preface, Strype, J. (1720) www.hrionline.ac.uk/strype/
2 Martin, G. H. & McConnell, Anita, 'Strype, John (1643–1737)', *Oxford Dictionary of National Biography* (Oxford University Press, Sept. 2004); online edn
3 Survey of London, vol. 27, ch. VI (http://www.british-history.ac.uk/ source.aspx?pubid=361)
4 ibid.
5 ibid.
6 ibid., ch. XIII
7 Hollis, L. (2008), pp. 297–8
8 Dillon, P. (2006), p.55
9 Rothstein, N. (1990), p.331
10 ibid., p.330
11 Gywnn, R. D. (1985)
12 Rothstein, N. (1990), p.371
13 Gywnn, R. D. (1985), p.69
14 Hollis, L. (2008), p.295
15 Richardson, J. (2000), p.172
16 Survey of London, vol. 27, ch. XII
17 Summerson, J. (2003), p.280
18 Betjeman, J. (1993), p.370
19 Summerson, J. (2003), p.284
20 Survey of London, vol. 27, ch. XII
21 Noorthouck, J. (1773), Book 5, ch.2
22 Hollis, L. (2008), p.192
23 ibid., p.196
24 ibid., p.142
25 ibid., p.248
26 ibid., p.199
27 Survey of London, vol. 27, p.205
28 Gwynn, R. D. (1985), p.71
29 Hollis, L. (2008), p.199
30 Feltwell, J. (1990), p.159
31 Rothstein, N., in Vigne, C. & Littleton, C., eds (2001), p.33
32 ibid., p.42
33 Ginsburg, M., 'Garthwaite, Anna Maria (1688–1763?)', *Oxford Dictionary of National Biography* (Oxford University Press, Sept. 2004); online edn
34 Mayhew, H. (1881) from 'And Ye Shall Walk in Silk Attire'
35 ibid.
36 ibid.
37 Page, W., ed. (1911), 'Industries: Silk-weaving', *A History of the County of Middlesex*, vol. 2. (http://www.british-history.ac.uk/ report.aspx?compid=22161)

CHAPTER 6
HOME HOUSE

1 Lewis, L. (1997), p.50
2 Whinney, M. (1969), p.13
3 Leslie, C. (1740), p.240
4 ibid., p.120
5 ibid., p.17
6 Gragg, L. (2000), p.29
7 Walvin, J. (1997), p.140
8 Leslie, C. (1740), p.36
9 Lewis, L. (1997), p.46
10 Wilson, B. (2009), p.29
11 Porter, R. (2001), p. xxi
12 Longstaffe-Gowan, T. (2006–7), pp.78–93
13 Thorold, P. (1999), p.30
14 ibid., p.113
15 ibid.
16 Reed, C., 'The Damn'd South Sea', *Harvard Magazine*, May 1999. (http://harvardmagazine.com/1999/05)
17 Thorold, P. (1999), p.138
18 Gwynn, J. (1996), p.5
19 ibid.
20 From 'The West Indian' (http://openlibrary.org/books/OL7148229M/West_Indian)
21 Sheridan, Richard B., 'Beckford, William (bap. 1709, d. 1770)', *Oxford Dictionary of National Biography* (Oxford University Press, Sept. 2004); online edn
22 Sennett, R. (2002), p.63
23 Miller, S. (2006), p.13
24 Schnorrenberg, Barbara Brandon, 'Montagu, Elizabeth (1718–1800)', *Oxford Dictionary of National Biography* (Oxford University Press, Sept. 2004); online edn
25 Eger, E. & Peltz, L. (2008), p.26
26 ibid., p.24
27 Whinney, M. (1969), p.13
28 Survey of London, vols 31 and 32: St James Westminster, part 2 (1963), ch. XVIII (http://www.british-history.ac.uk/report.aspx?compid=41477)
29 Von La Roche, S. (1933), p.241
30 Harris, E. (2001), p.1
31 Parissien, S. (1992), p.41
32 Hughes, R. (1972)
33 Harris, E. (2001), p.4
34 Harris, E. (1967)
35 ibid.
36 Saumarez Smith, C. (2000), p.164
37 Parissien, S. (1992), p.49
38 Harris, E. (2001), p.313
39 Saumarez Smith, C. (2000), p.147
40 Whinney, M. (1969), p.13
41 Longford, P. (1989), p.580
42 Williamson, A. (1974), p.140
43 Blackstock, F., 'Luttrell, Henry Lawes, second earl of Carhampton (1737–1821)', *Oxford Dictionary of National Biography* (Oxford University Press, Sept. 2004); online edn.

CHAPTER 7
REGENT STREET

1 Suggett, R. (1995), p.10
2 Summerson, J. (1980), p.2
3 ibid., p.3
4 ibid., p.5
5 ibid., p.7
6 Tyack, Geoffrey, 'Nash, John (1752–1835)', *Oxford Dictionary of National Biography* (Oxford University Press, Sept. 2004); online edn.
7 From Berkeley, G. (1897)
8 White, J. (2008), p.4
9 http://www.historyguide.org/intellect/reflections
10 Murray, V. (1998), p.96
11 Summerson, J. (2000), p.60

12 Saunders, A. (1969), p.65
13 Tyack, Geoffrey, 'Nash, John (1752–1835)', *Oxford Dictionary of National Biography* (Oxford University Press, Sept. 2004); online edn
14 Summerson, J. (1980), p.21
15 Batey, M. (1994), p.126
16 Tyack, Geoffrey, 'Nash, John (1752–1835)', *Oxford Dictionary of National Biography*, (Oxford University Press, Sept. 2004); online edn
17 Summerson, J. (2000), p.179
18 ibid., p.174
19 Saunders, A. (1969), p.69
20 Mordaunt Crook, J. (2000), p.7
21 Summerson, J. (2000), p.115
22 Saunders, A. (1969), p.80
23 Summerson, J. (1935), p.195
24 Arnold, D. (2000), p.4
25 Adams, A. (2005), p.17
26 Fox, C., ed. (1992), p.75
27 Elmes, J., ed. Shepherd, T. M. (1978), pp.1–2
28 Hobhouse, H. (2008), p.20
29 Summerson, J. (1935), p.130
30 ibid., p.84
31 ibid., p.126
32 ibid., p.108
33 Hobhouse, H. (2008), p.48
34 Elmes, J., ed. Shepherd, T. M. (1978), ch. 3
35 Hobhouse, H. (2008), p.21
36 ibid., pp. 43–4
37 Von La Roche, S. (1933), p.87
38 Hobhouse, H. (2008), p.10
39 ibid., p.50
40 ibid., p.63
41 Healey, E. (1997), p.91
42 ibid., p.94
43 Summerson, J. (1935), p.164
44 ibid., p.181
45 ibid., p.182
46 ibid., p.274

CHAPTER 8
THE HOUSES OF PARLIAMENT

1 Field, J. (2002), p.177
2 *The Times*, 20 October 1834
3 ibid.
4 ibid.
5 Barry, A. (1867), p.145
6 ibid., p.146
7 Field, J. (2002), pp. 178–9
8 Hamilton, J. (2007), p.262
9 *The Times*, 17 October 1834
10 *The Times*, 18 October 1834
11 Watkin, David, 'Soane, Sir John (1753–1837)', *Oxford Dictionary of National Biography* (Oxford University Press, Sept. 2004); online edn
12 ibid.
13 Cannadine, D. et al., eds (2000), p.243
14 Hill, R. (2009), p.87
15 Hilton, B. (2006), p.426
16 Hill, R. (2009), p.105
17 Field J. (2002), p.162
18 Cooke, Sir R. (1987), p.80
19 Rorabaugh, W. J. (Dec. 1973), p.165
20 Barry, A. (1867), p.239
21 Hill, R. (2009), p.144
22 Cannadine, D. et al., eds (2000), p.163
23 Cooke, Sir R. (1987), p.89
24 Hill, R. (2008), p.119
25 ibid., pp.213–14
26 Hunt, T. (2005), p.66
27 ibid., p.103
28 Hill, R. (2009), p.155
29 Rorabaugh, W. J. (Dec. 1973), p.172
30 Cannadine, D. et al., eds (2000), p.225
31 ibid., p.227
32 Boase, T. S. R. (1954), p.324
33 ibid., p.345
34 Port, M. H. (1976), p.122
35 ibid., p.125
36 ibid., p.139
37 ibid., p.113

38 ibid., p.103
39 ibid., p.115
40 Cooke, Sir R. (1987), p.129
41 Cannadine, D. et al., eds (2000), p.41
42 Cooke, Sir R. (1987), p.129
43 Port, M. H. (1976), p.149
44 Cannadine, D. et al., eds (2000), p.229
45 ibid., p.232
46 Cooke, Sir R. (1987), p.259
47 Colvin, H. M., ed. (1973), p.625
48 Hill, R. (2009), p.476
49 ibid., p.486
50 MacDonald, P. (2004), p.24
51 ibid., p.28
52 Barry, A. (1867), p.170

CHAPTER 9
VICTORIA EMBANKMENT

1 Johnson, S. (2007), p.160
2 On the Mode of Communication of
   Cholera (http://www.ph.ucla.edu/
   epi/snow/broadstreetpump.htl)
3 Armstrong, I. (2008), p.134
4 ibid., p.135
5 Metcalfe, P. (1972), p.80
6 Hollingshead, J. (1861), p.120
7 Armstrong, I. (2008), p.135
8 White, J., *London in the Nineteenth
   Century* (2008), p.51
9 Halliday, S. (1999), p.18
10 ibid., p.71
11 ibid., p.72
12 ibid., p.40
13 Owen, D. E (1982), p.26
14 Halliday, S. (1999), p.127
15 Porter, R. (2000), p.317
16 Schneer, J. (2005), p.148
17 Mayhew, H. (1881), p.375
18 Porter, R. (2000), p.322
19 Halliday, S. (1999), p.26
20 ibid., p.53
21 ibid. p.54
22 Oliver, S. (2000), p.232
23 Porter, R. (2000), p.320
24 MBW Handbook (1857), p.1
25 ibid., p.6
26 Halliday, S. (1999), p.67
27 Bazalgette, J. (1864–5), p.17
28 Halliday, S. (1999), p.71
29 Bazalgette, J. (1864–5), p.19
30 ibid.
31 Hollingshead, J. (1861), p.120
32 Porter, D. (1998), p.191
33 Wolmar, C. (2004), p.22
34 Porter, D. (1998), p.207
35 Wolmar, C. (2004), p.57
36 *New York Times*, 30 August 1892
    (http://select.nytimes.com/gst/
    abstract.html?res=F70F15FB395
    C17738DDDA 80B94D0405B8285
    FoD3#)

CHAPTER 10
WEMBLEY STADIUM

1 Rennell, T. (2000), p.4
2 Schneer, J. (2001), p.67
3 ibid., p.10
4 ibid., p.42
5 Marr, A. (2009), pp.14–15
6 Schneer, J. (2001), p.23
7 Inwood, S. (1998), p.201
8 Ferguson, N. (2003), p.318
9 ibid., p.318
10 *Places in Brent: Wembley and
    Tokyngton*, Grange Museum of
    Community History and Brent
    Archive, p.1
11 Elsley, H. W. R. (1953), p.157
12 Grossman, G. & W. (1938), p.17
13 Clarke, W., ed. (1881), p.vi
14 ibid., p.241
15 ibid., p.242
16 ibid., p.402
17 Jackson, A. A. (1986), p.75

18 ibid., p.82
19 Jay, R. (1987), p.146
20 Rasmussen, S. E. (1939), p.369
21 Jackson, A. A. (2006), p.59
22 ibid., p.42
23 Jensen, F. (2007), p.162
24 Ferguson, N. (2003), p.319
25 Knight, D. & Sabey, D. (1984), p.3
26 ibid., p.8
27 Lawrence, G. C., ed. (1924), p.xx
28 Knight, D. & Sabey, D. (1984), p.1
29 Lawrence, G. C., ed. (1924), p.52
30 ibid., p.33
31 Ferguson, N. (2003), p.319
32 Jackson, A. A. (2006), p.96
33 Barker, 23 (?) Mumford Quote
34 Saint, A. (1999), p.114

CHAPTER 11
KEELING HOUSE

1 *The Times*, 1 July 2000
2 *The Sunday Times*, 7 February 1993
3 English Heritage brochure
4 *The Sunday Times*, 17 October 1999
5 Wilkinson, L. (2001), p.70
6 Smith, L. (2007), pp.176–7
7 Porter, R. (2000), p.416
8 For maps and more information on
   Booth's survey, see www.booth.lse.
   ac.uk
9 Wise, S. (2009), p.59
10 Wilkinson, L. (2001), p.28
11 Glass, R. (1964)
12 Hanley, L. (2007), p.74
13 Kynaston, D. (2008), p.160
14 Young, M. & Willmott, P. (2007),
    p.122
15 ibid., p.128
16 Kynaston, D. (2008), p.161
17 Hanley, L. (2007), p.80
18 Kynaston, D. (2009), p.30
19 Hanley, L. (2007), p.78

20 Kynaston, D. (2008), p.435
21 Kynaston, D. (2009), p.61
22 ibid.
23 Mullins, C. (2007), p.48
24 Curtis, W. (1994), p.21
25 ibid.
26 ibid., p.36
27 ibid., p.26
28 ibid., p.223
29 Allan, J. (2002), p.21
30 Gold, J. R. (1995), p.248
31 Curtis, W. (1994), p.40
32 *Architects' Year Book* 4 (1952), p.10
33 Curtis, W. (1994), p.44
34 Glendinning, M. & Muthesius, S.
    (1994), p.109
35 *Architects' Year Book* 7 (1956),
    p.203
36 *Architects' Year Book* 4 (1952), p.137
37 ibid., p.138
38 Powers, A. (2007), p.114
39 Curtis, W. (1994), pp.52–3
40 Inwood, S. (1998), p.821
41 Young, M. & Willmott, P. (2007),
    p.186
42 ibid., p.199
43 *The Times*, 7 October 1957
44 Curtis, W. (1994), p.216
45 ibid., p.223
46 Bennett, C. (1990)
47 Curtis, W. (1994), p.51
48 *The London Plan*, February 2010, 2.1
49 ibid., 2.2. i

CHAPTER 12
30 ST MARY AXE

1 Eaton, K., 'Cisco to Turbo Boost
   South Korean City to "smart" Future
   City Status', *Fast Company*, 30 March
   2010
2 Gopnik, A., 'Not Scared', *The New
   Yorker*, 25 July 2005

3 Massey, D. (2007), p.3
4 ibid., p.4
5 Bagehot, W. (1999), p.12
6 McSmith, A. (2010), p.173
7 Kynaston, D. (2001), p.710
8 ibid., p.716
9 Augar, P. (2010), p.15
10 Schneer, J. (2005), p.268
11 GLA (May 2009), p.31
12 ibid., p.253
13 ibid., p.254
14 ibid., p.256
15 The Big Dig (1998), p.31
16 Jenkins, D., ed. (2000), p.375
17 ibid., p.701
18 ibid., pp.704–5
19 Sudjic, D. (2010), p.146

20 Jenkins, D., ed. (2000), p.518
21 Kynaston, D. (2001), p.699
22 ibid., p.700
23 Powell, K. (2006), p.45
24 ibid. p.63
25 ibid., p.40
26 ibid., p.49
27 ibid., p.191
28 ibid., p.195
29 http://www.london-se1.co.uk/
    news/view/2734
30 Moore, R., *Evening Standard*, 15
    December 2009
31 Jenkins, S., *Guardian*, 27 September
    2007
32 Fraser, S., *City A.M.*, 9 August 2010,
    p.16

BIBLIOGRAPHY

GENERAL

The Endless City: The Urban Age Project (Phaidon, 2007)

Ackroyd, P., *London: the Biography* (Chatto and Windus, 2000)

Ackroyd, P., *Sacred Thames* (Chatto and Windus, 2007)

Adams, A., *London in Poetry and Prose* (Enitharmon Press, 2005)

Bacon, E. N., *Design of Cities* (Thames and Hudson, 1974)

Baron, X., *London 1066–1914: Literary Sources and Documents*, 3 vols (Helm International, 1997)

Black, J., *London: A History* (Carnegie Press, 2009)

British Geological Survey, *Geology of London* (Keyworth, 2004)

Clayton, A., *The Folklore of London: Legends, Ceremonies and Celebrations Past and Present* (Historical Publications, 2008)

Curtis, W., *Denys Lasdun: Architecture, City, Landscape* (Phaidon, 1994)

Dorling, D., *Injustice: Why Social Inequality Exists* (Polity Press, 2010)

Fettwell, J., *The Story of Silk* (St Martin's Press, 1990)

Fox, C., *Londoners* (Thames and Hudson, 1987)

Foxell, S., *Mapping London: Making Sense of the City* (Black Dog Publishing, 2007)

Glinert, E., *East End Chronicles* (Penguin, 2006)

Glinert, E., *West End Chronicles* (Penguin, 2008)

Hollis, L., *The Phoenix: St Paul's Cathedral and the Men Who Made Modern London* (Weidenfeld and Nicolson, 2008)

Hunt, T., *Building Jerusalem: The Rise and Fall of the Victorian City* (Phoenix, 2005)

Inwood, S., *A History of London* (Macmillan, 1998)

Inwood, S., *Historical London* (Macmillan, 2008)

Keene, D.; Burns, A.; Saint, A., eds, *St Paul's: The Cathedral Church of London 604–2004* (Yale University Press, 2004)

Koolhas, R. et al., *Mutations* (Actas, 2002)

Lewis, J., ed., *London: The Autobiography* (Constable, 2008)

Mayhew, H., *London Characters* (Chatto and Windus, 1881)

Mitchell, R. J. & Leys, M. D. R., *A History of London Life* (Pelican, 1963)

Nuttgens, P., *The Landscape of Ideas* (Faber, 1972)

Olsen, D. J., *The City as a Work of Art: London, Paris, Vienna* (Yale University Press, 1986)

Porter, R., *London: A Social History* (Penguin, 2000)

Rasmussen, S. E. *London: The Unique City* (MIT Press, 1991)

Richardson, J., *The Annals of London* (Cassell, 2000)

Ross, C. & Clarke, J., *The London Museum History of London* (Penguin, 2008)

Schneer, J., *The Thames: England's River* (Little, Brown, 2005)

Sennett, R., *The Fall of Public Man* (Penguin, 1978)

Sennett, R., *The Conscience of the Eye* (Faber, 1991)

Sennett, R., *Flesh and Stone* (Faber, 1995)

Sheppard, F., *London: A History* (Oxford University Press, 1998)

Stow, J., ed. Kingsford, C. L., *Stow's Survey of London*, 2 vols (Clarendon Press, 1908) (http://www.british-history.ac.uk/source.aspx?pubid = 593)

Summerson, J., *Architecture in Britain, 1530–1830* (Yale University Press, 1993)

Summerson, J., *Georgian London* (Yale University Press, 2000)

Sutcliffe, A., *London: An Architectural History* (Yale University Press, 2006)

Thornbury, W., *Old and New London*, 6 vols, 1878 (http://www.british-history.ac.uk/place.aspx?gid= 79&region =1)

Vance, J. E., *The Continuing City: Urban Morphology in Western Civilization* (Johns Hopkins University Press, 1990)

Von La Roche, S., *Sophie in London 1731–1807* (Jonathan Cape, 1933)

White, J., *London in the Nineteenth Century* (Vintage, 2008)

White, J., *London in the Twentieth Century* (Vintage, 2008)

CHAPTER I

Vindolanda Tablet Project, Oxford (http://vindolanda.csad.ox.ac.uk/)

Archaeology of the City of London (Dept of Urban Archaeology, Museum of London, 1980)

Archaeology of Greater London: An assessment of the archaeological evidence from human presence in the area now covered by greater London (Dept of Urban Archaeology, Museum of London, 2000)

Baker, T., *Medieval London* (Cassell, 1970)

Bell, W., *London Wall through Eighteen Centuries* (Council for Tower Hill Improvements, 1937)

Birley, A., trans., *Lives of the Later Caesars* (Penguin, 1976)

Daniels, C. M., 'The role of the Roman in the spread and practice of Mithraism' *Mithraic Studies*, vol. 2 (Manchester University Press, 1971)

De La Bedoyere, G., *Hadrian's Wall* (Tempus, 1998)

De La Bedoyere, G., *Gods with Thunderbolts: Religion in Roman Britain* (Tempus, 2002)

De La Bedoyere, G., *Roman Britain: A New History* (Thames and Hudson, 2006)

Dio, Cassius, trans. Cary, E., *Roman History*, 9 vols (Loeb Classical Library, 1914)

Gibbon, E., ed. Womersley, D., *History of the Decline and Fall of the Roman Empire* (Allen Lane, 1994)

Green, M. J., *The Gods of Roman Britain* (Shire, 1983)

Grimes, W. F., 'Roman Britain', *The Classical Journal*, April 1947

Haynes, H. W., 'The Roman Wall in Britain', *Journal of the American Geographical Society of New York*, vol. 22, 1890

Hingley, R. & Unwin, C., *Boudica: Iron Age Warrior Queen* (Hambledon and London, 2005)

Hinnells, J. R., ed. *Mithraic Studies*, 2 vols (Manchester University Press, 1971)

Hobley, B., 'The archaeoloy of London Wall', *London Journal*, vol. 7, 1981

Hollaender, A. E. J. & Kellaway, W., eds, *Studies in London History* (Hodder and Stoughton, 1969)

Howe, E., *Roman Defences and Medieval Industry, Excavations at Baltic House* (City of London MoLAS Monograph, 7)

Howe, E., *Roman and Medieval Cripplegate* (City of London MoLAS Mongraph 21)

Lethaby, W. R., *Londinium Architecture and the Crafts* (Duckworth and Co., 1923)

Marsden, P., *Roman London* (Thames and Hudson, 1980)

Marsden, P., *Roman Forum Site in London* (HMSO, 1985)

Mattingly, D., *An Imperial Possession* (Penguin, 2007)

Milne, G., *The Port of Roman London* (B.T. Batsford, 1985)

Milne, G., *Roman London* (English Heritage, 1995)

Monmouth, Geoffrey of, *The History of the Kings of Britain* (Penguin, 1976)

Morris, J., *Londinium: London in the Roman Empire* (rev. edn) (Weidenfeld and Nicolson, 1982)

Nennius, ed. Morris, J., *British History and the Welsh Annals* (Phillimore, 1980)

Perrings, D., *Roman London* (Seaby, 1991)

Pierce, P., *Old London Bridge: The Story of the Longest Inhabited Bridge in the World* (Headline, 2001)

Price, J. E., *On a Bastion of London Wall in Camomile Street, Bishopsgate* (Westminster, 1880)

Shepherd, J., ed., *Post-war Archaeology in the City of London: 1946–72* (Museum of London, 1998)

Shepherd, J., *The Temple of Mithras, London* (English Heritage, 1998)

Suetonius, trans. Graves, Robert, *Lives of the Caesars* (Penguin, 1989)

Tacitus, *The Annals of Imperial Rome* (Penguin, 1958)

Tacitus, trans. Ogilvie, R.; Richmond, I., *De Vita Agricolae* (Clarendon Press, 1967)

Toynbee, J. M. C., 'The Roman Art Treasures from the Temple of Mithras', Special Paper 7 (London and Middlesex Archaeology Society, 1986)

Ulansey, D., *Origins of the Mithraic Mysteries* (Oxford University Press, 1991)

Ulansey, D., 'Solving the Mithraic Mysteries', *Biblical Archaeology Review*, vol. 20, Sept/Oct 1994

Watson, B; Brigham, T; Dyson, T., eds, *London Bridge: 2000 years of a River Crossing* (Museum of London Archaeology Service, 2001)

CHAPTER 2

Augustine, ed. Dyson, R. W., *The City of God Against the Pagans* (Cambridge University Press, 1998)

Ball, P., *Universe of Stone: Chartres Cathedral and the Triumph of the Medieval Mind* (Bodley Head, 2008)

Barlow, F., ed., *The Life of King Edward who Rests at Westminster* (Thomas Nelson and Sons, 1962)

Bevan, B., *Royal Westminster Abbey* (Robert Hale, 1971)

Blair, J., 'The Westminster Corridor: An Exploration of the Anglo-Saxon

History of Westminster Abbey and Its Nearby Lands and People', *The English Historical Review*, February 1997

Bony, J., *The English Decorated Style: Gothic Architecture Transformed 1250–1350* (Phaidon, 1979)

Carpenter, D. A., *The Reign of Henry III* (Hambledon Press, 1991)

Carpenter, D. A., *The Struggle for Mastery: Penguin History of Britain 1066–1284* (Penguin, 2004)

Coldstream, N., *Medieval Architecture* (Oxford University Press, 2002)

Colvin, H. M., *History of the King's Works*, vol. 1: *The Middle Ages* (HMSO, 1963)

Colvin. H. M., ed., *Building Accounts of Henry III* (Clarendon Press, 1971)

Field, J., *Kingdom, Power and Glory: A Historical Guide to Westminster Abbey* (James and James, 1996)

Foster, R., *Patterns of Thought: The Hidden Meaning of the Great Pavement of Westminster Abbey* (Jonathan Cape, 1991)

Frankl, P., Gothic Architecture (rev. edn) (Yale University Press, 2000)

Gerhold, D., *Westminster Hall: Nine Hundred Years of History* (James and James, 1999)

Grant, L. & Mortimer, R., ed, *Westminster Abbey: the Cosmati Pavements* (Ashgate, 2002)

Harvey, B., *Westminster Abbey and its Estate in the Middle Ages* (Clarendon Press, 1977)

Harvey, J., *The Master Builders* (Thames and Hudson, 1971)

Holland, T., *Millennium* (Little, Brown, 2008)

Hutton, E., *The Cosmati: The Roman Marble Workers of the 12th and 13th Centuries* (Routledge and Kegan Paul, 1950)

Hutton, W. H., ed., *The Misrule of Henry III* (David Nutt, 1887)

Jenkyns, R., *Westminster Abbey* (Profile, 2004)

Jordan, W. C., 'Abbots Ascending' *History Today*, vol. 59 (8), August 2009

Jordan, W. C., *A Tale of Two Monasteries: Westminster and Saint-Denis in the Thirteenth Century* (Princeton Univeersity Press, 2009)

Lethaby, W. R., *Westminster Abbey and the King's Craftsmen: A Study of Medieval Building* (Duckworth & Co., 1909)

Malmsbury, William of, *Chronicles of the Kings of England* (G. Bell and Sons, 1904)

Mason, E., ed., *Westminster Abbey and its People: c.1050-c.1216* (Boydell Press, 1996)

Mason, E., ed., *Westminster Abbey Charters, 1066-c.1214*, http://www.british-history.ac.uk/source.aspx?pubid=580)

Mortimer, R., ed., *Edward the Confessor: the Man and the Legend* (Boydell Press, 2009)

O'Daly, G., *Augustine's City of God: a Reader's Guide* (Clarendon Press, 1999)

Palliser, D. M., ed., *The Cambridge Urban History of Britain*, vol. 1 (Cambridge University Press, 2000)

Recht, R., *Seeing and Believing: The Art of Gothic Architecture* (University of Chicago Press, 2008)

Rosser, G., *Medieval Westminster: 1200–1540* (Clarendon Press, 1989)

Sullivan, D., *The Westminster Circle* (Historical Publications, 2006)

Swaan, W., *The Gothic Cathedral* (Elek, 1969)

Westminster Abbey (Annenberg School Press, 1972)

Westminster, Matthew of, *The Flowers of History*, 3 vols (Henry G. Bohn, 1853)

Wilson, C., *The Gothic Cathedral* (Thames and Hudson, 1990)

CHAPTER 3

The Competitive Role of London as a Global Financial Centre (Corp. of London/ YZen 2001)

'London Lickpenny', from *Medieval English Political Writings*, ed. Dean, J. M. (http://www.lib.rochester.edu/camelot/teams/dean1.htm

William Fitzstephen's *Florilegium Urbanum* http://users.trytel.com/ ~tristan/ towns/florilegium/introduction/intro01.html#p19)

Ames-Lewis, F., ed., *Sir Thomas Gresham and Gresham College* (Ashgate, 1999)

Anon., *Brief Memoir of Sir Thomas Gresham . . .*, BL 1082.d.16

Arrighi, G., *The Long Twentieth Century* (Verso, 1994)

Bindoff, S.T., *The Fame of Sir Thomas Gresham* (Jonathan Cape, 1973)

Burgeon, J. W., *The Life and Times of Sir Thomas Gresham*, 2 vols (Robert Jennings, 1839)

Braudel, F., *Civilization and Capitalism*, vol. 1: *The Structures of Everyday Life* (Collins, 1981)

Braudel, F., *Civilization and Capitalism*, vol. 3: *The Perspective of the World* (Collins, 1984)

Bryson, A., 'The Legal Quays: Sir William Paulet, First Margquis of Winchester', a talk given at Gresham College (http://www.gresham.ac.uk/audio_video-.asp?PageId=108)

Challis, C. E., *Currency and the Economy in Tudor and Early Stuart England* (The Historical Association, 1989)

Craig, Sir J., *The Mint: A History of the London Mint: AD 287 to 1948* (Cambridge University Press)

de Roover, R., *Gresham on Foreign Exchange* (Harvard University Press, 1949)

Dietz, B., 'Antwerp and London: The Structure and Balance of Trade in the 1560s', *Wealth and Power in Tudor England,* Ives, E.; Knecht, R.; Scarisbrick, J., eds (Athlone Press, 1978)

Divine, A., *The Opening of the World* (Collins, 1973)

Gascoigne, G., *A Larum for London* (Longmans, 1872)

Green, B., 'Shakespeare and Goethe on Gresham's Law and the Single Gold Standard', BL 8227aa 60

Guicciardini, L., *Description of the Low Countreys* (London, 1593; Teatrum Orbis Terrarum, 1976)

Hanson, N., *The Dreadful Judgement: The True Story of the Great Fire of London* (Corgi, 2002)

Isreal, J. I., *Dutch Primacy in World Trade, 1585–1740* (Clarendon Press, 1989)

Marnef, G., 'Gresham and Antwerp', a talk given at Gresham College (http://www.gresham.ac.uk/audio_video.asp?PageId=10)

Merritt, J. F., *Imagining Early Modern London: Perceptions and Portrayals of the City from Stow to Strype 1598–1720* (Cambridge University Press, 2001)

Picard, L., *Elizabeth's London: Everday Life in Elizabethan London* (Phoenix, 2003)

Ramsay, R. D., *The City of London in International Politics at the Accession of Elizabeth Tudor* (Manchester University Press, 1975)

Ronald, S., *The Pirate Queen: Queen Elizabeth I, her Pirate Adventurers and the Dawn of Empire* (HarperCollins, 2007)

Salter, F. R., *Sir Thomas Gresham* (Leonard Parsons, 1925)

Saunders, A., *The Royal Exchange* (London Topographical Society, no. 152, 1997)

Simpson, R., ed., *School of Shakespeare 1: A Larum for London* (Longman, Green and Co., 1872)

Teague, S. J., *Sir Thomas Gresham: Financier and College Founder* (Synjon Books, 1974)

Weddington, J., *A Breffe instruction, and manner, how to kepe, merchantes bokes, of accomptes,* (Scolar Press, 1979)

Wilson, E., *Wilson's Description of the New Royal Exchange ...* (Effingham Wilson, 1844)

Woodall, J., 'Trading Identities: The Image of the Merchant', a talk given at Gresham College (http://www.gresham.ac.uk/audio_video.asp?PageId= 108)

CHAPTER 4

Anderson, C., *Inigo Jones and the Classical Tradition* (Cambridge University Press, 2007)

Anon., A description of the Royal Hospital for Seamen at Greenwich, BL 10351 CC 32

Aslet, C., *The Story of Greenwich* (Fourth Estate, 1999)

Balakier, A. & J., *The Spatial Infinite at Greenwich in Works by Christopher Wren* ... (Edwin Mellen Press, 1995)

Bevington, D. & Holbrooke, P., eds, *The Politics of the Stuart Court Masque* (Cambridge University Press, 1998)

Bold, J., *Greenwich: An Architectural History of the Royal Hospital for Seamen and the Queen's House* (Yale University Press, 2000)

Brotton, J., *The Sale of the Late King's Goods* (Macmillan, 2006)

Callender, G., *The Queen's House, Greenwich, a short history 1617–1937* (Yelf Bros, 1937)

Downes, K., *Nicholas Hawksmoor* (Zwemmer, 1959)

Evelyn, J., *Navigation and Commerce* ... (1674)

Evelyn, J., ed. De Beer, E. S., *Diaries* vols 1–6 (1955)

Fraser, A., *King James* (Weidenfeld and Nicolson, 1974)

Harris, J. & Higgott, G., *Inigo Jones: Complete Archtectural Drawings* (Zwemmer, 1989)

Harris, J.; Orgel, S.; Strong, S., eds, *The King's Arcadia: Inigo Jones and the Stuart Court* (Arts Council of Great Britain, 1973)

Hawksmoor, N., 'Remarks on the Founding and Carrying on the Buildings of the Royal Hospital at Greenwich', Wren Society, vol. VI, 1929

Hooke, R., eds. Robinson, W. & Adams, W., *The Diary of Robert Hooke, 1672–80* (Taylor and Francis, 1935)

Horne, A., *The Seven Ages of Paris* (Weidenfeld and Nicolson, 2003)

Inwood, S., *The Man Who Knew too Much* (Macmillan, 2002)

Jones, I., intro. by Piggott, S., *Stone-Heng* (Gregg International, 1971)

Jones, I., ed. Johnson, A. W., *Three Volumes Annotated by Inigo Jones* (Abo Akademi University Press, 1997)

Jonson, B., *The Works of Ben Jonson*, vol 7: *Masques at Court* (1816)

Leapman, M., *Inigo: The Troubled Life of Inigo Jones, Architect of the English Renaissance* (Review, 2003)

Leggett, D., 'The Manor of East Greenwich and the American Colonies', *Transactions of the Greenwich and Lewisham Antiquary Society*, vol. 8, 1972

McCrae, W. H., *The Royal Observatory, Greenwich* (HMSO, 1975)

Mowl, T. & Earnshaw, B., *Architecture without Kings: The Rise of Puritan Classicism under Cromwell* (Manchester University Press, 1995)

Newell, P., *Greenwich Hospital 1692–1983* (Trustees of Greenwich Hospital, 1984)

Nicholson, A., *Earls of Paradise* (HarperCollins, 2007)

Oman, C., *Henrietta Maria* (White Lion Publishers, 1976)

Orrell, J., *The Theatre of Inigo Jones and John Webb* (Cambridge University Press, 1985)

Peacock, J., *The Stage Designs of Inigo Jones: the European Context* (Cambridge University Press, 1995)

Roy, I., 'Greenwich in the Civil War', *Transactions of the Greenwich and Lewisham Antiquary Society*, vol. 10, 1984–5

Sharpe, K., *The Personal Rule of Charles I* (Yale University Press, 1992)

Stewart, A., *The Cradle King: A Life of James VI and I* (Chatto and Windus, 2003)

Stoye, J., *English Travellers Abroad 1604–1667* (Yale University Press, 1989)

Summerson, J., *Inigo Jones* (Penguin, 1966)

Tinniswood, A., *His Inventions So Fertile: A Life of Christopher Wren* (Jonathan Cape, 2001)

Thornhill, J., *An Explanation of the Paintings in the Royal Hospital at Greenwich* (1726)

Whitaker, K., *A Royal Passion: The Turbulent Marriage of Charles I and Henrietta Maria* (Weidenfeld and Nicolson, 2010)

Williams, E. C., *Anne of Denmark: Wife of James VI of Scotland: James I of England* (Longman, 1970)

Wittkower, R., *Palladio and English Palladianism* (Thames and Hudson, 1974)

Worsley, G., *Inigo Jones and the European Classicist Tradition* (Yale University Press, 2006)

Wren, S., *Parentalia*... facsimile of Heirloom edn (1965)

Wren Society, vol. XIX (Wren Society, 1942)

CHAPTER 5

Noorthouck, J., *A New History of London* (1773) (http:/www.british-history.ac.uk/source.aspx?pubid=332)

Smith, G., Laboratory of the School of Arts (www.archive.org/stream/laboratoryorschooosmit)

19 Princelet Street (www.19princeletstreet.org.uk/ index.html)

Strype, J., *A Survey of London, 1720* (www.hrionline.ac.uk/strype/)

Survey of London, vol. 27: *Spitalfields and Mile End New Town* (www.history.ac.uk/)

Barbon, N., *A Discourse Shewing the Great Advantages that New Buildings, and the Enlarging of Towns and Cities Do bring to a Nation* (1678)

Barbon, N., *An Apology for the Builder* (1685)

Bayliss, M., 'The unsuccessful Andrew and other Ogiers: A Study in Failure in the Huguenot Community', *Proceedings of the Huguenot Society*, vol. XXVI, 1994–97

Berg, M., *Luxury and Pleasure in Eighteenth-century Britain* (Oxford University Press, 2005)

Betjeman, J., *John Betjeman's Guide to English Parish Churches* (HarperCollins, 1993)

Black, J., *A Subject for Taste: Culture in Eighteenth-century England* (Hambledon and London, 2005)

Brett-James, N. G., *The Growth of Stuart London* (Allen and Unwin, 1935)

Brewer. J., *Pleasures of the Imagination* (HarperCollins, 1997)

Burton, N. & Guillery, P., *Behind the Facade: London House Plans, 1660–1840* (Spire Books, 2006)

Cherry, B.; O'Brien, C.; Pevsner, N., eds, *The Buildings of England: London 5: East* (Yale University Press, 2005)

Coleman, D. C., *Courtaulds: An Economic and Social History* (Clarendon Press, 1969)

Courtauld, C., 'The Reburial of Louisa Perina Courtauld (neé Ogier)', *Proceedings of the Huguenot Society*, XXVII (5), 2002

Cox, M., *Life and Death in Spitalfields, 1700–1850* (Council for British Archaeology, 1996)

Cruickshank, D. & Burton, N., *Life in the Georgian City* (Viking, 1990)

Defoe, D., *A Tour Throu' the Whole Island of Great Britain*, vols I, II (Peter Davies, 1927)

Defoe, D., ed. Furbank, P. N. & Owen, R., *A True Born Englishman and Other Writings* (Penguin, 1997)

Defoe, D., *The Great Storm* (Penguin, 2005)

de la Ruffiniere du Prey, P., *Hawksmoor's London Churches: Architecture and Theology* (University of Chicago Press, 2000)

Dillon, P., *The Last Revolution: 1688 and the Creation of the Modern World* (Jonathan Cape, 2006)

Downes, K., *Hawksmoor* (Thames and Hudson, 1994)

Flanagan, J. F., *Spitalfields Silks of the 18th and 19th Centuries* (F. Lewis, 1954)

'Fournier Street Outstanding Conservation Area'. Tower Hamlets Council, June 1979

Girouard, M., 'The Georgian Houses of Spitalfields', *Proceedings of the Huguenot Society*, XXIII, 1977–82

Guillery, P., *The Small House in Eigtheenth Century London* (Yale University Press, 2004)

Gywnn, R. D., *Huguenot Heritage* (Routledge and Kegan Paul, 1985)

Gwynne, R. D., *The Huguenots of London* (Alpha Press, 1998)

Hammond, J. & Hammond B., *The Skilled Labourer* (new edn) (Longman, 1979)

Hatton, E., *A New View of London (1708)*

Leech, K., 'The Decay of Spitalfields', *East London Papers*, vol. 7.2, 1964

Maddocks, S., *The Copartnership Herald*, vol. 1, no. 10, 1931

Marsh, G., *18th Century Embroidery Techniques* (Guild of Master Craftsman Publications, 2006)

McKellar, E., *The Birth of Modern London* (Manchester University Press, 1999)

Molleson, T. & Cox, M., *The Spitalfields Project*, vol. 2: *The Anthropology* (CBA Research Report 86, 1993)

North, R., 'Life of the Honorable Sir Dudley North', *Lives of the Norths* (G. Bell and Sons, 1890)

Porter, G. E., *Treatise on . . . the Silk Manufacture* (1831)

Rothstein, N., 'The Calico Campaign of 1719–1721', *East London Papers*, vol. 7.1, 1964

Rothstein, N., *Silk Designs of the Eighteenth Century* (Thames and Hudson, 1990)

Rule, F., The Worst Street in London (Ian Allan, 2008)

Sabin, A. K., *The Silk Weavers of Spitalfields and Bethnal Green* (Bethnal Green Museum, 1931)

Vigne, C. & Littleton, C., eds, *From Strangers to Citizens: the Integration of Communities in Britain, Ireland and Colonial America, 1550–1759* (Sussex Academic Press, 2001)

CHAPTER 6

Beckfordiana: A website for William Beckford (http://beckford.c18.net/beckfordiana.html)

Cumberland, R., *The West Indian: a Play* (http://openlibrary.org/books/OL7148229M/West_Indian)

Shepherd, F. H. W., *Survey of London*, vols 31 and 32: St James's, Westminster (http://www.british-history.ac.uk/source.aspx?pubid=290)

Adburgham, A., *Shopping in Style: London from Restoration to Edwardian Elegance* (Thames and Hudson, 1979)

Anon., Critical Observations on the Buildings and Improvements of London, 1771, BL 105.e.40

Ayres, J., *Domestic Interiors: The British Tradition 1500–1850* (Yale University Press, 2003)

Black, J., *The British Seaborne Empire* (Yale University Press, 2004)

Brewer, J., *The Pleasures of the Imagination: English Culture in the Eighteenth Century* (HarperCollins, 1997)

Burton, E., *The Georgians at Home* (Longmans, 1967)

Chancellor, E. B., *Wanderings in Marylebone* (Dulau and Co., 1926)

Colley, L., *Britons: Forging the Nation* (2nd edn) (Yale University Press, 2005)

Cundall, F., *The Governors of Jamaica in the first half of the eighteenth century* (The West India Commitee, 1937)

Draper, N., 'Possessing Slaves: Ownership, compensation and Metropolitan Society in Britain at the Time of Emancipation 1834–40', *History Workshop Journal*, vol. 64(1), 2007

Eger, E. & Peltz, L., *Brilliant Women: 18th Century Bluestockings* (National Portrait Gallery, 2008)

Gore, A. and A., *The History of English Interiors* (Phaidon, 1991)

Gragg, L., 'The Port Royal Earthquake', *History Today*, September 2000

Gwynn, J., *London and Westminster Improved (1766)* (Gregg International, 1969)

Hampson, N., *The Enlightenment* (Penguin, 1990)

Harris, E., 'Home House: Adam Versus Wyatt', *Burlington Magazine*, vol. 109, 1967

Harris, E., *The Genius of Robert Adam: His Interiors* (Yale University Press, 2001)

Home, Elizabeth, Countess of, Last Will (National Archives PROB 11/1112)

Hughes, R., 'Palaces of the Mind', *Time* magazine, 10 April 1972

Jenkins, S., *Landlords to London: The Story of a Capital and its Growth* (Constable, 1975)

Leslie, C., *A New and Exact Account of Jamaica* (Edinburgh, 1740)

Lewis, L., 'Elizabeth, Countess of Home and her House in Portman Square', *Burlington Magazine*, vol. 139(i), 1997

Longford, P., *A Polite and Commercial People: England 1727–1783* (Oxford University Press, 1989)

Longstaffe-Gowan, T., 'Portman Square Gardens: The Montpelier of England', *The London Gardener*, vol. 12, 2006–7

Mackay, C., *Extraordinary Popular Delusions and the Madness of Crowds* (Wordsworth Reference, 1995)

Miller, S., *Conversation: A History of a Declining Art* (Yale University Press, 2006)

O'Connell, S., ed., *London 1753* (The British Museum Press, 2003)

Parissien, S., *Adam Style* (Phaidon, 1992)

Peck, L., *Consuming Splendour* (Cambridge University Press, 2005)

Picard, L., *Dr Johnson's London* (Weidenfeld and Nicolson, 2000)

Porter, R., *The Enlightenment* (Allen Lane, 2001)

Robinson, J. M., *The Wyatts: An Architectural Dynasty* (Oxford University Press, 1975)

Rude, G., *Hanoverian London, 1714–1818* (Secker and Warburg, 1971)

Saumarez Smith, C., *The Rise of Design: Design and the Domestic Interior in Eighteenth-century England* (Pimlico, 2000)

Sennett, R., *The Fall of Public Man* (Penguin, 2002)

Shaftesbury, ed. Klein, L., *Characteristiks …* (Cambridge University Press, 1999)

Summerson, J., *The Architecture of the Eighteenth Century* (Thames and Hudson, 1986)

Sykes, C. S., *Private Palaces: Life in the Great London Houses* (Chatto and Windus, 1985)

Tait, A. A., *Robert Adam Drawings and Imagination* (Cambridge University Press, 1993)

Thomas, P. D. G., *John Wilkes: A Friend to Liberty* (Oxford University Press, 1996)

Thorold, P., *The London Rich: The Creation of a Great City from 1666 to the Present Day* (St Martin's Press, 1999)

Vickery, A., *Behind Closed Doors* (Yale University Press, 2009)

Voltaire, trans. Tancock, L., *Letters on England* (Penguin, 1984)

Walvin, J., *Fruits of Empire: Exotic Produce and English Taste* (Macmillan, 1997)

Whinney, M., *Home House: No. 20 Portman Square* (*Country Life*, 1969)

Williamson, A., *Wilkes A Friend of Liberty* (Allen and Unwin, 1974)

Wilson, B., *What Price Liberty: How Freedom was Won and is Being Lost* (Faber, 2009)

Wroth, W., *London Pleasure Gardens of the 18th Century* (Macmillan and Co., 1896)

CHAPTER 7

Arnold, D., *Representing the Metropolis: Architecture, Urban Experience and Social life in London 1800–1840* (Ashgate, 2000)

Batey, M., 'The Picturesque: An Overview', *Garden History*, vol. 22, winter 1994

Berkeley, G., *Reminiscences of a Huntsman* (Edward Arnold, 1897)

Burke, E., *Reflections on the French Revolution* (http://www.historyguide.org/intellect/reflections)

Cameron, D. K., *London's Pleasures* (Sutton, 2001)

Colvin, H. M., ed., *The History of the Office of King's Works*, vol. VI (HMSO, 1963–1982)

Davis, T., *John Nash: The Prince Regent's Architect* (Country Life, 1966)

Draper-Stumm, T. & Kendall, D., *London's Shops: The World's Emporium* (English Heritage, 2002)

Elmes, J., ed. Shepherd, T. H., *Metropolitan Improvements* (Arno Press, 1978)

Epstein Nord, D., 'The City as Theater: from Georgian to Early Victorian London', *Victorian Studies*, Winter, 1988

Fox, C., ed., *London World City: 1800–1840* (Yale University Press, 1992)

Gay, J., ed. Walsh, M., *Selected Poems* (Carcanet, 2003)

Hamilton, J., *London Lights: The Minds that Moved the City that Shook the World* (John Murray, 2007)

Harvey, R., *War of Wars* (Constable, 2006)

Healey, E., *The Queen's House: A Social History of Buckingham Palace* (Michael Joseph, 1997)

Hill, D., *Regency London* (Macdonald, 1969)

Hill, D., *Georgian London* (Macdonald, 1970)

Hobhouse, H., *The Mile of Style: A History of Regent Street* (Phillimore, 2008)

Hod, J., *Trafalgar Square: A Visual History of London's Landmark through Time* (Batsford, 2005)

Mordaunt Crook, J., 'London's Arcadia: John Nash and the Planning of Regent's Park', Annual Soane Lecture, 2000

Murray, V., *High Society in the Regency Period 1788–1830* (Penguin, 1998)

Palmer, A., *George IV* (Weidenfeld and Nicolson, 1972)

Pevsner, N. & Cherry, B., *The Buildings of England: London 3: North West* (Penguin, 1991)

Samuel, E. C., 'The Villas in Regent's Park and their Residents', St Marylebone Society Publication, no. 1, 1959

Saunders, A., *Regent's Park: A Study of Development of the Area from 1086 to the Present Day* (David & Charles, 1969)

Sheppard, F. H. W., ed. *The London Survey*, vol. 21: *St Martin in the Fields and Trafalgar Square* (1940)

Sheppard, F. H. W., ed., *The London Survey*, vols 31 and 32; *St James's Westminster* (1963)

Suggett, R., *John Nash, Architect in Wales* (Royal Commission on the Ancient and Historical Monuments of Wales, 1995)

Summerson, J., *John Nash: Architect to King George IV* (George Allen and Unwin, 1935)

Summerson, J., *The Life and Work of John Nash, Architect* (George Allen and Unwin, 1980)

Summerson, Sir J., 'John Nash's "Statement", 1829', *Architectural History*, vol. 34, 1991

Townsend, D., 'The Picturesque', *Journal of Aesthetics and Art Criticism*, Fall 1997

White, J., *London in the 19th Century* (Vintage, 2008)

White, R. J., *Life in Regency England* (Botsford, 1963)

Whitehead, J., *The Growth of St Marylebone and Paddington* (Jack Whitehead, 2001)

CHAPTER 8

Barry, A., *The Life and Works of Sir Charles Barry, RA FRS* (John Murray, 1867)

Boase, T. S. R., 'The Decoration of the New Palace of Westminster: 1841–1863', *Journal of Warburg and Courtauld Institutes*, vol. 17, no. 3/4, 1954

Brookes, C., *The Gothic Revival* (Phaidon, 1999)

Cannadine, D. et al., eds, *The Houses of Parliament: History, Art and Architecture* (Merrell, 2000)

Clark, K., *The Gothic Revival* (Constable, 1950)

Colvin, H. M., ed., *The History of King's Works*, vol. 6: 1782–1851 (HMSO, 1973)

Cooke, Sir R., *The Place of Westminster: Houses of Parliament* (Burton Skira, 1987)

Cust, E., 'Thoughts on the Expedience of a Better System of Control', Hume Tracts (1837) (JSTOR 60209685)

Dixon, R. & Muthesius, S., *Victorian Architecture* (Thames and Hudson, 1978)

Field, J., *The Story of Parliament in the Palace of Westminster* (Politicos, 2002)

Hamilton, J., *London Lights: The Minds that Moved the City that Shook the World* (John Murray, 2007)

Hastings, M., *Parliament House: The Chambers of the House of Commons* (Architectural Press, 1950)

Hill, R., *God's Architect: Pugin and the Building of Romantic Britain* (Penguin, 2008)

Hilton, B., *A Mad, Bad and Dangerous People?* (Oxford University Press, 2006)

MacDonald, P., *Big Ben, the Clock and the Tower* (Sutton, 2004)

Pearce, E., *Reform! The Fight for the 1832 Reform Act* (Jonathan Cape, 2003)

Port, M. H., *The Houses of Parliament* (Yale University Press, 1976)

Pugin, A. W. N., *Contrasts . . .* (Leicester University Press, 1969)

Quinault, R., 'Westminster and the Victorian Constitution', *Transactions of the RHS*, vol. 2, 1992

Reid, D. B. (David Boswell), 'Narrative of Facts as to the New Houses of Parliament', *Hume Tracts* (1849) (JSTOR 60207891)

Rorabaugh, W. J., 'Politics and the Architectural Competition for the Houses of Parliament 1834–1837', *Victorian Studies*, vol. 17, no. 2, Dec. 1973

Sawyer, S., 'Delusion of National Grandeur: Reflections on the Intersection of Architecture and History at the Palace of Westminster, 1789–1834', *Transactions of the RHS*, vol. 13, 2003

Stevenson, J., ed., *London in the Age of Reform* (Basil Blackwell, 1977)

Weitzman, G. H., 'The Utilitarians and the Houses of Parliament', *Journal of the Society of Architectural Historians*, vol. 20, no. 3, Oct. 1961

CHAPTER 9

The Handbook for the Metropolitan and District Board of Works, 1857 (http://www.jstor.org/stable/60244750)

UCLA Epidemiology Department, John Snow site (http://www.ph.ucla.edu/epi/snow/broadstreetpump.htl)

The Victorian Dictionary (http://www.victorianlondon.org/)

Armstrong, I., *Victorian Glassworlds: Glass, Culture and the Imagination* (Oxford University Press, 2008)

Bazalgette, J., *Of the Metropolitan System of Drainage* (Institute of Civil Engineers, 1864–5)

Bennett, A. R., *London etc. in the Eighteen Fifties and Sixties* (Fisher Unwin, 1924)

Bradford, T., *The Groundwater Diaries* (Flamingo, 2004)

Buchanan, R. A., 'Gentlemen Engineers: the Making of a Profession', *Victorian Studies*, vol. 26., no. 4, Summer 1983

Clifton, G., *Professionalism, Patronage and Public Service in Victorian London* (Athlone, 1992)

Colquhoun, K., *A Thing in Disguise: The Visionary Life of Jospeh Paxton* (Fourth Estate, 2003)

Davis, J. R., *The Great Exhibition* (Sutton, 1999)

Dickens, C., *Our Mutual Friend* (Chapman and Hall, 1887)

Dobraszczyk, P., 'Historicizing Iron: Charles Driver and the Abbey Mills Pumping Stations (1865–8)', *Architectural History*, vol. 49, 2006

Halliday, S., *The Great Stink of London: Sir Joseph Bazalgette and the Cleansing of the Victorian Metropolis* (Sutton, 1999)

Hamlin, C., 'Edwin Chadwick and the Engineers: 1842–1854', *Technology and Culture*, vol. 33, no. 4, Oct. 1992

Harley, R. J., *London's Victoria Embankment* (Capital History, 2005)

Hollingshead, J., *Ragged London in 1861* (Smith, Elder and Co., 1861)

Humphreys, A., 'Knowing the Victorian City: Writing and Representation', *Victorian Literature and Culture*, 2002

Inwood, S., *City of Cities: The Birth of Modern London* (Macmillan, 2005)

Johnson, S., *The Ghost Map: A Street, an Epidemic and the Two Men who Battled to Save Victorian London* (Penguin, 2007)

Metcalfe, P., *Victorian Britain* (Cassell, 1972)

Nead, L., *Victorin Babylon: People, Streets and Images in Nineteenth Century London* (Yale University Press, 2000)

Oliver, S., 'The Thames Embankment and the disciplining of Nature in modernity', *The Geographical Journal*, vol. 166, no. 3, Sept. 2000

Owen, D. E., *The Government of Victorian London 1855–89* (Belknap Press, 1982)

Picard, L., *Victorian London* (Weidenfeld and Nicolson, 2005)

Porter, D., *The Thames Embankment: Environment, Technology, Society in Victorian London* (University of Akron Press, 1998)

Spufford, F. & Uglow, J., eds, *Cultural Babbage: Technology, Time and Inventions* (Faber, 1996)

Summer, J., *Soho* (Bloomsbury, 1989)

Wilson, A. N., *The Victorians* (Arrow, 2003)

Wolmar, C., *The Subterranean Railway: How the London Underground was Built and How it Changed the City Forever* (Atlantic, 2004)

CHAPTER 10

TfL: Annual Report and Statement of Accounts, 2008–9 (http://www.tfl. gov.uk/corporate/abcut-tfl/investorrelations/1458.aspx)

Adshead, A. D., 'The Town Planning of Greater London after the War', *The Town Planning Review*, vol. 7, no. 2, 1917

Adshead, A. D., 'The Town Planning of Greater London after the War: Part II', *The Town Planning Review*, vol. 7, no. 3/4, 1918

Barclay, P. & Powell, K., *Wembley Stadium: Venue of Legends* (Prestel, 2007)

Barres-Baker, M. C., 'Wembley in the First World War: 1914–1919', *Wembley Historical Society*, 15 Sept. 2006

Bell, W., *Where London Sleeps: Historical Journeys into the Suburbs* (Bodley Head, 1926)

Clarke, W., ed., *The Suburban Homes of London . . .* (Chatto and Windus, 1881)

Elsley, H. W. R., *Wembley Through the Ages* (*Wembley News*, 1953)

Ferguson, N., *Empire: How Britain Made the Modern World* (Penguin, 2003)

Ford, F. Madox, *The Soul of London: Survey of a Modern City* (Alston Rivers, 1905)

Gee, H., *Wembley: Fifty Great Years* (Pelham Books. 1972)

Glass, R., *London: Aspects of Change* (MacGibbon & Key, 1964)

Green, O., intro, *Metro-Land*, British Empire Exhibition Number, 1924 (Southbank Publishing, 2004)

Grossman, G. & W., *Diary of a Nobody* (Arrowsmith, 1938)

Harding Thompson, W., 'The Arterial Roads of Greater London in Course of Construction', *The Town Planning Review*, vol. 9, no. 2, 1921

Hoffenberg, P. H., *An Empire on Display: English, Indian and Australian Exhibitions from the Crystal Palace to the Great War* (University of California Press, 2001)

Howard, E., *Garden Cities of Tomorrow* (Faber, 1945)

Inwood, S., *City of Cities: The Birth of Modern London* (PanMacmillan, 2006)

Jackson, A. A., *London's Metropolitan Railway* (David and Charles, 1986)

Jackson. A. A., *The Middle Classes 1900–1950* (David St John Thomas Publishers, 1991)

Jackson, A. A., *London's Metro-Land* (Capital History, 2006)

James, H., *Essays in London* (James R. Osgood, McIlvaine and Co., 1893)

Jay, R., 'Taller than Eiffel's Tower: The London and Chicago Tower Projects: 1889–1894, *Journal of the Society of Architectural Historians*, vol. 46, no.2, 1987

Jefferys, R., *After London* (Cassell, 1885)

Jensen, F., *The English Semi-Detached House* (Ovolo Books, 2007)

Judd, D., *Empire: The British Imperial Experience from 1765 to the Present* (HarperCollins, 1996)

Knight, D. & Sabey, D., *The Lion Roars at Wembley* (Barnard and Westwood, 1984)

Lawrence, G. C., ed., *The British Empire Exhibition, 1924: Official Guide* (Fleetway Press, 1924)

Marr, A., *The Making of Modern Britain* (Macmillan, 2009)

Mee, A., ed. Saunders, A., *The King's England: London North of the Thames, except the City and Westminster* (Hodder and Stoughton, 1972)

Muthesius, H., *The English House* (Frances Lincoln, 2007)

Pevsner, N. & Cherry, B., *The Buildings of England: London 3: North West* (Penguin, 1991)

Pugh, Martin, '*We Danced All Night*': A Social History of Britain Between the Wars* (Bodley Head, 2008)

Rasmussen, S. E., *London: The Unique City* (Jonathan Cape, 1939)

Rennell, T., *Last Days of Glory: The Death of Queen Victoria* (Viking, 2000)

Saint, A., intro., *London Suburbs* (Merrell Holberton, 1999)

Schneer, J., *London 1900: the Imperial Metropolis* (Yale University Press, 2001)

Service, A., *London 1900* (Granada, 1979)

Thraves, A., *The History of the Wembley FA Cup Final* (Weidenfeld and Nicolson, 1994)

Tomsett, P. & Brand, C., *Wembley: Stadium of Legends* (Dewi Lewis, 2007)

Wade, C., *Hampstead Past* (Historical Publications, 1989)

White, H. P., *A Regional History of the Railways of Great Britain*, vol. III: *Greater London* (Phoenix House, 1963)

William, O., et al., *Wembley: First City of Concrete* (Concrete Utilities Bureau, 1924)

Young, P., *A History of British Football* (Stanley Paul, 1968)

CHAPTER 11

Architects' Year Book 4 (Paul Elek, 1952)

Architects' Year Book 7 (Paul Elek 1956)

'Heritage group vies to save council block for the nation', *The Sunday Times*, 7 Feb. 1993

'Crumbling block of flats saved for nation; Keeling House', *The Times*, 24 Nov. 1993

A Language and a Theme: The Architecture of Denys Lasdun & Partners (RIBA Publications, 1996)

Abercrombie, P., *Greater London Plan 1944* (HMSO, 1945)

Allan, J., *Berthold Lubetkin* (Merrell, 2002)

Baker, T. F. T., ed., *A History of the County of Middlesex*, vol. 11 (Victoria County History, 1998)

Bennett, C., 'La Poesie Concrète: A Love Story', *Guardian*, 15 November 1990

Dench, G., et al., *The New East End: Kinship, Race and Conflict* (Profile Books, 2006)

Dunleavy, P., *The Politics of Mass Housing in Britain, 1945–1975* Clarendon Press, 1981)

Elwall, R., *Building a Better Tomorrow: Architecture in Britain in the 1950s* (Wiley Academic, 2000)

Glendinning, M. & Muthesius, S., *Tower Block: Modern Public Housing in England, Scotland, Wales and Northern Ireland* (Yale University Press, 1994)

Gold, J. R., 'The MARS Plan for London 1932–1942: Plurality and Experimentation in the City. Plans of the Early British Modern Movements', *The Town Planning Review*, June 1995

Hall, P., *Cities of Tomorrow* (3rd edn) (Blackwell, 2002)

Hall, P., et al., *The Containment of Urban England*, 2 vols (George Allen and Unwin, 1973)

Hanley, L., *Estates: An Intimate History* (Granta, 2007)

Hughes, J., 'Born Again: The High Rise Slum', *The Times*, 1 July 2000

Humphries, S. & Taylor, J., *The Making of Modern London* (Sidgwick and Jackson, 1986)

Jay, B. & Warburton, N., eds, *Brandt: The Photography of Bill Brandt* (Thames and Hudson, 1999)

Kynaston, D., *Austerity Britain: 1945–51* (Bloomsbury, 2008)

Kynaston, D., *Family Britain: 1951–57*, (Bloomsbury, 2009)

Lasdun, D., 'Second Thoughts in Housing on London', *Architects' Year Book 4*, 1952

Lasdun, D., *MARS Group 1953–57 Architects' Year Book 9*, 1957

Lasdun, D., 'Freedom to Build', letter to the editor of *The Times*, 7 October 1957

Lasdun, D., *Architecture in an Age of Scepticism, a Practitioners' Anthology* (Heinemann, 1984)

Lasdun, D. & Davies, J. H. V., 'Thoughts in Progress', *Architectural Design*, Dec. 1956–Dec. 1957

Lynch, K., 'A New Look at Civic Design', *Journal of Architectural Education*, vol. 19, no. 1, 1955

Mullins, C., *A Festival on the River: The Story of the South Bank Centre* (Penguin, 2007)

O'Neill, G., *Our Street: East End Life in the Second World War* (Penguin, 2004)

Powers, A., *Britain: Modern Architectures in History* (Reaktion, 2007)

Ravetz, A., *The Government of Space: Town Planning in Modern Society* (Faber, 1986)

Reading, M. & Coe, P., *Lubetkin and Tecton: An Architectural Study* (Triangle Architectural Publishing, 1992)

Smit, J., 'They bought a tower block', *The Sunday Times*, 17 Oct. 1999

Smith, L., *Young Voices: British Children Remember the Second World War* (Viking, 2007)

Sudjic, D., 'The Bull about Bunkers', *Guardian*, 6 Feb. 1997

Summerson, J., intro, *Ten Years of British Architecture; an Arts Council Exhibition* (Arts Council, 1956)

Waller, M., *London, 1945: Life in the Debris of War* (John Murray, 2004)

Wilkinson, L., *Watercress but no Sandwiches: 300 years of the Columbia Road* (JHERA, 2001)

Wise, S., *The Blackest Streets: The Life and Death of a Victorian Slum* (Vintage, 2009)

Wright, P., *A Journey Through Ruins: The Last Days of London* (Oxford University Press, 2009)

Young, M. & Willmott, P., *Family and Kinship in East London* (Penguin, 2007)

CHAPTER 12

The Big Dig: Archaeology and the Jubilee Line Extension (Museum of London Archaeology Service, 1998)

'Unlock the Digital City', *Wired UK*, Nov. 2009

Augar, P., *The Death of Gentlemanly Capitalism* (Penguin, 2008)

Augar, P., *Reckless: The Rise and Fall of the City* (Vintage, 2010)

Bagehot, W., *Lombard Street: A Description of the Money Market* (Wiley Investment Classics, 1999)

Burdett, R., ed., *Richard Rogers Partnership: Works and Projects* (Monacelli Press, 1999)

Cable, V., *The Storm* (Atlantic, 2009)

Coggan, P., *The Money Machine: How the City Works* (Penguin, 2009)

Cohen, P. & Rustin, M. J., eds, *London's Turning: The Making of Thames Gateway* (Ashgate 2008)

Corporation of London, *Global Financial Centres 7*, March 2010

Elrington, C. R., ed., *A History of the County of Middlesex*, vol. 9 (Victoria County History, 1989)

Foster, N. + Partners, *Foster Catalogue 2001* (Prestel, 2001)

GLA, The London Plan: Spatial Development for Greater London (Feb. 2008)

GLA, Draft Revised Supplementary Planning Guidance (May 2009)

GLA, Taking London to the World: An Export Promotion Programme for the Capital (May 2009)

Glancey, J., *London: Bread and Circuses* (Verso, 2001)

Hebbert, M., *London: More by Fortune than Design* (Wiley, 1998)

Jenkins, D., ed., *On Foster – Foster On* (Prestel, 2000)

Kerr, J. & Gibson, A., eds, *London from Punk to Blair* (Reaktion, 2003)

Kynaston, D., *The City of London: A Club No More 1945–2000* (Chatto and Windus, 2001)

Lewis, M., *Liar's Poker: Two Cities, True Greed* (Hodder and Stoughton, 1989)

Massey, D., *World City* (Polity Press, 2007)

McSmith, A., *No Such Thing as Society* (Constable, 2010)

Michie, R. C., ed., *The Development of London as a Financial Centre*, vol 4: 1945–2000 (I. B. Tauris, 2000)

Pawley, M., *Norman Foster: A Global Architecture* (Thames and Hudson, 1999)

Plender, J. & Wallace, P., *The Square Mile: A Guide to the New City of London* (Century, 1985)

Powell, K., 30 *St Mary Axe: A Tower for London* (Merrell, 2006)

Powell, K., *New London Architecture 2* (Merrell, 2007)

Rogers, R., *Architecture: a Modern View* (Thames and Hudson, 1990)

Sudjic, D., *The Edifice Complex: How the Rich and Powerful Shape the World* (Allen Lane, 2005)

Sudjic, D., *Norman Foster* (Weidenfeld and Nicolson, 2010)

ACKNOWLEDGEMENTS

My fascination with London began when I was young, and has kept with me ever since. More than anything, it has been a search for a place called home; to make sense of the place around me in which I have chosen to grow roots as well as an attempt to unravel why this need is so strong. But home is not an abstract quality to be uncovered in a library, googled or downloaded. It is more often people than a pile of bricks. This book is dedicated to Rose, who is everything that home means and more. Also to Louis and Theadora.

This book would not exist without the many other friends, colleagues and family who helped and believed that it might just work. So thanks to Mum, Ed, Emma, Tim and Daisy. To Patrick and Clare and all at Conville and Walsh for being everything an agency should be – friends and guides. To Bea, Alan, Elizabeth and all at Weidenfeld and Nicolson – one could not ask for a better team. In particular, special thanks to Linden Lawson, who worked so hard on the text and improved it beyond my greatest hopes.

Finally, I want to thank the librarians and archivists who were so kind and unstinting in their help. It is a difficult time for our public libraries. Closing them down is a threat to our collective memory. The many libraries, archives and collections around the city are as essential to London's future as they are to preserving its past. Cutting funds and laying off valuable staff is a false economy and reduces our metropolitan hopes.

INDEX